Cross-cultural Perspectives
in Human Development

Cross-cultural Perspectives in Human Development

THEORY, RESEARCH AND APPLICATIONS

Edited by
T.S. SARASWATHI

SAGE PUBLICATIONS
New Delhi ∞ Thousand Oaks ∞ London

First published in 2003 by

Sage Publications India Pvt Ltd
B-42, Panchsheel Enclave
New Delhi 110 017

Sage Publications Inc   **Sage Publications Ltd**
2455 Teller Road   6 Bonhill Street
Thousand Oaks, California 91320   London EC2A 4PU

Published by Tejeshwar Singh for Sage Publications India Pvt Ltd, type-set in 10 pt Palatino by Star Compugraphics Private Limited, New Delhi and printed at Chaman Enterprises, New Delhi.

Library of Congress Cataloging-in-Publication Data

Cross-cultural perspectives in human development: theory, research and applications/edited by T.S. Saraswathi.
    p. cm.
    Includes index.
    1. Developmental psychology. 2. Ethnopsychology.   I. Saraswathi, T.S.
    BF713.5.C76   155—dc22   2003   2003013078

ISBN: 0–7619–9768–7 (US–Hb)   81–7829–252–1 (India–Hb)
        0–7619–9769–5 (US–Pb)   81–7829–253–X (India–Pb)

Sage Production Team: Payal Mehta, Mathew P.J., Neeru Handa and Santosh Rawat

I dedicate this volume to Professor R.C. Patel,
former Vice-Chancellor of Maharaja Sayajirao University
of Baroda, who facilitated the institution of the Nehru Chair
in Human Development and Family Studies, but did not
live to see it actualize his vision

Contents

List of Tables

List of Figures

Foreword

Forty years ago, the cross-cultural study of human development as a coherent field of study with a definitive identity simply did not exist. The overwhelming majority of human development textbooks published in North America and Western Europe ignored cross-cultural developmental variations altogether or relegated them to a few tangential pages. In practice, the study of human development meant the study of American and European children, adolescents and some adults. In contrast to this situation, the contributors to this volume are convinced that developmental trajectories vary widely (but not randomly!) from one ecological and sociocultural context to the next. Many of them have been prominently involved with the International Association for Cross-Cultural Psychology and see it as their mission to create a new and truly international field of study: the cross-cultural study of human development in an ecocultural context. For many of them, this mission is part of a broader viewpoint that aims at the creation of a global psychology appropriate to the new century and to the new world that is in the making.

It may prove useful in this context to briefly review the history of cross-cultural developmental psychology and its antecedents to better understand the broader situation within which this volume evolved. The academic discipline of developmental psychology was established between 1885 and 1930 when many of its early giants—William Preyer, Sigmund Freud, G. Stanley Hall, James M. Baldwin, Charlotte and Karl Bühler, Heinz Werner, Jean Piaget, Lev S. Vygotsky—succeeded in placing the discipline on the "academic map". With the exception of Vygotsky, none of them were attuned to the power of cultural influences. Indeed, it was cultural anthropologist Margaret Mead's pioneering but controversial fieldwork in the South Seas during the late 1920s that for the first time threw into doubt the cross-cultural validity of a leading developmental theory, namely, G. Stanley Hall's storm-and-stress theory of adolescence. However, the contributions of Margaret Mead and the other members of the culture and personality school had only a limited impact on developmental and personality psychology, in part because of their methodological limitations and because American psychology had become largely monocultural in character. It was the central ambition of the leading developmentalists of the time to create an overarching and (supposedly) universal theory capable of describing and explaining childhood development and its lasting effects on adult personality. As part of this actually quite ethnocentric enterprise, the developmental histories of "exotic natives" were only of tangential interest.

As late as the 1960s, cross-cultural human development researchers led a mostly unnoticed life at the margins of the discipline. But beneath the quiet and rather traditional surface of developmental psychology, change was brewing. In 1972, both the International Association for Cross-Cultural Psychology (IACCP) and the Society for Cross-Cultural Research (SCCR) were founded while a number of cross-culturally-oriented journals began to appear between 1966 and 1978. Many of the contributors to this volume—John W. Berry, Pierre Dasen, Lutz H. Eckensberger, Cigdem Kagitcibasi, and Bame Nsamenang—have indeed played a prominent role in the affairs of the IACCP while the anthropologist Alice Schlegel has been an influential member of the SCCR. Furthermore, the contributors to this volume represent a variety of Western and non-Western countries (and academic traditions) including Cameroon, Canada, Germany, India, Switzerland, Turkey, and the United States of America. This fact alone will convey to the attentive reader that a broad variety of viewpoints and research populations can be expected to make their appearance in the pages to follow.

As cross-cultural psychologists began to grope for an appropriate general theoretical framework for their studies, John W. Berry's ecocultural perspective on human development and adaptation began to make its influence felt. This framework has not only been employed to help coordinate several leading textbooks in cross-cultural psychology, but it has also proved useful in keeping the focus of cross-cultural psychologists on the sustained investigation of possibly universal psychological processes underlying a wide range of culturally and individually variable behaviour. It is thus fitting that his contribution to this volume follows Saraswathi's introductory chapter.

In the 1960s and 1970s, at the same time when cross-cultural psychology began to adopt a definite identity, evolutionary theories in biology underwent a number of trenchant changes and elaborations. Increasingly, evolutionary hypotheses began to be applied to humans and their behaviour in a variety of sociocultural settings. Unlike most mainstream psychologists, evolutionary theorists have always understood that their hypotheses cannot be considered valid unless they have been shown to hold true both among different species and among highly varied human populations living in different ecologies and cultural settings. The more general implication of this statement is that no cross-cultural life cycle psychology should be considered complete unless it can be shown to be in alignment with the general postulates of evolutionary biology and psychology. Moreover, the dialectic between the evolutionary viewpoint stressing the psychobiological adaptation of organisms to different ecologies and the viewpoint of cultural psychology with its emphasis on culturally constituted meaning systems is tailor-made for spirited debates among cross-cultural researchers. Thus it should come as no surprise that both of these perspectives are well represented in this multifaceted volume.

As psychology began to spread around the globe in recent decades, cultural psychologists as well as scholars in non-Western countries began to demand that indigenous conceptualizations of human nature be integrated into the Western perspectives that were, and still are, dominating mainstream psychology. One of these scholars is the Cameroonian developmentalist, A. Bame Nsamenang. In his contribution, he asks that African conceptions of personhood, social thought, socialization and education, and modes of constructing knowledge become part of psychology as taught and practised in sub-Saharan Africa—and hopefully elsewhere! Otherwise, he argues, the enterprise of psychology in Africa is doomed to failure and irrelevance. A "mixed" psychology interweaving strands of Western thought with strands of African thought would be especially appropriate in his view, since contemporary African societies and individuals have taken on a hybrid cultural character in which native and imported lifestyles and mentalities coexist in a more or less uneasy balance. Arguments such as these imply that a more global psychology of the future will incorporate contributions stemming from scholars around the world who can mine their cultures as rich sources of insight in order to expand the discipline of developmental psychology.

From a methodological point of view, several essays such as those by Anita Rampal, Reed Larson, and Sevda Bekman focus on a central idea: psychological theories and research need to emphasize much more than has hitherto been true, experience-near conceptualizations and methods that reflect the interpenetration of sociocultural context and human development, environment and organism, culture and biology, culture and mind, social and non-social psychological processes, and so on. The goal is not to create a psychology in which all traditional dichotomies have been covered with the soft plaster of postmodern thought, but rather to arrive at a more complex, process-oriented, socioculturally informed theory of human development systematically backed up by cross-cultural and, where appropriate, cross-species data. Such a theory will not only be more comprehensive and realistic, but also more suitable for successful application. This theme is emphasized in the second part of this volume, which centres on the application of developmental principles and findings especially in those countries constituting the non-Western "majority world".

In that world—where the large majority of today's children and adolescents live—psychology is frequently considered some kind of luxury. In such a context, it is all the more important that psychologists prove their usefulness to society by applying their knowledge to schools, parental education programmes, companies, and other key institutions. At the same time, the analysis of their interventions can contribute to better psychological theorizing, since psychosocial theories need to prove their mettle by being successfully applied. Many contributors to the second part of this volume share this Lewinian viewpoint by demonstrating intricate interactions between theory, methodology, and application in a broad variety of cultural settings.

The last three chapters demonstrate a special concern for Indian research findings in the context of cross-cultural comparison. Such a focus is not only appropriate for holders of the Nehru Chair in Human Development, but should also remind us that India may be considered a gigantic and inexhaustible laboratory for human development researchers. Possessed of a culture that includes some of humanity's oldest systematic theories about the human life cycle and its ultimate meaning, India presents a picture of enormous ecological, cultural, linguistic, and religious diversity. More children and adolescents live in India than in Western Europe and Anglo-Saxon North America combined. Ancient Indian customs continue to thrive side by side with ways of thinking derived from today's information age. In many ways, those psychological research findings holding true across India's cultural and sociological divides may add more to the psychological understanding of humanity than the endless series of American–European findings that continue to dominate developmental psychology textbooks around the world. In this context, it can only be hoped that Indian theorists and researchers will increasingly contribute to the international literature on psychological development.

This volume makes a powerful contribution to the internationalization of life cycle psychology. In this, it does not stand alone. Recent related books include, for instance, Patricia M. Greenfield and Rodney R. Cocking's *Cross-cultural roots of minority child development*, John W. Berry, Pierre R. Dasen, and T.S. Saraswathi's *Basic processes and human development* (Vol. 2 of *Handbook of cross-cultural psychology*), Anna L. Comunian and Uwe P. Gielen's *International perspectives on human development*, Harry W. Gardiner and Corinne Kosmitzski's *Lives across cultures: Cross-cultural human development*, together with several volumes to come. The cross-cultural study of human development, it seems, is finally coming of age. In many ways, it represents the cutting edge of research on socioemotional and sociocognitive development. Although still treated as upstarts and dubious outsiders by many mainstream developmentalists, cross-cultural researchers have been at least moderately successful in shaking up academic and ethnocentric complacency. They have been indispensable in moving psychology away from its monocultural American base, a development of special interest to psychologists in non-Western countries.

Today's global village demands a global psychology, and cross-cultural psychologists are at the forefront of those who are seriously endeavouring to construct such a psychology. Cross-cultural theories of human development lend themselves especially well to this enterprise because they demand that ecological conditions, evolutionary considerations, demographic shifts, cultural belief systems, enabling and constraining factors, family systems, psychosocial changes occurring over prolonged periods, and many other factors are simultaneously taken into account. At the same time, it is sheer fun to encounter so much cultural diversity while trying to identify some of the underlying psychological processes that might account for the origins of the diversity. We are thus engaged in the age-old search for an enhanced understanding of human nature and human destiny(ies), but are in a better position to avoid some of the more naïvely ethnocentric and anthropocentric conceptions that have until now bedevilled the search.

At the same time, the reader is in the hands of excellent guides assembled for this purpose by India's leading developmental psychologist. As scientists, they do not promise us ultimate truth, but offer us instead something that I find more nourishing: Hard, conceptual work, diverse yet often complementary perspectives, challenging applications, and a rich multicultural stew. The reader is in for an excellent meal: filling, blending together a variety of seemingly opposing flavours, and at times spicy in the Indian fashion!

June 2002   UWE P. GIELEN
                                    Institute for International and
                                    Cross-cultural Psychology
                                    St. Francis College, New York

Preface

This volume is based on lectures delivered by 12 cross-cultural psychologists/anthropologists, under the auspices of the Nehru Chair Professorship in the Department of Human Development & Family Studies, at the Maharaja Sayajirao University of Baroda. The lectures by these eminent scholars drawn from seven countries, address critical issues related to knowledge construction in human development and allied disciplines. The series of lectures deal with theoretical concerns, methodological alternatives, and issues of social intervention.

The Nehru Chair was instituted in 1990, the birth centenary year of Jawaharlal Nehru, in order to facilitate eminent scholars in human development and allied disciplines such as psychology, education, sociology, social work and women's studies to interact with graduate students and faculty, share their scholarship, and enrich the department's programme. The Chair was awarded on the basis of an open competition for university departments across the state, and the proposal I submitted for the department as Department Chair, was selected for the award, opening the windows of the world to our graduate programme. Two other professional developments that took place in the early 1990s served to strengthen the Nehru Chair programmes: (*a*) I was invited to co-edit one of the 3-volume *Handbook of cross-cultural psychology*. That enabled me to renew international professional contacts as well as develop some new ones with other scholars, who later became potential visiting scholars under the auspices of the Nehru Chair. (*b*) The University Grants Commission, the apex body for higher education in India, in special recognition of the contributions of the Department of Human Development & Family Studies (HDFS) at Baroda, awarded a special grant to enable us to invite leading scholars to participate in our programme of teaching–learning and also provide a forum for academic exchange.

The Nehru Chair Professors are selected every year, from a panel of internationally renowned scholars, by a committee chaired by the Vice Chancellor of the University (President) with the Dean of the Faculty of Home Economics, Head of the Department of Human Development & Family Studies (HDFS), and all senior professors in the department of HDFS, as its members. Letters are sent out every year to select scholars with interest in cross-cultural work and the panel drawn on the basis of letters of interest. The careful selection process has resulted in a rich assembly of scholars, worldviews, and theoretical perspectives. Special mention must be made here of the extremely supportive role played by the Vice Chancellors in the 1990s both in enabling us to secure the Chair, as well as in selecting the nominees. Late Professor R.C. Patel helped us in establishing the Chair in 1990 and Ms Padma Ramachandran, Vice Chancellor in the late 1990s was tremendously appreciative of the exchange of eminent international scholars in the field.

The visiting scholars from various countries (the USA, Canada, Switzerland, Germany, Turkey, Africa, and India) represent several social science disciplines. Such a representation added to the wealth of ideas reflecting the interdisciplinary and cross-cultural perspectives. It is this richness that I wish to share in the form of this edited volume. This volume stands as an exemplar of a successful endeavour by a small department in a developing country, which facilitated the coming together of renowned scholars in the field, during a period of high productivity in their own careers.

June 2002   **T.S. Sᴀʀᴀsᴡᴀᴛʜɪ**

Acknowledgements

Many people have in various ways played a role in facilitating the work published in this volume. While it is not possible to thank each one individually, my sincere appreciation is due to:

- each of the authors, whose contributions extended beyond the preparation of their chapters in this volume. Their lectures at the Department of Human Development & Family Studies, Maharaja Sayajirao University of Baroda, opened the windows of the world of cross-cultural psychology to graduate students;
- several other scholars who held the Nehru Chair between 1992 and 2001, but whose contribution is not represented in this volume;
- the MS University administration for facilitating the operation of the grants, and the Guest House Manager and staff who ensured a comfortable residence for the visitors;
- the staff of the University Grants Commission Special Assistance Programme who assisted in several ways with friendly cheer. Special mention must be made of Mahesh Soni, who spent countless hours finalizing the manuscript for the press and incorporating the revisions;
- my colleagues in the department, and especially to Professor Amita Verma, former Chairperson of the department, who extended their hospitality to the visitors;
- Ms Padma Ramachandran, former Vice Chancellor of MS University (1996–99), who took a special interest in the visitors and their academic contributions, and encouraged efforts to broaden our perspective;

– Juin Dutta who meticulously checked the citations and reference listings, relieving me of the authors' ire for nit picking!
– several others, from office boy to the Chief Accounts Officer, who helped in keeping the ball rolling.

Baroda, June 2002   **T.S. SARASWATHI**

Introduction

T.S. SARASWATHI

One of the most satisfying experiences in the preparation of this volume occurred to me at the time of organizing the contents page of the collected works. What became evident was that due partly to fortuitous circumstances, and partly to conscious design, the volume represents scholars from each of the major schools of thought and theoretical orientations that currently dominate the field. These include cross-cultural psychology, cultural psychology, cultural anthropology, evolutionary psychology, indigenous psychology, as well as those with a plea for addressing socially relevant and practical problem-oriented issues, and link theory to practice and social policy. I consider this representation a major strength of this volume, complementing a more comprehensive coverage of similar concerns in volume one of the *Handbook of cross-cultural psychology* (Berry, Poortinga, & Pandey, 1997).

It is beyond the purview of the introductory chapter to deal with the alternative perspectives in substantial detail. Only a brief account of the core characteristics of each of the schools of thought is presented to acquaint the reader who may not be very familiar with the literature. The reader is referred to key references in the area for a detailed treatment of the topic. Further, each of the chapters delineate critical issues of relevance to the theme they have chosen to address.

Beginning with an overview of salient ideas in each of the major schools of thought that coexist with a certain degree of tension and mutual criticism, I conclude the section by arguing for a possible and necessary interface among the apparently diverse perspectives, in order to promote a healthy and holistic growth of the field of human development.

Cross-Cultural Psychology

As stated by Kagitcibasi and Poortinga (2000, p. 133), "Cross-cultural psychology as a field of research has come about as a reaction against the tendency in psychology to ignore cultural variations and to consider them nuisance variables." (For a critical appraisal of the field, see Berry, Poortinga, & Pandey, 1997; Berry, Poortinga, Segall, & Dasen, 1992/2002; Segall, Dasen, Berry, & Poortinga, 1999.)

Segall et al. (1999) identified the two main goals of cross-cultural psychology as: (*a*) to test the generality of existing psychological knowledge and theories; and (*b*) to discover psychological variations that are not present in a single social setting. The two goals complement each other; the first addresses the issue of psychological universals, and the second the coexistence of diversity. The ultimate goal, however, is to determine how sociocultural variables influence human behaviour and discover the relationship between culture and individual behaviour. Hence, Berry et al. (1992/2002) highlighted the third goal of cross-cultural psychology as an attempt to assemble and *integrate* into a broadly based psychology, the results obtained when pursuing the first two goals, and then generate a more universal psychology that will be valid for a broad range of cultures.

The basic search is for universals in psychological processes, whether based on biological roots and/or similarity in cultural institutions that foster human development. This position of universalism, while recognizing differences, has important methodological implications. As stated by Kagitcibasi and Poortinga (2000, p. 131), "In so far as there is non identity of psychological processes cross-culturally, there is non-comparability of data.... Thus, the entire enterprise of culture comparative research collapses if the assumption of psychic unity of human kind is rejected." Cross-cultural research is both implicitly and explicitly comparative (Segall et al., 1999).

The so-called "modern era" of cross-cultural psychology (Lonner, 2000, p. 4), with active contributions from the mid-1960s, the launch of the *Journal of Cross-Cultural Psychology* in 1970, and the establishment of the International Association for Cross-Cultural Psychology in 1972, affirm that cross-cultural psychology as a field has come to stay as a major player in psychology, unless of course it gets integrated and all psychology becomes "culture-inclusive" (Valsiner, 1989; see also Berry, Segall, & Kagitcibasi, 1997).

One of the major criticisms against cross-cultural psychology, especially by cultural psychologists (see Miller, 1997), has been that it oversimplifies the role of culture by viewing it as an independent variable, whereas in reality culture and individual cannot be isolated. This has led to interesting debates on the issue in recent years (Jahoda & Krewer, 1997). Recently, Berry (2000) argued that from the perspective of cross-cultural psychology, culture be viewed as both an organismic and an independent variable. Being both "outside the skin", i.e., having an existence that transcends the individual members of the culture, and "inside the head" in that it is interactive and mutually influencing in its relation to the individual, is an argument also addressed by Dasen in his paper in this volume.

Cultural Psychology

Cultural psychology, with its focus on cultural relativism, has leading contributions from somewhat varied schools of thought, each with its own distinctive framework, but with a consensus on cultural relativism and the co-construction of culture and individual behaviour (see Cole, 1996; Greenfield, 1997; Miller, 1997; Shweder et al., 1998 for detailed discussions).

Mistry and Saraswathi (2003) highlighted three core features of cultural psychology in its study of culture and human development: (*a*) a focus on understanding culturally constructed meaning systems; (*b*) the assumption that culture and individual psychological functioning are mutually constitutive and cannot be understood in isolation; and (*c*) an emphasis on interpretive methodology with a focus on subjective meaning (rather than the experimental/

and psychometric approach adopted by cross-cultural psychology).

In her comprehensive review of cultural approaches to psychology, Miller (1997) stated:

> The dominant stance within cultural psychology is to view culture and psychology as mutually constitutive phenomena,... which make up each other or are integral to each other. In such a view, it is assumed that culture and individual behavior cannot be understood in isolation, yet are also not reducible to each other (p. 88).

In his foreword to Cole's (1996, p. xii) *Cultural psychology: A once and future discipline*, Sheldon White provides a succinct summary of the characteristic features of the cultural approaches to psychology. These include an emphasis on mediated action in context; the use of the "genetic method" understood broadly to include historical, ontogenetic, and microgenetic levels of analysis; the grounding of analysis in everyday life events; the assumption that the mind emerges in the joint activity of people (is co-constructed); a view of individuals as active agents in their own development; and an acknowledgement of a central role for interpretation in its explanatory framework. Cole (1996) captured the essence of the cultural approach to ontogeny that draws together the cultural–historical time (embedded in geological time and phylogeny), the life of the individual (ontogeny), and the history of the moment-to-moment lived experience (microgenesis) (see Figure).

While theoretically sophisticated and intuitively appealing, cultural psychology is yet to provide convincing answers to the presence/absence of psychic unity of basic psychological processes and consequently the issue of generalizability across contexts (Greenfield, 1997; Jahoda, & Krewer, 1997; Miller, 1997). Both cross-cultural and cultural psychology share the interest in understanding the role of culture in human development. However, the seemingly wide disparity in approach to understanding the role of culture has created a cleavage not exactly growth promoting in the discipline.

Eckensberger's paper on action theory provides a perspective of cultural psychology and is implicit in some of Dasen's postulations.

Figure

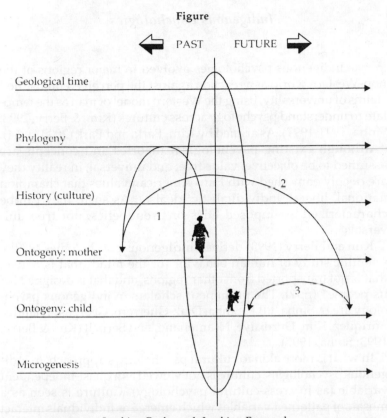

Looking Backward, Looking Forward

Note: The horizontal lines represent time scales corresponding to the history of
the physical universe, the history of life on earth (phylogeny), the history
of human beings on earth (cultural–historical time), the life of the individual
(ontogeny), and the history of moment-to-moment lived experience (microgenesis). The vertical ellipse represents the event of a child's birth. The
distribution of cognition in time is traced sequentially into (1) the mother's
memory of her past, (2) the mother's imagination of the future of the child,
and (3) the mother's subsequent behaviour. In this sequence, the ideal
aspect of culture is transformed into its material form as the mother and
other adults structure the child's experience to be consistent with what
they imagine to be the child's future identity. Reprinted by permission of
the publisher from *Cultural psychology: A once and future discipline* by
Michael Cole, p. 185, Cambridge, Mass: The Belknap Press of Harvard
University Press, Copyright © 1996 by the President and Fellows of Harvard College.

Indigenous Psychologies

Indigenous psychologies evolved in major regions of the non-Western world as a reaction against the perceived unjustified claims of universality, using the Western model of man as the template to understand psychology across cultures (Kim, & Berry, 1993; Sinha, 1993; 1997). As argued by Kim, Park, and Park (2000, p. 64), "Although existing psychological theories and concepts are assumed to be objective, value free, and universal, in reality they are deeply enmeshed with Euro American values that champion national, liberal, individualistic ideals.... As such, they can be characterized as imposed etics or pseudoetics, not true universals".

Kim and Berry (1993) defined indigenous psychologies as "the scientific study of human behavior (or the mind) that is native, that is not transported from other regions, and that is designed for its people" (p. 2). The prominent scholars in indigenous psychology are D. Sinha, J.B.P. Sinha, Diaz-Guerrero, Georgas, Triandis, Enriquez, Kim, Durojaiye, Nsamenang, and Serpell (Kim & Berry, 1993; Sinha, 1997).

In what is more akin to cultural psychology's approach, in indigenous psychologies, culture is not viewed as a quasi-independent variable (as in cross-cultural psychology). Culture is seen as a mosaic of patterned variables which emerge as individuals interact with their natural and human environments (Kim, Park, & Park, 2000).

Kagitcibasi and Poortinga (2000) drew attention to a significant difference between an indigenous orientation as a means as against indigenization as a goal. Indigenous orientation helps uncover the diversity of human behaviours and the circumstances in which they occur. They cited as exemplars such constructs as the nurturant task leader proposed by J.B.P. Sinha (1980) in the Indian organizational setting, and the autonomous–relational self proposed by Kagitcibasi (1996) in the context of Turkish families. Indigenization as a goal in itself can, on the other hand, create an unwieldy body of knowledge that remains insular and isolationist. Used in the former sense, an integration of knowledge gained from indigenous psychologies and subjected to cross-cultural testing could enrich the emergence of a truly universal psychology (Kim & Berry, 1993).

Anita Rampal's paper on everyday mathematics in the Indian context provides an interesting exemplar of indigenous psychology related to numeracy. Nsamenang makes an eloquent plea for accommodating alternative worldviews, examining the same in the context of Africa. Kagitcibasi's description of the autonomous–relational self is another significant contribution to this volume.

Anthropological Perspectives

Munroe and Munroe (1997) described the defining characteristic of cultural anthropology as its emphasis on the study of human beings in situ. The focus is on the use of qualitative field research and the explication of natural situations, rather than research under controlled conditions. Comparative anthropology, with which cross-cultural psychology has historical links, is a flourishing subdiscipline comprising both field studies and archival research. Schlegel describes this briefly in her paper.

Psychological anthropology is another allied discipline (see Lonner & Adamopoulos, 1997 for a detailed treatment of the subject). The Six Cultures Project is a good example of the kinds of research done by psychological anthropologists and which cross-cultural psychology has cross-fertilized.

Two themes highlighted by Munroe and Munroe (1997) in their essay on a comparative anthropological perspective, are particularly relevant in the context of this volume. First, is the emphasis on *universality*, stating that "All classes of phenomena, whether concepts, processes, or covariations among factors, whether within cultures or across cultures, will display central tendencies, not simply a rectangular distribution of equally likely and unique variates" (p. 176).

The emphasis is on the possibility of cultural comparisons and reasons to expect central tendencies in many classes of human behaviour, even while accounting for variations or culturally unique phenomena. This stance is similar to the one adopted by cross-cultural psychology. Reviewing the literature in the areas of perception, cognition, language, and sex typing, Munroe and Munroe argued that the uniformities observed in psychological behaviours "resonate with those we have seen for the expression of biological needs. While emphasizing universality we have also drawn attention to the impressive cultural diversity ..." (p. 186).

Second, is the attention to levels of analysis, namely, individual level variables, interpersonal level variables, and institutional level variables that have implications for the measurement and mode of aggregation of data (see Berry et al., 1992/2002, ch. 9, for discussions on the interface between cross-cultural psychology and the subdisciplines of anthropology both in theory and method).

Schlegel's paper on adolescence best illustrates the interface between the anthropological approach and cross-cultural methods.

Evolutionary Approaches

Because of my own limited familiarity with literature in this area, the ideas expressed in this section are essentially drawn from the comprehensive review on the topic by Keller (1997). Her paper in this volume presents the key theoretical ideas and their application in the area of infant development.

E.O. Wilson's (1975) book *Sociobiology: The new synthesis* may be viewed as a landmark in modern sociobiological conception. Wilson's challenging postulate that it is the genes and not the phenotypic individual that forms the unit of analysis, and that the successful transfer of genes to the next generation forms the metatheoretical formulation of the meaning of life from an evolutionary biological perspective, has generated much debate as well as theoretical and empirical work in the area (cf. Keller, 1997).

The major assumptions of the evolutionary approaches, as summarized succinctly by Keller (1997), include: (a) humans are primarily egoistic and altruism is also based on cost-benefit calculations; (b) social interactions are not based on equality and justice, but on their contribution to the inclusive fitness of the participants; (c) the necessity of regulating social interactions in terms of fitness calculations is regarded as the reason for the evolution of intelligence; (d) due to central tendencies that complement individual competition, biological marker variables like age and sex influence differential reproductive strategies; (e) reproductive strategies are developed within specific resource situations prevalent in particular environments; and (f) culture can be understood as an attempt to avoid unnecessary individual constructions that would delay ontogenetic development, because it summarizes and conceptualizes the more stable and even invariant contextual features, as environmental knowledge that is passed on from one generation to the next (Keller, 1997, p. 246). The evolutionary approaches present a synthesis between the biological and social sciences. Of particular interest to cross-cultural psychology is the fact that the evolutionary approaches take into account behavioural universals as well as universals in the contexts of development.

Culture and Human Development

Beyond the differential paradigmatic approaches, in the final analysis, all the disciplines and subdisciplines reviewed briefly in this section aim at understanding the intricate relations between culture and human development. This brings the developmental perspective centre stage. The potential of the developmental approach to capture the interplay of biological and cultural influences is best articulated by Gauvain (1995): "The inextricable connection between human biological processes, cultural systems of meaning and action, and their joint passage through time and historical circumstances constitutes the landscape of human development" (p. 27).

Even in the 1970s, when the modern *avatar* of cross-cultural psychology had found a firm footing, Eckensberger (1979) had pointed out that since the impact of culture upon individual behaviour is assumed to work "in time", it was important for cross-cultural psychology to be developmentally-oriented so as to unravel the interaction between the contributions of biology and culture to development. His own action theory model analyses development at three levels: *microgenesis* as in the unfolding of a single action; individual development or *ontogeny*; and historical development as viewed in sociocultural change.

Commenting on the "reciprocal and parallel blind spots of developmental and cross-cultural psychologies", Valsiner and Lawrence (1997) lamented, "[B]oth the life-span focus within developmental psychology and comparative cross-cultural psychology have advanced without giving sufficient attention to the mechanisms of human development by which culture and life-long personal development constrain each other" (p. 71). Their model of lifespan development is anchored on the idea that the pathways of human development are constrained or canalized and directed by the collective culture and person–culture transactions that mutually effect change. Valsiner and Lawrence argued that the lifespan perspective "... requires that we take up the call for culture-inclusive, open-systemic, whole-life approaches to the study of development" (p. 99). A tall order indeed, but something that calls for serious reflection.

Keller and Greenfield (2000) pointed out that while cultural and cross-cultural psychology have exerted a major influence on many areas of developmental psychology, the inverse influence is barely visible. They cited two reasons for this: one is intellectual in that developmentalists are interested in the *process* of socialization and enculturation, a perspective that is at variance with comparative psychology's view of culture as an independent variable. The second reason is the dominant role of social psychology and social psychologists in giving direction to cross-cultural psychology (informal discussions reveal that this may be a gendered issue with male dominance in social and female predominance in developmental psychology). The consequence is that the cross-cultural study of development "... is simultaneously a central player in developmental psychology and a marginal player in cross-cultural psychology" (Keller & Greenfield, 2000, p. 53).

The significant contributions that developmental study can make and has made to the theory and method in psychology have received fairly wide recognition (Best, 2000; Bornstein, 1980; Gielen, in press; Keller & Greenfield, 2000). All of them point out that developmental psychology has had a head start in the use of contextualized procedures such as naturalistic observation so critical for cultural studies. Similarly, developmental studies illustrate that the culturally constructed behaviour of adults can be viewed as an end point along a developmental pathway and that the vertical transmission of culture occurs through child socialization (Keller & Greenfield, 2000). Further, as is evident from every handbook or textbook on human development, developmental studies offer scope for the identification of early periods for effective intervention in health and education or the inculcation of prosocial behaviour (see Berry, Dasen, & Saraswathi, 1997; Dasen & Mishra, 2000).

There are reasons for optimism about the more visible recognition of developmental studies in the field. Gielen (in press) traced the history of cross-cultural human development studies during the twentieth century, starting from Kidd's (1906) pioneering work on savage childhood to contemporary literature including his own edited volume. His meticulous listing of nearly 60 publications as milestones in the cross-cultural study of childhood and adolescence is an extremely useful reference for scholars in this field. Contributions of non-Western scholars are particularly noteworthy. Of these I would like to make a special mention of Kagitcibasi's (1996) work in Turkey, Nsamenang's (1992) African worldview, and Saraswathi's (1999) work in the Indian subcontinent. Among the textbooks, those by Cole and Cole (2001), Gardiner and Kosmitzki (2002), Munroe and Munroe (1975/1994), and Segall et al. (1999) are particularly useful for introductory courses in cross-cultural human development.

Gielen (in press) listed 10 general assumptions structuring current cross-cultural investigations in human development. As they provide a useful framework for viewing the themes in this volume, some of the key ideas are summarized here: (*a*) human development is the outcome of complex and continuous interactions between biological predispositions, psychological processes, eco-cultural environment, and cultural belief systems; (*b*) culture is not simply an external variable; rather culture, mind, and behaviour "make each other up"; (*c*) cultural determinism and cultural relativism constitute outdated points of view; (*d*) human development, in all its complexity, can only be understood from a cross-cultural perspective. This calls for a multimethod and a multidisciplinary approach; (*e*) increasing contributions by non-Western social scientists are welcome and useful in easing the Western stranglehold over the discipline, at the same time strengthening culture sensitive alternative perspectives; and (*f*) a significant conceptualization that emerges from this is the possibility of alternative pathways in human development across cultures.

In sum, it may be concluded, "... the incorporation of cultural issues in the field of developmental psychology, be it in theory building or in its application to field situations, can serve as a mutually enriching experience for expanding the theoretical horizons as well as the extension of knowledge to promote the well-being of children ..." (Saraswathi & Dasen, 1997, p. xxxv). Reviewing the literature on cross-cultural developmental psychology till the 1980s, Bornstein's (1980) concluding comment continues to be pertinent:

> cross-cultural developmental comparison has caused us to rethink the origins and developmental course of behavior. Without it, our conclusions about some of the basics of human nature, as exemplified in motor development, perception, cognition, language acquisition, and social behavior *are at best shortsighted, ethnocentric, and suspect.* In the absence of cross-cultural developmental research, our psychology would be incorrect (pp. 266–267; emphasis added).

Integration

Having provided a bird's-eye view of the major disciplines, subdisciplines and schools of thought that dominate the field of cross-cultural and cultural psychology today, and that find representation in the contributions included in this volume, I conclude this section with a plea for integration. In an area of study that is barely a century old and in a discipline which has so many unchartered territories in several substantive areas, it seems paradoxical to waste energy like the six blind men who set out to construct their independent knowledge of the elephant's physique.

In my own search for companions in distress regarding the futility of insularity, in what can be enrichment through complementarity, I found several soul mates in literature. Expressed in many voices, the dominant idea that comes through is the need for and the possibility of interface, if not integration, among allied disciplines, schools of thought, methodological approaches, and between theory and practice.

The plea is also voiced implicitly or explicitly in many of the contributions included here such as those by Berry, Dasen, Keller, Schlegel, Kagitcibasi, Rampal, and Katz.

In the millennium special issue of the *Journal of Cross-Cultural Psychology*, Kagitcibasi and Poortinga (2000) drew attention to the converging theme of integration across the articles. These include, for example, the complementarity of the biological and cultural perspectives (Kashima, 2000; Keller & Greenfield, 2000), the possible contribution of differential indigenous psychologies to universal psychology (Kim, Park, & Park, 2000), the convergence of quantitative and qualitative methods (Kagitcibasi & Poortinga, 2000; Singelis, 2000), and the interdependency of theory and practice (Harkness & Keefer, 2000).

Similarly, in the 1997 edition of the *Handbook of cross-cultural psychology*, several authors have taken a stand that calls for complementarity along with a clear appreciation of the basic assumptions in one's own paradigmatic position (Jahoda & Krewer—historical; Miller—theoretical; Sinha—indigenous; Munroe & Munroe—anthropological; Keller—evolutionary; Greenfield—methodological; and Poortinga—convergence).

Poortinga's (1997) chapter on convergence is perhaps the most comprehensive attempt at building bridges. Poortinga argued for the need to "transgress self-imposed paradigmatic boundaries" especially between cultural and cross-cultural psychology, to examine the possible complementarity of the different approaches used to study the culture–behaviour–development interface. He stressed the significant but limited role played by different approaches or paradigms in explaining the culture–behaviour interaction, leaving much unexplained variance.

After critically examining the distinctions between culture–comparative and cultural approaches in terms of theory, methodology, conceptualization of culture, and possible generalizations, Poortinga reiterated his earlier proposal (1992; cf. 1997) that culture be viewed as a set of shared constraints and affordances. The other constraints include biological and genetic; the ecological context; the socioeconomic and historical context; and that of the specific concrete situation wherein the person's choices are limited by all the other constraints. Poortinga viewed this definition of culture as a set of shared constraints that limit the behaviour repertoire of members of a given group and distinguishes them from others, "as one possible way in which seemingly incompatible orientations to behavior–culture relationships can be defined as compatible and complementary" (p. 378). This view warrants further dialogue among adherents of alternative paradigms (also see Dasen & Mishra, 2000).

Within the context of cultural psychology, Miller (1998) made an eloquent plea for greater understanding and interchange between the diverse perspectives. "This means working to overcome the present disciplinary insularity as psychological investigators fail in certain cases to appreciate the strengths of interpretative anthropological research, and as anthropological investigators at times are dismissive of quantitative psychological research ..." (p. 6). The plea is for "achieving" a better synthesis or convergence "of the contrasting assumptions, goals, and multiple commitments informing the multiple theoretical perspectives represented in cultural approaches to psychology and of ways in which these perspectives overlap with, ... or even complement each other" (p. 7). The last caveat applies beyond the boundaries of cultural psychologies also to others devoted to understanding the culture–mind interface.

Eckensberger's paper in this volume may also be viewed as an attempt at integration, focusing on the dialectical relationship between person and environment through actions. Persons are seen as constructing their own reality and making choices between possible actions to reach a goal. Eckensberger views the model of the reflexive person who acts with agency and future goal orientation as the most inclusive paradigm among the five "worldviews" or alternative models of man examined by him in as early as 1979.

The controversial stand between cultural and cross-cultural psychology needs a clearer resolution for constructive progress in the field (Dasen & Mishra, 2000; Saraswathi, 1998). Even in the 1960s, Berry (1969) had postulated the complementarity of "the emic and etic position to capture both culture-specific and culture-general aspects of behavior" (Kagitcibasi & Poortinga, 2000, p. 131). This position is reiterated in Berry et al. (1992/2002) and Segall et al. (1999) with the concepts of universalism and cultural relativism, acknowledging the differential manifestations of basic psychological processes. Berry (2000) brought together his own and others' plea for a symbiosis of cultural and comparative approaches made over the last three decades (1969–2000) of active contributions to the field. He argued that the cultural, indigenous and comparative traditions of research are mutually compatible, and allow for a symbiotic approach. According to him, the three traditions can be incorporated into the generic field of cross-cultural psychology that will lead to the pursuit of a universal psychology. (The special issue of the *Asian Journal of Social Psychology* in which Berry's [2000] article appears also includes other contributions on related topics.) In his paper in this volume, Berry offers further arguments to bridge the seemingly different yet complementary positions. A recent book by Keller, Poortinga, and Scholmerich (2002) includes several articles that interface biology and culture.

I would like to conclude by drawing on the words of Jahoda and Krewer (1997), who on the basis of a historical overview of cross-cultural and cultural psychology, commented: "In any case, there is a lesson to be learned: being more familiar with the work of our historical ancestors not only helps to give a clearer awareness of our own hidden assumptions, but may also reduce the danger of a periodic reinvention of the wheel" (p. 31). This must necessarily include the goals of the discipline, the basic assumptions and controversial issues of the past and their resolution. As in politics and good governance, the option of working together, rather than adopting a path of confrontation, may pay rich dividends in the construction of knowledge.

Organizational Framework of the Present Volume

INTEGRATION OF THEORETICAL FRAMEWORKS EXPLICATING CULTURE AND DEVELOPMENT

The 12 chapters in the book are organized into two major sections. The first section focuses primarily on theoretical perspectives with some reference to methodological issues. The chapters are authored by leading cross-cultural psychologists/cultural anthropologists who have made significant contributions to theory building in the area of cross-cultural psychology. The second section deals with research on topics with which the authors have been associated for more than a decade.

John W. Berry presents the historical evolution of the ecocultural perspective that he has been advocating since 1966 (Berry, 1966; 1976). Over a period of three and a half decades, the ecocultural model proposed by Berry has been used for empirical research on a wide range of topics such as socialization, perception and cognition, social behaviour, acculturation, and adaptation to social change. As articulated by the author,

> the ecocultural perspective is rooted in two basic assumptions, both deriving from Darwinian thought. The first ... is that all human societies exhibit commonalities ... and that the basic psychological *processes* are shared, species common characteristics of all human beings on which culture plays infinite variations.... The second ... is that *behaviour* is differentially developed and expressed in response to ecological and cultural contexts ... (pp. 51–52).

allowing for comparisons across cultures. In sum, "the ecocultural framework considers human diversity (both cultural and psychological) as a set of collective and individual adaptations to the context" (p. 55). Methodological issues related to the level of analyses at the individual and cultural levels are also addressed briefly.

Lutz Eckensberger's work addresses the need for contextualizing psychological theories and details the action theory paradigm. The empirical evidence presented as exemplars addresses to some extent the concern whether action theory can lead to empirically testable propositions or whether it will remain an analytical device to fit any situation (see Miller, 1997). It also broadens the concept of agency to move beyond individual agency to the agency of the collective. Pierre Dasen attempts an integration of some of the current theoretical frameworks useful for the explication of human behaviour and development, with Berry's ecocultural framework and the concept of developmental niche (Super & Harkness, 1986) as the central focus. He also examines related theories with overlapping ideas such as Bronfenbrenner's ecological systems theory (1986; 1989), the ecological and social cross-cultural model by Georgas (1988; 1993; cf. Dasen, this volume), Ogbu's (1981) ecological and cultural model, and Kagitcibasi's (1996) model of family change. Work in the area of parental ethnotheories or parents' cultural belief systems and on cosmologies, religion, and cultural belief systems is used to examine the efficacy of the integrated framework as well as in identifying lacunae in research that can serve to generate knowledge regarding different levels of influence.

BIOLOGICAL AND CULTURAL TRANSMISSIONS:
EVOLUTIONARY CONSIDERATIONS

The unique contribution of Heidi Keller to this volume is the delineation of evolutionary considerations in understanding human development by examining ontogeny as the interface between biology and culture. The core assumptions of evolutionary theorizing are: (*a*) human phylogeny has been shaped by adaptations to selective pressures which arose due to contextual demands; and (*b*) not only somatic and biological systems, but also social behaviour and the complex psychology of human beings follow the reproductive logic. Evolutionary theorizing extends the idea to the conception of inclusive fitness of the individual resulting from own procreation and the procreation of relatives with whom the individual shares genes. Linked to the assumptions of evolutionary theorizing, the central thrust of Keller's paper is the delineation of the ontogenetic stage of relationship learning in early infancy as part of open genetic programmes for the developmental task of relationship formation. "It has been demonstrated that the mode and structure of early significant relationships influence the reproductive style of an individual ... the mode and structure of early relationships are related to the individual's own later parenting style, and thus constitute an essential part of the reproductive effort" (p. 110).

ALTERNATIVE PATHWAYS TO DEVELOPMENT

Two papers in the book address substantive issues related to human development in non-Western cultures (what Kagitcibasi refers to as the cultures of the majority world). Bame Nsamenang speaks in the voice of sub-Saharan Africa, and Cigdem Kagitcibasi deals with differential socialization in varied cultural contexts that result in alternative pathways for the development of various combinations of the autonomous and relational selves, and their implications for planned intervention programmes in the context of Turkish culture.

Nsamenang argues that different cultures value and socialize for different pathways in the human life course. Every cultural community has a worldview that includes an image of the human person and his or her ontogenesis. In most indigenous cultural worldviews, "socialization and education are organized to gradually integrate children from an early age into responsible roles through guided participation in valued cultural and economic activities at different stages of life" (p. 217). It is imperative that educationists and social scientists are trained to comprehend the significance of this diversity. Contemporary formal education in the school system as enforced in sub-Saharan Africa (and most of the non-Western countries) more often than not do not synchronize with the indigenous socialization or non-formal educational practices. This mismatch results in alienation and intergenerational conflicts not conducive to individual or societal development. This is a critical issue that psychologists and educators need to deal with and address.

Kagitcibasi extends the argument of alternative pathways in human development with the development of self and competence as the central focus. Her thesis is that in societies undergoing rapid socioeconomic change, the development of self and competence need to be understood from a contextual-functional perspective. She examines the socioeconomic–cultural contexts and differential family interaction pattern and child rearing orientations that lead to alternative expressions of self. Kagitcibasi argues that the constructs of autonomy or agency and relatedness are orthogonal and that while independence and separatedness are fostered in Western middle class, nuclear family settings, and interdependence and relatedness in agrarian societies, a third alternative style or type combining material independence and psychological relatedness is evident in the urban middle class in many parts of the majority world, including urban Turkey. Her theory of self examines the relation between ecocultural context, family socialization practices and consequent individual behaviour. The impact of social change facilitates the scrutiny of how cultures and consequently individuals adapt to changing circumstances, highlighting the fact that culture is dynamic and subject to change and reconstruction. Further, the author uses a large scale intervention programme of training mothers in early education, as an exemplar of how low SES parents can be supported and induced to value autonomy while continuing to uphold closeness to their children (Kagitcibasi, Bekman, & Goksel, 1995). Kagitcibasi opines that such a combination of autonomy and relatedness may be optimal, rather than an excessive emphasis on independence or interdependence, especially in the context of urbanization, formal schooling and changing sociocultural settings. This theoretical argument is used as a rationale for planned interventions in early childhood through mother involvement in Turkish families.

ADOLESCENCE IN A CROSS-CULTURAL PERSPECTIVE

Two papers in this collection provide a rich array of empirical data on adolescence and serve as excellent exemplars of methodological alternatives to standard experimental or survey methods in psychology. While the topical area chosen is adolescence, the methodology is applicable across the lifespan. Schlegel examines adolescence from an anthropological perspective. The empirical data was drawn from the histories and ethnographies of cultures in the Standard Cross-Cultural Sample (Murdock & White, 1980/1969), a sample of 186 tribal and traditional societies across the world. It mainly represents preindustrial societies in all world regions. The cross-cultural method uses cultures (and not individuals) as units of analysis. From the substantive point of view, the author makes a case for the social recognition of the stage called adolescence across all cultures. The content and duration of the stage, however, seem to vary. In many societies, adolescence is followed by a stage referred to as youth wherein marriage, and the social recognition of adulthood were delayed at least for males. Schlegel describes the social construction of adolescence in 186 societies included in the sample. The description includes variations in the observance of a ritual to formally recognize the life stage, gender differences in expectations regarding social behaviours, and in heterosexual interactions. The author contrasts the picture of adolescents as full participants in their families and communities in most preindustrial societies with that in America wherein adolescents are practically excluded from adult company, and expresses concern regarding such an exclusion. The apprenticeship programme for skill training of adolescents in Germany and the involvement of adolescents in community programmes in Northern Italy highlight the fact that meaningful participation of adolescents in the adult world is possible and productive in modern industrial societies also. India, at the crossroads of social change, can perhaps draw useful lessons from this.

The second paper on adolescence by Larson, Verma, and Dworkin examines the daily family lives of Indian middle class teenagers. As mentioned earlier, the work reported here is based on an innovative methodology called the Experience Sampling Method (ESM), wherein participants carried alarm watches for a week and filled out self-reports on their experience every time the alarm was sounded. Eight signals were sent at random times each day between 7.30 am and 9.30 pm, providing a total of 4,764 self-reports. Based on a comprehensive survey of 100 middle class adolescents, using the ESM method, the authors infer that Indian adolescents as compared to their American counterparts spend less time alone and with their peers, and much more time with their families. In terms of preference also, the family appears to be a high priority for Indian Grade 8 children while peers were the dominant choice for American adolescents. Further, in terms of affect, Indian adolescents reported feeling happier than Americans during time spent with their families; and did not experience the family as authoritarian. Based on their data, the authors conclude that the concern expressed by a number of Indian scholars regarding the negative impact of social change on family relations is not warranted.

EARLY INTERVENTION

Kagitcibasi's eloquent thesis on possible alternative pathways to development is complemented by Bekman's paper that describes a nationwide early intervention programme in Turkey. Bekman summarizes the major facets of the Turkish early enrichment project, which evolved from an applied research project conducted at the Bogacizi University in Istanbul. With its focus on home based intervention and mother training, the project known as the Mother-Child Education Programme (MOCEP) has expanded over the last two decades to touch the lives of more than 1,20,000 families across the nation (Kagitcibasi, this volume). MOCEP is implemented through the collaboration of the Mother-

Child Education Foundation and the Ministry of National Education in Turkey. The programme has three main components: to foster cognitive development of the child; to sensitize mothers to the overall development of the child; and to inform mothers about reproductive health and family planning. Spread over 25 weeks, the programme targets children who are "at risk" due to their environmental conditions. The results of the initial experimental study in the 1980s (Kagitcibasi, Sunar, & Bekman, 1988) and the follow-up study (Bekman, 1998; Kagitcibasi, Bekman, & Goksel, 1995) clearly reveal the impact of early home intervention not only on children but also on the mother, and on the relationship between the mother and the child. The likelihood that enhanced school readiness would pave the way for better academic performance was clearly confirmed by the results obtained on the cognitive performance and school achievement of children at the end of the first year of primary school. MOCEP also mitigates the negative effects associated with cognitively non-stimulating homes and inadequate study environments. In sum, MOCEP offers an excellent exemplar of the possibility of early enrichment to ensure the positive impact of formal schooling.

The paper by Rampal best illustrates an attempt to evolve grounded theory. Based on a rich array of information drawn from cross-cultural literature and folklore on everyday mathematics and her own provocative experience with numeracy education for adult learners, Rampal draws inferences that have significant import for understanding teaching and learning. These include the existence of a rich fund of indigenous knowledge that is found in everyday practice of mathematics; the failure of the formal education system to take advantage of the existing cultural practices to make formal learning more meaningful and useful; and the implications of this for teacher training and formal education.

In her thematic paper on early childhood education (ECE), Lilian G. Katz reviews the main trends, issues, and principles of practice in ECE, and draws implications for practice. Beginning with an outline of the principles of practice underlying a developmental approach to early education, she describes a major element of early childhood practice implied by them. The principles of practice for education in the early years address four basic questions: What should be learned? When it should be learned? How is it best learned? How can one assess how well the first three questions have been answered? The emphasis is on a developmental approach to early childhood practices. "A developmental approach to curriculum and teaching practices … is one that takes into account knowledge of development and principles derived therefrom … as they apply to decisions about curriculum content, teaching methods, and the developmental progression of the learners" (p. 358). Katz elaborates the developmental approach to early education in the form of 19 principles. Taken together, these principles suggest that young children need to be provided the contexts for learning in all four major categories: knowledge, skills, dispositions, and feelings, and have ample opportunity for the meaningful application and strengthening of the basic and essential literacy, numeracy, and social skills. They further suggest that young children should have frequent and continual opportunity to engage in small group efforts to investigate significant phenomena and events around them. Katz's contribution illustrates the integration of theory, research and practice.

Concluding Comment

In the pages that follow, the authors present a range of theoretical, methodological, and applied perspectives that are informative and thought provoking. Considering the range of cultures they represent, there is reason to believe that there is adequate universalism, at least in the process of the search for how culture and mind influence or construct and reconstruct each other. What is more, they communicate lucidly across cultural barriers be it East or West, North or South.

References

Bekman, S. (1998). *Fair chance: An evolution of the mother-education program.* Istanbul: Mother-Child Education Publication.

Berry, J.W. (1966). Temne and Eskimo perceptual skills. *International Journal of Psychology, 1,* 207–229.

Berry, J.W. (1969). On cross-cultural comparability. *International Journal of Psychology, 19,* 335–361.

Berry, J.W. (1976). *Human ecology and cognitive style: Comparative studies in cultural and psychological adaptation.* New York: Sage.

Berry, J.W. (2000). Cross-cultural psychology: A symbiosis of cultural and comparative approaches. *Asian Journal of Social Psychology, 3,* 197–205.

Berry, J.W., Dasen, P.R., & Saraswathi, T.S. (Eds). (1997). *Handbook of cross-cultural psychology. Vol. 2. Basic processes and human development.* Boston: Allyn & Bacon.

Berry, J.W., Poortinga, Y.H., & Pandey, J. (Eds). (1997). *Handbook of cross-cultural psychology. Vol. 1. Theory and method* (2nd ed.). Boston: Allyn & Bacon.

Berry, J.W., Poortinga, Y.H., Segall, M.H., & Dasen, P.R. (1992/2002). *Cross-cultural psychology: Research and applications.* Cambridge: Cambridge University Press.

Berry, J.W., Segall, M.H., & Kagitcibasi, C. (Eds). (1997). *Handbook of cross-cultural psychology, Vol. 3. Social behavior and applications* (2nd ed.). Boston: Allyn & Bacon.

Best, D.L. (2000). Recent trends in cross-cultural studies in human development: The role of current research traditions. In A.L. Comunian & U. Gielen (Eds), *International perspectives on human development.* Lengerich: Pabst Science Publications.

Bornstein, M.H. (1980). Cross-cultural developmental psychology. In M.H. Bornstein (Ed.), *Comparative methods in psychology* (pp. 231–281). Hillsdale, NJ: Lawrence Erlbaum.

Bronfenbrenner, U. (1986). Ecology of family as a context for human development: Research perspectives. *Developmental Psychology, 22,* 723–742.

Bronfenbrenner, U. (1989). Ecological systems theory. *Annals of Child Development, 6,* 185–246.

Cole, M. (1996). *Cultural psychology: A once and future discipline.* Cambridge, Mass: The Belknap Press of Harvard University Press.

Cole, M., & Cole, S. (2001). *The development of children* (4th ed.). New York: Worth.

Dasen, P.R., & Mishra, R.C. (2000). Cross-cultural views on human development in the third millennium. *International Journal of Behavioral Development, 24*(4), 428–434.

Eckensberger, L.H. (1979). A metamethodological evaluation of psychological theories from a cross-cultural perspective. In L. Eckensberger, W. Lonner, & Y.H. Poortinga (Eds), *Cross-cultural contributions to psychology* (pp. 255–275). Lisse: Swets & Zeitlinger.

Gardiner, H.W., & Kozmitzki, C. (2002). *Lives across cultures. Cross-cultural human development* (2nd ed.). Boston: Allyn & Bacon.

Gauvain, M. (1995). Thinking in niches: Sociocultural influences on cognitive development. *Human Development, 38,* 25–45.

Gielen, U.P. (in press). The cross-cultural study of human development. An opinionated historical introduction. In U.P. Gielen & J.L. Roopnaraine (Eds), *Childhood and adolescence in cross-cultural perspective.* Westport, CT: Greenwood Press.

Greenfield, P.M. (1997). Culture as process: Empirical methods for cultural psychology. In J.W. Berry, Y.H. Poortinga, & J. Pandey (Eds), *Handbook of cross-cultural psychology. Vol. 1. Theory and method* (2nd ed., pp. 301–346). Boston: Allyn & Bacon.

Harkness, S., & Keefer, C.H. (2000). Contributions of cross-cultural psychology to research and interventions in education and health. *Journal of Cross-Cultural Psychology*, 31(1), 92–109.

Jahoda, G., & Krewer, B. (1997). History of cross-cultural and cultural psychology. In J.W. Berry, Y.H. Poortinga, & J. Pandey (Eds), *Handbook of cross-cultural psychology. Vol. 1. Theory and method* (2nd ed., pp. 1–42). Boston: Allyn & Bacon.

Kagitcibasi, C. (1996). The autonomous–relational self: A new synthesis. *European Psychologist*, 1, 180–186.

Kagitcibasi, C., Bekman, S., & Goksel, A. (1995). Multipurpose model of nonformal education: The mother-child education program. *Coordinators' Notebook*, 17, 24–32.

Kagitcibasi, C., & Poortinga, Y.H. (2000). Cross-cultural psychology: Issues and overarching themes. *Journal of Cross-Cultural Psychology*, 31(1), 129–147.

Kagitcibasi, C., Sunar, D., & Bekman, S. (1988). *Comprehensive preschool education project. Final report.* Ottawa: International Development Research Center.

Kashima, Y. (2000). Conceptions of culture and person for psychology. *Journal of Cross-Cultural Psychology*, 31(1), 14–32.

Keller, H. (1997). Evolutionary approaches. In J.W. Berry, Y.H. Poortinga, & J. Pandey (Eds), *Handbook of cross-cultural psychology. Vol. 1. Theory and method* (2nd ed., pp. 215–255). Boston: Allyn & Bacon.

Keller, H., & Greenfield, P.M. (2000). History and future of development in cross-cultural psychology. *Journal of Cross-Cultural Psychology*, Millennium special issue, 31(1), 52–62.

Keller, H., Poortinga, Y.H., & Scholmerich, A. (Eds). (2002). *Between biology and culture: Perspectives on ontogenetic development.* Cambridge: Cambridge University Press.

Kim, U., & Berry, J.W. (Eds). (1993). *Indigenous psychologies: Research and experience in cultural context* (vol. 17). Cross-cultural research and methodology series. Newbury Park, CA: Sage.

Kim, U., Park, Y.S., & Park, D. (2000). The challenge of cross-cultural psychology: The role of the indigenous psychologies. *Journal of Cross-Cultural Psychology*, 31(1), 63–75.

Lonner, W. (2000). Foreword. *Journal of Cross-Cultural Psychology*, 31(1), 3–4.

Lonner, W.J., & Adamopoulos, J. (1997). Culture as antecedent to behavior. In J.W. Berry, Y.H. Poortinga, & J. Pandey (Eds), *Handbook of cross-cultural psychology. Vol. 1. Theory and method* (2nd ed., pp. 43–83). Boston: Allyn & Bacon.

Miller, J.G. (1997). Theoretical issues in cultural psychology. In J.W. Berry, Y.H. Poortinga, & J. Pandey (Eds), *Handbook of cross-cultural psychology. Vol. 1. Theory and method* (2nd ed., pp. 85–128). Boston: Allyn & Bacon.

Miller, J.G. (1998). Theory and method: Series introduction. *Cross-Cultural Psychology Bulletin*, 32(2), 6–7.

Mistry, J., & Saraswathi, T.S. (2003). The cultural context of child development. In R.M. Lerner, M.A. Easterbrooks, & J. Mistry (Eds), *Handbook of psychology: Vol. 6. Developmental psychology* (pp. 267–291). New York: Wiley.

Munroe, R.H., & Munroe, R.H. (1997). A comparative anthropological perspective. In J.W Berry, Y.H. Poortinga, & J. Pandey (Eds), *Handbook of cross-cultural* psychology. Vol. 1. Theory and method (2nd ed., pp. 171–213). Boston: Allyn & Bacon.

Munroe, R.L., & Munroe, R.H. (1975/1994). Cross-cultural human development. Prospect Heights, IL: Waveland Press.

Murdock, G.P., & White, D.R. (1980/1969). Standard cross-cultural sample. In H. Barry & A. Schlegel (Eds), Cross-cultural samples and codes (pp. 3–42). Pittsburg: University of Pittsburg Press.

Nsamenang, A.B. (1992). Human development in cultural context. A third world perspective. Newbury Park, CA: Sage.

Oghu, J (1981) Origins of human competence: A cultural-ecological perspective. Child Development, 52, 413–429.

Poortinga, Y. (1997). Towards convergence. In J.W. Berry, Y.H. Poortinga, & J. Pandey (Eds), Handbook of cross-cultural psychology. Vol. 1. Theory and method (2nd ed., pp. 347–387). Boston: Allyn & Bacon.

Saraswathi, T.S. (1998). Many deities, one God: Towards convergence in cultural and cross-cultural psychology. Culture & Psychology, 4(2), 147–160.

Saraswathi, T.S. (Ed.). (1999). Culture, socialization and human development: Theory, research and applications in India. New Delhi: Sage.

Saraswathi, T.S., & Dasen, P.R. (1997). Introduction to volume 2. In J.W. Berry, P.R. Dasen, & T.S. Saraswathi (Eds), Handbook of cross-cultural psychology. Vol. 2 (pp. xxv–xxxvii). Boston: Allyn & Bacon.

Segall, M.H., Dasen, P.R., Berry, J.W., & Poortinga, Y.H. (1999). Human behavior in global perspective (2nd ed.). Boston: Allyn & Bacon.

Shweder, R.A., Goodnow, J., Hatano, G., LeVine, R.A., Markus, H., & Miller, P. (1998). The cultural psychology of development: One mind, many mentalities. In R.L. Lerner (Ed.), Handbook of child psychology: Vol. 1. Theoretical models of human development (pp. 865–938). New York: Wiley.

Singelis, T.M. (2000). Some thoughts on the future of cross-cultural social psychology. Journal of Cross-Cultural Psychology, 31(1), 76–91.

Sinha, D. (1993). Indigenization of psychology in India and its relevance. In U. Kim & J.W. Berry (Eds), Indigenous psychologies: Research and experience in cultural context (pp. 30–43). Newbury Park, CA: Sage.

Sinha, D. (1997). Indigenizing psychology. In J.W. Berry, Y.H. Poortinga, & J. Pandey (Eds), Handbook of cross-cultural psychology. Vol. 1. Theory and method (2nd ed., pp. 129–169). Boston: Allyn & Bacon.

Sinha, J.B.P. (1980). The nurturant task leader. New Delhi: Concept.

Super, C.M., & Harkness, S. (1986). The developmental niche: A conceptualization at the interface of child and culture. International Journal of Behavioral Development, 9(4), 545–570.

Valsiner, J. (Ed.). (1989). Cultural context and child development. Toronto: C.J. Hogrefe and H. Huber.

Valsiner, J., & Lawrence, J. (1997). Human development in culture across the life span. In J.W. Berry, P.R. Dasen, & T.S. Saraswathi (Eds), Handbook of cross-cultural psychology. Vol. 2 (pp. 69–106). Boston: Allyn & Bacon.

Wilson, E.O. (1975). Sociobiology: The new synthesis. Cambridge/MA: Belknap Press.

‍‍‍‍‍‍ Part 1 ‍‍

Theoretical Perspectives

↜ 1 ↝

Ecocultural Perspective on Human Psychological Development

JOHN W. BERRY

Introduction

The Nehru Chair in Human Development serves as an excellent podium from which to review my approach to the development of human diversity. I have advocated an ecocultural perspective for many years (Berry, 1966). It has evolved through a series of research studies devoted to understanding similarities and differences in cognition and social behaviour (Berry, 1976; Berry, Bennett, & Denny, 2000; Berry et al., 1986; Mishra, Sinha, & Berry, 1996) to a broad approach to understanding human diversity. The core ideas have a long history (Jahoda, 1995), and have been assembled into conceptual frameworks (Berry, 1975; 1995) used in empirical research, and in coordinating textbooks in cross-cultural psychology (Berry, Poortinga, Segall, & Dasen, 1992/2002; Segall, Dasen, Berry, & Poortinga, 1990/1999). Similar ideas and frameworks have been advanced both by anthropologists (Whiting, 1977) and psychologists (Bronfenbrenner, 1977) who share the view that human activity can only be understood within the context in which it develops and takes place.

The ecocultural perspective is rooted in two basic assumptions, both deriving from Darwinian thought. The first (the "universalist" assumption) is that all human societies exhibit commonalities ("cultural universals") and that the basic psychological *processes* are shared, species common characteristics of all human beings on which culture plays infinite variations during the course of development and daily activity. The second (the "adaptation" assumption) is that *behaviour* is differentially developed and expressed in response to ecological and cultural contexts. This view allows for comparisons across cultures (on the basis of the common underlying process), but makes comparison worthwhile (using the surface variation as basic evidence). Whether derived from anthropology (Murdock, 1975) or sociology (Aberle et al., 1950), there is substantial evidence that groups everywhere possess shared sociocultural attributes. For example, all peoples have language, tools, social structures (norms, roles), and social institutions (marriage, justice). It is also evident that such underlying commonalities are expressed by groups in vastly different ways from one time and place to another. Similarly, there is parallel evidence, at the psychological level, for both underlying similarity and surface variation (Berry et al., 1997). For instance, all individuals have the competence to develop, learn and perform speech, technology, role playing and norm observance. At the same time, there are obviously vast group and individual differences in the extent and style of expression of these shared underlying processes. This combination of underlying similarity with surface expressive variation has been termed as "universal" by Berry, Poortinga, Segall, and Dasen (1992/2002) to distinguish it from two other theoretical views: "absolutism" denies cultural influence on behavioural development and expression; while "relativism" denies the existence of common underlying psychological processes. Of course, while variations in behavioural expression can be directly observed, the underlying commonalities are a theoretical construction and cannot be observed directly (Troadec, 2001). Paradoxically, this search for our common humanity can only be pursued by observing our diversity. This dual task is the essence of cross-cultural psychology (Berry, 1968; 2000; Bril, 1995).

In the following an outline of our current thinking on how people adapt culturally (as a group) to their long-standing ecological settings is presented. It continues with a proposal about how people develop and perform (as individuals) in adaptation to their eco-cultural situation.

Ecological and Cultural Adaptation

A continuing theme in cultural anthropology is that cultural variations may be understood as adaptations to differing ecological settings or contexts (Boyd & Richerson, 1983). This line of thinking usually known as *cultural ecology* (Vayda & Rappoport, 1968), *ecological anthropology* (Moran, 1982; Vayda & McKay, 1975), or the *ecosystem approach* (Moran, 1990) to anthropology has a long history in the discipline (see Feldman, 1975). Its roots can be traced back to Forde's (1934) classic analysis of relationships between the physical habitat and societal features in Africa, and Kroeber's (1917) early demonstration that cultural areas and natural areas co-vary in aboriginal North America. Unlike earlier simplistic assertions by the school of "environmental determinism" (Huntington, 1945), the ecological school of thought has ranged from "possiblism" (where the environment provides opportunities, and sets some constraints or limits on the range of possible cultural forms that may emerge) to an emphasis on "resource utilization" (where active and interactive relationships between human populations and their habitat are analysed).

Of particular interest to psychologists was Steward's (1955) use of what was later known as the *cognized environment*; this concept refers to the "selected features of the environment of greatest relevance to a population's subsistence". With this notion, ecological thinking moved simultaneously away from any links to earlier deterministic views, and towards the more psychological idea of individuals actively perceiving, appraising, and changing their environments.

The earlier ecological approaches have tended to view cultural systems as relatively stable (even permanent) *adaptations* (as a state), largely ignoring *adaptation* (as a process), or *adaptability* (as a system characteristic) of cultural populations (Bennett, 1976). However, it is clear that cultures evolve over time, sometimes in response to changing ecological circumstances, and at times due to contact with other cultures. This fact has required the addition of a more dynamic conception of ecological adaptation as a continuous as well as an interactive process (between ecological, cultural, and psychological variables). It is from the most recent position that we approach the topic. It is a view that is consistent with more recent general changes in anthropology, away from a "museum" orientation to culture (collecting and organizing static artifacts) to one that emphasizes cultures as constantly changing, and being concerned with creation, metamorphosis, and recreation.

Over the years ecological thinking has influenced not only anthropology, but also psychology. The fields of ecological and environmental psychology have become fully elaborated (see Werner, Brown, & Altman, 1997), with substantial theoretical and empirical foundations. In essence, individual human behaviour has come to be seen in its natural setting or habitat, both in terms of its development, and its contemporary display. The parallel development of cross-cultural psychology (see Berry et al., 1997) has also "naturalized" the study of human behaviour and its development. In this field, individual behaviour is accounted for to a large extent by considering the role of cultural influences on it. In my own approach, ecological as well as cultural influences are considered as operating in tandem, hence the term "ecocultural approach".

An Ecocultural Approach

The current interpretation of the ecocultural framework (see Figure 1.1) proposes to account for human psychological diversity (both individual and group similarities and differences) by taking into account two fundamental sources of influence (ecological and sociopolitical), and two features of human populations that are adapted to them: cultural and biological characteristics. These population variables are transmitted to individuals by various "transmission variables" such as enculturation, socialization, genetics, and acculturation. Our understanding of both cultural and genetic transmission has been greatly advanced by recent work on culture learning (Tomasello, Kruger, & Ratner, 1993) and on the human genome project (Paabo, 2001). The essence of both these domains is the fundamental similarity of all human beings (at a deep level), combined with variation in the expression of these shared attributes (at the surface level). Work on the process and outcomes of acculturation has also advanced (Marin, Balls-

Organista, & Chung, 2001), necessitated by the dramatic increase in intercultural contact and change.

Figure 1.1
An Ecocultural Framework Linking Ecology,
Cultural Adaptation, and Individual Behaviour

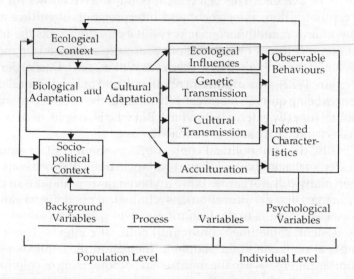

To summarize, the ecocultural framework considers human diversity (both cultural and psychological) as a set of collective and individual adaptations to the context. Within this general perspective, it views cultures as evolving adaptations to ecological and sociopolitical influences, and views individual psychological characteristics in a population as adaptive to their cultural context, as well as to the broader ecological and sociopolitical influences. It also views (group) culture and (individual) behaviour as distinct phenomena at their own levels, that need to be examined independently.

Within psychology, the findings of the burgeoning field of environmental psychology have attempted to specify the links between the ecological context and individual human development and behaviour. Cross-cultural psychology has tended to view cultures (both one's own and others with which one has contact) as *differential contexts* for development, and view behaviour as adaptive to these varying contexts.

The ecocultural approach offers a "value neutral" framework for describing and interpreting similarities and differences in human behaviour across cultures (Berry, 1994). As adaptive to context, psychological phenomena can be understood "in their own terms" (as Malinowski insisted), and external evaluations can usually be avoided. This is a critical point, since it allows for the conceptualization, assessment and interpretation of culture and behaviour in non-ethnocentric ways. It explicitly rejects the idea that some cultures or behaviours are more advanced or more developed than others (Berry, Dasen, & Witkin, 1983; Dasen, Berry, & Witkin, 1979). Any argument about cultural or behavioural differences being ordered hierarchically requires the adoption of some absolute (usually external) standard. But who is so bold, or so wise, to assert and verify such a standard?

Finally, the sociopolitical context brings about contact among cultures, so that individuals have to adapt to more than one context. When many cultural contexts are involved (as in situations of culture contact and acculturation), psychological phenomena can be viewed as attempts to deal simultaneously with two (sometimes inconsistent, sometimes conflicting) cultural contexts. These attempts at understanding people in their multiple contexts is an important alternative to the more usual pathologizing of colonized or immigrant cultures and peoples. Of course, these intercultural settings need to be approached from the same non-ethnocentric perspective as *cross-cultural* ones (Berry, 1985).

Studies of Perception and Cognition

Initially (Berry, 1966) the link between ecology, culture, and behaviour was elaborated into a framework in order to predict differential development of visual disembedding, analytic and spatial abilities between hunting based and agriculture based peoples. The first step was to propose that the "ecological demands" for survival that were placed on hunting peoples were for a high level of these perceptual–cognitive abilities, in contrast with people employing other (particularly agricultural) subsistence strategies. Second, it was proposed that "cultural aids" (such as socialization practices, linguistic differentiation of spatial information, and the use of arts and crafts) would promote the development of these abilities. As predicted, empirical studies of Inuit (or Eskimo) in the Canadian Arctic and Temne (in Sierra Leone) revealed marked differences in these abilities. Further work was done, and during the course of this empirical work, the ideas became further elaborated into an ecocultural framework. In each case, a consideration of ecological and cultural features of the group was taken as a basis for predicting differential psychological outcomes in a variety of domains. For example (Berry, 1967; 1979), differential degrees of reliance on hunting, and variations in social stratification (ranging from "loose" to "tight") (Pelto, 1968) and in child socialization practices (ranging from emphasis on "assertion" to "compliance") (Barry, Child, & Bacon, 1959) were used to predict variations in the development of these functional abilities.

Further work on perceptual and cognitive abilities (aligned in part to the theory of psychological differentiation, particularly the cognitive style of field dependence–field independence) (Witkin & Berry, 1975) led to the publication of three volumes (Berry, 1976; Berry et al., 1986; Mishra, Sinha, & Berry, 1996) reporting results of studies in the Arctic, Africa, Australia, New Guinea, and India.

The ecocultural framework has also been used to understand sources of variation in perceptual–cognitive development (Dasen, 1975; Nsamenang, 1992). This developmental focus is closely linked to an increasing interest in indigenous conceptions of cognitive competence and in the cognitive tasks faced by people in daily life (Berry & Irvine, 1986; Berry, Irvine, & Hunt, 1988). In this work, it is argued that the indigenous conceptions of competence need to be uncovered; competencies need to be seen as developments nurtured by activities of daily life ("bricolage"), and as adaptive to the ecological context. Understanding the indigenous conceptions of competence, cognitive values, daily activities, and contexts is an essential prerequisite for valid cognitive assessment. As in the case of cross-cultural and intercultural research strategies, these indigenous (within-culture) studies need to be undertaken from a non-ethnocentric perspective (Berry & Bennett, 1992).

Dimensions of Ecological and Cultural Variation

In order to conceptualize a number of possible human adaptations to varying habitats, a unidimensional ecocultural dimension was developed and operationalized (Berry, 1966; 1976) over the range of subsistence economic activities from hunting to agriculture. Around the same time, Lomax and Berkowitz (1972) found evidence of *two independent factors* of cultural variation over the ecological range from gatherers through hunters to agriculturalists to urban dwellers and they called these "differentiation" and "integration". The first refers to the number and kinds of role distinctions made in society, while the second refers to "groupiness" or degree of cohesion among members of a society, and to the social coordination of their day-to-day activities. While there are two independent dimensions, over the *middle range* of subsistence strategies the two dimensions are *positively correlated*. It is precisely at this middle range (hunters to agriculturalists) that my earlier (1966; 1976) unidimensional conceptualization and operationalization took place. Thus, the unidimensional nature of my earlier ecocultural dimension was not fundamentally incorrect; it was just restricted in range. (As an aside, this is a clear demonstration of the necessity of carrying out cross-cultural research across broad cultural sweeps.) A more general conceptualization, taking into account gatherers and urban societies, would need to adopt the two-dimensional view of ecological and cultural variation.

In a series of papers, Boldt and colleagues (Boldt, 1976; Boldt & Roberts, 1979; Roberts, Boldt, & Guest, 1990) pursued the possibility that there are indeed two independent dimensions (see also Gamble & Ginsberg, 1981). They argued that "structural complexity" and "structural tightness" need to be distinguished. The first refers to the number and diversity of roles in society, which "should expand the range of courses of action available to an actor, and therefore, enhance choice and individual autonomy" (Roberts, Boldt, & Guest, 1990, p. 69). The second refers to the degree to which social expectations are imposed on individuals, which should "reduce an actor's autonomy by narrowing the opportunities for negotiating a preferred course of action" (Roberts et al., 1990, p. 69).

This structural complexity–structural tightness distinction corresponds to the differentiation–integration distinction of Lomax and Berkowitz (1972). At the same time, it can be broken down into two components: the more general sociocultural indexes such as "cultural complexity" (McNett, 1970), "tightness–looseness" (Pelto, 1968), and my own ecocultural index (Berry, 1976). More specifically, for the ecocultural index, it places the ecological variables of settlement pattern and mean size of local community together with the cultural variable of political stratification into one construct ("structural complexity"), but puts the other cultural variables of social stratification and socialization emphases on compliance into another construct ("structural tightness").

Triandis (1994) introduced the concept of "cultural syndromes" that draws together some of these cultural dimensions. He adopted the "tight–loose" and the "cultural complexity" notions, and incorporated them into a framework linking them to the psychological dimension(s) of "individualism and collectivism". This framework shifts the focus from cognitive behaviours towards social behaviour, particularly to an interest in how, and how much, individuals become embedded in their social context. This area will be considered briefly.

Studies of Social Behaviour

While the ecocultural framework has been largely used in the study of perception and cognition, it has also been effectively employed to explore aspects of social behaviour. For example, studies of social conformity (Berry, 1967; 1979) have shown that greater conformity to a suggested group norm is likely to occur in cultures that are structurally tight (with high norm obligation). The relationship is robust, whether examined at the individual level, or by using the group's mean score as the variable related to ecology (see Bond & Smith, 1996, for a review). Another example has proposed links between ecocultural indicators and the currently popular concepts of "individualism" and "collectivism" (Berry, 1993). It is suggested that individualism may be related to the differentiation (structural complexity) dimensions, with greater differentiation in a society being predictive of greater personal individualism. However, it is argued that collectivism is related more to the integration (structural tightness) dimensions, with higher integration predictive of greater collectivism. It is further suggested that when individualism and collectivism are found to be at the opposite ends of one value dimension it is because data are usually obtained in societies (industrial urban) where the two cultural dimensions (differentiation and integration) are strongly distinguished; if data were to be collected over a broader range, in other types of societies (such as hunting or agricultural) where the two dimensions coincide, then this value opposition or incompatibility may not be observed.

Recent work (Georgas & Berry, 1995; Georgas, van de Vijver, & Berry, 2000) has further extended this interest in social aspects of behaviour. The first study sought to discover ecological and social indicators that may allow societies to be clustered according to their similarities and differences on six dimensions: ecology, education, economy, mass communications, population, and religion. The second study examined ecosocial indicators across cultures, and then sought evidence of their relationships with a number of psychological variables (such as values and subjective well-being). Results showed that many of the indicators came together to form a single economic dimension (termed "Affluence"), and this was distinct from "Religion" in the pattern of relationships with the psychological variables. Specifically, across cultures, a high placement on Affluence (along with Protestant Religion) was associated with greater emphasis on individualism, utilitarianism, and personal well-being. In contrast, for other religions, coupled with low Affluence, there was an emphasis on power, loyalty, and hierarchy values.

Theoretical Issues

Two basic assumptions of the ecocultural approach were articulated at the outset: universalism and adaptation. While no claim can be made that these two assumptions have been verified, they have served as a useful and important heuristic in the field (see Troadec, 2001). Another theoretical issue that has not yet been addressed is the question: Is "culture" conceptualized as an "independent" or as an "organismic" variable in the framework? My answer (Berry, 2000) is that it is both.

To justify this view, it is helpful to recall the argument (Kroeber, 1917) that culture is "superorganic", "super" meaning above and beyond, and "organic" referring to its individual biological and psychological bases. Two arguments were presented by Kroeber for the independent existence of culture, at its own level. First, particular individuals come and go, but cultures remain more or less stable. This is a remarkable phenomenon; despite a large turnover in membership with each new generation, cultures and their institutions remain relatively unchanged. Thus, a culture does not depend on particular individuals for its existence, but has a life of its own at the collective level of the group. The second argument is that no single individual "possesses" all the culture of the group to which one belongs; the culture as a whole is carried by the collectivity, and indeed is likely to be beyond the biological or psychological capacity (to know or to do) of any single person in the group. For example, no single person knows all the laws, political institutions and economic structures that constitute even this limited sector of one's culture.

For these two reasons, Kroeber perceived cultural phenomena as collective phenomena, above and beyond the individual person, and hence his term "superorganic". This position is an important one for cross-cultural psychology since it permits us to employ the group–individual distinction in attempting to link the two, and possibly to trace the influence of cultural factors on individual psychological development.

From the superorganic perspective, which holds that culture exists prior to any particular individual, we can consider culture as "lying in wait" to pounce on newcomers (be they infants or immigrants), and to draw them into its fold by the processes of cultural transmission and acculturation (see Figure 1.1). Hence, we can claim that culture is, in important ways, an *independent variable* (or more accurately, a complex set of interrelated independent variables).

However, these two transmission processes lead to the incorporation of culture into the individual; hence culture also becomes an *organismic variable*. It is simultaneously outside and inside the individual. Being both "out there" and "in here" (Berry, 2000), the interactive, mutually influencing, character of culture–behaviour relationship becomes manifest. This view is indicated by the feedback loop shown in Figure 1.1, where individuals are in a position to influence, change, and even destroy their ecosystem and cultural accomplishments.

Methodological Issues

The view that cultural and behavioural phenomena can be conceptualized and measured in their own right has methodological implications. One of these lies in a pair of distinctions: between two levels of observation (cultural/individual); and between two levels of analysis of the data obtained by such observations (cultural/individual). These two distinctions are presented in relation to each other in Figure 1.2. For each, the distinction between the cultural (population) level and the individual level is made, producing a classification of four methodological types of cross-cultural studies.

Figure 1.2
Classification of Types of Cross-cultural Studies

Level of Analysis	Level of Observation	
	Cultural	*Individual*
Cultural	1. Holocultural (e.g., HRAF)	2. Aggregation (e.g., values)
Individual	4. Ecocultural (e.g., cognitive style)	3. Individual difference (e.g., traits, abilities)

In the first type (Holocultural), the data are collected at the cultural level, usually by anthropologists using ethnographic methods, and are interpreted at that level, leading to the typical ethnographic report. These cultural observations can also be related to each other, comparing various customs or institutions with other factors across cultures, leading to holocultural studies (such as using the HRAF). Such studies have revealed broad patterns of co-variation among elements of culture. For example, the study by Barry, Child, and Bacon (1959) showed that child rearing practices (ranging on a dimension from those emphasizing "assertion" to those emphasizing "compliance") were correlated with ecological factors (such as subsistence economy) and with social structural factors (such as hierarchy in social relationships). While no individual psychological data are collected in this type of study, they serve the important role of providing basic contextual information for studies in cross-cultural psychology.

In the second type (Aggregation), the data are collected at the individual level (such as using interviews and questionnaires) with samples drawn from a population. These data are then used to calculate scores for each culture, by aggregation, from the individual responses. Here the level of observation is the individual, but the level of analysis is the culture. Culture (or country) scores may claim to represent the population if individual data are from representative samples of individuals. Such country scores can be related to other aggregated scores, or to (independent) country indicators, such as GNP. They can also be related to other (independent) cultural descriptions obtained with holocultural research methods (type 1). These aggregated country scores are sometimes used in correlations with individual scores on very similar scales (such as in countries with a high collectivism score, individuals usually score high on a collectivism scale). That is, the same set of data is used twice in the correlation: once at the individual level of observation and once at the cultural level of analysis. However, this practice may lack sufficient independence in conceptualization and measurement to be entirely valid.

In the third type of study (Individual Difference), data are collected and analysed at the individual level. These studies are the common and basic type generally conducted in psychology. Usually mean scores are calculated for a particular test, and the relationships among scores are correlated or factor analysed. The vast majority of these individual difference studies are not used for cross-cultural comparisons, and remain focused on distributions and relationships among variables within one population. However, when cross-cultural comparisons are made, they are usually of these mean scores, sometimes taken to represent only the sample, but also at times taken to represent the culture as a whole. If factors are produced, comparisons of the factors are made, usually to establish equivalence or provide evidence of bias. These cross-cultural comparisons remain at the individual level of observation and analysis; cultural factors are not usually invoked in any attempt to explain mean score differences that may be obtained.

Occasionally post hoc "cultural" explanations are proposed to account for mean score differences. Studies of personality traits, emotions or other behaviours like conformity (Bond & Smith, 1996) are of this type.

The fourth type (Ecocultural) represents a hybrid, combining elements of the first and third types. Here, cultural level findings (the first type, from ethnographic sources) are examined for their relationships with individual level data (from the third type, individual difference studies). The sampling of cultures can provide a range of variation in contexts, and allow the prediction of variation (similarities and differences) in individual psychological development and behaviour. Since the two sets of data are independent of each other (due to their different levels of observation and analysis), it is valid to examine relationships between them. Examples of these are the ecocultural studies of cognitive style (Berry, 1976) mentioned earlier, where ecological and cultural information was used to select cultural groups (as contexts for development), followed by predictions and assessment of individual behaviour in these various settings.

The second methodological issue centres on the very meaning of "cross-cultural" in any research design. As we have just discussed, some cross-cultural studies do not include cultural variables in their research design (type 3), while others only create "cultural" variables by aggregating psychological data to the population level (type 2). Yet all four types of study are routinely called "cross-cultural". In my view, we need to make some distinctions between those studies that explicitly incorporate cultural factors and those that do not; the former are truly "cross-cultural", while the latter are more properly termed "international".

This distinction is made in Figure 1.3: on the left, studies not including cultural variables in their research design can only be international. In such studies, it is possible to achieve generalizations based on patterns of similarities and differences found in the phenomena of interest (such as abilities, values, developmental stages). Which group is low, which groups cluster with others, and is there evidence for some universality, are the only questions that can be answered. Since no cultural variables are included in the design, it is not possible to say *why* such patterns exist in the data. Unfortunately, in many international studies, there are post hoc attempts at such explanations, which usually fall well short of being convincing: any one can dream up a "cultural" variable to explain behavioural variation!

Figure 1.3
Classification of Types of Comparative Psychological Research

Comparative Psychological Research		
No Cultural Variables	Cultural Variables Explicit in Research	
"International Studies"	"Cross-cultural Studies"	
• Generalizations possible (similarities and differences) • Explanations not possible (culture–behaviour relationships)	No contact among cultures "Culture-comparative" studies	Contact among cultures "Intercultural" studies
	• Generalizations and explanations both possible	• Generalizations possible if done comparatively • Explanations possible even if not done comparatively

In contrast, in studies that incorporate cultural variables explicitly (and preferably independently) such as in type 4 ecocultural studies, both generalizations and explanations are possible. There are two varieties of these "cross-cultural" studies. In the first, societies that are widely dispersed, and that have little contact with each other, can be sampled to provide large variation in ecological and cultural contexts. Ideally, these contexts can be studied at the population level. Individuals can also be sampled within these societies to provide psychological data. Because cultural level and psychological level data are obtained separately, and because societies are relatively independent of each other, it is possible to look at both for culture–behaviour relationships across societies in the study. These may be termed as "culture comparative" studies.

The second type of cross-cultural study focuses on cultural groups living in contact with each other in culturally plural societies. These studies include groups that are not independent of each other and hence they can be termed as "intercultural". In such studies, if the groups in contact (the larger society and ethnocultural groups) are studied at both the cultural and individual levels, explanations of culture–behaviour relationships are possible to achieve. If only one plural society is studied, generalizations are not possible. However, if such intercultural studies are conducted across a number of plural societies, it is possible to achieve generalizations as well. For example, an intercultural study of Chinese immigrants in Australia can examine culture–behaviour relationships as they take place and change during intercultural interaction. If the study were also to be done in Canada, New Zealand and the USA, then some more general statements about Chinese immigrant acculturation can be made, taking cultural features of the various societies of settlement into account.

Summary and Conclusion

In this paper, I have addressed the question of the origins of similarities and differences in human behaviour across cultures. I have argued that we can go a long way to providing an answer if we adopt an ecocultural perspective, in which we assume that psychological processes are "universal" in the species, and that behaviours are "adaptive" to contexts, both ecological and sociopolitical. Within such a framework, we can conceptualize cultural and individual behaviour as separate phenomena: culture exists apart from particular individuals, but becomes incorporated into all individuals through two main transmission processes (enculturation and acculturation). Hence, culture is both an independent variable and an organismic variable in such a framework. Given this conception, it is possible to undertake empirical work at the two levels. Analyses can be conducted within levels (the classical ethnographic and individual difference studies). The major advantage, however, is when cultural level data are used to predict individual and group similarities and differences in behaviour. The ecocultural strategy is both "cultural" and "comparative", allowing for a "cross-cultural" understanding of human diversity.

References

Aberle, D.F., Cohen, A., Davis, A., Levy, M., & Sutton, F. (1950). Functional prerequisites of society. *Ethics, 60*, 100–111.

Barry, H., Child, I., & Bacon, M. (1959). Relations of child training to subsistence economy. *American Anthropologist, 61*, 51–63.

Bennett, J. (1976). *The ecological transition.* London: Pergamon.

Berry, J.W. (1966). Temne and Eskimo perceptual skills. *International Journal of Psychology, 1*, 207–229.

Berry, J.W. (1967). Independence and conformity in subsistence-level societies. *Journal of Personality and Social Psychology, 7*, 415–418.

Berry, J.W. (1968). On cross-cultural comparability. *International Journal of Psychology, 4*, 119–128.

Berry, J.W. (1975). An ecological approach to cross-cultural psychology. *Nederlands Tijdschrift voor de Psychologie, 30*, 51–84.

Berry, J.W. (1976). *Human ecology and cognitive style: Comparative studies in cultural and psychological adaptation.* New York: Sage/Halsted.

Berry, J.W. (1979). A cultural ecology of social behaviour. In L. Berkowitz (Ed.), *Advances in experimental social psychology, vol. 12* (pp. 177–206). New York: Academic Press.

Berry, J.W. (1985). Cultural psychology and ethnic psychology. In I. Reyes-Lagunes & Y.H. Poortinga (Eds), *From a different perspective* (pp. 3–15). Lisse: Swets & Zeitlinger.

Berry, J.W. (1993). Ecology of individualism and collectivism. In U. Kim, Harry C. Triandis, C. Kagitcibasi, Sang-Chin Choi, & Gene Yoon (Eds), *Individualism and collectivism: Theory, method, and applications* (pp. 77–84). Thousand Oaks, CA: Sage.

Berry, J.W. (1994). An ecological approach to cultural and ethnic psychology. In E. Trickett (Ed.), *Human diversity* (pp. 115–141). San Francisco: Jossey-Bass.

Berry, J.W. (1995). The descendants of a model. *Culture & Psychology, 1*, 373–380.

Berry, J.W. (2000). Cross-cultural psychology: A symbiosis of cultural and comparative approaches. *Asian Journal of Social Psychology, 3*, 197–205.

Berry, J.W., & Bennett, J.A. (1992). Cree conceptions of cognitive competence. *International Journal of Psychology, 27*, 73–88.

Berry, J.W., Bennett, J.A., & Denny, J.P. (2000). *Ecology, culture and cognitive processing.* Paper presented at the International Association of Cross-Cultural Psychology Congress, Pultusk, Poland.

Berry, J.W., Dasen, P.R., & Witkin, H.A. (1983). Developmental theories in cross-cultural perspective. In L. Alder (Ed.), *Cross-cultural research at issue* (pp. 13–21). New York: Academic Press.

Berry, J.W., & Irvine, S.H. (1986). Bricolage: Savages do it daily. In R. Sternberg & R. Wagner (Eds), *Practical intelligence: Nature and origins of competence in the everyday world* (pp. 271–306). New York: Cambridge University Press.

Berry, J.W., Irvine, S.H., & Hunt, E.B. (Eds.) (1988). *Indigenous cognition: Functioning in cultural context.* Dordrecht: Nijhoff.

68 ᴄᴀ *John W. Berry*

Berry, J.W., Poortinga, Y.H., Pandey, J., Dasen, P.R., Saraswathi, T.S., Segall, M.H., & Kagitcibasi, C. (1997). *Handbook of cross-cultural psychology, 3 volumes. Vol. 1: Theory and method, Vol. 2: Basic processes and human development, Vol. 3: Social behavior and applications.* Boston: Allyn & Bacon.

Berry, J.W., Poortinga, Y.H., Segall, M.H., & Dasen, P.R. (1992/2002). *Cross-cultural psychology: Research and applications.* New York: Cambridge University Press.

Berry, J.W., van de Koppel, J.M.H., Sénéchal, C., Annis, R.C., Bahuchet, S., Cavalli-Sforza, L.L., & Witkin, H.A. (1986). *On the edge of the forest: Cultural adaptation and cognitive development in central Africa.* Lisse: Swets & Zeitlinger.

Boldt, E.D. (1976). Acquiescence and conventionality in a communal society. *Journal of Cross-Cultural Psychology, 7,* 21, 36.

Boldt, E.D., & Roberts, L.W. (1979). Structural tightness and social conformity. *Journal of Cross-Cultural Psychology, 10,* 221–230.

Bond, R., & Smith, P. (1996). Culture and conformity: A meta-analysis. *Psychological Bulletin, 119,* 111–137.

Boyd, R., & Richerson, P. (1983). Why is culture adaptive? *Quarterly Review of Biology, 58,* 209–214.

Bril, B. (1995). Les apports de la psychologie culturelle comparative à la compréhenson du développement de l'enfant. In J. Lautrey (Ed.), *Universel et différentiel en psychologie* (pp. 327–349). Paris: PUF.

Bronfenbrenner, U. (1977). Toward an experimental ecology of human development. *American Psychologist, 32,* 513–531.

Dasen, P.R. (1975). Concrete operational development in three cultures. *Journal of Cross-Cultural Psychology, 6,* 156–172.

Dasen, P.R., Berry, J.W., & Witkin, H.A. (1979). The use of developmental theories cross-culturally. In L. Eckensberger, W. Lonner, & Y.H. Poortinga (Eds), *Cross-cultural contributions to psychology* (pp. 69–82). Lisse: Swets & Zeitlinger.

Feldman, D. (1975). The history of the relationship between environment and culture in ethnological thought. *Journal of the History of the Behavioural Sciences, 110,* 67–81.

Forde, D. (1934). *Habitat, economy and society.* New York: Dutton.

Gamble, J.J., & Ginsberg, P.E. (1981). Differentiation, cognition and social evolution. *Journal of Cross-Cultural Psychology, 12,* 445–459.

Georgas, J., & Berry, J.W. (1995). An ecocultural taxonomy for cross-cultural psychology. *Cross-Cultural Research, 29,* 121–157.

Georgas, J., van de Vijver, F., & Berry, J.W. (July, 2000). *The ecocultural framework and psychological variables in cross-cultural research.* Paper presented at the International Association of Cross-Cultural Psychology Congress, Pultusk, Poland.

Huntington, E. (1945). *Mainsprings of civilization.* New York: John Wiley.

Jahoda, G. (1995). The ancestry of a model. *Culture & Psychology, 1,* 11–24.

Kroeber, A. (1917). The superorganic. *American Anthropologist, 19,* 163–213.

Lomax, A., & Berkowitz, W. (1972). The evolutionary taxonomy of culture. *Science, 177,* 228–239.

Marin, G., Balls-Organista, P., & Chung, K. (Eds). (2001). *Acculturation.* Washington: APA Books.

McNett, C.W. (1970). A settlement pattern scale of cultural complexity. In R. Naroll & R. Cohen (Eds), *Handbook of method in cultural anthropology* (pp. 872–886). New York: Natural History Press.

Mishra, R.C., Sinha, D., & Berry, J.W. (1996). *Ecology, acculturation and psychological adaptation: A study of Adivasis in Bihar.* New Delhi: Sage Publications.

Moran, E. (1982). *Human adaptability: An introduction to ecological anthropology.* Boulder: Westview Press.

Moran, E. (Ed.). (1990). *The ecosystem approach in anthropology.* Ann Arbor: University of Michigan Press.

Murdock, G.P. (1975). *Outline of cultural materials.* New Haven: Human Relations Area Files.

Nsamenang, A.B. (1992). *Human development in cultural context.* Newbury Park, CA: Sage.

Paabo, S. (2001). The human genome and our view of ourselves. *Science, 291,* 1219–1220.

Pelto, P. (1968). The difference between "tight" and "loose" societies. *Transaction, 5,* 37–40.

Roberts, L.W., Boldt, E.D., & Guest, A. (1990). Structural tightness and social conformity: Varying the source of external influence. *Great Plains Sociologist, 3,* 67–83.

Segall, M.H., Dasen, P.R., Berry, J.W., & Poortinga, Y.H. (1990/1999). *Human behavior in global perspective.* Boston: Allyn & Bacon.

Steward, J.H. (1955). *Theory of culture change.* Urbana: University of Illinois Press.

Tomasello, M., Kruger, A., & Ratner, H. (1993). Culture learning. *Behavioral and Brain Sciences, 16,* 495–552.

Triandis, H.C. (1994). *Culture and social behavior.* New York: McGraw-Hill.

Troadec, B. (2001). Le modèle écoculturel: un cadre pour la psychologie culturelle comparative. *International Journal of Psychology, 36,* 53–64.

Vayda, A.P., & McKay, B. (1975). New directions in ecology and ecological anthropology. *Annual Review of Anthropology, 4,* 293–306.

Vayda, A.P., & Rappoport, R. (1968). Ecology, cultural and non-cultural. In J. Clifton (Ed.), *Cultural anthropology* (pp. 477–497). Boston: Houghton Mifflin.

Werner, C., Brown, B., & Altman, I. (1997). Environmental psychology. In J.W. Berry, M.H. Segall, & C. Kagitcibasi (Eds), *Handbook of cross-cultural psychology, vol. 3: Social behavior and applications* (pp. 253–290). Boston: Allyn & Bacon.

Whiting, J.W.M. (1977). A model for psychocultural research. In P.H. Leiderman, S.R. Tulkin, & A. Rosenfeld (Eds), *Culture and infancy: Variations in the human experience* (pp. 29–48). New York: Academic Press.

Witkin, H., & Berry, J.W. (1975). Psychological differentiation in cross-cultural perspective. *Journal of Cross-Cultural Psychology, 6,* 4–87.

‰ 2 ‱

Wanted: A Contextualized Psychology: Plea for a Cultural Psychology Based on Action Theory

LUTZ H. ECKENSBERGER*

Prologue

This paper presents a condensed version of the lectures I had the opportunity and honour to give on the Nehru Chair (Department of Human Development, Maharaja Sayajirao University of Baroda). Teaching in this context was not a one-way process: I also learned much from the students. One thing I learnt is to share with them their love of a booklet written by Richard Bach (1977), titled *Illusions*. It deals with the problem of reality (facts) and its construction (illusions) in non-scientific language, a topic which came up during our discussions on naive empiricism and con-structivism in science. This book refers to a *Handbook of the messiahs* which offers numerous wisdoms. I chose three of them as guiding principles for my lectures. Therefore, I also want to use them as epigraphs for the following text.

Learning is finding out what you already know.
Doing is demonstrating that you know it.

* I would like to thank Dr Ingrid Plath for improving the style of the text and Stephan Roth for preparing the figures.

Teaching is reminding others that they know just as well as you do.
You are all learners, doers, teachers.
> *There is no such thing as a problem*
> *without a gift for you in its hands.*
> *You seek problems because you need their gifts.*
You teach best what you most need to learn.

A Personal Justification of the Topic

After having finished my studies in psychology in 1965, I got my first job in a German research institute that was rather unique in those days: it was aimed at the role of education in developing countries, it therefore did not aim at basic but at applied research; it aimed at helping German developmental aid policy in evaluation programmes, and it was therefore interdisciplinary. My own task under this umbrella was to evaluate technical school programmes in Afghanistan and Thailand (cf. Eckensberger, 1968). This early experience helped me move away from "social" and "scientific" preoccupations to think about the relation between "basic research" and its "application". Second, it forced me to think about culture as the context; and it helped me to realize that culture is not a genuine part of psychological theories, but that mainstream psychology does not integrate culture but uses it just as an independent variable.

My early experiences resulted in two major consequences that have determined my personal thinking about this issue ever since. First, on a pragmatic level I propose that one should not talk of psychological theories and their application (basic research and applied research) when it comes to the solution of real life problems, but rather distinguish *two genuinely different types of activities: theory construction and practical problem solving*. On the other hand, practical problem solving would be much easier, if psychological theories contained as much sociocultural–historical context as possible. It is evident that not all psychological theories are equally suitable for this task. Therefore, I began turning intensively to those psychological theories that *include context* from the very beginning and I identified *context with culture* (Eckensberger, 1976; 1979; 1990; 1996).

Theory Building and Practical Problem Solving:
Two Activities or One?

My first argument is quite simple: instead of trying to translate and back-translate the structure of scientific discourse into political (societal) decisions, and instead of trying to answer political questions by empirical research and thereby falling into the trap of mutual misunderstanding and wrong expectations, we should simply accept that the two action domains, theory construction and sociopolitical decision-making, are different in quality. This genuine difference on various dimensions is presented in Table 2.1.

Table 2.1
Attributes of "Scientific Action" and "Social/Technical Action"
which Constitute the Domains of Scientific Theory Building
and Technical/Social Problem Solving

Attribute	"Scientific Action"	"Social/Technical Action"
Goal	Formulation/test of hypotheses; *explanation* of the world, formulation of theories that allow generalizations of results	Solving of concrete (single) problems in reality; *creation/changing* the world; improvement of living conditions
Means	*Basic research* by various means, accumulation of knowledge	Counselling; task force, survey research (e.g., Delphi)
Result	A hypothesis may be wrong (principle of falsification)	An intervention should work (not be incorrect)
Orientation towards Reality	*Instrumental* (with reference to question)	*Normative*
Time Constraints	Relatively low	Usually high
Confidence Margin	*Absolute* (theoretically derived; significance, satiation)	Pragmatic: the *relatively* best solution
Interdisciplinarity	Desired but difficult	Necessary

First, the goals (and possible outcomes) of these activities are different and evaluated differently. In theory building, the goal is to explain or understand the (social, spiritual, material) world so that generalizations of results are possible, whereas in politics, the goal is to change the world, to improve the living conditions, etc. by solving concrete single problems. Hence, the orientation towards reality is descriptive (instrumental) in the case of theory building. It is clearly normative in political actions. In this context it is entirely clear that *logically a deduction* of normative consequences from empirical work is not possible (cf. Eckensberger & Gähde, 1993 for an extensive discussion of this issue). What is possible at best, is defining the limits of and preconditions for change as well as the mechanisms involved which allow or impede interventions. Because of these normative implications, the evaluation of "scientific" action and political intervention is also quite different. A scientific hypothesis can be falsified (in some science of science orientations this is even intended), a politically (socially) motivated intervention should *work*, however. Another obvious, but important, difference is the *urgency* of decision-making. Although it is true that in basic research time is not an unlimited resource, but time constraints are usually only defined by the internal structure of the research process itself. This is different in political decision-making: here, external constraints or pull factors usually define strong time limitations. This implies by necessity that the standard procedures of science cannot be applied to political decision-making. Not only are different criteria for "confidence" in the results adopted (in science significance levels are developed, in politics the *relatively* best solution should be chosen), but also the application of different means. Whereas in theory building *basic research* (in all its variations) is advocated and possible, in policy making much simpler survey methods, discussions among experts (Delphi) in task forces should be used and cultivated. I am convinced that in the political domain research in many cases is neither possible nor necessary for decision-making. What is necessary is having the courage to think in "analogies". There exists a vast body of knowledge (in different domains of psychology) that could be evaluated and transposed into another domain. Of course, the results of political decisions should also be understood as reforms. At a higher level of abstraction, reforms therefore can be interpreted as experiments and can be made topics of research themselves (Campbell, 1969).

Searching for a Context Inclusive Theory— Plea for a "Cultural Psychology"

One reason for the emergence of indigenous psychology (IP) was precisely the limitation of direct application of Western (nomothetical) psychology to other cultures (Sinha, 1997). When Berry et al. (1992) argued, "of course, *Western psychology is one such indigenous psychology...*" (p. 381, emphasis added), this sounds fine and somehow even modest. But, on a certain level, these authors are not correct as far the *mainstream of Western psychology* is concerned. This is so, because traditional American psychology is understood as a *nomothetical* science which is intentionally *culture free*. This means that it also *lacks the content of the American culture*. From this point of view, it does not fit the definition of an IP. On another level this statement contains a grain of truth, which is, however, probably not intended by the authors. This truth is that psychology, although aiming at universal laws, in fact seems to include structures similar to some (cultural) conditions of Western societies, that it appears as if psychology mirrors Western cultural content. In a similar vein, Schwartz (1997) cited the example of Skinnerian psychology which assumes that virtually all behaviour is controlled by contingencies and reinforcements, but that this is only "ecologically valid" for some parts of Western culture because the latter is based upon the same principle:

> rats pressing levers for food had a great deal in common with, for example, human beings pressing slacks in a clothing factory... this similarity is not a reflection of the basic universal facts about human nature, but rather a reflection of the conditions of human labor ushered in by industrial capitalism (p. 22).

From a bird's-eye view, the *main problem* underlying the discussion of indigenization of psychology is *not* to develop culture specific theories, i.e., theories that are based upon *particular cultural contents,* but to *develop a theory that allows for the integration or inclusion of particular cultural contents into a general theory.*

I pointed out on different occasions (Eckensberger, 1979; 1990; 1996) that psychology should not primarily be viewed as a natural science, but as a *cultural science.* It should not deal with culture as an independent variable, but as a *constitutive condition* for humans in general. My arguments for a paradigmatic shift originated to a large extent as a result of an article published by Reese and Overton (1970). Following a Kuhnian perspective (Kuhn, 1969), these authors claimed that different theories following different "models of man" exist as metaphors (paradigms) in psychology. Since these models of man differ qualitatively, and are mutually exclusive, this is also true for the theories that are derived from them. The authors distinguished the organismic theories of the Piagetian tradition from the mechanistic theories of classical learning. This analysis implied that theories cannot be evaluated in terms of being better or worse, or right or wrong, but can only be evaluated in terms of their fruitfulness. The choice of a theory is primarily dependent upon the question of the concern one has. In applying this rationale to my problem (to include culture in psychology), I expanded the number of relevant paradigms in psychology to five theory families or paradigms and attempted to explicate (*a*) their model assumptions as well as to test (*b*) how well they would allow the inclusion of culture in psychology (Eckensberger, 1979). I cannot go into the details of these (old) arguments here, nor can I summarize their revisions (Eckensberger, 2002), but it may be sufficient to note that according to these analyses two types of theories allow the definition of individual *and* cultural development at the same time, which means that they are truly "contextualized": theories based on the idea of biological systems which include the organism and environment (culture) in one system, and *action theories.* The first paradigm is represented by all theories which are based on the idea of the ecosystem, like Berry's (1976) eco-behavioural model or Barker's (1969) "ecopsychology", and the recent "socio-biological" approaches (Dawkins, 1976). They are, however, purely functional and do not consider the self-reflectivity and intentionality of humans beyond their functional phylogenetic adaptiveness. I therefore argued that these approaches are deficient in adequately grasping the main characteristics of humans (Eckensberger, 1979;

2002). In the following therefore I want to elaborate on some of the features of action theory.

SOME HISTORICAL REMARKS ON ACTION THEORIES

As this subheading indicates, there are more than one action theories. In fact, they have a long history that goes back to Aristotle, and they should be aptly called a perspective on psychology rather than a coherent theory. Although this perspective varied in saliency during the history of Western psychology, it has been in existence since its very beginning in the last century both in Europe and North America. In 1874 in Germany Brentano, a teacher of Freud's, focused on *intentionality* as a basic feature of consciousness leading to the concept of *"acts of consciousness"*. Ten years later, Dilthey distinguished between an *explanation* of *nature* and an *understanding* of the *mind/soul*, a dichotomy which paved the way for the ongoing discourse on the *dichotomy of explanation and understanding* (Wright, 1971). In 1920, Stern criticized mainstream psychology of his time because it neglected *intentionality* as well as *cultural change* as a created framework for human development. In Paris, Janet wrote his dissertation on "Automatisme" in 1889. This was the beginning of an elaborated action theoretical system of neuroses (see Schwartz, 1951). At the end of the nineteenth century, James developed a sophisticated theory of action which anticipated a remarkable number of action theory concepts (see Barbalet, 1997). At the turn of the century Münsterberg, a disciple of Wundt, also proposed *action as the basic unit* of psychology instead of sensations. Unfortunately, these early conceptualizations were overruled by the neopositivistic *logic of explanation* expounded by the Vienna circle in philosophy and by behaviourism in psychology. Even during the 70s and 80s of the last century this perspective was considered (at least) somewhat strange in psychology and particularly in cross-cultural psychology. It was criticized for being subjective (and therefore not part of science) and for not relying on causality (Poortinga & Malpass, 1986). Today, action theory is far more accepted in different fields and by different authors: Bruner (1990) published his *Acts of meanings*; Bandura (2001) talked of an "Agentic perspective"; Russell (1996) published a book on the role of agency in mental development; Malle, Moses, and Baldwin (2001) published a work in which intentions and intentionality formed the foundation of social cognition; and even the latest edition of the *Handbook of child psychology* includes a chapter on action theory by Brandtstädter (1998). Cole's work is an exception to these recent developments in the action theory perspective (Laboratory of Comparative Human Cognition, 1983), just as the work of Valsiner (1987) and Wertsch (1985), who follow the Russian activity theory, which is, however, similar to the action theory perspective (Eckensberger, 1995) in that it shares one root of action theory, namely, Janet's work. Evidently, it is more acceptable nowadays to discuss the whole issue of the "language game" as these examples show and probably the ideas now also have a greater chance of being accepted.

The framework, which is elaborated in the following, is largely based on the theoretical and empirical research of my teacher Ernst Boesch (1976; 1991), as well as on the work of Habermas (1981), Janet (in Schwartz, 1951), Piaget (1970), Wright (1971), and of course on my own work during the last 25 years.

AN ACTION THEORETICAL VIEW
OF PSYCHOLOGY: CONCEPT OF MAN

We claimed (Eckensberger, 1979) that in action theory the *concept of man* is the *potentially* self-reflective subject, the *homo interpretans*. Man is an interpreting being who tries throughout his lifespan to understand the world and his experiences, and at the same time makes plans for the future. Self-reflectivity and intentionality are, therefore, *the* basic features of human beings, which distinguish them from other animals (Eckensberger, 2000). However, it is important to understand that this model of man does not represent a one-sided "cognitive monster". (*a*) The focus on intentionality and reflectivity does not mean that *every* human activity is self-reflective and intended. On the contrary, there may be countless daily routines and automatisms which are not. Yet, most of these actions *can* be made self-reflective or conscious by the actor, and *can* also be altered in principle by intentional decisions. These aspects clearly differentiate action from behaviour. (*b*) Beyond this, automatisms have at least two origins. One is biological, and these automatisms function naturally such as the basis for walking, but they also can be made conscious, the object of reflection, as in marching or dancing, which are a type of walking too. Others are reflective and intended at first, but become routine thereafter. Learning to write, for instance, is a concentrated, intentional action, which one is very much aware of initially. After several years of practice, one may not even be aware of how one writes as when drafting a letter or preparing a scientific paper. One focuses on the content, not on the process of writing any longer. In other words, this activity has become automatized. But one *can* also decide to improve one's handwriting at anytime, thereby making the act of writing itself the object of reflection once again.

A second caution should be made explicit. The focus on culture as a unique human phenomenon does not deny the utmost importance of biological and neurophysiological preconditions for human actions and, therefore, for culture. This topic is far too complex to be discussed here (cf. Eckensberger, 2002), but a brief comment is in order. There is no doubt that human beings have a phylogenetic continuity with other species, but this does not mean that their achievements can be explained by "ultimate causes", by phylogenetic explanations alone. Potential self-reflectivity and intentionality certainly developed during phylogeny (supported by brain development and social coordinations via language, which in themselves were probably triggered and supported by cultural development). However, these phenomena allow human beings to create conditions of living which may or may not be biologically adaptive. Hence, they cannot be adequately explained by their biological adaptation. Thus, I consider the interpretation of culture as "man's peculiar elaborate way of expressing the vertebrate biogram" (Count, 1958, p. 1049) as rather misleading or empty. To understand culture as an "epiphenomenon" and as "a product of selfish individuals, who are forced to live in groups" (Chasiotis & Keller, 1994, p. 77, translation by Eckensberger) is also shortsighted. Instead, it appears to be more fruitful to argue that despite this continuity there is a qualitative shift in phylogeny in the case of human beings (some behaviour patterns in animals that look like "cultures" are "proto-cultures" from this point of view). Yet, there is no doubt that the biological conditions set a frame, enabling and limiting conditions to human actions, their interpretations and the development of culture (Eckensberger, 2000).

Recent neurophysiological interpretations of actions in the context of new brain research, which refer to (biological) proximate causes for human activities (Roth, 1997; Singer, 2000), also do not "explain" cognitive processes as such, although they clearly are their basis (Eckensberger, 2002). Consequently, I also do not follow a "radical constructivism", in which the construction of meaning and the creation of culture is totally arbitrary (Eckensberger, 1990).

There is an old saying which originates from Tolman. It goes as follows: in order to explain a psychology in terms of biology or physiology, there first has to be a psychology that can be explained by these sciences. In the following therefore, the focus will be on developing a theory that is genuinely psychological and allows for understanding the interplay between the individual and culture, which we consider as the most important task of psychology as a science.

Although people relate directly to their non-social and material or natural surroundings, this process always takes place *in a cultural context and together with other subjects*. Writing, for instance, is inextricably linked to the script of a language—Latin letters differ strikingly from Devnagiri script, and both diverge from Arabic ones, and are totally different from Chinese characters. Thus, the cultural context provides shared schemas of writing, including the semantic meanings that refer to the world. These schemas, on the one hand, serve as a sort of a template for individual and collective experiences, and on the other hand, they are constructed and modified by human beings during the course of history or rather cultural history.

The *interpretation* of man as a potentially self-reflective being who, in addition to constructing culture, also "creates him- or herself" (thinks of the person he or she wants to be, develops norms about right and wrong, which more or less implies upholding one's character) calls for an integration of the individual as well as cultural rules and interpretation systems. Human beings create and form cultural and social rules which are in turn preconditions for their actions. This explains why these rules are always intertwined with teleological structures (they serve a purpose), and why Shweder (1990) interpreted culture as an "intentional world", a perspective which implies that they can be altered to varying degrees. However, it is true that after a while the particular purpose is often, perhaps even usually, forgotten, which means that they can become "functionally autonomous" as individual actions, thereby constituting customs or habits. This explains why Smedslund (1984) perceived culture as "the invisible obvious".

Interestingly, an action theory which includes culture implies a genuine developmental perspective. The interrelationship between the individual and culture is not just that "they make each other up" (Triandis, 2000), but this interrelationship is based upon *intentional* processes over time. But development is conceptualized on different levels: the phylogenetic level (phylogeny), the individual level (ontogeny), the action level (actual genesis), and the cultural level (history and cultural change). These levels are depicted in Figure 2.1

Figure 2.1
Different Kinds and Levels of Development in an Action Theory Framework

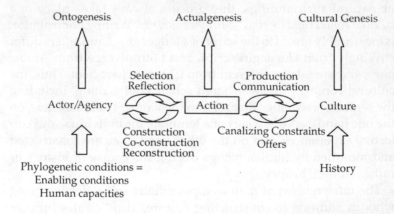

THE STRUCTURE OF THE CONCEPT OF ACTION—
SELF-REFLEXIVITY AND RESPONSIBILITY

Conceptually, actions can be seen as *future-oriented* and *potentially reflective* activities that the acting subject (agency) is *potentially* aware of. This implies that there is at least a subjective "point" at which a decision to do or not to do something is taken.

But this once again is of a potential quality. This very aspect clearly separates action from behaviour.

The uses of action concepts in empirical research are manifold. One approach is to study the emergence, the course of execution and termination of actions in real life contexts. Here, the dynamic course of concrete (and idealized) actions can be analysed in terms of phases that can be reconstructed by affective/evaluative, structural/cognitive, and energetic aspects (see Boesch, 1976; 1991; Schwartz, 1951). In the beginning phase one anticipates goals (outcomes of actions), specifically conditions that one strives to attain or avoid. During the course of an action important *regulative processes* (which can be of cognitive, evaluative and energetic quality) take place. Finally, in the end phase one evaluates the results of an action as to whether the anticipated conditions or change in conditions occurred.

Action concepts may also be used as a framework for analysing the understanding of other persons as well as cultural contexts. That is, action concepts may be used as a framework for psychological and cultural concepts as well as their interplay in general. For developing such a broad conceptual framework, it is useful to first examine the general structure of actions, which also allows one to distinguish different action types, and subsequently to use the action concept at different levels.

ACTION TYPES

In Figure 2.2 two kinds or types of actions are distinguished: instrumental, and social/norm-oriented actions. It is assumed that they have a different ontology or quality, although they are similar in structure. The agency is at the centre of an action. Traditionally, this is an individual, but from a cultural perspective, this may also be a group (for instance, the family). In the two types of actions, the instrumental action is carried out by an agency vis-à-vis the physical/natural environment (agency A and agency B horizontally in the upper and lower part of the figure), while an action, which aims at another person or group, is based on the process of understanding (depicted vertically on the left side of the figure). In both cases the agency has a goal (upon which he or she can

Figure 2.2
Two Main Action Types: Instrumental and Social/Norm-oriented Actions

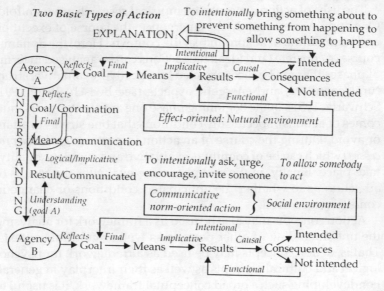

reflect) and he or she can choose some means in order to reach this goal. The application of means can involve either doing something or omitting to do something (not doing something intentionally is also an action!). This choice is based on a *final* operation, that is, the means are chosen *in order to* reach a goal (this is neither a reflection nor a causal process). In the case of the instrumental action the goal is to *produce some effect* (to bring about something by doing something, to prevent something from happening or to allow something to happen by not doing anything against its happening). This structure is appropriate for the object "physical/natural world", which is governed by causal laws. For example, a farmer wants to improve the harvest (goal). He chooses artificial fertilizers as the means (in this case the farmer does something). When he has done so, the fertilizer is in the soil (this is the result, which is a logical implication of the action). The intended consequence is that crops grow faster and the yield is greater on the basis of causal (biological) laws. Hence, the goal has been achieved, the (causal effect) is intended, and at the same time it is a function of the fertilizer. Clearly, the increase in the harvest can be *explained* by causal laws, although triggered by an intentional act. At the same time, the selfsame action may pollute the groundwater, which was, however, not intended (yet it is a causal consequence of the same action). It is clear that unintended consequences can also be taken into account from the very beginning, and that one is taking a risk if one uses fertilizer nonetheless. So risks are the inevitable implications of actions. In general, however, effect-oriented or instrumental actions are appropriate for the natural/physical world.

A social action is different, although it has a similar structure. For example, a farmer (agency A) is ill, which means that he cannot take the action of applying fertilizer to the soil, but asks somebody else, a neighbour (agency B), to do it. This calls for coordinating his goal with the goals of the person, whom he asks. Three aspects are important in this example: (*a*) the farmer (agency A) has to recognize the goals of the other person (agency B), that is, he has to *understand* this other person, whether he has the time, whether he agrees to apply the fertilizer, etc. *Understanding a person therefore means understanding his goals or whole actions.* (*b*) Whether the other person does the work or not is not a causal process (as in instrumental actions), but in this case it is a *decision* (which implies a choice and, therefore, intentions) on the part of this other person. (*c*) Whether he does it or not also depends on whether he understands the farmer (agency A) who requested him and his situation, as well as on his knowledge about the possible unintended effects of what he has been asked to do. Probably, the farmer has to try to convince the neighbour to do the work, but in the end it is the neighbour who has to decide. This example clearly shows that understanding does not refer to causes but to reasons. Basically, understanding or communicative actions are appropriate for the object "social world".

This distinction leads to an interesting consequence. In the case of the example discussed earlier, the farmer treats the other person as a person, that is, he takes the other person's goals and situation into account, and respects him. However, the relationship between the two may be quite different. Agency B may be a servant, for instance, who has to follow orders. That can lead to an "instrumental" interpretation of agency B by agency A. In other words, agency A interprets the behaviour (adding fertilizer to the soil) as something like a cause that follows from the order like a natural law without any possibility of deciding not to do it (he *has* to do it). This means that agency A treats agency B *as if* he is a part of nature, which is governed by causal laws. We can talk of a *strategic action* in this case. At the same time, it is evident that these different action types are not only more or less appropriate for the natural and social world. Whether or not something is "part" of the "social" or "natural/causal" world is a matter of interpretation on the part of the agency. The world is constituted largely by the application of the respective action types.

LEVELS OF ACTION

In order to apply this structural scheme of actions to a variety of psychological concepts and to design a basic heuristic for psychology, we extended Janet's work (Schwartz, 1951), and postulated different *levels of action*. Even though these levels are presented in a sequential order in the following, it is obvious that they are intertwined and interdependent and that they are present simultaneously in any concrete action.

"Primary Actions": World-oriented Actions

Primary actions with specific concrete goals are executed in "real" situations. They not only change the environment (in this context, the agency's "natural organism" is part of this environment), but also change the subject's perception, knowledge and interpretation of the situation (see Figure 2.3).

We propose (Eckensberger, 1976; 1979) placing the action between the subject (agency) and the context (culture), as done in Figure 2.1. Thus, two action fields are formed, the "external action field" and the "internal action field", which overlap, and are interconnected by the action which is part of both, and which, therefore, acts as a bridge (or a pivot) between them. The "internal action field" contains the subjective meaning people attribute to a situation, and the "external action field" or cultural factors include existing shared cultural concepts such as shared interpretational patterns, scripts and expectancies. Hence, subjective and cultural structures and processes refer mutually to each other, neither one

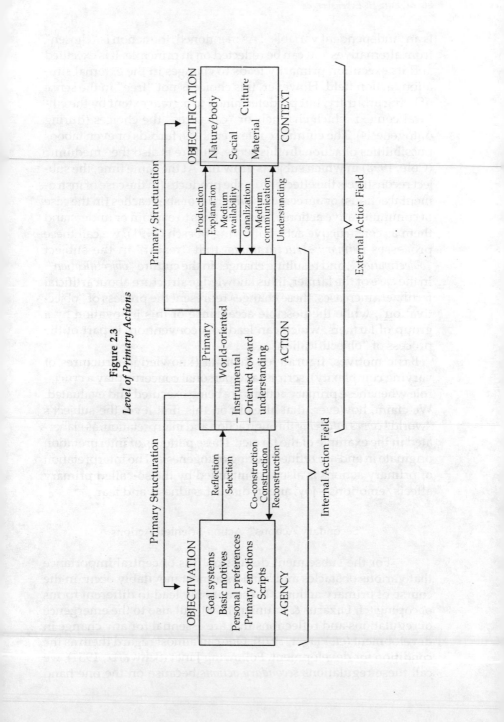

Figure 2.3
Level of Primary Actions

is an "independent variable". As mentioned, the action is "chosen" from alternatives and can be reflected on in principle. It is executed and its execution primarily leads to changes in the external situation/action field. However, this choice is not "free" in the sense of being arbitrary, but predetermined to a great extent by the cultural context which channels or "canalizes" the choices (during ontogenesis). The cultural context enables, forbids or even taboos possibilities of action. In this sense, culture is also the "medium" (Cole, 1998) in which subjects grow up. At the same time, the subject reconstructs the effects he or she produces (in the case of instrumental actions) or agreements which he or she reaches (in the case of communicative actions), or at least has to explain or understand them as constructive acts. Following Boesch (1991), we call these processes *primary structurations*, that "result" in the subject *"objectivation"*, and resulting changes in the culture *"objectification"*. In the case of the farmer, if his knowledge structure about artificial fertilizers increases, these changes represent the process of "objectivation", while the possible acceptance of this innovation by a group of farmers, which can lead to a convention, is part of the process of "objectification".

Basic motives, figurative schemata (knowledge structures of varying complexity), scripts, and personal concerns play a crucial role when these primary actions are being executed and evaluated. We claim, however, that already on this first level the subject's *"world" comes into being* through action and interpretation, as elaborated in the example of the farmer. These patterns of interpretation originate in and are refined during ontogenesis. The interpretation of primary actions is also accompanied by the so-called primary affects/emotions—joy, anger, disgust, sadness, and fear.

"Secondary Actions": Action-oriented Actions

For the subsequent discussion it is of central importance that various obstacles and barriers almost inevitably occur in the course of primary actions. These not only lead to different forms of coping (cf. Lazarus & Launier, 1978), but also to the emergence of regulations and reflections that are essential for any change in development (cf. Piaget, 1970). One can almost regard them as the condition for development. Following Janet (Schwartz, 1951), we call these regulations *secondary actions* because on the one hand they are, just as primary actions, future-oriented and possess a basic teleological structure (they are goal-oriented since they are supposed to re-establish and adapt primary actions, and they imply decisions and evaluations of outcomes). On the other hand, however, they are not oriented toward the world but toward primary actions. Hence, we call these secondary *"action-oriented actions"*.

In our conceptualization of the relationship between the objective world (ontology) and the subjective understanding of the world (epistemology), we claim that the barriers which lead to the schemata mentioned earlier, are not "objectively given", but basically come into being through interpretations. They achieve their specific quality primarily via interpretation, and more or less "adequate" ways of overcoming the barriers can be differentiated. Basically, two types of barriers are important. The first type is technical or instrumental in quality and can be called a problem. The second type has a social quality, implying that it is a conflict. If the farmer in our example cited earlier is unable to obtain any artificial fertilizer and assumes that there is a shortage in the region, then this is a problem, an obstacle. If, however, he interprets the shortage as being intentionally created by other farmers, who, say, distributed it unjustly, then this same situation (shortage of artificial fertilizer) is no longer a problem but it represents a conflict.

Secondary actions are regulations and reflections of primary actions. The first differentiation of these regulations can be made on the basis of interpreting a barrier as a problem or a conflict, because just as interpretations of the social world and the natural world can be more or less "adequate", overcoming the two types of barriers can be more or less "adequate" as well. In the case of an (instrumental) problem, the barrier has to be (technically) removed; in the case of a conflict, it has to be socially "solved". In light of the action types distinguished here, it is evident that these are rather different approaches.

It is of utmost importance that every definition of a barrier or obstacle in the course of an action implies some standard about how an action is usually carried out, or should be carried out. We call these phenomena "action-guiding frameworks" or "normative rule systems" for actions. These standards may be technical (for instance, that the artificial fertilizer should be available in sufficient quantity or within a certain time frame), or social (an expectancy based upon some convention, or a claim about the just distribution based on some ethical convictions, or a claim based on some religious convictions about the right time for adding fertilizer or harvesting). These standards are not only preconditions for defining barriers as barriers, but they also imply different "forms of overcoming" the obstacle that are more or less "adequate". For instance, barriers that are interpreted *causally* (materially/physically) are viewed as *problems* that have to be *removed*. Yet, barriers interpreted as *social phenomena* (because somebody created them intentionally) are considered *conflicts* that have to be *resolved* (for details see Eckensberger, 1993).

In the case of interpreting the absence of the artificial fertilizer as a technical problem, some alternative means of obtaining the fertilizer may be examined (which can also be understood as flexible re-framing or secondary control belief), or the farmer may expend more energy to get the right amount of fertilizer, which is an "actional" or primary control strategy. In the case of a social interpretation of the obstacle, the farmer could try to reach a consensus about better distribution, or might go to the police and try to enforce the right behaviour by law. Many kinds of regulations are possible, but they all depend upon the basic interpretation of the obstacle as being technical, conventional, legal or moral, to name the most important social standards for actions. (For a systematic depiction of the most significant types of rules, their distinctions and relations see Eckensberger, 1993; 1996).

These standards are not only used to evaluate courses of action, but they are themselves developed during ontogenesis by experiences in a specific cultural context, in which different expectations, customs, ethical principles or belief systems set the stage. Concepts from Piaget's (1970) theory are advocated as developmental principles or processes (assimilation/accommodation, decentration, reflective abstraction) that lead to a qualitative transformation of these standards during "stages" of development. These Piagetian principles have to be complemented by a cultural content dimension which seems to become ever more important as the concept of standard grows in complexity in the course of development, as revealed by research on Piaget's and Kohlberg's theory (Dasen & Heron, 1981; Eckensberger & Zimba, 1997). There is an urgent need to complement Piagetian developmental concepts with more content-oriented concepts of development, based on the tradition of socialization processes (Krishnan, 1999). These should particularly include cultural rituals of various kinds which all are normative in character. This approach would, however, also imply some weakening of the strict (internally consistent) stage concept.

Finally, it should be noted that the different interpretations of barriers also imply various types of emotions. We can distinguish manifold "shades" of affects that emerge as reactions to differently interpreted barriers or experiences (cf. Eckensberger & Emminghaus, 1982). For example, when a barrier is interpreted causally as a physical or material incident (a problem), we speak about a "frustrating emotion"—*anger or rage*. However, we talk about *wrath* in the case of a social barrier (a conflict), and of *guilt* and *shame* if the subject regards himself or herself responsible for the barrier. It is less important that our terms reflect everyday language exactly. Rather, the central point is to distinguish various emotional reactions to frustrations using different emotional concepts, depending on the barrier's interpreted source or origin.

In many cases one cannot presume that the acting subject is not involved in these regulative processes alone. The social world institutes co-regulations (supports, help), which in turn influence the emotional evaluation of the success or failure of a regulation (for instance, if one succeeds, one feels pride or triumph, one feels grateful towards others or appreciates their help) (cf. Valsiner, 1987).

Hence, all regulations aim at controlling or, generally speaking, at coordinating actions—to continue or to abandon an action, to reinterpret the situation, etc. Apart from this, as mentioned earlier, they differ, just as primary actions, in the affordances and possibilities a culture provides, as well as in the prohibitions and taboos—the "normative rule systems"—that already exist. These are, among other things, knowledge systems, but also morals and laws as outcomes of "time-tested" ways of solving conflicts in a culture (see Figure 2.4).

"Tertiary Actions": Actor-oriented Actions

It is only consistent to presume, especially when postulating that humans are "*potentially* self-reflective beings", that impediments to or disturbances of secondary actions inevitably compel the person to reflection or self-reflection (Piaget, 1974). One may ask questions like "What goals do I really have?", "How important

Figure 2.4
Level of Secondary Actions

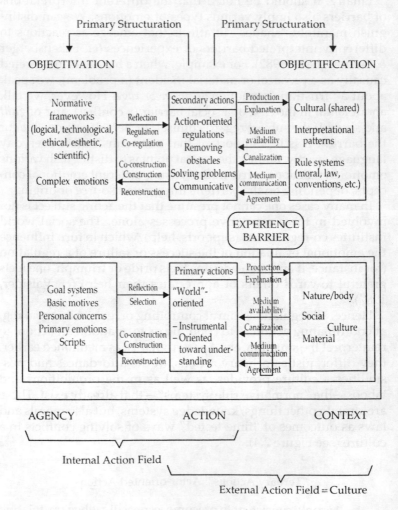

is a particular action outcome for me?", "What does some moral insight mean to me?", "Is it important for me to 'uphold' my personal convictions or character?", which leads to the question "Who am I?", or "What is the meaning of my existence?". Again, primarily the barriers of actions (this time of secondary actions) contain the developmental potentials for such questions. Our theoretical reflections are presented in Figure 2.5. At the level of tertiary actions, the process of primary structuration leads to role expectations or stereotypes oriented toward others (personhood) in a culture or society, and on the other hand, to the development of the subject's identity and his or her presentation to the outside world. These identity structures also have an action guiding potential. They can be considered identity stages, as outlined by Robert Kegan (1982), Erikson (1959) and others, and this implies that the subject constantly reconstructs and renews the understanding of his or her *relationship* to the social world, and thereby the relation between autonomy (independence) and attachment (interdependence) in the social world. Essentially, the subject reconstructs the balance between being entitled to personal needs and fulfilling those of others. Also, the relation of the subject to the natural/ material world (aspects of culture) is located here.

One barrier that is of utmost importance at the level of tertiary action is self-reflection related to knowledge of one's death or existence on earth. It is religion (on the cultural side) that offers an existence beyond death (although this may differ in various religions), thereby "outwitting" death. Religiosity is what individuals believe. As pointed out by Oser and Gmünder (1984), and Fowler (1981), religious structures are of an existential (religious) nature and can be described as stages that represent man's relation to the "ultimate" (Eckensberger, 1993). This is actually an interpretation scheme in its own right, it usually implies an entire theory of the structure of the world (relations amongst men, animals, plants) and its development (created by and governed by one or more ultimate being/beings). It also entails rules of conduct (what is right or wrong, or what is a sin). Some kinds of "regulation" are even prescribed in or afforded by a religion. These may be purifying rituals, prayers, etc. The farmer in our example may have some religious assumptions about why he cannot get fertilizer, he probably assumes that he has committed a sin (in some religions

Figure 2.5
Tertiary Level of Action

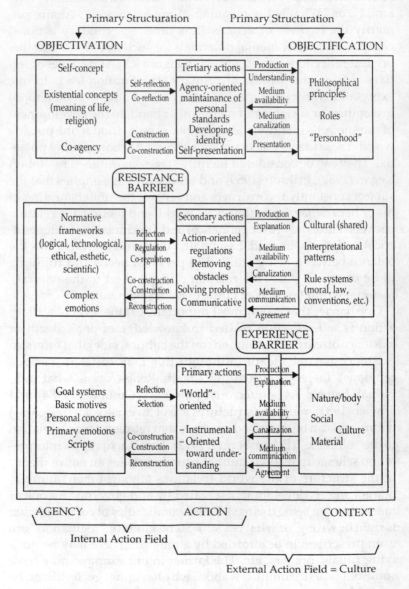

AGENCY   ACTION   CONTEXT

Internal Action Field

External Action Field = Culture

this could have been in a former life), and he may therefore pray for a better harvest.

"Agency" is characterized by four relations: by being (*a*) *reflexively* tied to one's own environment-oriented actions; (*b*) oriented to the social world by *understanding* the actions of others; (*c*) *self-reflexively* related to itself (the "Innenwelt" or "inside world"); and (*d*) related *contemplatively* to some transcendental or ultimate phenomenon.

Secondary Structurations

As in the case of primary structurations, evidently we also presume the existence of "secondary structurations". Boesch's (1976; 1991) terminology forms the basis of our notions presented here, even though he did not elaborate these concepts with respect to the action types mentioned, but primarily with reference to instrumental actions. Basically, they deal with the affective, dynamic processes, which lead to the subjectively unique meanings of processes and events at the individual level and to affectively enriched symbolic meanings of culturally preformed structures like myths. This topic is undervalued in psychology because of its more or less exclusive focus on general laws and principles. Not surprisingly, suppositions in this domain are at a rudimentary stage, and need to be developed in greater detail.

Boesch (1991) presumed that an action (he usually referred to instrumental actions) consists of two components: first, the "instrumental" aspect usually studied, for example, one uses a hammer to drive a nail into the wall; and second, the "subjective functional" aspect (see Figure 2.6). Hammering can be fun, one can let off steam or be proud of being able to hammer successfully. Boesch (1976; 1991) talked about the subject's "functional potentiality", which is similar to Bandura's (1993) concept of "self efficacy". According to Boesch, the action of hammering acquires a value that goes beyond instrumentality and provides feedback to the agency, but most importantly, an *affective relationship* to the agency (ego) is established. Apart from this, through this functional potentiality the whole situation (including the hammer) acquires an *idiosyncratic* meaning for the subject, a process known as *subjectivation*. The situation is not only constituted cognitively (due to the processes of a primary structuration), but also structured affectively, virtually symbolizing the functional potentiality, a process which is called *symbolization*.

Figure 2.6
Primary and Secondary Structurations

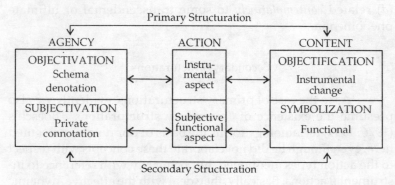

Even though Boesch's view is still quite speculative, it entails a very valuable aspect: the process of subjectivation (correspondingly symbolization in culture) exists on all three levels of action. *"Phantasms"* emerge at the level of secondary actions. They are superordinate, individual goals of actions. We call them content-oriented normative frameworks (they are meant to complement the structural stage concepts), they include notions of control (or harmony), ideals of autonomy (or relatedness), self-assurance, "leading a good life", conservation of nature, etc. (see Figure 2.7). With respect to farming, for instance, two rather contrasting "phantasms" exist in the West (Döring, Eckensberger, Huppert, & Breit, in press). One is "organic agriculture" and the other is "conventional agriculture". They not only entail diverse conceptions of risk taking, and different cognitive convictions about how to treat the soil as well as animals and customers, but also imply varying moral orientations. Both imply a high "personal involvement", which leads farmers to identify themselves with these orientations. Public debates on these two orientations do not only include a descriptive analysis of the different methods involved, but are also affectively loaded. This justifiably allows one to refer to the two "types of farming" as Western "myths".

Figure 2.7
The Level of Tertiary Actions

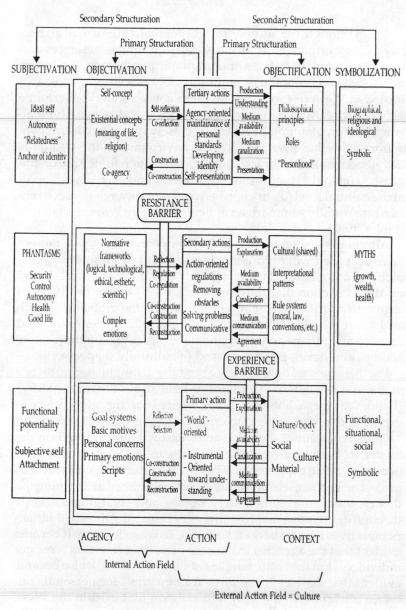

Epilogue

Although the motive for contextualizing or culturizing psychology originated from early cross-cultural experiences and the detection of limitations of nomothetic psychology, the theory developed and proposed is unquestionably as well as unavoidably rooted in Western thought. The main concepts are Western in a general sense. Agency is defined and understood as an individualistic concept, planning of actions is closely linked to control over action (as well as over the physical environment), the standards developed (moral, technical, logical, conventional, etc.) are distinguished on the basis of Western traditions, and even the examples at the cultural level (distinction between morality, religion, convention) are usually summarized as being typically Western in nature (Sinha, 1997).

Although I am aware of this I still hope that the *type of theory* I have proposed will permit the development of a framework that includes other cultural contents as well. This expectation is based on the conviction that the *frame itself is not Western but human*. I assume that all human beings struggle with the problem of death and existence, they try to make sense of their experiences, and develop and pursue goals, they relate to others via communicative actions, and develop in the context of culturally shaped scripts.

For this reason, I deliberately asked the distinguished audience at the Asian Regional Conference held in Kathmandu in 1991 (Pandey, Sinha, & Bhawuk, 1996), where I had the opportunity to expound this perspective, to criticize or complement it from an "Asian perspective". For the same reason, I also lectured on the theory in Baroda, asking the students to confront it with their personal Indian experiences. This is why I started a joint research project on partner selection, which not only aimed at applying the theory, but also at deliberately testing and enlarging its scope through discussions that from the very beginning included Indian perspectives (Eckensberger, Kapadia, & Wagels, 2000). It became evident that the agencies in the case of partner selection were not individuals but the entire families of those involved. It also became evident that distinct "normative frameworks" for personal concerns, conventions, morality and religion that exist in the West, do not operate in the same fashion in real life contexts of other cultures, particularly India. Actions in real life usually have more than one goal and they are hierarchized (understanding a book may be a goal that can only be reached, if one has the ability to read, but reading a book may be the prerequisite for the goal of passing a course, passing the course may be the means of qualifying for taking an exam, and being successful in the exam may be the precondition for being allowed to marry). This enables us to better understand the interrelationships among different rule systems that may also be hierarchized. The principle of goal hierarchy may be used in different cultures, but the hierarchies themselves may differ. Notions of control also differ. Sinha (1996) proposed that Indians were not so much interested in controlling the world, but rather in living in harmony with the world. I had argued earlier (Eckensberger, 1996) that this orientation may be understood as complementing the action types distinguished in Table 2.2.

Table 2.2
Four Types of Action Resulting from Attempts to Control or to Harmonize the Physical/Material/Biological or Social World

Reality is interpreted as being	Action Orientation	
	To control	To harmonize
Physical/Material/Biological	Instrumental	*Adaptive*
Social	Strategic	Communicative

More can be said about control beliefs. The application of control ideas from action theory (intrapsychic and action-oriented control) in the case of partner selection clearly showed that, for instance, horoscope is a central control method. The ideas underpinning the variety of ways of obtaining information about the future and minimizing risks by non-social and non-causal processes like horoscope and other types of prediction are far more openly accepted in India than in other cultures. The usual types of thinking (final, intentional, causal, functional, logical) should thus be supplemented by "analogical thinking" in non-Western cultures.

These examples show that when the assumption and concepts proposed in the theory are approached from a different cultural perspective, they probably have to be modified or complemented. However, we are convinced that the approach provides a general framework that allows psychology to include the culture concept into its theories and enables us to structure cross-cultural comparisons as well.

References

Bach, R. (1977). *Illusions: The adventures of a reluctant Messiah*. NY: Delacorte Press.

Bandura, A. (1993). Perceived self-efficacy in cognitive development and functioning. *Educational Psychology, 28*, 117–148.

Bandura, A. (2001). Social cognitive theory: A agentic perspective. *Annual Review, 52*, 1–26.

Barbalet, J.W. (1997). The Jamesian theory of action. *The Sociobiological Review, 45*(1), 102–121.

Barker, R. (1969). *Ecological psychology*. Stanford: Stanford University Press.

Berry, J.W. (1976). *Human ecology and cognitive style: Comparative studies in cultural and psychological adaptation*. New York: Sage/Halstead.

Berry, J.W., Poortinga, Y.H., Segall, M.H., & Dasen, P.R. (1992). *Cross-cultural psychology: Research and applications*. Cambridge, MA: Cambridge University Press.

Boesch, Ernst E. (1976). *Psychopathologie des Alltags. Zur Ökopsychologie des Handelns und seiner Störungen*. Bern: Huber.

Boesch, Ernst E. (1991). *Symbolic action theory and cultural psychology*. Berlin: Springer.

Brandtstädter, J. (1998). Action perspectives on human development. In W. Damon & R.M. Lerner (Eds), *Handbook of child psychology. Vol. 1: Theoretical models of human development* (5th ed., pp. 807–863). New York: John Wiley & Sons, Inc.

Bruner, J. (1990). *Acts of meaning*. Harvard: Harvard University Press.

Campbell, D.T. (1969). Reforms as experiments. *American Psychologist, 24*, 409–429.

Chasiotis, A., & Keller, H. (1994). Evolutionary psychology and developmental cross-cultural psychology. In A.-M. Bouvy, F.J.R. van de Vijver, P. Boski, & P. Schmitz (Eds), *Journeys into cross-cultural psychology* (pp. 68–82). Lisse: Swets & Zeitlinger.

Cole, M. (1998). *Cultural psychology: A once and future discipline*. Cambridge: The Belnap Press of Harvard University Press.

Count, E.W. (1958). The biological basis of human society. *American Anthropology, 60*, 1049–1089.

Dasen, P.R., & Heron, A. (1981). Cross-cultural tests of Piaget's theory. In H.C. Triandis & A. Heron (Eds), *Handbook of cross-cultural psychology. Vol. 4: Developmental psychology* (pp. 295–342). Boston: Allyn & Bacon.

Dawkins, R. (1976). *The selfish gene*. New York: Oxford University Press.

Döring, T., Eckensberger, L.H., Huppert, A., & Breit, H. (in press). Risk management and morality in agriculture: Conventional and organic farming in a German region. In M.J. Casimir & U. Stahl (Eds), *Culture and the changing environment. Uncertainty, cognition, and risk management in cross-cultural perspective.* Oxford & New York: Berghahn.

Eckensberger, L.H. (1976). Der Beitrag kulturvergleichender Forschung zur Fragestellung der Umweltpsychologie. In G. Kaminski (Ed.), *Umweltpsychologie-Perspektiven, Probleme, Praxis* (S. 73–98). Stuttgart: Klett.

Eckensberger, L.H. (1979). A metamethodological evaluation of psychological theories from a cross-cultural perspective. In L.H. Eckensberger, W.J. Lonner, & Y.H. Poortinga (Eds), *Cross-cultural contributions to psychology* (pp. 255–275). Amsterdam: Swets and Zeitlinger.

Eckensberger, L.H. (1990). From cross cultural psychology to cultural psychology. *The Quarterly Newsletter of the Laboratory of Comparative Human Cognition,* 12(1), 37–52.

Eckensberger, L.H. (1993). Moralische Urteile als handlungsleitende normative Regelsysteme im Spiegel der kulturvergleichenden Forschung. In A. Thomas (Hrsg), *Kulturvergleichende Psychologie* (S. 259–295). Göttingen: Hogrefe.

Eckensberger, L.H. (1995). Activity or action: Two different roads towards an integration of culture into psychology? *Psychology & Culture, 1,* 67–80.

Eckensberger, L.H. (1996). Agency, action and culture: Three basic concepts for cross-cultural psychology. In J. Pandey, D. Sinha, & D.P.S. Bhawuk (Eds), *Asian contributions to cross-cultural psychology* (pp. 72–102). New Delhi: Sage Publications.

Eckensberger, L.H. (2000, 16–21 July). *Self reflectivity and intentionality as key characteristics of humans: Consequences for a cross-cultural cultural psychology.* Keynote address to the XV International Congress of IACCP, Pultusk, Poland.

Eckensberger, L.H. (2001). Psychology of action theory. In N.J. Smelser & P.B. Baltes (Eds), *International encyclopedia of the social & behavioural sciences.* Oxford: Elsevier Science Ltd.

Eckensberger, L.H. (2002). Paradigms revisited: From immeasurability to respected complementarity. In H. Keller, Y.H. Poortinga, & A. Schölmerich (Eds), *Between culture and biology: Perspectives on ontogenetic development* (pp. 341–383). Cambridge: Cambridge University Press.

Eckensberger, L.H., & Emminghaus, W.B. (1982). Moralisches Urteil und Aggression: Zur Systematisierung und Präzisierung des Aggressionskonzeptes sowie einiger empirischer Befunde. In R. Hilke & W. Kempf (Eds), *Aggression. Naturwissenschaftliche und kulturwissenschaftliche Perspektiven der Aggressionsforschung* (pp. 208–280). Bern: Huber.

Eckensberger, L.H., & Gähde, U. (Hrsg). (1993). *Ethische Normen und empirische Hypothese.* Frankfurt: Suhrkamp.

Eckensberger, L.H., Kapadia, S., & Wagels, K. (2000, 11–14 July). *Social cognitive domains of thinking in marriage partner selection: The Indian context.* Paper presented at the symposium on the development of moral reasoning and diversity in the conceptions of the being, 16th ISSBD Meeting, Beijing.

Eckensberger, L.H. (unter Mitarbeit von H.J. Claus). (1968). *Unterrichtsprobleme an technisch gewerblichen Ausbildungsstätten in Entwicklungsländern.* Stuttgart: Klett.

Eckensberger, L.H., & Zimba, R.F. (1997). The development of moral judgment. In J.W. Berry, P.R. Dasen, & T.S. Saraswathi (Eds), *Handbook of cross-cultural psychology: Vol. 3: Developmental psychology* (2nd ed., pp. 299–338). Boston: Allyn & Bacon.

Erikson, E.H. (1959). *Identity and the life-cycle.* New York: International University Press.

Fowler, J.W. (1981). *Stages of faith.* NY: Harper & Row.

Habermas, J. (1981). *Theorie des kommunikativen Handelns. Band 1: Handlungsrationalität und geschlechtliche Rationalisierung.* Frankfurt am Main: Suhrkamp.

Kegan, R. (1982). *The emerging self.* Harvard: Harvard University Press. (Dt: 1986: Die Entwicklungsstufen des Selbst. München: Kindt Verlag).

Krishnan, L. (1999). Socialization and cognitive-moral influences on justice rule preferences: The case of Indian culture. In T.S. Saraswathi (Ed.), *Culture, socialization and human development: Theory, research and applications in India* (pp. 188–212). New Delhi: Sage.

Kuhn, T.S. (1969). *The structure of scientific revolutions.* Chicago: University of Chicago Press.

Lazarus, R.S., & Launier, R. (1978). Stress-related transactions between person and environment. In L.A. Pervin & M. Lewis (Eds), *Perspective in interactional psychology* (pp. 287–327). New York: Plenum.

Laboratory of Comparative Human Cognition (LCHC). (1983). Culture and cognition. In P. Mussen (Ed.), *Handbook of child psychology. Vol. 1: History, theory, and methods* (pp. 296–356). New York: Wiley.

Malle, B.F., Moses, L.J., & Baldwin, D.A. (Eds). (2001). *Intentions and intentionality. Foundations of social cognitions.* Cambridge: The MIT Press.

Oser, F., & Gmünder, P. (1984). *Der Mensch. Stufen seiner religiösen Entwicklung.* Zürich: Benziger.

Pandey, J., Sinha, D., & Bhawuk, D.P.S. (1996). *Asian contributions to cross-cultural psychology.* New Delhi: Sage Publications.

Piaget, J. (1970). Piaget's theory. In P.H. Mussen (Ed.), *Carmichael's handbook of child psychology* (Vol. 1, pp. 703–732). New York: Wiley.

Piaget, J. (1974). *La prise de conscience.* Paris: Presses Universitaires de France.

Poortinga, Y.H., & Malpass, R.S. (1986). *Making inferences from cross-cultural data. Field methods in cross-cultural research. Vol. 8: Cross-cultural research and methodology series* (pp. 17–46). Beverly Hills, CA: Sage.

Reese, H.W., & Overton, W.F. (1970). Models of development and theories of development. In L.R. Goulet & P.B. Baltes (Eds), *Life-span developmental psychology: Research and theory* (pp. 115–145). New York: Academic Press.

Roth, G. (1997). *Das Gehirn und seine Wirklichkeit: Kognitive Neurobiologie und ihre Philosophischen Konsequenzen* (5. überarb. Aufl.). Frankfurt am Main: Suhrkamp.

Russell, J. (1996). *Agency. Its role in mental development.* Cambridge: Erlbaum, Tayler & Francis.

Schwartz, L. (1951). *Die Neurosen und die dynamische Psychologie von Pierre Janet.* Basel, Switzerland: Schwabe.

Schwartz, B. (1997). Psychology, idea technology, and ideology. *American Psychological Society, 8*(1), 21–27.

Shweder, R.A. (1990). Cultural psychology—What is it? In J.W. Stigler, R.A. Shweder, & G. Herdt (Eds), *Cultural psychology: Essays on comparative human development* (pp. 1–43). Cambridge: Cambridge University Press.

Singer, W. (2000). Vom Gehirn zum Bewußtsein. In N. Elsner & G. Lüer (Hrsg), *Das Gehirn und sein Geist* (S. 189–204). Göttingen: Wallsteinverlag.

Sinha, D. (1996). Cross-cultural psychology: The Asian scenario. In J. Pandey, D. Sinha, & D.P.S. Bhawuk (Eds), *Asian contributions to cross-cultural psychology* (pp. 20–41). New Delhi: Sage.

Sinha, D. (1997). Indigenizing psychology. In J.W. Berry, Y.H. Poortinga, & J. Pandey (Eds), *Handbook of cross-cultural psychology. Vol. 1: Theory and method* (2nd ed., pp. 129–169). Boston: Allyn & Bacon.

Smedslund, J. (1984). The invisible obvious: Culture in psychology. In K.M.J. Lagerspetz & P. Niemi (Eds), *Psychology in the 1990s*. Amsterdam: Elsevier Science Publisher.

Stern, E. (1920). Probleme der Kulturpsychologie. *Zeitschrift für die gesamte Staatswissenschaft, 75*, 267–301.

Triandis, H.C. (2000). *Dialectics between cultural and cross-cultural psychology.* Keynote address to the XV Congress of the IACCP, Pultusk, Poland.

Valsiner, J. (1987). *Culture and the development of children's action.* Chichester: Wiley.

Wertsch, J.V. (1985). *Vygotsky and the social formation of mind.* Cambridge, MA: Harvard University Press.

Wright, G.H.v. (1971). *Explanation and understanding.* Ithaca and New York: Cornell University Press.

ॐ 3 ॐ

Ontogeny as the Interface between Biology and Culture: Evolutionary Considerations

HEIDI KELLER

Introduction

If social scientists acknowledge the role of biology in human behaviour and development, they would readily admit that there is an organic substrate which influences the co-ordination of behavioural and developmental processes with biochemical transactions. Yet, the conscious and intentional actions of humans are considered to be beyond biological control. This view is often connected with a dichotomous conception about the relationship between culture and biology (Eckensberger & Keller, 1998). However, evidence from such different areas as behavioural and developmental genetics and brain research has documented that biology and culture are rather mutually constitutive interactive systems than separate dimensions (Keller & Chasiotis, in press), thus confirming assumptions that were articulated by eminent scholars of psychology at the dawn of the last century (cf. Keller, Poortinga, & Scholmerich, 2002), but were more or less ignored during the intervening period. For example, maturation has been identified as an experience dependent process on the one hand, and on the other hand, it has been documented that experiences are processed on the basis of

informed hypotheses (Chisholm, 1996) which canalize the potentially unlimited environmental choices (Bischof-Köhler, 1991;
Crnic, 1984; Gottlieb, 1991; Keller, 2002). The evolutionary theory
has added another dimension to the proximate analysis of psycho-
biological processes by asking the ultimate question why specific
behavioural regulations contribute to reproductive success. Reproductive success represents the currency with which the interplay
of the biological and psychological system is evaluated, and thus
the ultimate goal of behavioural development (Hamilton, 1964;
Wilson, 1975). This stunning perspective on human behaviour and
development permits a fresh look at the dynamics of psychological
processes and their ontogeny. In the following section, the core
assumptions of evolutionary theorizing will be briefly introduced.

Core Assumptions of Evolutionary Theorizing

The basic and perhaps till today the most provocative assumption of the evolutionary theory is constituted by the Darwinian credo that humans do not play a special role in the array of
species. Human phylogeny has been shaped by adaptations to
selective pressures which arose due to contextual demands that
our ancestors had to face such as any other species development.
The recent contribution of sociobiology (Wilson, 1975) to this assumption was that not only somatic and biological systems in a
narrower sense follow the reproductive logic, but also social behaviour and the complex psychology of human beings.

The second landmark of evolutionary theorizing consists of the
transformation of the Darwinian formulation of preservation of
the species through reproduction of individuals (Darwin, 1859) to
the conception of inclusive fitness of the individual resulting from
own procreation (Darwinian fitness) and the procreation of relatives with whom the individual shares genes (indirect fitness)
(Hamilton, 1964). The focus on inclusive fitness implies that the
evolutionary perspective centres on the gene as the unit of analysis.
".... It is not the naked gene, that is exposed to selective forces
directly" (Mayr, 1994, p. 206) but the "realized animal" that lives
or dies, breeds or helps relatives (Daly & Wilson, 1983, p. 32). However, individuals are considered as "vehicles" (Dawkins, 1976) yet

"active replicators" (Dawkins, 1976), since changes in the genes must cause changes in the phenotype.

The shift from the species to the individual level has dramatic implications for the conception of human nature (Keller, 1996; Keller & Chasiotis, in press), since it implies, for example, that altruism results mainly from implicit and unconscious cost-benefit calculations and that relationships are genuinely conflictuous in nature (Hamilton, 1964; Trivers, 1971).

The individual life course constitutes a trade-off, mostly implicit and non-intentional between investment in own growth and development (somatic effort) and investment in reproduction, which comprises the functional systems of mating and parental investment (reproductive effort) (cf. Chisholm, 1996). This implies that the adult individual alone is not the end product of evolution, but the whole lifespan and its patterning is a result of selective forces and is thus evolutionarily shaped (Alexander, 1987; Schmid-Hempel, 1992).

Reproductive decisions—the heuristics of reproduction—are contingent upon environmental conditions, comprising material and ecological resources, as well as social complexity (cf. Dunbar, 1996) and niches that prior generations have created (Laland, Odling-Smee, & Feldman, 2000), forming a continuous scenario of change at the same time. Evolutionary theorizing integrates biological and cultural forces in a common framework. However, there is not only one version of evolutionary theory but varying approaches with different views on the link between culture and biology.

The earliest conceptualizations of culture in evolutionary theory are outlined in the classical "sociobiological" approach as proposed by E.O. Wilson (1975) in his landmark publication *Sociobiology—The new synthesis*. In this approach, culture is understood as one expression of genetic action like any other characteristic of the phenotype (Alexander, 1979; Trivers, 1985). Culture can affect genetic evolution "only" by influencing the gene frequencies in a population through differential reinforcement of particular reproductive patterns and styles. This rather restricted conception has been modified with respect to different assumptions about gene culture co-evolution (for a summary of approaches see, Hewlett & Lamb, 2002).

These approaches assume culture as an independent system of shared beliefs and values that is socially transmitted between individuals belonging to different generations as cultural heritage (Boyd & Richerson, 1985; Cavalli-Sforza & Feldman, 1981; Durham, 1991). Cultural activities may affect the environmental parameters and, therefore, establish modified selection pressures which may feed back into genetic evolution. Laland, Odling-Smee, and Feldman (2000) proposed to extend this model by including niche construction as the cultural way of humans to change the environment. Although other species also modify their environments, niche construction qualifies culture as the principle way in which humans adapt to their environments.

Crucial for any understanding of the links between genetic expression and cultural influences seems to be the course and pattern of ontogenetic development (Keller, 2002), and herewith the role of learning for adaptational processes. The role and modes of learning during ontogenetic development are substantially related to the respective conception of genetic activity.

Defining Genetic Programmes

Genes exert their effects on behaviour basically within two kinds of programmes which can be differentiated with respect to the directness of the genes–behaviour relationship. *Fixed genetic programmes* are invariably coded in the DNA of the genotype and expressed in phenotypical characteristics accordingly without further transmission mechanisms. However, there is no one-to-one relationship between individual genes and behavioural characteristics since most behaviours are coded in loci of different genes (pleiotropy). The translation of the genetic information into behaviour may occur during different stages of the human lifespan which is also part of fixed programmes. In fact, the influence of fixed genetic programmes may become stronger with developmental progress (Keller, 2000b).

Besides the action of fixed behavioural programmes, behaviour and behavioural development of higher animals and especially humans are organized to a great extent by *open genetic programmes* (Mayr, 1991). It is difficult to describe open genetic programmes in terms of an encompassing definition, since their modes of influencing and directing behaviour are "legion" (Mayr, 1991, p. 68). They are products of evolution like fixed programmes, but comprise "facultative" or "open" developmental processes (Laland, Odling-Smee, & Feldman, 2000). These processes are based on specialized information acquisition subsystems in individual organisms, covering single associations as well as domain specific functioning (MacDonald, 1988). For example, in the case of language acquisition, there may be a different interplay between genetic preparedness and learning than that for motor development or social competencies. Learning based in open genetic programmes, therefore, has to be understood as a highly specified mechanism: "... the more we have studied learning abilities, the more impressed we have become with their specificity" (Trivers, 1985, p. 102).

Open genetic programmes provide individuals with "epigenetic rules" (Wilson, 1975) or "central tendencies" (MacDonald, 1988) or "informed hypotheses" (Chisholm, 1996) for the acquisition of specific environmental information at definite phases of development. The openness or closedness of these predispositions varies according to the required specificity of the environmental information. The ethological conception of a sensitive period for imprinting builds on one of the most restricted cases (Lorenz, 1969), although even there environmental modifications are possible.

During the predisposed time windows for the acquisition of specific information, learning is easier than at any other time spans (Boyd & Richerson, 1985; Draper & Harpending, 1988) as has been demonstrated for different developmental domains (cf. Keller, 2000b).

Open genetic programmes provide individuals with a second asset of adaptation that allows them to respond variably and flexibly to environmental affordances and challenges within the boundaries of a reaction norm (Keller, in press). Learning is the major venue for human fitness and for cultural transmission at the same time; however, the range of possibilities is not unlimited since an evolved reaction norm (Keller & Chasiotis, in press) restricts indefinite variability (Figure 3.1).

One of the most controversial issues facing evolutionary scientists is the applicability of epigenetic rules for human functioning

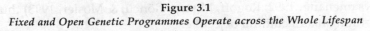

Figure 3.1
Fixed and Open Genetic Programmes Operate across the Whole Lifespan

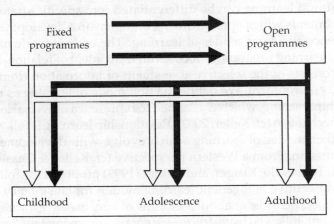

in complex industrialized knowledge based societies. Various scholars have questioned the usefulness of evolutionary reasoning about ultimate causes beyond subsistence level societies (Hrdy, 1987; Tooby & Cosmides, 1992). However, there is empirical support for the existence of central tendencies in modern environments for different domains like mating (Buss, 1994), parental investment (Keller & Zach, 2002), or the relationship between variables describing the childhood context and reproductive marker variables (Belsky, Steinberg, & Draper, 1991; Chasiotis, Scheffer, Restemeier, & Keller, 1998).

The Role of Learning for Development

As we have argued, learning capacities enormously increase the flexibility of humans' interactions with their environment, and thus adaptation. Learning is, however, a multifaceted construct which can occur in many different types and modes. We focus here on learning in social development, rather than on learning in cognitive development. Learning in social development is fitted into the matrix of cultural contexts and processes

(Nsamenang, 1992; Rogoff, Mistry, Göncü, & Mosier, 1993) thus defining it as a cultural objective.

Cultural learning can be differentiated into specific strategies and contents which operate during ontogeny in a developmental sequence and form modes of learning. The earliest mode of the social learning programme focuses on the content of relationships and consists of the selective assessment of information from the social environment. We define the first mode of learning as relationship learning, which is assumed to represent a universal learning mechanism (cf. Keller, 2002). Relationship learning is followed by other modes of learning which evolve with developmental progression. From a Western perspective (cf. Keller & Chasiotis, 1994), Tomasello, Kruger, and Ratner (1993) proposed the following consecutive ontogenetic learning models for late infancy and childhood periods: at about 9 months of age, *imitative learning* is prevalent, followed by *instructed learning* at approximately 4 years, and *collaborative learning* at around 6–7 years. For non-Western cultural contexts, different sequences and/or different modes of learning may be functional (Keller & Greenfield, 2000; Rogoff, 1990). The learning models become flexible devices or operational structures for the acquisition of information and the development of a knowledge storage within a cultural context. It is, however, important to note that the acquisition of knowledge is not a random enterprise, but operates within pre-selected filters or a priori biases. Due to these selective mechanisms, learning can be assumed to be adaptive (Laland, Odling-Smee, & Feldman, 2000). Thus, individuals assess the information from the environment that, in the ultimate sense, is relevant for developing reproductive styles which promise to optimize their inclusive fitness.

The evolution of learning as an asset for adaptation must have been a consequence of increasing variability and change in the environment between consecutive generations. When environments change very slowly, adaptive knowledge can be gained at the genetic level with genes incorporating the "experiences" of the ancestors (Delbrück, 1949; Mayr, 1991). When environmental conditions change very rapidly for adaptation at the genetic level, adaptation through environmental knowledge becomes necessary. During the course of human history, the tempo of environmental change has been generally slow, so that parents and offspring experienced similar environments. Therefore, intergenerational transmission from parent to offspring became a major pathway for genetic as well as cultural information. When environmental changes occur very rapidly, environmental conditions of parents and offspring may markedly differ, so that conformity with ancestral ways of life would not only be dysfunctional, but also decrease adaptation of the offspring. Under these circumstances, horizontal or within-generation learning becomes more important. Recent treatises on the power of peer socialization (Harris, 1998) may reflect the impact of rapidly changing environments of the "information society" (cf. Figure 3.2).

Figure 3.2
Vertical and Horizontal Influences on the Individual in Context

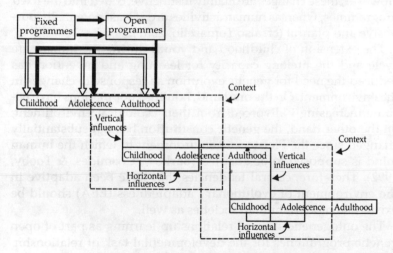

These vertical and horizontal influences are summarized in Figure 3.2. Each individual is part of a context that may change from generation to generation. Due to own childhood experiences, the parental generation creates socialization contexts (niches) for their offspring who also face horizontal influences over the course of their development, especially from peers. The individual integration of vertical and horizontal influences will be translated into the socialization contexts, that this generation creates for their offspring. Thus, ontogenetic development is the main mechanism of generational cultural change.[1]

The evolutionary basis of the capacity for social learning is constituted by the emergence of intelligence (Vogel, 1992) that enables humans not only to adopt but to also create knowledge that equips them to change the environment, for instance, by inventing niches for different proximate purposes. Super and Harkness (1996) described a developmental niche as the accumulation of ecological/contextual conditions, parental ethnotheories and the caregivers' psychology forming the environment for children's socialization (cf. also the general niche conception by Laland, Odling-Smee, & Feldman, 2000). Yet other species also change their environments and create niches like termites building hills and destroying trees or earthworms changing the chemistry of the soil they inhabit. However, these changes are mainly instinctive, coded into the fixed programmes, whereas human activities are at least potentially purposive and planful (cf. also Tomasello, 2001).

The extension of childhood and youth during the human life cycle and the lifelong capacity for learning and invention has reduced the need for genetic evolution as response to changes in the environment. On the one hand, hominid populations have become increasingly divorced from their ecological environment; on the other hand, the genetic constitution has not substantially changed since the Pleistocene environment to which the human mind is supposed to be adapted (Barkow, Cosmides, & Tooby, 1992). Therefore, central tendencies that have been adaptive in the environment of evolutionary adaptedness (EEA) should be existent in modern human societies as well.

The ontogenetic stage of relationship learning as part of open genetic programmes for the developmental task of relationship formation will be presented in the following. Relationship formation is part of the life histories of individuals (Alexander, 1989). It has been demonstrated that the mode and structure of early significant relationships influence the reproductive style of an individual. With this, the mode and structure of early relationships are related to the individual's own later parenting style, and thus constitute an essential part of the reproductive effort.

[1] This model does not assess horizontal layers of societal influences which, of course, are also important contributors to environmental change.

Relationship Formation: The Functional Mechanisms of Learning based in Open Genetic Programmes

There is consensus among different theoretical orientations that one of the first integrative developmental tasks that infants have to master is the acquisition of primary social relationships with significant others, i.e., the construction of a social matrix (Keller & Eckensberger, 1998). Although the solution of this task is a universal challenge of human development, cultures never-theless differ substantially with respect to the mode and structure of early relationship formation. With open genetic programmes, infants are prepared to assess actively the relevant information for mastering this task within their respective environment. Also, parents and caregivers in general are equipped with a universal repertoire of parenting systems, from which the cultural context selects components which form culturally informed parenting styles (Greenfield, 2002; Keller, 2000b).

INFANTS' PREPAREDNESS FOR THE ACQUISITION OF SOCIAL INFORMATION

During the last trimenon of pregnancy, infants' functional predispositions for social interaction become operative. They can be understood as proto-cognitions (Rochat, 1997) comprising behavioural propensities for growth and maturation like sucking and swallowing as well as for social interaction and information processing. Infants are altricial at birth, i.e., they need care and protection. It has been argued that this helplessness results from a "physiological preterm birth" (Prechtl, 1984) that became necessary due to hominid brain development. Evolutionary theorists, how-ever, argue that altriciality allows the infant to invest all available resources into growth and development which, together with the social capacities that are existent from birth on, promote the de-velopment of a *"better adult"* (better adult hypothesis, Alexander, 1989). In order to grow, develop and learn, infants have to attract the attention of caregivers and elicit their caregiving motivation. For this, they display a repertoire of characteristics that are part of their appearance as well as their inborn behavioural repertoire.

The display of the "Kindchenschema" (babyness), that Konrad Lorenz (1943) had first described, consisting of a large head in terms of body proportions, a distinct forehead and big eyes, is an effective bonding mechanism, in species other than humans as well. Infants possess an array of attachment behaviours for the expression of distress (like crying and fussing) as well as for the expression of positively tuned cues (like vocalization and smiling) which reliably evoke caregiving responses from the social environment. Infants attend selectively to their caregiving environment with central tendencies directing information acquisition. They prefer perceptual cues that characterize the human face like movement, brightness and contour over other perceptual displays, such as random patterns with the same informational characteristics from birth on (Fantz, 1963; Keller, 1992). They respond to the human face with eye contact and smiling; they recognize familiar sounds and voices. They expect responsiveness from their social environment as still face studies have demonstrated (Weinberg & Tronick, 1996).

Infants' predispositions for social interactions and social learning are supposed to have evolved as responses to environmental challenges during phylogeny, mainly the regulation of physiological and behavioural functioning (Hofer, 1987), protection from predators (Bowlby, 1969), development of group cohesion (Dunbar, 1996; Keller, 2000b), and finally and most recently, personality formation (cf. Keller, 2000a). Relationship learning is situated mainly in the early postnatal period covering the first 3–6 months of life. This period is demarcated by developmental transitions in different cultures. In Western literature, a first bio (social) behavioural shift is identified at about 3 months (Cole & Cole, 2001; Emde, 1984) with the adoption of the diurnal rhythm and a perceived change in the quality of social interaction: increase of eye contact (Keller, Gauda, Miranda, & Scholmerich, 1985), the emergence of a "true" social smile (Bayley, 1955) where the first developmental result of relationship formation is achieved (Keller, 1992) and a sense of an emergent self has been culturally shaped (Stern, 1985). Developmental transitions during this age span introducing the baby to new developmental contexts are also reported from other cultural environments like India (Saraswathi & Pai, 1997) or Africa (Yovsi, 2001). The acquisition of the diurnal rhythm does not converge cross-culturally, indicating its susceptibility to cultural practices.

PARENTING

Infants' needs and behavioural propensities are responded to by their caregivers within different systems of parenting (Keller, 2000a). The parenting systems form prototypical socialization contexts which constitute relatively independent functional units which define encompassing interactional experiences that supposedly have different developmental consequences. Several parenting systems usually overlap, so that various combinations constitute different parenting styles. Mainly five systems can be identified.

The Primary Care System

Providing primary care for infants in terms of food, shelter and hygiene characterizes any parenting effort and represents the phylogenetically oldest part of the parenting systems. The investments in primary care, however, may vary significantly across contexts. Under pressures of poverty and famine, nursing may constitute the major parenting effort (Minturn & Lambert, 1964), mainly as a response to infants' signals of distress. Accordingly, the psychological function would be the reduction of distress. The promptness and reliability with which an infant receives primary care and, therefore, experiences relief, initiates a basic sense of security and trust as a primary dimension of the emerging self (Bischof, 1985; Bowlby, 1969; Erikson, 1950).

The Body Contact System

A second system of parenting can be defined by extended body contact and carrying. In different cultural contexts, mothers carry their infants for a substantial part of the day, for example, tied to the back or astride the mother's hip with her arm around the baby. Aka Pygmy mothers carry their infants for nearly 8 hours a day (Hewlett, 1991), South American Ache infants spend about 93 per cent of the day in tactile contact with mainly the mother (Hill & Hurtado, 1996). Carrying the baby protects the infant from dangerous and life threatening events like fire and poisonous animals on the ground. Psychologically, body contact supports bonding and group cohesion (Dunbar, 1996; Harlow & Harlow, 1962) since the infant experiences to be part of a social system.

Body Stimulation System

The third system of parenting is also based on body experiences. It differs from body contact due to its exclusive dyadic nature. Mothers and other caregivers provide infants motor experiences through touch and movement, observe infants' reactions and modulate their behaviour accordingly. With affective expressions and reactions, infants communicate the pleasure and excitement they experience. It is assumed that body stimulation is functionally related to motor development. The motor precocity of African infants (Geber & Dean, 1957; Super, 1976) as compared to Western infants has been explained in terms of training (Konner, 1977). Also, Indian babies exposed to body massage outperformed American babies (Landers, 1989; Phatak, 1986).

In general, the psychological function of body stimulation may include intensifying body perception and, thus, the discovery of own body effectiveness in relation to resources of the environment. The body is experienced as an "agent" situated in the environment (Rochat, 1997, p. 99). Body stimulation may also enhance somatic development and prepare an organism for early reproduction.

Object Stimulation System

The object stimulation system of parenting has an exclusive attentional focus between the caregiver and the infant which is, however, localized outside the dyad. In many cultural environments, caregivers try to orient infants to objects from an early age. Object stimulation at an early age is especially popular in Western societies, where the object often replaces the person (Keller & Greenfield, 2000). Object stimulation supports the infants' exploratory tendencies and metacognitive processes. The psychological function of object stimulation during the early months of life is to nurture cognitive development and disengage the infant from the dependency of social relationships.

Face-to-Face System

This parenting system includes face-to-face exchange, which is especially characterized through mutual eye contact and the frequent use of language (Keller, 2000b). Face-to-face exchange constitutes an exclusive dyadic activity and follows the interactional rules of a pseudo-dialogue. The main interactional experience that the infant can derive from the on- and offsets of the behavioural exchange is the contingency experience. Through prompt response to the infant's signals, the infant can perceive himself or herself as the cause of the caregiver's action. Thus, the infant is informed about his or her uniqueness and self-efficacy. There is warmth in face-to-face episodes, mainly through the sharing of positive emotions as expressed in simultaneous facial displays. Whereas facial warmth is perceived to prompt interrelatedness, contingency is the medium for developing individuality and separateness (Keller, Lohaus, Voelker, Cappenberg, & Chasiotis, 1999; Voelker, Keller, Lohaus, Cappenberg, & Chasiotis, 1999).

INTERACTIONAL QUALITY

The systems of parenting described here set the stage for exchanges between individual caregivers and individual infants. The experiences are modulated by interactional mechanisms which individualize each behavioural exchange. The parenting systems may represent shared cultural activities (Keller, 2002), the individual regulations, however, may be directed by intuitive parenting programmes (Papoušek & Papoušek, 1991) that operate without conscious awareness or even intention. The fine grained regulations between caregivers and infants have been predominantly analysed within the face-to-face system. Intuitive parenting is automatically triggered by behavioural cues of the infant, since the intentional demonstration of this parenting style without the presence of a baby is usually experienced as difficult and unpleasant. The main constituents of intuitive parenting during the first months of life are monitoring the face-to-face distance of about 20 to 30 cm where the infants have a clear vision until convergence and accommodation have matured around the third month. Caregivers facilitate and focus on interactional exchange with visual feedback and imitate and modulate infants smiling or vocalizing with a feedback loop. They talk to the infant using a special language register, i.e., babytalk or motherese, consisting of high pitched, high frequency simple sentences, with many repetitions, long pauses and many nonsense utterances. These behavioural components may be considered as universals since they have been identified across individuals, being already existent in 3-year-olds as well as in different contexts and cultures (Keller, Scholmerich, & Eibl-Eibesfeld, 1988). The interactional quality and, thus, the basis for the developmental consequences for the child, are dependent upon the structural parameters with which these behaviours are implemented in the behavioural flow so that attuned dialogues can emerge. Mainly two structural components modulate interactional quality, i.e., warmth and contingency of caregiving behaviours. As has been discussed in the case of the face-to-face system, contingency denotes the prompt reactiveness of the caregiver with a time lag faster than 1 second (Lohaus, Keller, Voelker, Cappenberg, & Chasiotis, 1997; Lohaus, Voelker, Keller, Cappenberg, & Chasiotis, 1998) which qualifies the behaviour as intuitive (Papoušek & Papoušek, 1991). Warmth describes the emotional quality as expressed in sharing positive affect and empathizing with negative emotions and distress. Contingency and warmth form independent components of parenting (Keller, Lohaus, Voelker, Cappenberg, & Chasiotis, 1999; Lohaus, Keller, Ball, Elben, & Voelker, 2001; Voelker, Keller, Lohaus, Cappenberg, & Chasiotis, 1999). Although the different parenting systems favour the expression of warmth and contingency to varying degrees, both components are expressed within all systems, yet with different behavioural manifestations.

A third interactional structure that determines the quality of interaction concerns the exclusiveness of the dyadic exchange (Keller, 2000a; Keller & Eckensberger, 1998). Whereas body stimulation, object stimulation and face-to-face exchange are, by definition, exclusive dyadic activities directing the caregiver's attention completely to the infant, the primary care system as well as the body contact system may be part of co-occurring care (Saraswathi, 1994), where the babies' needs and behaviours are constantly monitored, but the caregiver continues with other activities at the same time (like household chores, fetching things, farming). The parenting systems as well as the interactive mechanisms within the systems represent differential parental strategies of investment allocation.

The Conception of Parental Investment

Evolutionary approaches conceive of parenting on the basis of the inclusive fitness theory as an investment that parents allocate individually and differentially to their offspring (Clutton-Brock, 1991). The dynamics of investment decisions have been summarized in the parental investment theory, mainly proposed by Trivers (1972; 1974; cf. Clutton-Brock, 1991). Any investment decision involves two aspects: on the one hand, physical, social, and psychological parental care contributes to the reproductive success of the offspring and thus enhances the parents' fitness. On the other hand, investment in a particular child compromises at the same time the parental possibilities to invest in other children. The timing of reproduction during the life cycle thus becomes crucial and the trade-off between current and future reproduction (C-F trade-off) (Schaffer, 1983) is the most important trade-off during the life cycle. Parental investment constitutes a hypothetical continuum which begins at conception and continues throughout the lifespan.

Investment decisions are based on the ecological and social conditions of the environment, defining the parental condition as outlined earlier. The mortality rate of the reference group, especially child mortality, informs the individual about the relevant ecological parameters for investment decisions. Since it has been demonstrated that individuals store fertility and mortality rates and co-variates without realizing that they do so (Hasher & Zacks, 1984; cf. Hill & Hurtado, 1996) and there is ample evidence for the functioning of an implicit (non-conscious) memory (Goschke, 1996), it can be inferred that reproductive decisions are mainly non-conscious and non-intentional, although the timing of reproduction may be intended and planned on the basis of conscious decisions.

Different contextual scenarios select different children's characteristics as a further basis for investment decisions. Poor health status and physical abnormalities are significant predictors of infanticide (Daly & Wilson, 1984; Vogel, 1989). The same tendency in Western parents may compel them to seek refuge in abortion after amniocentesis and other medical tests have detected trisomia or other fetal defects (Schiefenhoevel, 1993). Trivers and Willard (1973) proposed a relationship between social status and sex preference, when they claim that "... under certain well defined conditions, natural selection favors deviations from a 50:50 sex ratio at conception" (p. 90). This hypothesis has come to be seen as synonymous with any sex biased parental investment before or after birth since then (Hrdy, 1987, p. 101). The rationale for the Trivers–Willard hypothesis is based on the assumption of a higher variability of the reproduction potential of males as compared to females as a consequence of sexual selection and sexual reproduction in humans. Accordingly, parents from a high socioeconomic background with an intergenerationally stable and predictable socioeconomic frame can expect high reproductive success when investing in boys. Parents from the low economic strata optimize their reproductive success when investing primarily in girls. Reports from different cultures, historical times, and regions have confirmed differential investment patterns according to the sex of the child (Das Gupta, 1987; Keller & Zach, 2002). Although there is seeming support for the assumption that parents invest differentially in sons and daughters after birth, a number of studies have failed to confirm the predictions. Also, proximate psychological studies have reported contradictory evidence for sex biased interactions between infants and their primary caregivers (Bakeman & Brown, 1980; Moss, 1967; Seifer, Sameroff, Anagnostopolou, & Elias, 1992). Several reasons have to be considered including the parameters of assessment as well as sampling biases.

Children's characteristics that mark their developmental niche in a family comprise, other than the respective sex, the individual birth position, containing information about the parity of the parent as well as the sibship system of the child (Sulloway, 1996; in press). Specifically, differences in parenting in relation to first and later-born children have been reported from different cultures. First-borns are accorded more time and attention than laterborns and are more stimulated (Dunn & Kendrick, 1982). In many societies they are accorded a higher status than laterborns (LeVine,1977; Riesman, 1992). On the other hand, laterborns are less alone than firstborns (Keller & Zach, 2002) and experience more maternal warmth (Moore, Cohn, & Campbell, 1997) as revealed by studies of Western societies. Virtually none of the studies balance the effect of sex and sibling position with respect to parental investment (cf. Keller & Zach, 2002; Moss, 1967) as significant aspects of children's non-shared environments (cf. Plomin, 1994).

PARAMETERS OF PARENTAL INVESTMENT

Parental investment has been usually assessed in terms of quantitative parameters, and thus the relative amount invested in one descendant as compared with other descendants, like counting feeding rates in birds or egg fanning periods in fish (cf. Borgerhoff Mulder, 1990). Also, human parental investment has been mainly expressed in quantitative terms like the amount of carrying, or the length and frequency of nursing bouts as expressed in the energy spent. Accordingly, investment is reported as more or less of care ranging from neglect or even infanticide (Daly & Wilson, 1984) to "good" care, associated with a positive family climate (Belsky, Steinberg, & Draper, 1991). In order to be able to capture the complexity of human caregiving, it appears to be necessary to assess psychological strategies in addition to parameters of energy. The systems of parenting that have been introduced earlier are able to capture different psychological experiences. Moreover, the analysis of the psychological effort of the caregiver as expressed in the interactional mechanisms of warmth, contingency and the attentional structure becomes crucial for the understanding of human parental investment. In a study of North German male and female first and laterborn 3 month old infants, we (Keller & Zach, 2002) assessed time spent with the infant as well as body contact and face-to-face system in a middle class sample. We assumed that the face-to-face system constitutes a higher investment due to its exclusive dyadic nature than the body contact system which may occur jointly with other activities. Due to evolutionary predictions, we expected that differences in maternal investment in an affluent environment would be most pronounced with first-borns, favouring boys, and the least pronounced with laterborns.

Although our data did not confirm the hypotheses, we found evidence for the differential treatment of the four subsamples. Firstborn boys differed significantly from laterborn boys and girls with respect to the experience of the face-to-face system as expected. They did not differ from firstborn girls, who spent more time alone as compared to all the other subsamples. These dimensions of maternal care revealed differences in samples of a modern society that are in line with the central tendencies of evolutionary predictions.

Conclusion

We have addressed only the first months of an infant's life. It cannot, of course, be concluded that these few months imprint the reproduction style in a deterministic way. The developmental model presented here assumes a sequence of different developmental tasks during the course of ontogenetic development which forms meaningful developmental pathways. The mastery of earlier tasks influences the timing, the developmental course, and the result of later tasks. Unlike the attachment theoretical assumptions, we assumed that a first developmental result with respect to the task of relationship formation is already achieved at about 3 months of age. The primary matrix of relationships that the infant has acquired by then may set the stage for the conception of the self that should be best adapted to the ecological and social demands of the respective environment. Specifically, two conceptions of parenting that integrate experiences from different systems and interactional mechanisms have been described in the literature. A combination of primary care with nursing on demand and body contact by carrying the infant for a major part of the day and possibly also body stimulation with regular exercises or massaging form the agrarian or paediatric strategy (LeVine, 1974; 1994) or the non-Western style (Keller & Eckensberger, 1998), mostly prevalent in farming or pastoral communities. Primary care coupled with the face-to-face system as the main communication context for the caregiver–child interaction form the pedagogical (LeVine, 1994) or Western (Keller & Eckensberger, 1998) parenting style. The different combinations of the parenting systems together with the interactional modes of warmth and contingency not only form pervasive socialization climates but also define cultural scripts for self and personality development (Keller, 1996). It may be assumed that the long-term psychological consequences as initiated by the first socialization experiences may be related to interrelated or individualistic orientations in personality functioning, as described by social psychologists (Kagitcibasi, 1997; Triandis, 1995). Evolutionary theorizing would qualify these personality styles as concomitants of reproductive styles. However, empirical studies are needed to evaluate whether this framework provides a fruitful approach for explaining cross-cultural as well as interindividual variation.

References

Alexander, R.D. (1979). *Darwinism and human affairs*. Seattle, WA: University of Washington Press.

Alexander, R.D. (1987). *The biology of moral systems*. New York: Aldine de Gruyter.

Alexander, R.D. (1989). Über die Interessen der Menschen und die Evolution von Lebensabläufen. In H. Meier (Ed.), *Die Herausforderung der evolutionsbiologie* (pp. 129–171). München: Piper.

Bakeman, R., & Brown, J.V. (1980). Early interaction. Consequences for social and mental development at three years. *Child Development, 51*, 437–447.

Barkow, J.H., Cosmides, L., & Tooby, J. (1992). *The adapted mind. Evolutionary psychology and the generation of culture*. New York: Oxford University Press.

Bayley, N. (1955). On the growth of intelligence. *American Psychologist, 10*, 805–818.

Belsky, J, Steinberg, L., & Draper, P. (1991). Further reflections on an evolutionary theory of socialization. *Child Development, 62*, 682–685.

Bischof, N. (1985). *Das Rätsel Ödipus: Die biologischen Wurzeln des Urkonfliktes von Intimität und Autonomie*. München: Piper.

Bischof-Köhler, D. (1991). The development of empathy in infants. In M.E. Lamb & H. Keller (Eds), *Infant development. Perspectives from German speaking countries* (pp. 245–273). Hillsdale, NJ: Erlbaum.

Borgerhoff Mulder, M. (1990). Kipsigis women's preference for wealthy men: Evidence for female choice in mammals? *Behavioral Ecology and Sociobiology, 27*, 255–264.

Bowlby, J. (1969). *Attachment and loss. Vol. I: Attachment*. New York: Basic Books.

Boyd, R., & Richerson, P.J. (1985). *Culture and the evolutionary process*. Chicago: University of Chicago Press.

Buss, D.M. (1994). *Die Evolution des Begehrens. Geheimnisse der Partnerwahl*. Hamburg: Kabel.

Cavalli-Sforza, L.L., & Feldman, M.W. (1981). *Cultural transmission and evolution: A quantitative approach.* Princeton: Princeton University Press.

Chasiotis, A., Scheffer, D., Restemeier, R., & Keller, H. (1998). Intergenerational context discontinuity affects the onset of puberty: A comparison of parent–child dyads in West and East Germany. *Human Nature, 9*(3), 321–339.

Chisholm, J.S. (1996). The evolutionary ecology of attachment organization. *Human Nature, 7*(1), 1–38.

Clutton-Brock, T.H. (1991). *The evolution of parental care.* Princeton, NJ: Princeton University Press.

Cole, M., & Cole, S.R. (2001). *The development of children* (4th ed.). New York: Freeman & Company.

Crnic, L.S. (1984). Early experience effects. In R.N. Emde & R.J. Harmon (Eds), *Continuities and discontinuities in development* (pp. 355–368). New York: Plenum Press.

Daly, M., & Wilson, M. (1983). *Sex, evolution and behavior* (2nd ed.). Boston: PWS Publishers.

Daly, M., & Wilson, M. (1984). A sociobiological analysis of human infanticide. In G. Hausfater & S.B. Hrdy (Eds), *Infanticide: Comparative and evolutionary perspectives* (pp. 487–502). New York: Aldine de Gruyter.

Darwin, C. (1859). *On the origin of species by means of natural selection. Or the preservation of favoured races in the struggle for life.* London: John Murray.

Das Gupta, M. (1987). Selective discrimination against female children in rural Punjab. *Population and Development Review, 13*, 77–100.

Dawkins, R. (1976). *The selfish gene.* Oxford: Oxford University Press.

Delbrück, M. (1949). A physicist looks at biology. *Transactions of the Conneticut Academy of Arts and Sciences, 38*, 173–190.

Draper, P., & Harpending, H. (1988). A sociobiological perspective on human reproductive strategies. In K.B. MacDonald (Ed.), *Sociobiological perspectives on human development* (pp. 340–372). New York: Springer.

Dunbar, R. (1996). *Grooming, gossip and the evolution of language.* London: Faber & Faber.

Dunn, J., & Kendrick, C. (1982). *Siblings: Love, envy, and understanding.* Cambridge, MA: Harvard University Press.

Durham, W.H. (1991). *Coevolution: Genes, culture, and human diversity.* Stanford: Stanford University Press.

Eckensberger, L.H., & Keller, H. (1998). Menschenbilder und Entwicklungskonzepte. In H. Keller (Hrsg.), *Lehrbuch Entwicklungspsychologie* (S. 11–56). Bern: Huber Verlag.

Emde, R.N. (1984). The affective self: Continuities and transformations from infancy. In J.D. Call, E. Galenson, & R.L. Tyson (Eds), *Frontiers of infant psychiatry* (pp. 38–54). New York: Basic Books.

Erikson, E.H. (1950). *Childhood and society.* New York: Norton.

Fantz, R.L. (1963). Pattern vision in newborn infants. *Science, 140*, 296–297.

Geber, M., & Dean, R.F. (1957). The state of development of new-born African children. *Lancet, 272*, 1216–1219.

Goschke, T. (1996). Gedächtnis und Emotion: Affektive Bedingungen des Einprägens, Erinnerns und Vergessens. In D. Albert & K.-H. Stapf (Eds),

Enzyklopädie der Psychologie, Themenbereich C: Theorie und Forschung, Serie II: Kognition, Band 4: Gedächtnis (pp. 603–692). Bern: Hogrefe.

Gottlieb, G. (1991). Experiential canalization of behavioral development: Theory. *Developmental Psychology, 27*, 4–13.

Greenfield, P.M. (2002). The mutual definition of culture and biology in development. In H. Keller, Y.H. Poortinga, & A. Scholmerich (Eds), *Between culture and biology: Perspectives on ontogenetic development* (pp. 57–76). Cambridge: Cambridge University Press.

Hamilton, W. (1964). The genetical evolution of social behaviour (I + II). *Journal of Theoretical Biology, 7*, 1 52.

Harlow, H.F., & Harlow, M.K. (1962). Social deprivation in monkeys. *Scientific American, 207*, 136–146.

Harris, J.R. (1998). *The nurture assumption*. New York: Free Press.

Hasher, L., & Zacks, R.T. (1984). Automatic processing of fundamental information. *American Psychologist, 39*(12), 1372–1388.

Hewlett, B.S. (1991). *Intimate fathers: The nature and context of Aka Pygmy paternal infant care*. Ann Arbor: University of Michigan Press.

Hewlett, B.S., & Lamb, M.E. (2002). Integrating evolution, culture and developmental psychology: Explaining caregiver-infant proximity and responsiveness in Central Africa and the United States of America. In H. Keller, Y.H. Poortinga, & A. Scholmerich (Eds), *Between culture and biology: Perspectives on ontogenetic development* (pp. 241–269). Cambridge: Cambridge University Press.

Hill, K., & Hurtado, A.M. (1996). *Ache life history. The ecology and demography of a foraging people*. New York: Walter de Gruyter.

Hofer, M.A. (1987). Early social relationships: A psychobiologist's view. *Child Development, 58*, 633–647.

Hrdy, S.B. (1987). Sex biased parental investment among primates and other mammals: A critical evaluation of the Trivers–Willard hypothesis. In R.J. Gelles & J.B. Lancaster (Eds), *Child abuse and neglect—Biosocial dimensions* (pp. 97–147). New York: Aldine.

Kagitcibasi, C. (1997). Individualism and collectivism. In J.W. Berry, M.H. Segall, & C. Kagitcibasi (Eds), *Handbook of cross-cultural psychology. Volume 3: Social behavior and applications* (2nd ed., pp. 1–49). Boston: Allyn & Bacon.

Keller, H. (1992). The development of exploratory behavior. *The German Journal of Psychology, 16*(2), 120–140.

Keller, H. (1996). Evolutionary approaches. In J.W. Berry, Y.H. Poortinga, & J. Pandey (Eds), *Handbook of cross-cultural psychology, Volume 1: Theory and method* (2nd ed., pp. 215–255). Boston: Allyn & Bacon.

Keller, H. (2000a). Human parent-child relationships from an evolutionary perspective. *American Behavioral Scientist*, Special issue on Evolutionary psychology: Potential and limits of a Darwinian framework for the behavioral sciences, 43(6), 957–969.

Keller, H. (2000b). Sozial-emotionale Grundlagen des Spracherwerbs. In H. Grimm (Hrsg), *Enzyklopädie der Psychologie. Band 3: Sprachentwicklung* (S. 379–402). Göttingen: Hogrefe.

Keller, H. (2002). Development as the interface between biology and culture: A conceptualisation of early ontogenetic experiences. In H. Keller, Y.H.

Poortinga, & A. Scholmerich (Eds), Between culture and biology: Perspectives on ontogenetic development (pp. 215–240). Cambridge: Cambridge University Press.

Keller, H. (in press). Persönlichkeit und Kultur. In A. Thomas (Ed.), Kulturvergleichende Psychologie—ein Lehrbuch. Göttingen: Hogrefe.

Keller, H., & Chasiotis, A. (1994, April 5–8). A psycho-biological conceptualization of ethnotheories. Invited lecture at the International Congress on Education, famille et development en Afrique, Abijan, Ivory Coast.

Keller, H., & Chasiotis, A. (in press). Kultur und Entwicklung. In M. Hasselhorn & R. Silbereisen (Eds), Psychologie des Säuglings—und Kindesalters, Enzyklopädie der Psychologie, Band CV4. Göttingen: Hogrefe.

Keller, H., & Eckensberger, L.H. (1998). Kultur und Entwicklung. In H. Keller (Ed.), Lehrbuch Entwicklungspsychologie (pp. 57–96). Bern: Huber Verlag.

Keller, H., Gauda, G., Miranda, D., & Scholmerich, A. (1985). Die Entwicklung des Blickverhaltens im ersten Lebensjahr. Zeitschrift für Entwicklungspsychologie und Pädagogische Psychologie, 17(3), 258–269.

Keller, H., & Greenfield, P.M. (2000). History and future of development in crosscultural psychology. In C. Kagitcibasi & Y.H. Poortinga (Eds), Journal of Cross-Cultural Psychology, Millennium special issue, 31(1), 52–62.

Keller, H., Lohaus, A., Voelker, S., Cappenberg, M., & Chasiotis, A. (1999). Temporal contingency as an independent component of parenting behavior. Child Development, 70(2), 474–485.

Keller, H., Poortinga, Y.H., & Scholmerich, A. (Eds). (2002). Between culture and biology: Perspectives on ontogenetic development. Cambridge: Cambridge University Press.

Keller, H., Scholmerich, A., & Eibl-Eibesfeldt, I. (1988). Communication patterns in adult-infant interactions in Western and non-Western cultures. Journal of Cross-Cultural Psychology, 19(4), 427–445.

Keller, H., & Zach, U. (2002). Gender and birth position as determinants of parental behavior. International Journal of Behavioral Psychology, 26(2), 177–184.

Konner, M.J. (1977). Infancy among the Kalahari Desert San. In P.H. Leiderman, S.R. Tulkin, & A. Rosenfeld (Eds), Culture and infancy. Variations in the human experience (pp. 287–328). New York: Academic Press.

Laland, K.N., Odling-Smee, F.J., & Feldman, M.W. (2000). Niche construction, biological evolution, and cultural change. Behavioral and Brain Sciences, 23, 131–146.

Landers, C. (1989). A psychobiological study of infant development in south India. In J.K. Nugent, B.M. Lester, & T.B. Brazelton (Eds), The cultural context of infancy (pp. 169–207). Norwood: Ablex.

LeVine, R.A. (1974). Parental goals: A cross-cultural view. Teachers College Record, 76, 226–239.

LeVine, R.A. (1977). Child rearing as cultural adaptation. In P.H. Leiderman, S.R. Tulkin, & A. Rosenfeld (Eds), Culture and infancy: Variables in the human experience (pp. 15–28). New York: Academic Press.

LeVine, R.A. (1994). Child care and culture: Lessons from Africa. Cambridge: Cambridge University Press.

Lohaus, A., Keller, H., Ball, J., Elben, C., & Voelker, S. (2001). Maternal sensitivity: Components and relations to warmth and contingency. *Parenting, Science and Practice, 1*(4), 267–284.

Lohaus, A., Keller, H., Voelker, S., Cappenberg, M., & Chasiotis, A. (1997). Intuitive parenting and infant behavior: Concepts, implications, and empirical validation. *The Journal of Genetic Psychology, 158*(3), 271–286.

Lohaus, A., Voelker, S., Keller, H., Cappenberg, M., & Chasiotis, A. (1998). Wahrgenommene kindliche Problemlage und mütterliche Interaktionsqualität: eine längsschnittliche Zusammenhangsanalyse. *Zeitschrift für Entwicklungspsychologie und Pädagogische Psychologie, 30*(3), 111–117.

Lorenz, K. (1943). Die angeborenen Formen möglicher Erfahrung. *Zeitschrift für Tierpsychologie, 5*(2), 235–409.

Lorenz, K. (1969). Innate bases of learning. In K.H. Pribram (Ed.), *On the biology of learning* (pp. 13–93). New York: Harcourt.

MacDonald, K.B. (1988). *Social and personality development. An evolutionary synthesis.* New York: Plenum Press.

Mayr, E. (1991). Die Entwicklung von Artenschwärmen bei Fischen. In E. Mayr, *Eine neue Philosophie der Biologie* (pp. 300–318). München: Piper.

Mayr, E. (1994). Evolution—Grundfragen und Mißverständnisse. *Ethik und Sozialwissenschaften, 5*(2), 203–209.

Minturn, L., & Lambert, W.W. (1964). *Mothers of six cultures.* New York: Wiley.

Moore, G., Cohn, J., & Campbell, S. (1997). Mothers' affective behavior with infant siblings: Stability and change. *Developmental Psychology, 33*(5), 856–860.

Moss, H.A. (1967). Sex, age, and state as determinants of mother-infant interaction. *Merrill-Palmer Quarterly, 13*, 19–36.

Nsamenang, A.B. (1992). *Human development in cultural context. A third world perspective.* Newbury Park: Sage Publications.

Papoušek, H., & Papoušek, M. (1991). Innate and cultural guidance of infants' integrative competencies: China, the United States, and Germany. In M.H. Bornstein (Ed.), *Cultural approaches to parenting* (pp. 23–44). Hillsdale, NJ: Lawrence Erlbaum.

Phatak, P. (1986). *Manual for using Bayley Scales of Infant Development, based on Baroda studies and Baroda norms.* Report of the Department of Child Development. Baroda: The Maharaja Sayajirao University of Baroda, Faculty of Home Science.

Plomin, R. (1994). Nature, nurture, and social development: Response. *Social Development, 3*(1), 71–76.

Prechtl, H. (1984). *Continuity of neural functions from prenatal to postnatal life.* London: Spastics International Medical Publications.

Riesman, P. (1992). *First find your child a good mother: The construction of self in two African communities.* New Brunswick, NJ: Rutgers University Press.

Rochat, P. (1997). Early development of the ecological self. In C. Dent-Read & P. Zukow-Goldring (Eds), *Evolving explanations of development. Ecological approaches to organism-environment systems* (pp. 91–121). Washington, DC: American Psychological Association.

Rogoff, B. (1990). *Apprenticeship in thinking: Cognitive development in social context.* New York: Oxford University Press.

Rogoff, B., Mistry, J., Göncü, A., & Mosier, C. (1993). Guided participation in cultural activity by toddlers and caregivers. *Monographs of the Society for Research in Child Development, Serial No. 236, 58*(8).

Saraswathi, T.S. (1994). Women in poverty context: Balancing economic and child care needs. In R. Borooah, K. Cloud, S. Seshadri, T.S. Saraswathi, J.T. Peterson, & A. Verma (Eds), *Capturing complexity: An interdisciplinary look at women, households and development* (pp. 162–178). New Delhi: Sage.

Saraswathi, T.S., & Pai, S. (1997). Socialization in the Indian context. In H.S.R. Kao & D. Sinha (Eds), *Asian perspectives on psychology* (pp. 74–92). New Delhi: Sage Publications.

Schaffer, W. (1983). The application of optimal control theory to the general life history problem. *American Naturalist, 121*, 418–431.

Schiefenhoevel, W. (1993). Adaptiv oder pathogen? Kulturelle Einflüsse auf die Streßphysiologie. In E. Voland (Ed.), *Evolution und Anpassung: warum die Vergangenheit die Gegenwart erklärt* (S. 249–262). Stuttgart: Hirzel.

Schmid-Hempel, P. (1992). Lebenslaufstrategien, Fortpflanzungsunterschiede und biologische Optimierung. In E. Voland (Ed.), *Fortpflanzung: Natur und Kultur im Wechselspiel* (pp. 74–103). Frankfurt: Suhrkamp.

Seifer, R., Sameroff, A.J., Anagnostopolou, R., & Elias, P.K. (1992). Mother-infant interaction during the first year: Effects of situation, maternal mental illness, and demographic factors. *Infant Behavior and Development, 15*, 405–426.

Stern, D.N. (1985). *The interpersonal world of the infant: A view from psychoanalysis and developmental psychology.* New York: Basic Books.

Sulloway, F. (1996). *Born to rebel: Birth order, family dynamics, and creative lives.* New York: Pantheon Books.

Sulloway, F.J. (in press). Birth order, sibling competition, and human behavior. In P.S. Davies & H.R. Holcamb III (Eds), *The evolution of minds: Psychological and philosophical perspectives.* Dordrecht/Boston: Kluwer Academic Publishers.

Super, C., & Harkness, S. (1996). The cultural structuring of child development. In J.W. Berry, P.R. Dasen, & T.S. Saraswathi (Eds), *Handbook of cross-cultural psychology, vol. 2: Basic processes and human development* (2nd ed., pp. 1–39). Boston: Allyn & Bacon.

Super, C.M. (1976). Environmental effects on motor development: A case of African infant precocity. *Developmental Medicine and Child Neurology, 18*, 561–567.

Tomasello, M. (2001). Cultural transmission. A view from chimpanzees and human infants. *Journal of Cross-Cultural Psychologoy, 32*(1), 151–162.

Tomasello, M., Kruger, A.C., & Ratner, H.H. (1993). Cultural learning. *Behavioral and Brain Sciences, 16*, 495–552.

Tooby, J., & Cosmides, L. (1992). The psychological foundations of culture. In J.H. Barkow, L. Cosmides, & J. Tooby (Eds), *The adapted mind. Evolutionary psychology and the generation of culture* (pp. 19–136). New York: Oxford University Press.

Triandis, H.C. (1995). *Individualism and collectivism.* Boulder, CO: Westview.

Trivers, R.L. (1971). The evolution of reciprocal altruism. *Quarterly Review of Biology, 46*, 35–57.

Trivers, R.L. (1972). Parental investment and sexual selection. In B.G. Campbell (Ed.), *Sexual selection and the descent of man: 1871–1971* (pp. 136–179). Chicago: Aldine de Gruyter.

Trivers, R.L. (1974). Parent-offspring conflict. *American Zoologist, 14*, 249–264.

Trivers, R.L. (1985). *Social evolution.* Menlo Park, CA: Benjamin/Cummings.

Trivers, R.L., & Willard, D.E. (1973). Natural selection of parental ability to vary the sex ratio of offspring. *Science, 179*, 90–92.

Voelker, S., Keller, H., Lohaus, A., Cappenberg, M., & Chasiotis, A. (1999). Maternal interactive behaviour in early infancy and later attachment. *International Journal of Behavioral Development, 23*(4), 921–936.

Vogel, C. (1989). *Vom Töten zum Mord.* München: Hanser.

Vogel, C. (1992). Die Rolle der familie im biogenetischen Geschehen. In E. Voland (Ed.), *Fortpflanzung: Natur und kultur im Wechselspiel* (pp. 145–169). Frankfurt: Suhrkamp.

Weinberg, M.K., & Tronick, E.Z. (1996). Infant affective reactions to the resumption of maternal interaction after the still-face. *Child Development, 67*, 905–914.

Wilson, E.O. (1975). *Sociobiology: The new synthesis.* Cambridge, MA: Belknap Press.

Yovsi, R.D. (2001). *An investigation of breastfeeding and mother-infant interactions in the face of cultural taboos and belief systems. The case of Nso and Fulani mothers and their infants of 3–5 months of age in Mbvem, sub-division of the north-west province of Cameroon.* Unpublished doctoral dissertation, University of Osnabrueck.

℘ 4 ℘

Theoretical Frameworks in Cross-cultural Developmental Psychology: An Attempt at Integration[1]

PIERRE R. DASEN

Cross-cultural psychologists are often concerned about the minimal impact their research has on mainstream psychology; this has been attributed to the methodological difficulties of carrying out research in diverse cultural settings and attempting comparisons across settings, and to the lack of strong theoretical frameworks (Dasen & Mishra, 2000). It is this second aspect that I would like to tackle in this paper, since we now have a number of interesting theoretical frameworks in the field of cross-cultural developmental psychology. What do these have in common, and can they be integrated into one single overarching framework? This is what I will attempt to do in this paper.

I start by reviewing of a number of these frameworks, commenting briefly on their main advantages and mentioning some

[1] This chapter was first prepared under the title "The role of indigenous conceptions for developmental theories" for the workshop "Theories of individual development: Demarcating and integrating metaperspectives", held in Lutherstadt-Wittenberg, November 5–8, 1998 in honour of Lutz Eckensberger. It also benefitted from discussions at the workshop "Ethnotheories on child development and value of children in cultural context", University of Konstanz, July 11–13, 1999, and presentations at the Universities of Geneva and Paris-10 Nanterre. I wish to thank everyone who has contributed critical comments, in particular Ramesh Mishra, Elizabeth Reichel, Colette Sabatier, T.S. Saraswathi, Axel Scholmerich, and Fabienne Tanon.

criticisms, and then attempting an integration that combines their respective strengths. This review is limited to cross-cultural developmental psychology, and does not pretend to include recent developments in such areas as cognitive anthropology and evolutionary psychology. I am indebted to similar reviews by Gardiner, Mutter, and Kosmitzki (1998), Mistry and Saraswathi (2003), and Sabatier (1994a) that refer partly to the same frameworks. Clearly, a consensus emerges about their usefulness.

In particular, I will focus on the *ecocultural framework* developed over the years by Berry, and used as the basis of our textbooks on cross-cultural psychology (Berry, Poortinga, Segall, & Dasen, 1992/2002; Segall, Dasen, Berry, & Poortinga, 1999; see Berry, this volume) and on the *developmental niche* of Super and Harkness (1986; 1997). Both frameworks have led to important research programmes, that helped substantiate the conceptualization with empirical support. My own research over the years has been inspired by the former from its beginnings, and although much of it was done before the developmental niche was formalized, it can be usefully rephrased in the terms of the latter (Dasen, 1998). It has become progressively obvious to me that the two frameworks needed integration; while the developmental niche is said to be an open system, macro social variables are largely left unexplored, whereas they are more specifically taken into account in the ecocultural framework.

I will also briefly review other theoretical frameworks in the field, in particular Bronfenbrenner's (1989) *ecological systems theory*, which is another example of a framework in which the child is located within the concentric circles of contexts, from the microsystem to the macrosystem. Georgas (1988; 1993) combined the ecocultural framework with the ecological systems theory. Attention will also be drawn to Ogbu's (1981) *ecological and cultural model* geared towards explaining school success or failure in multicultural contexts, to Kagitcibasi's (1990; 1996a; 1996b) *model of family change* in relation to the construction of separated or relational self, and to Trommsdorff's (1999) contributions.

I will also attempt to add some structure to one component of the developmental niche. What is proposed is that most of the observations are at the level of "parents' ideas" that researchers can integrate into "social representations" or "parental ethnotheories". These are themselves part of more general value systems, capped by overarching "cultural belief systems" such as cosmologies and religion. While this is rather banal, it is striking that research on human development only rarely deals with all these levels, or with the relationships between these levels.

The Theoretical Frameworks Reviewed

THE ECOCULTURAL FRAMEWORK

An "ecocultural" approach in cross-cultural psychology was proposed by Berry since the first years of its development into a recognized discipline and the theoretical framework he developed over the years (Berry, 1976) has served as general guidelines for two textbooks on cross-cultural psychology (Berry et al., 2002; Segall et al., 1999) (see Figure 4.1; Berry, this volume).

I am not dealing with this framework in any detail, since it is presented by Berry (this volume), and is also described in Segall et al. (1999), and Berry et al. (2002). The main feature of this framework is to distinguish between the population and the individual levels of analysis. This reflects the originality of an interdisciplinary cross-cultural approach, that draws on various social sciences such as anthropology, demography, human geography, and sociology to set individual psychological functioning in a sociocultural context.

While the general flow of the framework is from left to right, feedback arrows represent influences by individuals back to the other variables in the framework; hence the framework is not limited to simple antecedent–consequence relationships, but is potentially open to interactive or dialectical relationships such as those emphasized in action theory and cultural psychology (Boesch, 1991; Eckensberger, this volume). Nevertheless, further work is needed on these feedback loops to make the framework more interactive.

As Jahoda (1995) and Berry et al. (2002) pointed out, the ecocultural framework has a long past in the history of ideas, including the functionalism of Malinowski and the psychocultural model of Whiting (1977). Berry (1995; this volume) and Troadec (2001) provided further links to the more recent and ongoing research inspired by the framework.

Figure 4.1
The Eco-cultural Framework

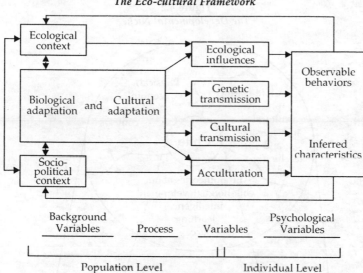

Note: Reprinted by permission of the publisher from M.H. Segall, P.R. Dasen, J.W. Berry, & Y.H. Poortinga (1999). *Human behavior in global perspective: An introduction to cross-cultural psychology. Revised second edition.* Boston: Allyn & Bacon, p. 26. Copyright © 1999 by Pearson Education.

The ecocultural framework is very broad, and although cultural transmission (enculturation and socialization) figures as a central process, the framework is not specifically designed to deal with human development. In the next framework that is reviewed, the developmental niche, the developing individual is taken as the focal point.

THE DEVELOPMENTAL NICHE

The framework developed by psychologist Super and anthropologist Harkness (Harkness & Super, 1983; 1996; Super & Harkness, 1986; 1997) as a means for integrating findings from psychology and anthropology, making the child within its context the unit of analysis is illustrated in the top part of Figure 4.2.

Surrounding the child are three components or subsystems: (*a*) the settings, or the physical and social contexts in which the child

Figure 4.2
The Developmental Niche

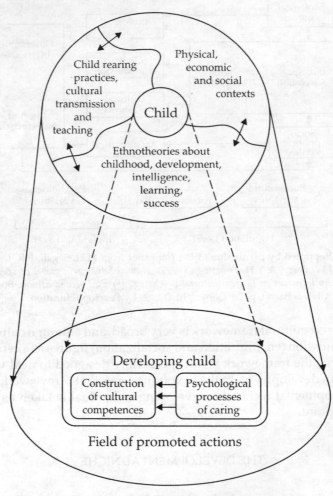

Note: Adapted with permission from B. Bril (1999). Dires sur l'enfant selon les cultures. Etat des lieux et perspectives. In B. Bril, P.R. Dasen, C. Sabatier, & B. Krewer (Eds), *Propos sur l'enfant et l'adolescent: quels enfants pour quelles cultures?* Paris: L'Harmattan, p. 26.

lives; (b) the customs, or culturally determined rearing and educational practices; and (c) the psychological characteristics of the caretakers, including parental ethnotheories of child development. Examples illustrating these three components are presented in Table 4.1, some of which will be discussed later.

Table 4.1
Components of the Developmental Niche

1. *Settings*

Physical settings
- Visual ecology, availability of objects (including print, media)
- Nutrition
- Size and organization of living space

Social settings
- Household size and density, sleeping arrangements
- Family structure (nuclear, extended)
- Family composition, multiple mothering, generations present, children as caretakers, size of peer group
- Prominence of father and mother
- Language(s)

2. *Customs/Child Rearing Practices*

- Postures and stimulations
- Caretaking practices, e.g., carrying, body contact, handling, massage, toilet training
- Opportunity for practice (e.g., sitting, walking)
- Routines: eating, sleeping (co-sleeping)
- Work and play (e.g., household chores)
- Maternal responsiveness; interpersonal communication (touching, talking; proximal/distal)
- Styles: authoritarian/authoritative, primary/secondary control
- Multiple vs dyadic interactions, and co-active vs exclusive attention structure
- Legitimate peripheral participation in communities of practice
- Education (informal, formal; teaching styles)

3. *Parental Ethnotheories, Cultural Belief Systems, Social Representations, Caretaker Psychology*

- Developmental theories (nature vs nurture)
- Developmental timetables
- Types of competencies expected
- Levels of skill mastery
- Evaluation procedures
- Final stage
- Definitions of "intelligence"

It is important to note that the developmental niche is a system in which the child and the three components interact in a coherent fashion, although there are inconsistencies at times, especially under the impact of acculturation. As the child adapts to his surroundings, the niche also adapts to the individual, and it thus changes itself in the course of ontogenesis. It is an open system where each component is linked with other aspects of the more general environment, but these links with the macrosystem are more explicit in the ecocultural framework, and in the ecological systems theory.

The lower part of Figure 4.2 represents an extension proposed by Bril (1999; Reed & Bril, 1996). The main idea is that the cultural organization of human life is so pervasive that even "biological skills" such as eating and walking are scaffolded by society.

Infants will be *selectively exposed* to only a subset of [the ecological] niche, to certain selected opportunities for experience and action. This selected subset of the niche we call the *field of promoted action*. Although each child probably inhabits a unique field of promoted action, it is very likely that fields of promoted action will tend to be organized in characteristic ways by each culture (Reed & Bril, 1996, pp. 439–440).

According to Reed and Bril (1996), the field of promoted action should be studied along the dimensions of intensity (how strongly an opportunity for action is promoted or prohibited), extensity (how frequently a child encounters an affordance), propriety (which refers to the "social rules about who may do what with what objects and in what circumstances", p. 440), and development (the change with age in the field of promoted action). This concept points to the fact that the niche favours some actions more than others, and that the child is not passive in the process.

In presenting the developmental niche as a field of promoted action, Bril (1999) emphasized the fact that attention paid to the context should not prevent us from studying the learning processes and how these allow the child to construct cultural competences. In diverse cultural contexts, different learning processes are emphasized as, for example, in the comparison between learning in everyday settings and learning in school (Dasen, 1988; 2000; Segall et al., 1999; Trommsdorff & Dasen, 2002).

BRONFENBRENNER'S ECOLOGICAL SYSTEMS THEORY

Over the years, Bronfenbrenner (1989; 1993) developed an "ecological systems theory" in the area of human development (see Figure 4.3).

Figure 4.3
Ecological Systems Framework

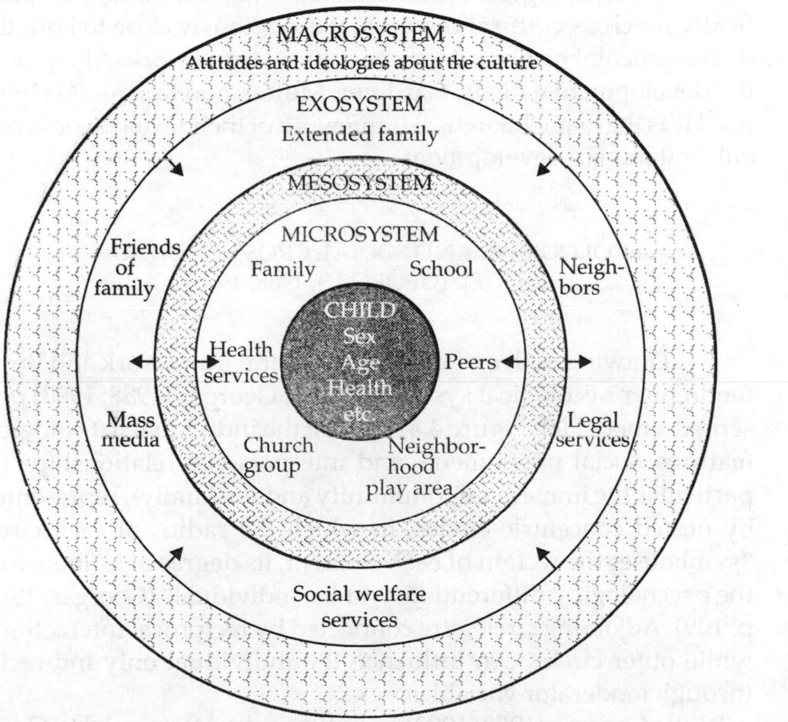

Note: Reprinted by permission of Pearson Education from C.B. Kopp & J.B. Kaslow (1982). *The child*. Reading, MA: Addison-Wesley, p. 648.

Just as in the case of the developmental niche, the developing child is in the middle, interacting actively, through bidirectional, reciprocal influences, with the environment. The latter is structured in terms of concentric circles representing the microsystem, the mesosystem, the exosystem, and the macrosystem. The microsystem represents experience with the immediate (physical or social) surroundings. The exosystem comprises settings of which the individual is not a part, but that nevertheless exert an influence; and the mesosystem contains the interactive processes between two or more settings. The macrosystem includes such general aspects of society as its values and belief systems; in other words, its "culture".

While the ecological systems theory was not designed specifically for cross-cultural research, it is obviously close to both the developmental niche and the ecocultural framework. Along with the developmental niche, Gardiner, Mutter, and Kosmitzki (1998) used it as the main theoretical framework of their textbook on cross-cultural human development.

ECOLOGICAL AND SOCIAL CROSS-CULTURAL MODEL (GEORGAS, 1988; 1993)

Drawing both on Berry's ecocultural framework and Bronfenbrenner's ecological systems theory, Georgas (1988; 1993) presented a model (cf. Figure 4.4) linking the individual to ecological features, social phenomena, and interpersonal relationships (in particular the immediate community and the family), represented by nested concentric circles, in which the radius of each circle "symbolises the weight of each element, its degree of influence on the psychological differentiation of the individual" (Georgas, 1988, p. 109). Adjoining circles are connected by reciprocal interactions, while outer circles can influence the individual only indirectly through moderator variables.

While Georgas (1988; 1993) initially applied the model to Greek society, ongoing research covering a large number of countries has examined the relationships between family bonds and family structure and function, comparing in particular the nuclear and the extended family (Georgas et al., 1997). The model does not

Figure 4.4
An Ecological and Social Cross-cultural Model

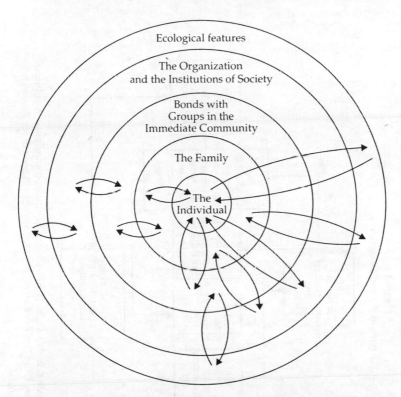

Note: Reprinted with permission from J. Georgas (1988). An ecological and social cross-cultural model: The case of Greece. In J.W. Berry, S.H. Irvine, & E.B. Hunt (Eds), *Indigenous cognition: Functioning in cultural context*. Dordrecht, The Netherlands: Nijhoff, pp. 105–123.

deal explicitly with human development, but the importance attributed to the family does make it relevant to our purpose here.

OGBU'S CULTURAL–ECOLOGICAL MODEL OF CHILD REARING

Ogbu (1981) proposed a framework (see Figure 4.5) in which the flow is from cultural ecology (A), in particular those

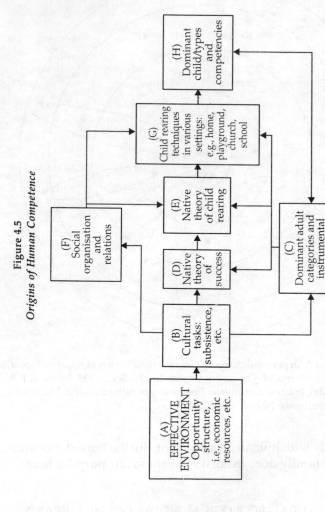

Figure 4.5
Origins of Human Competence

(A)
EFFECTIVE
ENVIRONMENT
Opportunity
structure,
i.e, economic
resources, etc.

(B)
Cultural
tasks:
subsistence,
etc.

(C)
Dominant adult
categories and
instrumental
competencies

(D)
Native
theory
of
success

(E)
Native
theory
of child
rearing

(F)
Social
organisation
and
relations

(G)
Child rearing
techniques
in various
settings:
e.g., home,
playground,
church,
school

(H)
Dominant
child/types
and
competencies

Note: Adapted with permission from J. Ogbu (1981). Origins of human competence: A cultural-ecological perspective. *Child Development, 52,* p. 422. Copyright © Society for Research in Child Development.

aspects that affect the quest for subsistence and protection from threats to physical survival (B), to social organization (F) and values (C), and to "native theories" of success (D) and child rearing (E), child rearing techniques (G), and finally to outcomes in terms of the major (dominant or modal) competencies of the child.

Ogbu's framework did not have a wide impact outside of educational sciences, probably because he applied it mainly to school performance in inner city ghettos in the United States. According to Ogbu, African Americans form a caste-like minority of involuntary migrants, with a history of exploitation and discrimination dating back to slavery; this induces parents to give their children ambivalent messages about schooling and school achievement. "Voluntary" migrants are more positive about their chances in school and in society. The framework draws attention to the fact that diversity exists within societies; as most societies are or are becoming multicultural, the distinction between intracultural and intercultural or cross-cultural research becomes blurred. Ogbu forcefully made the methodological point that competencies between different subgroups of a society cannot be meaningfully compared unless all the components of the framework are taken into account. The question whether Ogbu's framework is restricted to the American historical and political context or not has been dealt with in a special issue of the *Anthropology & Education Quarterly* (Gibson, 1997).

KAGITCIBASI'S MODEL OF FAMILY CHANGE

While the main focus of Kagitcibasi's (1990; 1996a; 1966b; this volume) theoretical framework (see Figure 4.6) is the family, the framework shows similarities with those discussed earlier in so far as it also presents links between antecedents in socioeconomic contexts, in particular living conditions (rural/urban, level of affluence), family structure, and family systems (socialization values, parenting styles—authoritarian, permissive, authoritative, and child rearing orientations—dependence and obedience, autonomy and self-reliance). Due to this focus on the family, it is specifically directed at human development.

Figure 4.6
Model of Family Change

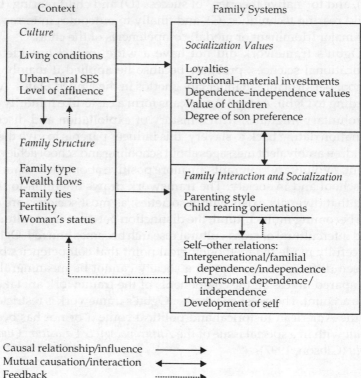

Note: Reprinted with permission from C. Kagitcibasi (1996). *Family and human development across cultures: A view from the other side*. Hillsdale, NJ: Lawrence Erlbaum.

Although the individual does not appear as a separate component in the framework, the psychological outcome that interests Kagitcibasi most is the development of the self, as either independent (separated) or interdependent (relational), or indeed the interesting combination of the autonomous–relational self (Kagitcibasi, 1996b), that is particularly found in collectivistic societies undergoing rapid urbanization and industrialization. This framework is interesting because it deals in greater detail with one of the components of the ecocultural framework, that of sociohistorical change.

TROMMSDORFF'S FUTURE ORIENTATION, VALUE OF CHILDREN AND INTERGENERATIONAL RELATIONS

Trommsdorff (1989; 1993; 1999) conducted research on various aspects of cross-cultural human development relevant to our interests. The theoretical framework she adopted in relation to future orientation in adolescents, following the summary presentation made by Seginer (in press), can best be depicted as a series of concentric circles, with the target behaviour in the innermost circle, surrounded by motivational antecedents (beliefs and values such as control beliefs and optimism), then social roles (linked to age, gender, occupation), socialization settings (family, school), and finally sociocultural settings (such as social class).

Another theoretical framework in Trommsdorff's work (summarized by Seginer, in press) presents reciprocal relationships between two antecedent variables, economic, social and political conditions and cultural values, that determine parents' beliefs, goals and practices, which together with the parent–child interaction determine the child outcomes. An overall feedback loop leads back from child outcomes to the socioeconomic and political contexts.

The first of these two frameworks is close to Bronfenbrenner's concentric circles; it could no doubt be generalized beyond future orientation as observed behaviour. The second framework is graphically more similar to the ecocultural framework, but focused on child outcomes like the developmental niche.

An Integrated Framework of Human Development from an Ecocultural Perspective

All these frameworks have their strengths as well as weaknesses, but they have much in common. They are fundamentally psychological, i.e., they explain the behaviour of the individual and particularly of the developing child; they focus on normal development, and not on pathological conditions. They agree with the basic tenet of cross-cultural psychology, namely that "human behaviour *must* be viewed in the sociocultural context in which it occurs if we are truly to understand it" (Segall et al., 1999, p. 1). Hence, the individual is embedded, in various but complementary ways, in a series of contexts that can best be conceptualized as a nested set, from the more proximal (microsystem) to the more distal (macrosystem). Bronfenbrenner, Georgas, and Trommsdorff explicitly used concentric circles in the graphic expression of their frameworks, because this format adequately captures this essential feature, particularly if the circles are taken not to represent separating borders but reciprocal interactions.

I have tried to combine both this general overview and particular points drawn from each of the different frameworks in Figure 4.7. Of course, it is quite impossible to integrate the wealth of detail of each, but readers may well fill in some of the gaps according to their own interests and preferences.

The link between this schematic representation and its predecessors discussed earlier is obvious—the use of concentric circles drawing on Bronfenbrenner, Georgas, and Trommsdorff. The outer circle of the macro- and exosystems includes the ecological and sociopolitical contexts and biological and cultural adaptation drawn from the ecocultural framework; cosmology, religion and values are set at this most general level. Contrary to most of the other frameworks, components are not presented in boxes or compartments, but are separated by arrows showing reciprocal interactions.

The second circle represents the processes linking these variables to the microsystem of the developmental niche (third circle inwards). It should be noted that genetic transmission is by definition not a reciprocal process (nor are usually direct ecological influences, although that is a debatable issue), while all other interactions proceed both ways. Within the developmental niche, the three components also interact; they are depicted without separation to emphasize the fact that all three components interact through the mesosystem with the exo- and macrosystems. The developing child is at the centre, with an emphasis on learning processes, and an explicit distinction between observable behaviour and inferred characteristics (i.e., constructs), drawn from the ecocultural framework; this is akin to the performance/competence distinction, to which I have drawn attention repeatedly

Figure 4.7
An Integrated Theoretical Framework for
Cross-cultural Human Development

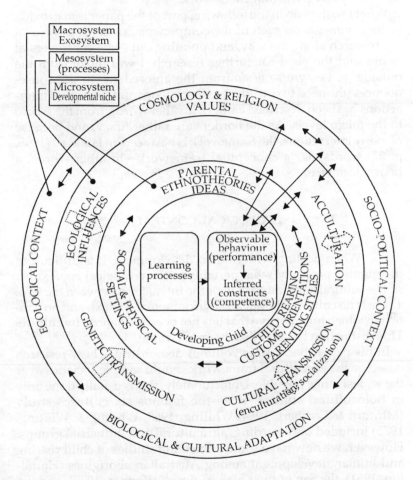

(Dasen, 1982), and which is particularly important for the methodology of cross-cultural studies.

Theoretical frameworks are always heuristic devices that simpli-
fy complexity into manageable schemes, and this is particularly
apparent when they are presented, as is Figure 4.7 and all those
that I have reviewed so far, in a graphical format. In cross-cultural

psychology, we have to be particularly suspicious of oversimplifications, because reality is always more complex than can be described by any particular framework.[2]

What I wish to do in the following part of the paper is to provide some comments on each of the components, reviewing some of the research along the way, and pointing out some controversial issues and the need for further research. I will move from the outside in, i.e., *grosso modo* from the antecedents to the consequences (the need to consider feedback loops and dialectical interactions has been described earlier); in other words, from the macro to the micro levels. As the borders are rather fuzzy, and because of many interactions, the framework is best seen, in Jahoda's (1995, p. 23) words, as "a conceptual framework—in other words, a heuristic device".

ECOLOGICAL CONTEXT

When dealing with human development, it is difficult to distinguish precisely what pertains to the ecological context *per se*, the cultural adaptation to it, or the interaction between the two. There is no culture without an environmental context, and no context in which humans live that has not been influenced by culture. This distinction has mainly a heuristic value.

In his paper, Berry (this volume) demonstrates how research based on the ecocultural framework should sample societies over the widest range possible. Unfortunately, this is usually done only in holocultural studies. Even the famous six cultures study (Minturn & Lambert, 1964; Whiting, 1963; Whiting & Whiting, 1975) included only herding, agricultural and industrial groups. However, we now have some interesting studies of child rearing and human development among Australian aborigines (Hamilton, 1981), the San of the Kalahari desert (Konner, 1977), and the

---

[2] One particularly frequent oversimplification takes the form of what Segall et al. (1999, p. 132) called "great divide" theories: primitive vs civilized, illiterate vs literate, non-Western vs Western, majority vs minority world, and so on. Individualism and collectivism (I/C), that currently has the favour of many cross-culturalists (Kim, Triandis, Kagitcibasi, Choi, & Yoon, 1994; Triandis, 1995), is in danger of being one of these great divide schemes that pretends to explain all cultural differences. In her review of I/C, Kagitcibasi (1997) showed how complex this distinction really is.

pygmies of Central Africa (Hewlett, 1991). Some of the studies explicitly compare hunting and gathering and agricultural groups in the same geographical area, for example, among the Efe foragers and the Lese farmers of the Congo (formerly Zaïre) (Morelli & Tronick, 1991), and among different groups of Adivasi, or the so-called "tribals" in India (Mishra, Sinha, & Berry, 1996).

Overall, the impression one gains from research linked to subsistence patterns is an overarching coherence between the latter and the developmental niche, be it in terms of the particular settings provided, the indigenous conceptions, and the child rearing practices. The cultural similarities between various hunting and gathering societies all over the world are quite striking (Coon, 1971; Testart, 1982), particularly the important role of fathers in caregiving.

Another theoretical strand that is directly linked to the ecological contexts deals with the basic health conditions provided by these settings. In his theory of the "universal hierarchy of parental goals", LeVine (1977; LeVine et al., 1994; Richman et al., 1988) argued that the caregivers' primary concern is the child's survival. Only if that is insured that adults focus on imparting knowledge and skills that contribute to economic capabilities, and the transmission of cultural values is their last priority.

No doubt, several aspects of the developmental niche can be explained by this scheme. For example, in many societies which have high infant mortality, the baby is not considered to be a full person before quite some time—until the infant has been named, or several weeks after birth, or until weaning (Erny, 1968; 1972a; 1972b). Among Australian aborigines (Hamilton, 1981), for instance, an infant may even be killed if birth spacing was not adequate. If an infant died, it was because the spirit of the ancestor had decided to come back at another time. Functionally, such an indigenous conception reduces the bereavement associated with the loss of an infant.

On the other hand, the hierarchical nature of LeVine's theory, and its Darwinian evolutionary leanings (LeVine, 1973) lead, I believe, to an oversimplification that does not do justice to a variety of observations. In many West African contexts, for example, while infant mortality is high, caregivers spend a great deal of time interacting with infants emotionally, verbally and socially in a manner that goes well beyond insuring simple survival (Baoulé of Côte d'Ivoire: Dasen, Inhelder, Lavallée, & Retschitzki, 1978;

Nso of Cameroon: Nsamenang, 1992; Wolof of Senegal: Rabain, 1979). Ho (1994) demonstrated that the theory does not fit parent–child relationships in China. In LeVine's scheme, some of the observations seem to be widely confirmed, namely that the infant is constantly near the caretaker's body, and crying is immediately attended to, especially through feeding. That there is little organized concern about the infant's behavioural development and relatively little treatment of him as an emotionally responsive individual (as in eye contact, smile elicitation, or chatting) may be true for the Gusii in Nyansongo, Kenya (LeVine & LeVine, 1963) as well as some other societies (Richman et al., 1988), but cannot be generalized to Africa or Asia.

SOCIOPOLITICAL CONTEXT

There are obviously reciprocal relationships, or co-constructions, between culture and context. It is, nevertheless, useful to ensure that the sociopolitical context is viewed as a separate component, because it draws attention to the need to always introduce a diachronic perspective; sociopolitical, herein, also implies sociohistorical. Indeed, culture is not just a static given, but is in constant change (which is also revealed by the use of the term cultural "adaptation"). Also, this component draws attention to the fact that much of current psychological theory is in effect a Western indigenous conception, linked to the present historical period, and that various aspects of human development may change according to historical periods (for historical changes in parental ethnotheories see Bril, Dasen, Sabatier, & Krewer, 1999).

This component draws attention to the processes of acculturation (Berry & Sam, 1997; Dasen, 2001), that are usefully distinguished from enculturation and socialization; while the latter apply to human development in any society, the former deal with the contact between societies. Of course, today there are hardly any isolated societies, as most of them have become multicultural. Hence, a large part of cross-cultural psychology is devoted to studying the processes of contacts between cultures. Camilleri and Malewska-Peyre (1997), for example, dealt with the "identity strategies" through which migrant adolescents cope with their bicultural upbringing (see also Dasen & Ogay, 2001). The number of studies of human development under conditions of social change and acculturation, in particular with migrants (Rabain-Jamin & Wornham, 1990; Sabatier, 1994b), is rapidly increasing, and those combining studies of immigrant minority groups as well as those still living in their cultures of origin (Greenfield & Cocking, 1994) are particularly interesting.

An important aspect of the sociohistorical context is informal and formal education, with which I have dealt elsewhere (Dasen, 2000; Segall et al., 1999; Trommsdorff & Dasen, 2002). A fact that is at times forgotten is that schooling, although now a pervasive institution worldwide, is historically fairly recent even in Western countries, and carries with it a particular set of contexts, customs, and conceptions (Serpell & Hatano, 1997).

BIOLOGICAL AND CULTURAL ADAPTATION

The ecocultural framework recognizes the complementarity of biological and cultural adaptation (Berry et al., 1992/2002). Just as there are ecological constraints, there are biological constraints, and the two are intertwined. Greenfield and Childs (1991) illustrated this through the restrained motor activity they observed as a constant stylistic feature of Zinacantec development, present at birth and attributed to genetic factors, reinforced throughout maturity by Zinacantec child rearing practices, and congruent with the adult restrained style of movement. In their writings on the developmental niche, Harkness and Super repeatedly stressed the importance of temperament and individual differences that may be linked to genetic underpinnings. While it is evident that culture and biology interact, there are some extreme forms of sociobiology that amount in the very least to an oversimplification of the complexities of human development, and sometimes to great divide theories. For example, Rushton (1995) represented nineteenth century social evolutionism and racism in scientific disguise (see Segall et al., 1999, pp. 135–156). Because of these ethnocentric overtones of some of the biologically-oriented literature, I have not given it as much attention as the more sophisticated current thinking, particularly in anthropology and evolutionary psychology, may warrant. The interested reader will find it easy to refer to current literature to bridge this gap.

Cultural adaptation is, by definition, the centrepiece of any cultural or cross-cultural perspective. Yet, because in a way "culture" is present everywhere, it is difficult to distinguish it from other components of the framework, not only within the ecocultural framework (cf. the difficult distinction between contexts and culture, discussed earlier), but also within the developmental niche, in which culture is all-pervasive. This is especially true if we abandon the definition of culture as being purely outside the individuals who constitute a society, i.e., not as a collection of antecedent variables, but as a co-construction in the minds of individuals.[3]

The paradox is that, if everything is cultural, the explanatory power of the concept tends to disappear, unless it is "unpackaged" (Whiting, 1976). Cultural adaptation therefore has to be broken down into manageable subunits, which is where the epistemological problems start. How can this be done without destroying the systemic character of culture as an overarching structure? Can we split it up into so many categories, as in the HRAF database? At what level should we aggregate the data? It is not easy to answer these questions. The symbolism of concentric circles is an attempt to show that we should focus attention on the level at which we decide to work, and establish links up and down to the other levels of analysis.

It is, of course, impossible to review all the relevant aspects of cultural adaptation. However, two topics are of particular importance, because they cap, as it were, parental ethnotheories—cosmology and religion, and values. I therefore devote more space to these topics than to others.

COSMOLOGIES, RELIGION, AND CULTURAL BELIEF SYSTEMS

At the most general level, there are overarching cultural belief systems, such as cosmologies or religions, that deal with fundamental issues such as the place of humans in nature. In the Judaeo-Christian or Islamic worldviews, nature is to be dominated and controlled, whereas in Hinduism, Buddhism, Taoism and

[3] This raises the more general issue of "culture as antecedent vs culture as co-construction", and hence the issue of choice of scientific paradigms.

especially in various forms of animism, humans are a part of nature, and often responsible for maintaining the balance. According to Nsamenang (this volume), worldview is "a shared frame of reference or psychosocial outlook by which members of a particular culture perceive or make sense of the universe and the place of the human being in it". Cosmologies and worldviews are usually shared by large segments of a society. However, Reichel (1999) argued that strictly speaking the term cosmology has as its scope the universe or cosmos, while the worldview deals with the world. These terms should not be conflated for analytical purposes, because in some societies they give rise to different, gender based knowledge systems.

Another characteristic of cosmologies and religion is that they are often resistant to cultural change, or they may coexist with new conceptions brought about by acculturative contacts without being perceived as contradictory (Camilleri & Malewska-Peyre, 1997; Saraswathi & Ganapathy, 2002).

While much is known, through ethnographic documents, about differences in cosmology and worldviews, the far-reaching consequences they may have for human development remain mainly speculative. It is obvious that they will influence value systems, parental ethnotheories, and child rearing practices, but unfortunately there is little empirical research demonstrating these links.

For example, the belief in reincarnation appears, in different forms, in many societies. Intuitively, it is obvious that this should fundamentally change the very view of what a child is, and different forms should lead to varying consequences, but I have not found many studies which actually demonstrate this. In the Hindu worldview, the belief in an endless cycle of birth and death is linked to the concepts of *karma* and *guna*, the latter pointing to the dominant role attributed to innate predispositions that cannot be easily altered by child training and socialization (Saraswathi & Ganapathy, 2002). Nevertheless, I would speculate that the idea of being able to influence the process through one's behaviour should lead to far more stringent socialization, through which adults try to instil "good" behaviour in children. This would be quite different from Australian aborigines, for whom children are ancestors who are reborn with a developed personality, and do not have to be shaped or taught in any way, which explains what Western people perceive as extremely lenient child rearing practices (Hamilton,

1981). Children are not expected to show respect for adults, but adults for their reborn ancestors!

In his numerous works on African infancy and childhood,[4] Erny (1968; 1972a; 1972b) extensively discussed African cosmologies and reincarnation in particular. Erny (1972b, pp. 40–41) pointed to the complexity of beliefs about reincarnation that can represent: (*a*) the return of part of the spiritual principle of an ancestor (i.e., the newborn child represents the ancestor ontologically); (*b*) the name of the child represents the ancestor socially; and (*c*) the ancestor can be seen as a protective patron. Erny (1968, p. 144) schematically represented the life cycle according to African philosophy, in which the individual passes from this life to the other world at death, becomes an ancestor, and is reborn. The passage to the present world, however, does not occur at birth, but only after successful weaning.

This has important consequences for the ethnotheory of what a child, or indeed any individual, really is:

> Society is not expected to intervene actively, but to welcome [the child], to place it in optimal conditions of development; there is nothing to be added to the new being, that contains within itself all the potentials necessary to its full realisation. The child is not to be moulded like clay, is not to be conditioned, is not to be imposed with any outside will, but is to be placed in an adequate environment, that will pay attention to its wishes and will fulfil its needs (Erny, 1972b, p. 57, my translation).

Recent writings on African worldviews as they influence human development can be found in Tapé (1994) with examples from the Bété of Côte d'Ivoire, Zeitlin (1996) on Yoruba (Nigeria) worldview and reincarnation, and Nsamenang (1992) on the Nso of Cameroon.

Worldviews or the belief systems people hold about the universe and their place in it, elaborated and encoded in cultural traditions during evolutionary history, prime human social action in a manner analogous to how genes undergird biology.

---

[4] These seem to have been largely ignored by anglophone writers, despite their partial availability in English (Erny, 1973; 1981).

Worldview is thus a cultural blueprint for social functioning [...], orienting and guiding occupants of developmental niches in how to picture, relate to, and deal with the world, as well as how to organize life in order to maximize not just inclusive fitness but also human welfare (Nsamenang, 1992, p. 19).

Another interesting example of how cosmology influences parental ethnotheories and child rearing practices was described by Chamoux (1986; see Segall et al., 1999 for a summary in English) for the Nahuas of Mexico. In the Nahuas' ethnotheory, the soul is not present at birth but develops gradually. An individual has "soul levels", one of which is inborn and connotes character or destiny while another may be acquired through personal effort. The progressively acquired soul may also be lost, and it is the duty of adults to conduct rites designed to ward off this possibility. Soul loss would be manifest in illness, or in developmental retardation, which are not attributed to the child's constitution, but rather to external perturbations.

VALUE SYSTEMS

Cosmologies and worldviews carry with them value systems; values express a society's moral and ethical guidelines, implying rules and standards of conduct. They are shared by a majority of a social group, but are set at a slightly lower level of generality than cosmologies, and are reflected at a still lower level in beliefs, attitudes, and behaviours. In many cases, these value systems come close to political ideologies (Triandis, 1995), but note should be made of the important methodological distinction between studying values at the level of cultural productions (proverbs, tales, and myths) and at the individual level (using questionnaires and scales, individual scores being aggregated as means by countries).

The latter approach is current in cross-cultural psychology, particularly the focus on the dimension of independence/interdependence, known as idiocentrism/allocentrism at the individual level, and individualism/collectivism at the societal level (Kagitcibasi, 1997; Triandis, 1995). Kagitcibasi (1996b; 1998) and Trommsdorff (1999) applied this scheme to the area of human development.

Greenfield and Cocking (1994) used it as a basic underlying scheme of research on socialization.

"PARENTAL ETHNOTHEORIES" OR "SOCIAL REPRESENTATIONS"

While cosmologies and values have usually not been discussed as part of the developmental niche, most of the research has concentrated on what have variously been called "social representations" (Chombard de Lauwe & Feuerhahn, 1991), "parental conceptions" (Sabatier, 1994b), "parental ethnotheories" (Bril & Lehalle, 1988; Bril, Zack, & Nkounkou-Hombessa, 1989; Saraswathi & Ganapathy, 2002), "parents' cultural belief systems" (Harkness, & Super, 1996; Sigel, McGillicuddy-DeLisi, & Goodnow, 1992), "parents' ideas" (Goodnow & Collins, 1990), "implicit theories of development" (Vandenplas-Holper, 1987), "subjective child-rearing theories" (Friedlmeier, 1995), or "caretaker psychology" (Super & Harkness, 1997).

I personally have a preference for "parental (or caretakers') ethnotheories". In every society, adults (particularly parents and other caretakers, including professionals such as teachers when these role distinctions exist) share "ideas", i.e., conceptions about what a child is, the landmarks or stages of development and their timing, and how these can be assessed, or how learning occurs (e.g., whether teaching is necessary or not); ideas about expected gender differences, definitions of illness, of appropriate foods, or of sleeping arrangements and routines are other examples.

Some of these ideas are rather isolated and are therefore likely to be idiosyncratic; at times they may even appear to be contradictory. Often these ideas form a more or less coherent set. Of course, the requirements of a *theory* may not really be met, insofar as ethnotheories are not always very systematic nor fully conscious; I still like the term, because it suggests, as in "ethnoscience" (ethnomathematics, ethnomedicine, etc.), that each society has its system of knowledge, of which the Western (and even that of professionals) is only one. These systems of conceptions may not be shared by a whole society, but are shared at least by smaller social groups. Hence, the term "social representations" may be a good alternative, although it is itself polysemic.

Instances of ethnotheories or social representations are conceptions of the respective roles of nature and nurture in development, or the definition of developmental goals (the "end stage") (cf. Greenfield, 1976) illustrated by various definitions of intelligence (Dasen, 1984; Dasen et al., 1985; Serpell, 1993). Extensive literature is available on parental ethnotheories or parents' cultural belief systems, references to which have been provided by Super and Harkness (1997), and Bril et al. (1999). These, of course, do not concern only parents, but also all caretakers, including professionals such as teachers and paediatricians. For example, Harkness et al. (1996) studied the "root metaphors" used by American paediatricians while discussing sleep patterns with parents, and how these have changed over time.

The observable behaviour that the researcher notes when interviewing informants is usually at the level of sporadic "ideas"; at times one gets the impression that "ethnotheories" emerge during the interview, because of the interviewer's prompting. In any case, ethnotheories are always a construction or inference made by the researcher.

Of course, we also have to study the links between these different levels, or the absence thereof. Specific parents' ideas or ethnotheories may or may not be congruent with the value system and cosmology, and across the components of the developmental niche (between ethnotheories and practices and settings). Because of these links, the precise location of an item in the structure may be open to discussion. For example, according to a Baoulé parent in a village of Côte d'Ivoire, a good child should spontaneously and obediently perform chores for the family. This is observable behaviour, and would be at the level of a caretaker's *idea*. But this statement goes together with many other ideas of this sort; it is part of the Baoulé definition of *n'glouèlê*, that we would translate as (predominantly social) "intelligence" (Dasen et al., 1985; Fournier, Schurmans, & Dasen, 1999). Hence, the researcher may conclude that there is a Baoulé *ethnotheory* of what is valued as an end state of human development. Fostering a social rather than a technological intelligence (or, better said, putting the latter at the service of the former) is congruent with an interdependent or collectivistic *value system*, which is itself in line with the African *worldview* of how a person fits into the social group and into nature.

Research on these links has to be done from a sociohistorical perspective, taking into account social change and acculturation, that are in particular likely to explain any incongruence between the levels (Kagitcibasi, 1998).

PHYSICAL AND SOCIAL SETTINGS AND CUSTOMS AND CHILD REARING PRACTICES

I will not attempt to review the two other parts of the developmental niche in detail, but provide only a few comments. In cultural and psychological anthropology, many descriptive studies have documented these in various societies (Munroe, Munroe, & Whiting, 1981), and the main elements are listed in Table 4.1. The precise attribution of the different elements to one part of the niche or another is open to discussion. For example, Table 4.1 includes nutrition in the physical settings, while it could also be construed as part of the ecological context. Nutrition is a good example of the interactions between various components of the framework: it is basically linked to the ecological context and productive activities, but as far as malnutrition and child development are concerned, the most important factor is not food production but food distribution, that depends on sociopolitical decisions, and a whole complex system of variables, including infectious diseases and patterns of mother–infant interactions (for a detailed discussion, see Dasen & Super, 1988). Or, visual ecology refers, for example, to the studies initiated by Segall, Campbell, and Herskovits (1966; reviewed in Segall et al., 1999), showing how features of the environment such as the number of right angles projected on the retina (the so-called "carpenteredness") influences the susceptibility to specific visual illusions. The degree of carpenteredness is an unconscious aspect of our living space, yet this ecological feature is brought about by culture, in the strict sense of its definition by Herskovits (1948, p. 17) as the "man made part of the human environment".

The component of child rearing practices refers mainly to what caretakers *do* rather than what they *say*. As Bril (1999) argued, the relationship between the two is far from simple. Sometimes they match perfectly. In Zack and Bril's (1989) research on French and Bambara mothers, the latter held that a baby should be able to sit alone by 3–4 months, and on the average they do, whereas French mothers mentioned 6–7 months, which is the French norm on infant tests. The observed child rearing practices are obviously helpful in leading to such an early achievement of this motor skill among the Bambara. As Super (1976; 1981) demonstrated, there is an almost perfect correlation between parental ethnotheory, practices, and the outcome in terms of motor development. In other cases, however, what the caretakers say does not correspond to what they do. For example, co-sleeping is strongly discouraged by Western ethnotheories (such as psychoanalysis, and paediatricians' lore found in numerous books giving advice to parents), and most Western parents will deny that it ever happens. This is not supported by empirical facts (Morelli, Rogoff, Oppenheim, & Goldsmith, 1992; Wolf, Lozoff, Latz, & Paludetto, 1996): co-sleeping is a normal practice not only in Central America, but also in Europe and in the United States (particularly among African Americans), and even in Japan.

That people do not necessarily do what they say is, of course, rather banal; social psychologists dealing with attitudes and values have been aware of this for a long time. In anthropology, Wassmann (1995) discussed some compelling examples of how ethnoscience (such as the classification of foods) as elaborated from language does not correspond to daily practices.

It should be noted that in Table 4.1, education (formal and informal) is listed under this component, while it obviously ranges beyond the category of practices. It provides particular settings and includes ethnotheories, and hence concerns the whole of the developmental niche. Like enculturation and socialization, it could also be dealt with at the level of underlying processes. It is interesting to note that the style of informal education may be influenced by representations of schooling (Rogoff, Mistry, Göncü, & Mosier, 1993).

THE CHILD

The focus of the developmental niche is the child. The major methodological lesson from this theoretical framework is that the object of study should be neither the child alone nor the cultural context alone, but the child in context.

Viewing the individual as an active participant in the co-construction of the niche (and hence of "culture") is an important part of current theorizing on the cultural construction of human development; other key words in this respect are "community of practice" and "guided participation in cultural activity" (Lave & Wenger, 1991; for a review see Segall et al., 1999; Super & Harkness, 1997). Conceptions of socialization have changed over the years (for cross-cultural studies of socialization, see Saraswathi, 1999; Saraswathi & Pai, 1997; Trommsdorff, 1989). Initially, the child was seen as a passive recipient of socialization practices. It was "being socialized" by "socialization agents". Today, socialization is viewed as far more interactive, with individuals assuming an active role in their own socialization. In complex societies particularly where many social roles are distinguished and numerous social groups interact, individuals partly choose their own socialization (Camilleri & Malewska-Peyre, 1997).

Bril's (1999) rendition of the developmental niche draws attention to learning processes, and Dasen (1988; Segall et al., 1999) reviewed relevant cross-cultural research particularly in relation to everyday cognition. The socio-constructivist perspective based on Vygotsky emphasized the social context of learning processes, such as the constructs of zone of proximal development, scaffolding, and "legitimate peripheral participation" (Lave & Wenger, 1991; Super & Harkness, 1997). Since adults are involved in these learning processes (even if unconsciously at times, as in Greenfield's [1984] study of scaffolding in the learning of weaving among the Zinacantec Indians), they could also be placed in the component of child rearing practices.

Greenfield's (1999; 2000) longitudinal study describes the impact of the sociopolitical context on learning processes. She found that the learning process in the same Zinacantec community had changed over the course of 20 years from Vygotskyan scaffolding to Piagetian trial and error. Weaving occurs in the context of economic production, mainly for tourists, and instead of being confined to two traditional patterns, innovation is encouraged.

One key issue is how the various components of the system, and of interactions between the components, determine developmental outcomes. Depending on the interests of a researcher, this could be motor development, cognition, emotions, social competencies, the construction of the self, or any other aspect of psychological development. Piecing together a puzzle from a large number of specific studies, each covering only a small part of the overall framework, would require a separate chapter.

Conclusion

How useful is such an attempt at integration? Do we not lose the most important features of each particular theory when we concentrate them into a single figure? For graphical reasons, it is impossible to do justice to all the components that should be included. However, the end result may not be the most interesting aspect of the enterprise; going through the process has served to draw attention to the existence of these theories and their respective strengths. It shows that the study of cross-cultural human development is gradually becoming self-critical and less ethnocentric (Dasen, 1993; Nsamenang, 2001), bridging the gap between indigenous conceptions and a more general, if not universal, psychological theory.

Commenting on the ecocultural framework, Jahoda (1995, p. 23) said, "it is doubtful whether in the present state of knowledge and technical resources, a full operationalisation of such a model as a whole would be feasible". This would be even more true of an integrated framework such as the one presented here. We cannot hope to have a model that can be empirically tested in all its elements and in a single study. The number of variables that are involved, and that interact with each other, is so large that a simple causal link is not only difficult to demonstrate empirically, but in fact does not make sense. The fact that we have to deal with the full complexity of social systems (Saraswathi, 1994) in their ecocultural contexts should not deter us from undertaking research, but to conduct it with attention to the various levels of analysis (Berry, this volume). The framework should also help us to put the existing research results into a broader and more integrated perspective. And if it demonstrates only one thing, it is that cross-cultural human development is no longer lacking in theory, and that it has really become "an outlook that takes culture seriously" (Dasen & Jahoda, 1986, p. 413), something that was little more than wishful thinking a couple of decades ago.

References

Berry, J.W. (1976). *Human ecology and cognitive style: Comparative studies in cultural and psychological adaptation*. New York: Sage Publications.

Berry, J.W. (1995). The descendants of a model. *Culture & Psychology, 1*(3), 373–380.

Berry, J.W., Poortinga, Y.H., Segall, M.H., & Dasen, P.R. (2002). *Cross-cultural psychology. Research and applications* (rev. 2nd ed.). Cambridge: Cambridge University Press.

Berry, J.W., & Sam, J. (1997). Acculturation and adaptation. In J.W. Berry, M.H. Segall, & C. Kagitcibasi (Eds), *Handbook of cross-cultural psychology. Vol. 3, Social psychology* (2nd ed., pp. 291–326). Boston: Allyn & Bacon.

Boesch, E.E. (1991). *Symbolic action theory for cultural psychology*. Berlin: Springer.

Bril, B. (1999). Dires sur l'enfant selon les cultures. Etat des lieux et perspectives. In B. Bril, P.R. Dasen, C. Sabatier, & B. Krewer (Eds), *Propos sur l'enfant et l'adolescent: Quels enfants pour quelles cultures?* (pp. 5–40). Paris: L'Harmattan.

Bril, B., Dasen, P.R., Sabatier, C., & Krewer, B. (Eds). (1999). *Propos sur l'enfant et l'adolescent: Quels enfants pour quelles cultures?* Paris: L'Harmattan.

Bril, B., & Lehalle, H. (1988). *Le développement psychologique est-il universel? Approches interculturelles*. Paris: PUF.

Bril, B., Zack, M., & Nkounkou-Hombessa, E. (1989). Ethnotheories of development and education: A view from different cultures. *European Journal of Psychology of Education, 4,* 307–318.

Bronfenbrenner, U. (1989). Ecological systems theory. *Annals of Child Development, 6,* 185–246.

Bronfenbrenner, U. (1993). The ecology of cognitive development: Research models and fugitive findings. In R. Wozniak & K.W. Fischer (Eds), *Development in context* (pp. 3–44). Hillsdale, NJ: Erlbaum.

Camilleri, C., & Malewska-Peyre, H. (1997). Socialization and identity strategies. In J.W. Berry, P.R. Dasen, & T.S. Saraswathi (Eds), *Handbook of cross-cultural psychology. Vol. 2, Basic processes and human development* (2nd ed., pp. 41–68). Boston: Allyn & Bacon.

Chamoux, M.-N. (1986). Apprendre autrement: aspects des pédagogies dites informelles chez les Indiens du Mexique. In P. Rossel (Ed.), *Demain l'artisanat?* (no. 16, pp. 211–335). Genève: Cahiers de l'Institut Universitaire d'Etudes du Développement.

Chombard de Lauwe, M.J., & Feuerhahn, N. (1991). La représentation sociale dans le domaine de l'enfance. In D. Jodelet (Ed.), *Les représentations sociales* (pp. 320–340). Paris: PUF.

Coon, C.S. (1971). *The hunting peoples*. Boston, MA: Little, Brown & Co.

Dasen, P.R. (1982). Cross-cultural aspects of Piaget's theory: The competence/performance model. In L.L. Adler (Ed.), *Cross-cultural research at issue* (pp. 163–170). New York: Academic Press.

Dasen, P.R. (1984). The cross-cultural study of intelligence: Piaget and the Baoulé. In P.S. Fry (Ed.), *Changing conceptions of intelligence and intellectual functioning: Current theory and research* (pp. 107–134). Amsterdam: North-Holland. (Reprinted from *International Journal of Psychology, 19*, 407–434).

Dasen, P.R. (1988). Cultures et processus d'apprentissage. *Bulletin du CILA (Centre de Linguistique Appliquée, Univ. de Neuchâtel), 47*, 52–64.

Dasen, P.R. (1993). L'ethnocentrisme de la psychologie. In M. Rey (Ed.), *Psychologie clinique et interrogations culturelles* (pp. 155–174). Paris: L'Harmattan.

Dasen, P.R. (1998). Cadres théoriques en psychologie interculturelle. In J.G. Adair, D. Bélanger, & K.L. Dion (Eds), *Advances in psychological science/Récents développements en psychologie scientifique, vol. 1, Social, personal, and cultural aspects/Aspects sociaux, personnels et culturels* (pp. 205 227). London: Psychology Press.

Dasen, P.R. (2000). Développement humain et éducation informelle. In P.R. Dasen & C. Perregaux (Eds), *Pourquoi des approches interculturelles en sciences de l'éducation?* (pp. 107–123). Bruxelles: DeBoeck Université (Collection « Raisons éducatives » vol. 3).

Dasen, P.R. (2001). Intégration, assimilation et stress acculturatif. In C. Perregaux, T. Ogay, Y. Leanza, & P.R. Dasen (Eds), *Intégrations et migrations: Regards pluridisciplinaires* (pp. 187–210). Paris: L'Harmattan.

Dasen, P.R., Inhelder, B., Lavallée, M., & Retschitzki, J. (1978). *Naissance de l'intelligence chez l'enfant Baoulé de Côte d'Ivoire*. Berne: Hans Huber.

Dasen, P.R., & Jahoda, G. (1986). Preface to special issue on cross-cultural human development. *International Journal of Behavioral Development, 9*(4), 413–416.

Dasen, P.R., & Mishra, R.C. (2000). Cross-cultural human development in the third millennium. *International Journal of Behavioral Development, 24*, 428–434.

Dasen, P.R., & Ogay, T. (2000). Pertinence d'une approche comparative pour la théorie des stratégies identitaires. In J. Costa-Lascoux, M.-A. Hily, & G. Vermès (Eds), *Pluralité des cultures et dynamiques identitaires. Hommage à Carmel Camilleri* (pp. 55–80). Paris: L'Harmattan.

Dasen, P.R., Dembélé, B., Ettien, K., Kabran, K., Kamagate, D., Koffi, D.A., & N'Guessan, A. (1985). N'glouèlê, l'intelligence chez les Baoulé. *Archives de Psychologie, 53*, 293–324.

Dasen, P.R., & Super, C.M. (1988). The usefulness of a cross-cultural approach in studies of malnutrition and psychological development. In P.R. Dasen, J.W. Berry, & N. Sartorius (Eds), *Health and cross-cultural psychology: Towards applications* (pp. 112–138). Newbury Park, CA: Sage.

Erny, P. (1968). *L'enfant dans la pensée traditionnelle de l'Afrique Noire*. Paris: Le livre africain.

Erny, P. (1972a). *L'enfant et son milieu en Afrique noire*. Paris: Payot.

Erny, P. (1972b). *Les premiers pas dans la vie de l'enfant d'Afrique noire*. Paris: L'Ecole.

Erny, P. (1973). *Childhood and cosmos: The social psychology of the black African child. Translation of: L'enfant dans la pensée traditionnelle de l'Afrique noire*, by A. Mboukou (original, 1968). Washington, DC: Black Orpheus Press.

Erny, P. (1981). *The child and his environment in black Africa: An essay on traditional education. Translation of: L'enfant et son milieu en Afrique noire, by G.J. Wanjohi* (original published 1972). New York: Oxford University Press.

Fournier, M., Schurmans, M.-N., & Dasen, P.R. (1999). Représentations sociales de l'intelligence: Effets de l'utilisation de langues différentes. In B. Bril, P.R. Dasen, C. Sabatier, & B. Krewer (Eds), *Propos sur l'enfant et l'adolescent: Quels enfants pour quelles cultures?* (pp. 279–296). Paris: L'Harmattan.

Friedlmeier, W. (1995). Subjektive Erziehungstheorien im Kulturvergleich. In G. Trommsdorff (Ed.), *Kindheit und Jugend im Kulturvergleich* (pp. 43–64). Weinheim: Juventa.

Gardiner, H., Mutter, J., & Kosmitzki, C. (1998). *Lives across cultures: Cross-cultural human development.* Boston: Allyn & Bacon.

Georgas, J. (1988). An ecological and social cross-cultural model: The case of Greece. In J.W. Berry, S.H. Irvine, & E.B. Hunt (Eds), *Indigenous cognition: Functioning in cultural context* (pp. 105–123). Dordrecht, The Netherlands: Nijhoff.

Georgas, J. (1993). Ecological-social model of Greek psychology. In U. Kim & J.W. Berry (Eds), *Indigenous psychologies: Research and experience in cultural context* (pp. 56–78). Newbury Park, CA: Sage.

Georgas, J., Christakopoulou, S., Poortinga, Y.H., Goodwin, R., Angleitner, A., & Charalambous, N. (1997). The relationship of family bonds to family structure and function across cultures. *Journal of Cross-Cultural Psychology, 28,* 303–320.

Gibson, M.A. (Ed.). (1997). Ethnicity and school performance: Complicating the immigrant/involuntary minority typology. *Anthropology & Education Quarterly,* special issue, *28*(3).

Goodnow, J.J., & Collins, W.A. (1990). *Development according to parents. The nature, sources and consequences of parents' ideas.* East Sussex: LEA.

Greenfield, P.M. (1976). Cross-cultural research and Piagetian theory: Paradox and progress. In K.F. Riegel & J.A. Meacham (Eds), *The developing individual in a changing world, vol. 1* (pp. 322–333). The Hague: Mouton.

Greenfield, P.M. (1984). A theory of the teacher in the learning activities of everyday life. In B. Rogoff & J. Lave (Eds), *Everyday cognition* (pp. 117–138). Cambridge, MA: Harvard University Press.

Greenfield, P.M. (1999). Cultural change and human development. *New Directions for Child and Adolescent Development* (83), 37–59.

Greenfield, P.M. (2000). Culture and universals: Integrating social and cognitive development. In L. Nucci, G. Saxe, & E. Turiel (Eds), *Culture, thought, and development* (pp. 231–277). Mahwah, NJ: Erlbaum.

Greenfield, P.M., & Childs, C.P. (1991). Developmental continuity in bicultural context. In R. Cohen & A.W. Siegel (Eds), *Context and development* (pp. 135–159). Hillsdale, NJ: Erlbaum.

Greenfield, P.M., & Cocking, R.R. (Eds). (1994). *Cross-cultural roots of minority child development.* Hillsdale, NJ: Lawrence Erlbaum.

Hamilton, A. (1981). *Nature and nurture: Aboriginal child-rearing in North-Central Arnhem land.* Canberra: Australian Institute of Aboriginal Studies/Atlantic Highlands, NJ: Humanities Press.

Harkness, S., & Super, C.M. (1983). The cultural construction of child development. *Ethos, 11,* 221–231.

Harkness, S., & Super, C.M. (Eds). (1996). *Parents' cultural belief systems. Their origins, expressions, and consequences.* New York: Guilford Press.

Harkness, S., Super, C.M., Keefer, C.H., Raghavan, C.S., & Campbell, E.K. (1996). Ask the doctor. The negotiation of cultural models in American parent-pediatrician discourse. In S. Harkness & C.M. Super (Eds), *Parents' cultural belief systems. Their origins, expressions, and consequences* (pp. 289–310). New York: Guilford Press.

Herskovits, M.J. (1948). *Man and his works: The science of cultural anthropology*. New York: Knopf.

Hewlett, B.S. (1991). *Intimate fathers: The nature and context of Aka Pygmy paternal infant care*. Ann Arbor, MI: University of Michigan Press.

Ho, D.Y.F. (1994). Cognitive socialization in Confucian heritage cultures. In P. Greenfield & R. Cocking (Eds), *Cross-cultural roots of minority child development* (pp. 285–313). Hillsdale, NJ: Lawrence Erlbaum.

Jahoda, G. (1995). The ancestry of a model. *Culture & Psychology, 1*(1), 11–24.

Kagitcibasi, C. (1990). Family and socialization in cross-cultural perspective: A model of change. In J.J. Berman (Ed.), *Nebraska symposium on motivation 1989: Cross-cultural perspectives* (pp. 135–200). Lincoln: University of Nebraska Press.

Kagitcibasi, C. (1996a). *Family and human development across cultures: A view from the other side*. Hillsdale, NJ: Lawrence Erlbaum.

Kagitcibasi, C. (1996b). The autonomous relational self: A new synthesis. *European Psychologist, 1*, 180–186.

Kagitcibasi, C. (1997). Individualism and collectivism. In J.W. Berry, M.H. Segall, & C. Kagitcibasi (Eds), *Handbook of cross-cultural psychology. Vol. 3, Social psychology* (2nd ed., pp. 1–50). Boston: Allyn & Bacon.

Kagitcibasi, C. (1998). Human development: Cross-cultural perspectives. In J. Adair, D. Bélanger, & K.L. Dion (Eds), *Advances in psychological science: Vol. 2. Developmental, personal, and social aspects* (pp. 475–494). London: Psychology Press.

Kim, U., Triandis, H.C., Kagitcibasi, C., Choi, S.-C., & Yoon, G. (Eds). (1994). *Individualism and collectivism: Theory, method, and applications*. Thousand Oaks, CA: Sage.

Konner, M.J. (1977). Infancy among the Kalahari desert San. In P.H. Leiderman, S.R. Tulkin, & A. Rosenfeld (Eds), *Culture and infancy* (pp. 287–328). New York: Academic Press.

Kopp, C.B., & Kaslow, J.B. (1982). *The child*. Reading, MA: Addison-Wesley.

Lave, J., & Wenger, E. (1991). *Situated learning. Legitimate peripheral participation*. Cambridge: Cambridge University Press.

LeVine, R.A. (1973). *Culture, behavior, and personality*. Chicago, IL: Aldine.

LeVine, R.A. (1977). Child-rearing as cultural adaptation. In P.H. Leiderman, S.R. Tulkin, & A. Rosenfeld (Eds), *Culture and infancy: Variations in the human experience* (pp. 15–27). New York: Academic Press.

LeVine, R.A., Dixon, S., LeVine, S., Richman, A., Leiderman, P.H., Keefer, C.H., & Brezelton, T.B. (1994). *Child care and culture: Lessons from Africa*. Cambridge: Cambridge University Press.

LeVine, R.A., & LeVine, B. B. (1963). Nyansongo: A Gusii community in Kenya. In B.B. Whiting (Ed.), *Six cultures: Studies of child-rearing* (pp. 15–202). New York: Wiley.

Minturn, L., & Lambert, W.W. (1964). *Mothers of six cultures: Antecedents of child rearing*. New York: John Wiley.

Mishra, R.C., Sinha, D., & Berry, J.W. (1996). *Ecology, acculturation and psychological adaptation: A study of Adivasis in Bihar*. New Delhi: Sage.

Mistry, J., & Saraswathi, T.S. (2003). The cultural context of child development. In R.M. Lerner, M.A. Easterbrooks, & J. Mistry (Eds), *Handbook of psychology. Vol. 6: Developmental psychology* (pp. 267–291). New York: Wiley.

Morelli, G.A., Rogoff, B., Oppenheim, D., & Goldsmith, D. (1992). Cultural variation in infants' sleeping arrangements: Questions of independence. *Developmental Psychology, 28*, 604–613.

Morelli, G.A., & Tronick, E.E. (1991). Parenting and child development in the Efe foragers and the Lese farmers of Zaïre. In M.H. Bornstein (Ed.), *Cultural approaches to parenting* (pp. 91–114). Hillsdale, NJ: Lawrence Erlbaum.

Munroe, R.H., Munroe, R.L., & Whiting, B.B. (Eds). (1981). *Handbook of cross-cultural human development*. New York: Garland STPM.

Nsamenang, A.B. (1992). *Human development in cultural context*. Beverly Hills, CA: Sage.

Nsamenang, A.B. (2001). Perspective africaine sur le développement social: Implications pour la recherche développementale interculturelle. In C. Sabatier & P.R. Dasen (Eds), *Cultures, développement et éducation. Autres enfants, autres écoles* (pp. 39–52). Paris: L'Harmattan.

Nsamenang, A.B. (in press). Conceptualizing human development and education in sub-Saharan Africa at the interface of indigenous and exogenous influences. In T.S. Saraswathi (Ed.), *Cross-cultural perspectives in human development: Theory, research and applications*. New Delhi: Sage.

Ogbu, J. (1981). Origins of human competence: A cultural-ecological perspective. *Child Development, 52*, 413–429.

Rabain, J. (1979). *L'enfant du lignage*. Paris: Payot.

Rabain-Jamin, J., & Wornham, W.L. (1990). Transformations des conduites de maternage et des pratiques de soins chez les femmes migrantes originaires d'Afrique de l'Ouest. *Psychiatrie de l'enfant, 23*, 287–319.

Reed, E.S., & Bril, B. (1996). The primacy of action in development. In M.L. Latash & M.T. Turvey (Eds), *Dexterity and its development* (pp. 431–451). Mahwah, NJ: Lawrence Erlbaum.

Reichel, E. (1999). Cosmology, worldview and gender-based knowledge systems among the Tanimuka and Yukuna (Northwest Amazon). *Worldviews: Environment, Culture, Religion, 3*, 213–242.

Richman, A.L., LeVine, R.A., New, R.S., Howrigan, G.A., Welles-Nystrom, B., & LeVine, S.E. (1988). Maternal behavior to infants in five cultures. In R.A. LeVine, P.R. Miller, & M.M. West (Eds), *Parental behavior in diverse societies* (pp. 82–97). San Francisco, CA: Jossey-Bass.

Rogoff, B., Mistry, J., Göncü, A., & Mosier, C. (1993). Guided participation in cultural activity by toddlers and caregivers. *Monographs of the Society for Research in Child Development*, Serial no. 236, *58*(8).

Rushton, J.P. (1995). *Race, evolution, and behavior: A life history perspective*. New Brunswick, NJ: Transaction.

Sabatier, C. (1994a). Niche développementale et psychologie écologique du développement humain: apports du comparatif. In M. Deleau & A. Weil-Barais (Eds), *Le développement de l'enfant. Approches comparatives* (pp. 65–86). Paris: Presses Universitaires de France.

Sabatier, C. (1994b). Parental conceptions of early development and developmental stimulation. In H. Bloch & M.H. Bornstein (Eds), *Francophone perspectives on early development* (pp. 299–314). Hillsdale, NJ: Lawrence Erlbaum.

Saraswathi, T.S. (1994). Women in poverty context: Balancing economic and child care needs. In K.C.R. Borooah, S. Seshadri, T.S. Saraswathi, J.I. Peterson, & A. Verma (Eds), *Capturing complexity: An interdisciplinary look at women, households and development* (pp. 162–178). New Delhi: Sage.

Saraswathi, T.S. (Ed.). (1999). *Culture, socialization and human development: Theory, research and applications in India*. New Delhi: Sage.

Saraswathi, T.S., & Ganapathy, H. (2002). Indian parents' ethnotheories as reflections of Hindu scheme of child and human development. In H. Keller, Y.H. Poortinga, & A. Scholmerich (Eds), *Between culture and biology: Perspectives on ontogenetic development* (pp. 80–88). Cambridge: Cambridge University Press.

Saraswathi, T.S., & Pai, S. (1997). Socialisation in the Indian context. In H.S.R. Kao & D. Sinha (Eds), *Asian Perspectives on Psychology* (pp. 74–92). New Delhi: Sage.

Segall, M.H., Campbell, D.T., & Herskovits, M.J. (1966). *The influence of culture on visual perception*. Indianapolis: Bobbs-Merrill.

Segall, M.H., Dasen, P.R., Berry, J.W., & Poortinga, Y.H. (1999). *Human behavior in global perspective: An introduction to cross-cultural psychology* (rev. 2nd ed.). Boston: Allyn & Bacon.

Seginer, R. (in press). Human development in multiple contexts: The seminal work of Gisela Trommsdorff. In W. Friedlmeier, B. Schwarz, P. Chakkarath, & E. Schäfermeier (Eds), *Proceedings of the symposium culture and human development. The importance of cross-cultural research to the social sciences*. University of Konstanz, 1–3 March 2002.

Serpell, R. (1993). *The significance of schooling. Life-journeys in an African society*. Cambridge: Cambridge University Press.

Serpell, R., & Hatano, G. (1997). Education, schooling, and literacy. In J.W. Berry, P.R. Dasen, & T.S. Saraswathi (Eds), *Handbook of cross-cultural psychology. Vol. 2: Basic processes and human development* (2nd ed., pp. 339–376). Boston: Allyn & Bacon.

Sigel, I.E., McGillicuddy-DeLisi, V., & Goodnow, J.J. (Eds). (1992). *Parental belief systems: The psychological consequences for children* (2nd ed.). Hillsdale, NJ: Lawrence Erlbaum.

Super, C.M. (1976). Environmental effects on motor development: The case of "African infant precocity". *Developmental Medicine and Child Neurology, 18*, 561–567.

Super, C.M. (1981). Behavioral development in infancy. In R.H. Munroe, R.L. Munroe, & B.B. Whiting (Eds), *Handbook of cross-cultural human development* (pp. 181–270). New York: Garland STPM.

Super, C.M., & Harkness, S. (1986). The developmental niche: A conceptualization at the interface of child and culture. *International Journal of Behavioral Development, 9*(4), 545–570.

Super, C.M., & Harkness, S. (1997). The cultural structuring of child development. In J.W. Berry, P.R. Dasen, & T.S. Saraswathi (Eds), *Handbook of cross-cultural psychology. Vol. 2, Basic processes and human development* (2nd ed., pp. 1–39). Boston: Allyn & Bacon.

Tapé, G. (1994). *L'intelligence en Afrique. Une étude du raisonnement expérimental.* Paris: L'Harmattan.

Testart, A. (1982). *Les chasseurs-cueilleurs ou l'origine des inégalités.* Paris: Société d'Ethnographie.

Triandis, H.C. (1995). *Individualism and collectivism.* Boulder, CO: Westview.

Troadec, B. (2001). Le modèle écoculturel: Un cadre pour la psychologie culturelle comparative. *Journal International de Psychologie, 36,* 53–64.

Trommsdorff, G. (Ed.). (1989). *Sozialisation im Kulturvergleich.* Stuttgart: Ferdinand Enke.

Trommsdorff, G. (1993). *Entwicklung im Kulturvergleich.* In A. Thomas (Ed.), *Kulturvergleichende Psychologie* (pp. 103–144). Göttingen: Hogrefe.

Trommsdorff, G. (1999). Autonomie und Verbundenheit im kulturellen Vergleich von Sozialisationsbedingungen. In H.R. Leu & L. Krappmann (Eds), *Zwischen Autonomie und Verbundenheit* (pp. 392–419). Frankfurt/Main: Suhrkamp.

Trommsdorff, G., & Dasen, P.R. (2002). Cross-cultural study of education. In N.J. Smelser & P.B. Baltes (Eds), *International encyclopedia of the social and behavioral sciences* (pp. 3003–3007). Oxford: Elsevier Science.

Vandenplas-Holper, C. (1987). Les théories implicites du développement et de l'éducation. *European Journal of Psychology of Education, 11,* 17–39.

Wassmann, J. (1995). The final requiem for the omniscient informant? An interdisciplinary approach to everyday cognition. *Culture and Psychology, 1,* 167–201.

Whiting, B.B. (1963). *Six cultures: Studies of child rearing.* Cambridge, MA: Harvard University Press.

Whiting, B.B. (1976). The problem of the packaged variable. In K.F. Riegel & J.A. Meacham (Eds), *The developing individual in a changing world* (vol. 1, pp. 303–309). La Haye: Mouton.

Whiting, B.B., & Whiting, J.W.M. (1975). *Children of six cultures: A psycho-cultural analysis.* Cambridge, MA: Harvard University Press.

Whiting, J.W.M. (1977). A model for psychocultural research. In P.H. Leiderman, S.R. Tulkin, & A. Rosenfeld (Eds), *Culture and infancy: Variations in the human experience* (pp. 29–48). New York: Academic Press.

Wolf, A.W., Lozoff, B., Latz, S., & Paludetto, R. (1996). Parental theories in the management of young children's sleep in Japan, Italy, and the United States. In S. Harkness & C.M. Super (Eds), *Parents' cultural belief systems. Their origins, expressions, and consequences* (pp. 364–384). New York: Guilford Press.

Zack, M., & Bril, B. (1989). Comment les mères françaises et bambara du Mali se représentent-elles le développement de leur enfant? In J. Retschitzki,

M. Bossel-Lagos, & P.R. Dasen (Eds), *La recherche interculturelle* (vol. 2, pp. 7–17). Paris: L'Harmattan.

Zeitlin, M. (1996). My child is my crown. Yoruba parental theories and practices in early childhood. In S. Harkness & C.M. Super (Eds), *Parents' cultural belief systems. Their origins, expressions, and consequences* (pp. 407–427). New York: Guilford Press.

ಕೂ 5 ಲಃ

Human Development Across Cultures: A Contextual-functional Analysis and Implications for Interventions

CIGDEM KAGITCIBASI

Some significant aspects of human development across cultures are examined in this paper. Particularly in societies undergoing rapid socioeconomic change, the development of self and of competence need to be better understood. I will deal with these developmental phenomena and the psychological processes underlying them from a contextual-functional perspective. Thus questions such as these will be dealt with here: What kinds of family interaction patterns and child rearing orientations lead to the development of particular types of selves and why? What kinds of socioeconomic cultural contexts produce (or necessitate) those particular family patterns and why?

Human development occurs in a cultural context. Family socialization is of crucial significance here, as it reflects the sociocultural, historical, and economic aspects of the larger society. I will be dealing selectively with some aspects of the socialization process to throw light on both cross-cultural diversity and unity. Diversity will emerge mainly in the study of the development of the self, and unity will emerge mostly in the development of competence in changing urban contexts.

Development of the Self

Psychological theory and practice, particularly as influenced by the psychoanalytic perspective, considers the development of well-defined self boundaries and individuation–separation to be requisites for healthy personality and family relations. Thus, it affirms one type of self—the separated self. The separation is not only at the basic existential level, in the sense of some early cognitive process of differentiation, which must indeed take place for everyone, since each person is aware of being a separate entity from others. It goes beyond that into the psychological construal of self–other relations, defining healthy and pathological functioning. The theoretical perspectives used by psychology claim to be universally valid. Yet, there is an important lesson that psychology can learn from cross-cultural research which points to diversity. The separated self may be a culture bound phenomenon.

To highlight the diversity of the family contexts in which the self develops, I would like to start with some examples. The first example is taken from some parent education classes in the US where young mothers are often taught "to let go" of their toddlers. If mothers have to be taught this, it is obviously not a "natural" tendency, but needs to be cultivated in them, possibly counteracting their tendencies to engulf or protect the child. This is done to allow for the individuation–separation of the young child and for the development of autonomy, both of which are considered necessary for healthy personality development. Otherwise, psychology cautions that an unhealthy symbiotic relationship between the mother and the child may develop. Clearly, this practice in parent education is based on psychological theory.

The other example is taken from the descriptions of mother–child interaction in Japan by Azuma (reported in Kornadt, 1987, p. 133). When a child is troublesome, the typical message of the Japanese mother to her non-cooperative child is, "I am one with you; we can be and will be of the same mind". But this is exactly the definition of a symbiotic relationship. Families containing such symbiotic relationships, without clear boundaries of the selves, are considered "enmeshed" and not healthy in Western psychology. A hypothetical Turkish clinical psychologist, fresh out of his/her professional training in the United States, who goes to a

Turkish village would face a similar dilemma. Observing the human relationships there, he or she would declare the whole village to be enmeshed, with everybody overlapping with everybody else! Obviously a whole village or a whole society is not "pathological". What is wrong is the inappropriate application of the theory. What we see here is the cultural limitation of the theory. While it may be perfectly valid in some sociocultural contexts, its universal validity is questionable.

AUTONOMY AND RELATEDNESS

What these examples reflect is a basic dimension of self–other relations. It pertains to human merging and separation; I call it the psychology of relatedness. This is also a dimension extending from interdependence to independence. It can be studied as a characteristic of interpersonal relations, or as a characteristic of the self, contrasting well-defined boundaries with fluid boundaries. It can be conceptualized at the individual, group or cultural levels. For example, we can talk about the culture of relatedness, or the culture of separateness or we can talk about the independent self or the interdependent self and all the gradations in between these extremes.

Indeed, we find that many conceptualizations that are quite similar to this dimension of independence–interdependence have been proposed. For example, we find it in the conflict theories of personality, as surrender vs autonomy of Angyal (1951), or communion vs agency of Bakan (1966), and in general in the recent theorizing along individualism–collectivism distinction in cross-cultural psychology. They refer to two basic but apparently conflicting human needs—the need for agency and the need for relatedness. Agency and relatedness are really not conflicting tendencies; they are, however, conceptualized as conflicting because Western psychology teaches that early separation is a requisite for the development of autonomy.

An individualistic construal of autonomy thus often implies separateness from others and is seen to result from a separation–individuation process. Yet, it is neither logically nor psychologically necessary for autonomy to imply separateness if it is recognized that agency and interpersonal distance comprise two different spheres or dimensions of interpersonal relations. The two poles of the agency dimension are autonomy and heteronomy; those of the interpersonal distance dimension are separateness and relatedness (Kagitcibasi, 1996a). The two dimensions are confounded when agency is pitted against relatedness.

A number of questions become relevant here that have both theoretical and empirical significance. One has to do with the different types of selves (separated–relational, autonomous–heteronomous) and how they differ from one another in terms of several psychological processes, ranging from self-perceptions to emotions. A second question inquires into the different kinds of socialization processes that engender these different selves. A third question asks why a certain kind of socialization occurs in a particular sociocultural context and when a change in the resultant development of the self may be expected.

Recent cross-cultural research and theory regarding the self have mainly dealt with the first question in terms of the correlates of the independent and the interdependent selves. Often taxonomies in terms of individualism–collectivism are used, and the consequences or behavioural correlates of the different types of selves are examined along several psychological processes (Markus & Kitayama, 1991). The causes or antecedents of the separated–relational and autonomous–heteronomous (agentic-dependent) selves (the second and third questions) are not adequately examined.

Addressing the last question is highly challenging, as it requires an examination of the functional underpinnings of the society–family–socialization interfaces, not commonly ventured by psychologists. For example, there is a need to understand how family interaction patterns and socialization values are affected by the socioeconomic–cultural context and how the former, in turn, affect child rearing. Any changes in the context would have implications for changes in the chain of relationships. This kind of a conceptualization cannot remain only at the psychological level of analysis but has to situate the self within family and culture. The family would play a mediating role in the causal relationships between the self and society.

FAMILY AS A DEVELOPMENTAL CONTEXT

I have developed a model of family change that throws light on the development of three different types of self within three different prototypical family interaction patterns (Kagitcibasi, 1990; 1996b). The model aims to discover the societal and familial antecedents of the separated and the relational selves. It also examines the implications of socioeconomic development for family change and for the emergence of the self that integrates both autonomy and relatedness. The three prototypical family interaction patterns are: the traditional family of (total) interdependence (characterized by material and psychological interdependence), the individualistic model based on independence, and a dialectical synthesis of the two, involving material independence but psychological interdependence. These interaction patterns are studied at the intergenerational level.

The family pattern of interdependence is prevalent in a traditional rural agrarian society, though not limited to it, where intergenerational interdependence is a requisite for family livelihood with low levels of affluence. The individual contributes to the family well-being both as a young child and later as an adult by providing old age security to his/her parents. Thus, the child's economic/utilitarian value has salience for parents, and high fertility is implicated, as the economic value of the child (VOC) is cumulative with child numbers (Kagitcibasi, 1982; 1990). In the family model of interdependence, the independence of the child is not functional and may even be seen as a threat to the family livelihood because independent offspring may look after his/her own self-interest rather than that of the family. Thus, obedience orientation is seen in child rearing that leaves no room for autonomy.

The family model of independence forms a contrast to that of interdependence. It is typical of the affluent Western middle class nuclear family, at least in its professed ideals. Child rearing is oriented toward engendering self-reliance and autonomy, since intergenerational independence is valued. Separation–individuation is considered a requisite for healthy human development where objective conditions of social welfare and affluence render family interdependence unnecessary, if not dysfunctional.

It is commonly assumed that with socioeconomic development a shift occurs from the former model of family interdependence to the latter model of family independence. This assumption is based on a general view of modernization and is not questioned much though modernization theory has lost its popularity in sociology. However, this assumption is being challenged today with increasing evidence of continuities in closely-knit interaction patterns despite increased urbanization and industrialization in collectivistic cultures, which I will discuss later (see Kagıtcıbası, 1990; 1996b for a review). What appears to happen is that *material* interdependencies weaken in the family with increased affluence and urban lifestyles, but *psychological* interdependencies continue, since they are not incompatible with the changing lifestyles.

These changes have significant implications for child rearing. When material interdependencies decrease, autonomy can emerge in child rearing. This is because when the material contribution of the offspring is no longer required for family livelihood, his/her autonomy is not seen as a threat. Nevertheless, since psychological interdependencies continue to be valued, the *closeness* (connectedness/relatedness) of the growing child is aspired for. Though autonomy is valued and complete obedience (and loyalty) of the child is no longer demanded, there is still control (not permissive child rearing) in child rearing because separation of the child is not the goal.

Thus, in the family model of psychological interdependence[1] autonomy *can* enter child rearing because of decreasing material interdependencies. Why it *should* enter, however, has to do more with its adaptiveness in urban living conditions. With changing lifestyles, autonomous, agentic orientations become more functional in coping with specialized tasks requiring individual responsibility rather than following age-old traditions. Obedience does not ensure success in school or in jobs that go beyond mechanical work in nonagricultural contexts (Kohn, 1969; Nunes, 1993; Okagaki & Sternberg, 1993).

Child rearing is oriented toward obedience in the family model of total interdependence, since an obedient child is more likely to

---

[1] This was initially referred to as "emotional interdependence", but the term proved to be misleading, appearing to refer to family affection, which the model does not assume.

grow up to be a loyal offspring. Autonomy and separateness of the growing child are encouraged in the family model of independence, since these characteristics contribute to greater self-reliance and self-sufficiency. In the family model of psychological interdependence, a dialectic synthesis of the other two models is seen in child rearing that integrates autonomy with relatedness. The self that develops in the family model of interdependence is the relational self; it is characterized by relatedness and heteronomy. The self that emerges in the family model of independence is the separated self; it involves autonomy and separateness. The self that develops in the family model of psychological interdependence is the autonomous–relational self, manifesting autonomy and relatedness.

Authoritarian and obedience-oriented parenting contribute to the development of the relational self in the family model of interdependence. Relatively permissive and self-reliance-oriented parenting engenders the separated self in the family model of independence. In the family model of psychological interdependence there is a combined autonomy and control orientation in parenting, which is akin to "authoritative parenting" (Baumrind, 1980), that leads to the development of the autonomous–relational self (Figure 5.1).

Figure 5.1
Agency, Interpersonal Distance and the Types of Selves in Context

	AGENCY	
	AUTONOMY	HETERONOMY
RELATEDNESS	Autonomous–relational self Family model of psycho-logical interdependence	Relational self Family model of interdependence
INTERPERSONAL DISTANCE	Authoritative parenting (control and autonomy orientation)	Authoritarian parenting (obedience orientation)
SEPARATION	Separated self Family model of inde-pendence Relatively permissive parenting (self-reliance orientation)	Separated–heteronomous self Hierarchical family Autocratic parenting (rejecting, neglecting)

A summary of the interpersonal distance and agency dimensions in terms of the type of self, family and parenting they implicate is presented in Figure 5.1. The three combinations of relatedness–autonomy, relatedness–heteronomy, and separation–autonomy have been described here as autonomous–relational self (psychological interdependence), relational self (interdependence), and separated self (independence), respectively. The fourth pattern has not been dealt with. It points to a situation where the person lacks both autonomy of action and closeness to others. This may be the case where there is indifferent parenting (Baumrind, 1980), or where the individual is pushed into a subordinate and separate position. This may be seen in the hierarchical family involving autocratic power differentials between generations (and genders) that interfere with intimacy and relatedness (Fisek, 1991). The resultant separated–heteronomous self would have neither of the two basic needs (for agency and relatedness) satisfied. Or, it may characterize abusive family relations depriving the person of both autonomy and relatedness. An example would be an Indian widow with no support but dominated by the late husband's family (Saraswathi, 2001).

CROSS-CULTURAL RESEARCH SUPPORTING THE AUTONOMOUS–RELATIONAL SELF

The autonomous–relational self (Kagitcibasi, 1996a) may be considered to be self-contradictory if the two underlying dimensions, interpersonal distance and agency, are confounded. However, the logical and psychological distinctness of these two separate dimensions (separateness–relatedness and autonomy–heteronomy) allows for this possible combination. Indeed, a great deal of recent comparative research points to the distinctness of autonomy and relatedness and to their possible combination, providing evidence for the validity of the autonomous–related self and the family model of psychological interdependence. For example, Kim, Butzel, and Ryan (1998), in a study of Korean and US samples, pointed to a more positive relation between autonomy and collectivistic attitudes (relatedness) than between autonomy and individualistic attitudes (separateness), providing support to the independence of the agency and the interpersonal distance dimensions.

Lin and Fu (1990) reported that Chinese parents were high on both control in child rearing and encouragement of independence. Similarly, Cha (1994) noted that Korean parents granted autonomy to their children while accepting ingroup obligations. Thus, apparently conflicting tendencies are found to coexist in child rearing that combines autonomy and control orientations, further substantiating the independence of the interpersonal distance and agency dimensions.

Studies of Turkish parents revealed parental values combining autonomy and relatedness. While low SES parents (family model of interdependence) expected their children to be grateful to them (insuring loyalty), high SES parents (family model of psychological interdependence) did not expect gratitude and valued autonomy, but they nevertheless wanted their children to be close to them (Imamoglu, 1987). Furthermore, low SES parents could be supported and induced (through an intervention programme) to value autonomy while continuing to uphold closeness to their children (Kagitcibasi, Sunar, & Bekman, 2001).

In a study of Turkish minority families in Germany, Phalet and Schonpflug (2001) reported that parental positive autonomy goals for adolescents did not imply separateness, and that achievement values were associated with (parental) collectivism, not individualism. In Hong Kong, Chou (2000) found that separation from parents was associated with depression in adolescents. Even in the individualistic US culture, positive, rather than negative, links between relatedness to parents and autonomy were observed among teenagers (Ryan & Lynch, 1989; Ryan, Stiller, & Lynch, 1994).

Stewart, Bond, Deeds, and Chung (1999) studied upper middle class Asian and Caucasian teenagers at an international school in Hong Kong as well as their mothers with regard to intergenerational patterns of values and autonomy expectations. The family change model (Kagitcibasi, 1990; 1996b) was tested and supported by the findings; there was persistence of family interdependencies despite adoption of some "individualistic" values. Even in these most "modern" Asian families "family relatedness and expectations of parental control [were found to] persist" (p. 589).

Working with Chinese, Chinese American, and Euro-American parents and children, Jose, Huntsinger, Huntsinger, and Liaw (2000) found support for the family model of psychological interdependence (Kagitcibasi, 1990; 1996b), as they noted that Chinese parents endorsed both values of relatedness and autonomy. Both samples of Chinese parents showed a combination of high control and closeness to their children, demonstrating more control than Euro-American parents even while being equally warm in their interactions. The last finding is parallel to the results of an early study comparing Turkish and American adolescents' perceptions of parental control and warmth (Kagitcibasi, 1970). While Turkish adolescents reported more parental control, there was no difference between the two groups in perceived parental warmth. A recent study of Turkish adolescents (Aydin & Oztutuncu, 2001) observed that depression and negative schema were associated with separateness, but not with high control in the family.

The development of the autonomous–relational self is best understood from a contextual/functional perspective. This type of an integrative synthesis emerges in the family context of psychological interdependence, rather than in one of total interdependence or independence. This is because in the model of psychological interdependence both autonomy and closely-knit connectedness are functional. This would be more typical in the developed (urban, educated) sectors of collectivistic societies with cultures of relatedness, rather than in traditional societies. Urban lifestyles render autonomy, rather than heteronomy, functional, as discussed earlier. However, culture lag may slow down the process of change, and obedience-oriented child rearing may persist even though no longer needed or functional. Such a maladaptive situation may call for intervention (Kagitcibasi, 1996b).

There may be shifts from a model of independence to a model of psychological interdependence as the latter model better satisfies the two basic human needs for autonomy and relatedness. Indeed, recent evidence points to such reaffirmation of relatedness values in a posttechnological postmodern society. For example, Inglehart and Baker (2000), and Young (1992) noted the increasing importance of human relational values in several technological societies; and Saal (1987), Jansen (1987), and Weil (1987) pointed to new living arrangements recreating the community in the Netherlands and Israel. Recent social criticism of unbridled individualism in the Western, especially American, context calls for relatedness rather than separateness (Smith, 1994; Spence, 1985; Wallach & Wallach, 1990). From a different perspective, feminist theory and research in family psychology propose a better recognition and appreciation of relatedness *together with* autonomy (Kegan, 1994; Lerner, 1988; Vannoy, 1991).

All this amounts to a call for a corrective to too much of an emphasis in psychology on individual autonomy and too little on human relatedness (Guisinger & Blatt, 1994). The recognition of this imbalance would be facilitated by an understanding of the two independent dimensions of interpersonal distance (separateness–relatedness) and agency (autonomy–heteronomy). Autonomy should be recognized for what it is, as agency, not as separateness. The agency dimension should not be confused with the interpersonal distance dimension. The recognition of the possible coexistence of relatedness with autonomy would provide the needed corrective. Such a corrective in our thinking promises to promote a more balanced human development.

Development of Competence

In an early anthropological study in a Turkish village, Helling (1966) noted the prevalence of a parental teaching style based on demonstration, imitation, and motor learning rather than verbal explanation and reasoning. As a husband–wife team, they observed informal teaching–learning activities and reported the case of a father "teaching" his son how to cut wood by just doing it himself, expecting his son to imitate his actions without giving any explanations. The Hellings revisited the village 20 years later and did not observe any appreciable change in this non-verbal orientation to "teaching by doing" (Helling, 1986).

Similar descriptions of teaching and learning have been reported from many cultures, especially among rural populations. For example, other early work points to similar patterns in Africa (Gay & Cole, 1967; LeVine & LeVine, 1966), and more recently it has been noted among the Australian aborigines (Teasdale & Teasdale, 1992). These patterns are not only widespread, but they also work. Children learn to cut wood or acquire manual skills over time to produce exquisite handicrafts, mainly through imitation without being given any verbal instruction or positive reinforcement (LeVine, 1989). In Western urban contexts, similar non-verbal and low positive reinforcement parental teaching styles have been observed among Hispanic minorities in the USA (Laosa, 1984) and Turkish minorities in the Netherlands (Leseman, 1993; Van Tuijl, Leseman, & Rispens, 2001).

The general cultural conceptions of childhood may also have something to do with whether there is extensive verbalization with the child. Specifically, whether caregivers see themselves in an active, child development-oriented, consciously goal directed "child rearing" role and whether childhood is considered special or not are important. This type of self-role definition is common among educated middle class (Western and particularly American) parents (Coll, 1990; Goodnow, 1988; Laosa, 1980). In contrast, Kakar (1978) noted that Indian caregivers emphasized pleasure between the adult and the child and experienced little pressure to mould the child in a given direction. In traditional societies, children are expected to learn adult roles and behaviours mainly through observation and imitation.

Observation and imitation occur in all contexts and throughout the lifespan. However, there are limitations to observational learning. For example, it has been found to be not effective for transfer to new tasks (Laboratory of Comparative Human Cognition, 1983; Segall et al., 1990). Also, observational learning is only one type of learning among others, and at least some of these others involve verbal reasoning. If verbalization with the child, especially verbal communication involving adult reasoning and decontextualized language is lacking or infrequent, there may be serious developmental implications.

Obedience orientation is another commonly observed characteristic of traditional child rearing. This is also a key characteristic of child socialization in the family model of interdependence. In more traditional family contexts, especially in rural agrarian and low socioeconomic conditions, a high value is assigned to obedience in child rearing, and this value is reflected in a cultural conceptualization of cognitive competence which includes a social component, especially social responsibility and social sensitivity.

Research has pointed to the so-called "social" definitions of intelligence in Africa (as reviewed by Berry, 1984); this has been termed as "African social intelligence" (Mundy-Castle, 1974). However, it is not unique to Africa but is commonly seen in "traditional" societies which emphasize "socio-affective" aspects of cognitive competence. Berry and Bennett (1992) noted that the Cree

of northern Canada did not differentiate between the cognitive
and social/moral aspects of competence. This is in contrast to the
purely cognitive conceptualization of intelligence in Western technological societies. Obviously, as intelligence tests are products of
the Western technological society, they reflect the latter notions of
intelligence.

In a classic study, Serpell (1977) demonstrated the contrast
between the "folk" conceptions of intelligence and what is measured by intelligence tests. He asked five adults in a Zambian village
to rate children of about 10 years of age in terms of which children
they would select to perform an important task. He also asked
them to rank the children as per the local definition of intelligence.
The children thus rated were administered a number of intelligence
tests, including three developed for use with non-schooled children
in Zambia. Children's scores on the intelligence tests did not correlate with the adults' ratings. The reason for this was that even
though free of specific school bias, the tests measured pure cognitive skills rather than social skills and social responsibility which
the adults used as criteria.

Child socialization aims to develop valued characteristics in children, in this case social skills and social responsibility, rather than,
say, abstract reasoning, which is associated with intelligence by
psychologists. Clearly, children's cognitive competence in culturally valued domains is boosted whereas development in other
domains lags behind, if recognized at all. Thus, learning is adaptive
to environmental demands. The main problem emerges, however,
when stable functional relations or adaptive mechanisms are challenged by modifications in lifestyles, accompanying social structural and economic changes.

Particularly with urbanization, involving rural to urban migration of populations, and with international migration, what was
adaptive in child socialization can become maladaptive. This problem becomes relevant in studies examining ethnic and social class
differences in Western urban contexts. Most ethnic minorities in
the industrialized countries of Europe, North America, and Australia are recent immigrants from less developed countries and
especially from rural areas (Blacks in the USA, and native peoples
being the main exception). Many of the child rearing patterns of
these ethnic minority populations reflect the kinds of parental conceptions of cognitive competence that I have discussed here. Specifically, a socially rather than a cognitively-oriented conception

of competence is valued, stressing conformity–obedience goals, and early learning in the family is based mainly on observation and imitation.

Research on ethnic minority families in the US has revealed this type of parental conception and has observed a misfit between this cultural conception of competence and that of the school culture in the host society. Nunes (1993) noted that immigrant Mexican parents in the USA believed, erroneously, that if their children were quiet and obedient and listened to the teacher, they would succeed in school. Okagaki and Sternberg (1993) reported that for immigrant parents from Cambodia, Mexico, the Philippines and Vietnam, noncognitive characteristics (i.e., motivation, social skills, and practical school skills) were equally or even more important than cognitive characteristics (problem solving skills, verbal ability, and creative ability) to their conceptions of an "intelligent first-grade child", but this was not true for Anglo-American parents. Further, parents' beliefs about the importance of conformity were correlated negatively with children's school performance, and American-born parents favoured developing autonomy over conformity.

DISADVANTAGE

Research in this area has demonstrated that some cultural conceptions of cognitive competence held by caregivers and their corresponding behaviours may conflict with mainstream (school) conceptions. If school performance is used as a developmental outcome variable, such home orientations may be considered a "disadvantage".

An important point is the extent of verbal communication with and the responsiveness to the child. For example, whether or not the child's requests are attended to even when adults are engrossed in some other activity like conversing among themselves. The greater verbal responsiveness of American middle class parents compared with working class parents has been documented in research (Laosa, 1980; McLoyd, 1990; Sameroff & Fiese, 1992). In contrast, in a nationwide study in Turkey more than 6,000 mothers were interviewed (Turkish Family Research Institute, 1995) and

73 per cent of them reported that a child behaviour that was "not tolerated" was "the child interrupting adult conversation". Since a nationally representative sample was selected, this finding reflected cultural standards. In cultural contexts, where childhood is not viewed as special, verbal responsiveness to children may be less. When one considers that the traditional motto "children are to be seen and not heard" was widespread in the West, too, until recently and is still prevalent among lower SES groups, changes over time as well as across cultures become apparent.

In a longitudinal study (Kagitcibasi, 1991; 1996a; Kagitcibasi, Sunar, & Bekman, 2001) we interviewed mothers of young children living in low income areas of Istanbul. To determine the degree of others' involvement/interaction with their 3–5-year-olds, we asked them how often they gave their full attention to the child outside of meal times. It was observed that 22 per cent answered "never" or "almost never". Along with those who responded "seldom", low involvement was observed among more than 40 per cent of the mothers. When asked what they commonly did when they were with their children at home, 89.7 per cent of the mothers stated that they did their household chores (and a small proportion mentioned tasks like knitting and embroidery), with little direct interaction with their children.

A lack of responsiveness, especially in terms of verbal inter-action, can become a disadvantage for the child. I have already referred to the misfit between school expectations and child rearing goals among marginal groups. A background of observational learning without verbal reasoning can be a disadvantage in school (Nunes, 1993). Indeed, early verbal interaction with adults appears to be a crucial antecedent of early language development. Language skills are, in turn, indicative of better school performance.

Research on the development of oral language skills and literacy has highlighted the importance of extensive adult–child verbal interactions, involving reasoning, asking and answering questions, storytelling, book reading and discussions of ongoing events (Snow, 1991; 1993). A growing body of research in the area of literacy has shown that early home experience with oral language skills and the "culture of literacy" (involving familiarity with printed media, world knowledge, vocabulary, etc.) predict advanced literacy achievement. Children who lack such experience would not only be disadvantaged in school, but also as adults in a literate society.

Early research in Turkey reported large differences in the vocabulary of middle and working class Grade 5 children (Semin, 1975). It has been found that vocabulary is the best single predictor of reading success (Anderson & Freebody, 1981). Similarly, Ataman and Epir (1972) observed that Turkish children from low income families formed concepts of lower level of complexity as compared to middle class children. Savasir and Sahin (1988), and Savasir, Sezgin, and Erol (1992) reported persistent social class differences in vocabulary and verbal competence in Turkey. Studying the children of Turkish migrant workers in The Netherlands, Leseman (1993) noted that lower SES Turkish children (age 3–3½ years) had lower levels of vocabulary and concept formation skills (in Turkish) than Dutch middle and working class children (in Dutch). Similar results were obtained in other studies on larger cohorts of Dutch children and different groups of immigrant children in the age group of 3–6 years (Van Tuijl, Leseman, & Rispens, 2001).

In a study of Mexican-American mothers and their children, Laosa (1982; 1984) highlighted the significance of low maternal education, low social class standing, and minority language status as determinants of children's poor cognitive performance. Mothers' teaching strategies and verbal communication with the child were mediating factors. Specifically, there was less verbal interaction between less educated Hispanic mothers and their young children, they also used less praise and less inquiring but more modelling, directives and negative physical control than Anglo mothers. Laosa (1984) found differences between Hispanic and Anglo children's performance (on the McCarthy scales of children's abilities) as early as 2½ years of age, indicating the importance of early language development. Similarly, Slaughter (1988) noted the lack of decontextualized communication and play in a sample of young children in Black families in the US. She pointed to this as a factor explaining why Black infants who surpassed White infants in early sensorimotor intelligence lagged behind them in later language based cognitive performance.

Other researchers have also highlighted the importance of early adult–child verbal communication. Wachs and Gruen (1982) observed that verbal stimulation was particularly important after the first year, and the amount of parent–child interaction after 24 months of age had an impact on developmental outcomes. The second year appears to be critical for early syntactic and semantic development, and starting from age 2, the amount and complexity of parental verbal communication with the child is consequential for the child's cognitive development. Goodnow (1988) identified "parental modernity" as a probable important moderator variable. This outlook is associated with "stimulating academic behaviour", "stimulating language", and "encouraging social maturity". Parents with such an outlook provide a stimulating environment to their young children and actively prepare them for school. Applegate, Burleson, and Delia (1992) proposed a model of communication development focusing on the complexity dimension. It purports that the complexity of parental social cognition leads to the complexity of parental communication, which in turn gives rise to the complexity of the child's social cognition and, finally, to the complexity of the child's communication. The key in this process model is what they have referred to as "reflection-enhancing parenting", which is found to be positively related to the mother's social class and social cognitive development.

Social Change and Implications for Intervention

The two different spheres of human development and socialization that have been discussed here, namely, the development of the self and of competence, demonstrate several common points of mutual influence. A contextual and functional analysis provides us with insights for understanding why and how certain patterns of child rearing lead to the development of certain patterns of self and competence. Such an approach also indicates when a change in these patterns is needed and how it can be achieved.

When developmental contexts change, as in the case of rural to urban or international migration, new environmental demands emerge. In particular, urban lifestyles, involving public schooling, more specialized tasks and jobs require different outlooks affecting both the self and competence. Clearly, change is called for. However, what kind of change is optimal is an empirical question that again requires functional analysis. A functional perspective proposes that those human traits and interpersonal orientations that are incompatible with the emerging environmental demands should and would disappear. Others that are not incompatible with new lifestyles, and particularly those that are adaptive to them would continue. This is indeed the theoretical basis of my model of family change.

On the basis of a contextual-functional analysis, what I have come up with regarding the family and the self is a new synthesis—the family model of psychological interdependence and the autonomous–relational self. Though this is a new synthesis in terms of psychological teaching, I believe that it may be a universal trend. Despite the fact that the evidence for this synthetic model of human/family relations comes mainly from research conducted in collectivistic societies undergoing urbanization and economic development, it has universal relevance. This is because such a synthesis does more justice to the two basic human needs for autonomy and relatedness.

Regarding the development of competence, a universally valid cognitive competence model is implicated. This is because global patterns of urbanization, industrialization, and technological development require greater degrees of education and specialization than ever before. All societies need to socialize their children to be competent in changing lifestyles. This does not mean, however, that the so-called "social intelligence" of the traditional society, involving social sensitivity and responsibility, needs to be discarded. What is needed is the *addition* of cognitive competence to social competence.

Though functional analysis is useful in understanding what kind of change is needed, it cannot guarantee that such change will in fact take place. Culture is often resistant to change, and "cultural lag" may impede progress. Also, cultural diffusion from the West, especially from the US, through the media can push Western models of human/family relations even though such an independence pattern may not be the most functional one for adapting to human and societal needs. Thus, what is called for is intervention that is informed by scientifically sound and socially responsible research to counteract both the resistance to change of traditional culture and cultural diffusion from the individualistic West.

With regard to the issues I have discussed here, intervention needs to address two spheres of child socialization. The first one would be designed to increase such parental orientations as heightened responsiveness to the child, extensive verbal communication with the child, the use of reasoning in child discipline, valuing cognitive skills and education, while at the same time nurturing close relations. The second one would promote autonomy within the relational self by introducing autonomy as a child rearing goal. These intervention goals are summarized in Figure 5.2 which also shows the main shifts in contexts and their concomitant functional correlates in human traits and behaviours.

Figure 5.2
Contextual Change and its Outcomes

Context	Rural/traditional ⟶	Urban
	Less specialized tasks	More specialized tasks
	Low levels of schooling	Increasing schooling
Family	Family model of total ⟶ interdependence	Family model of psychological interdependence
	Old age security VOC important	Material interdependence decreasing
	Material interdependence	
Child rearing and the self	Obedience orientation ⟶ functional	Autonomy becomes functional
	The related self	The autonomous-related self
Teaching and learning	Teaching through ⟶ demonstration and modelling Apprenticeship in everyday life	School-like learning, cognitive language skills become functional

In a longitudinal study conducted in Istanbul (Kagitcibasi, 1991; 1996a; Kagitcibasi, Sunar, & Bekman, 2001), a mother training programme was devised to encourage mothers to develop a positive self-concept, feelings of competence, and efficacy as well as specific cognitive skills and positive orientations to provide their children with more cognitive stimulation and enrichment at home. This was achieved by reinforcing the existing close mother–child relationship on the one hand, and by capitalizing on the existing communal support systems, on the other. The latter were utilized in group meetings of mothers in the community and paraprofessional home instruction. The impact of intervention on both mothers and their children was impressive in the fourth year of the study (Kagitcibasi, 1991; 1996a; Kagitcibasi et al., 2001).

In this study that came to be known as the Turkish Early Enrichment Project (TEEP), mothers and their preschool aged children in low income areas of Istanbul were studied first to establish the baselines. Subsequently, in the second and third year of the study, a randomly selected sample of mothers attended a mother–child training programme that focused on the cognitive development of children (the Turkish adaptation of the Home Instruction Program for Preschool Youngsters—HIPPY) (Lombard, 1981), and also on supporting mothers in their child rearing roles and empowering them in general. The mothers implemented the cognitive development programme for their children in their homes. Long-term effects were examined through a follow-up study 7 years later and it was found that the gains from the intervention had been maintained (Kagitcibasi, 1996a; Kagitcibasi et al., 2001). Both following the intervention and 7 years later, children whose mothers had participated in the mother training programme surpassed the control group in cognitive performance and school achievement. They also exhibited greater autonomy, more positive self-concept, and better family and social adjustment. Trained mothers interacted more positively with their children, were pleased with them, and had higher educational aspirations for them. These mothers also had higher intrafamily status and reported better and closer family relations in general compared with the control group.

This is an example of a model of intervention that was successful, as it built upon the existing human relational patterns and the family culture, rather than ignoring them. As the focus expanded holistically from the individual child to interactions between the child and the environment, multiple and expanding benefits accrued from the intervention. This model has great potential for use in intervention/development programmes because it works through and builds upon the existing strengths in the family and promotes them for overall individual–family–community development.

An important goal of the Turkish Early Enrichment Project was modifying child rearing orientations. Specifically, an attempt was made to introduce "autonomy" in child rearing while reinforcing "closely knit human/family ties". Results of the fourth year and at follow-up showed that a greater number of trained mothers appreciated their children's autonomy while remaining as close to them as the control group of mothers. This is in line with the model of psychological interdependence. Another way in which a modification in child rearing orientations was accomplished in the Turkish Early Enrichment Project was by getting mothers to be more responsive to their children and to help support their children's cognitive development to prepare them for school.

The first year baseline assessments revealed generally low levels of responsiveness to children among mothers and low levels of environmental stimulation at home (Kagitcibasi, Sunar, & Bekman, 2001). This is in line with research conducted in socioeconomically disadvantaged homes in the US and other Western societies (see Kagitcibasi, 1996b for a review). The project intervention aimed to improve the situation by sensitizing mothers to the importance of early learning environments and by involving them directly in the early education of their children. The results showed increased levels of mother–child interaction as well as more supportive mother teaching styles, greater verbalization, and heightened responsiveness in general among the trained group compared with the control group. These positive orientations were sustained over time and were also shared by the fathers, as evidenced by the follow-up results. Such parenting had doubtless much to do with the satisfactory overall development and achievement of the children.

Conclusion

There is accumulated knowledge in developmental psychology regarding the indicators of early human development and school readiness. Research has informed us particularly about the development of language, problem solving and other cognitive skills, social competence, emotional development, and self-help skills in early childhood. However, this knowledge needs to be put to more effective use in wide scale intervention work in different sociocultural contexts, especially in non-Western settings and in contexts of migration. To ascertain inadequate development and to promote optimal development, culturally valid measures are needed that would build upon both cross-cultural research as well as within each sociocultural context. Both commonalities and differences would need to be taken into consideration, integrating comparative standards and culture sensitive conceptualization.

It is with these considerations that we undertook the Turkish Early Enrichment Project. Encouraging mothers to support their children's overall development and school readiness entailed using comparative school related cognitive standards, but this was done within a culturally relevant contextual approach. Our research experience as well as the applications emerging from our project have reinforced my belief in the feasibility of such an integrative approach, combining comparative standards of human development with culturally sensitive endogenous conceptualizations of well-being.

TEEP is extensively used in Turkey. A mother–child education programme has been based on it, replacing HIPPY, that is operative across the country, having reached nearly 1,20,000 mothers and children. An evaluation research (Bekman, 1998) revealed important gains even in the case of large scale application. These gains were seen in both children's school preparation and school performance, as well as in the child rearing orientations and self-concept of mothers.

Psychologists and educators have an important role to play here. This role can be summarized in terms of sensitizing and training people, forming public opinion, and informing social policies to help bring about changes that promote human well-being. Social policies need to be much more informed than they are at present by conducting research in human development, developmental science, and human sciences in general. When such research is culturally sensitive and cognizant of social change, it would help improve social policies and render them more supportive of human adjustment to culture change.

References

Anderson, R.C., & Freebody, P. (1981). Vocabulary knowledge. In J.T. Guthrie (Ed.), *Comprehension and teaching: Research reviews*. Newark, NJ: IRA.
Angyal, A. (1951). A theoretical model of personality studies. *Journal of Personality, 20*, 131–142.
Applegate, J.L., Burleson, B.R., & Delia, J.G. (1992). Reflection enhancing parenting as an antecedent to children's social-cognitive and communicative development. In I.E. Sigel, A.V. McGillicuddy DeLisi, & J.J. Goodnow (Eds),

Parental belief systems (pp. 3–40). Hillsdale, NJ: Lawrence Erlbaum Associates.

Ataman, J., & Epir, S. (1972). Socio economic status and classificatory behavior among Turkish children. In L.J.C. Cronbach & P.J.D. Drenth (Eds), *Mental test and cultural adaptation* (pp. 329–337). The Hague: Mouton.

Aydin, B., & Oztutuncu, F. (2001). Examination of adolescents' negative thoughts, depressive mood, and family environment. *Adolescence, 36,* 77–83.

Bakan, D. (1966). *The duality of human existence.* Chicago: Rand McNally.

Baumrind, D. (1980). New directions in socialization research. *American Psychologist, 35,* 639–652.

Bekman, S. (1998). *A fair chance: An evaluation of the Mother–Child Education Program.* Istanbul: MOCEF.

Berry, J.W. (1984). Toward a universal psychology of cognitive competence. *International Journal of Psychology, 19,* 335–361.

Berry, J.W., & Bennett, J.A. (1992). Cree conceptions of cognitive competence. *International Journal of Psychology, 27,* 73–88.

Cha, J.H. (1994). Aspects of individualism and collectivism in Korea. In U. Kim & H.C. Triandis (Eds), *Individualism and collectivism: Theory, method, and applications.* Cross-cultural research and methodology series (vol. 18, pp. 157–174). Thousand Oaks, CA: Sage.

Chou, K-L. (2000). Emotional autonomy and depression among Chinese adolescents. *Journal of Genetic Psychology, 161,* 161–169.

Coll, C.T.G. (1990). Developmental outcome of minority infants: A process-oriented look into our beginnings. *Child Development, 61,* 270–289.

Fisek, G.O. (1991). A cross-cultural examination of proximity and hierarchy as dimensions of family structure. *Family Process, 30,* 121–133.

Gay, J., & Cole, M. (1967). *The new mathematics and an old culture.* New York: Holt, Rinehart & Winston.

Goodnow, J.J. (1988). Parents' ideas, actions, and feeling: Models and methods from developmental and social psychology. *Child Development, 59,* 286–320.

Guisinger, S., & Blatt, S.J. (1994). Individuality and relatedness; evolution of a fundamental dialectic. *American Psychologist, 49,* 104–111.

Helling, G.A. (1966). *The Turkish village as a social system.* Los Angeles, CA: Occidental College.

Helling, G.A. (1986). Personal communication.

Imamoglu, E.O. (1987). An interdependence model of human development. In C. Kagitcibasi (Ed.), *Growth and progress in cross-cultural psychology* (pp. 138–145). Lisse: Swets & Zeitlinger.

Inglehart, R., & Baker, W.E. (2000). Modernization, cultural change, and the persistence of traditional values. *American Sociological Review, 65*(1), 19–51.

Jansen, H.A.M. (1987). The development of communal living in the Netherlands. In L. Shamgar-Handelman & R. Palomba (Eds), *Alternative patterns of family life in modern societies.* Rome: Collana Monografie.

Jose, P.E., Huntsinger, C.S., Huntsinger, P.R., & Liaw, F-R. (2000). Parental values and practices relevant to young children's social development in Taiwan and the United States. *Journal of Cross-Cultural Psychology, 31,* 677–702.

Kagitcibasi, C. (1970). Social norms and authoritarianism: A Turkish-American comparison. *Journal of Personality and Social Psychology, 16,* 444–451.

Kagitcibasi, C. (1982). Sex roles, value of children and fertility in Turkey. In C. Kagitcibasi (Ed.), *Sex roles, family and community in Turkey* (pp. 151–180). Bloomington, Indiana: Indiana University Press.

Kagitcibasi, C. (1990). Family and socialization in cross-cultural perspective: A model of change. In J. Berman (Ed.), *Cross-cultural perspectives: Nebraska symposium on motivation, 1989* (pp. 135–200). Lincoln, NE: Nebraska University Press.

Kagitcibasi, C. (1991). The early enrichment project in Turkey. *UNESCO-UNICEF-WFP. Notes/comments.* No. 193. Paris: UNESCO.

Kagitcibasi, C. (1996a). The autonomous-relational self: A new synthesis. *European Psychologist, 1,* 180–186.

Kagitcibasi, C. (1996b). *Family and human development across cultures: A view from the other side.* Mahwah, NJ: Lawrence Erlbaum.

Kagitcibasi, C., Sunar, D., & Bekman, S. (2001). Long-term effects of early intervention: Turkish low-income mothers and children. *Journal of Applied Developmental Psychology, 22,* 333–361.

Kakar, S. (1978). *The inner world: A psychoanalytic study of childhood and society in India.* Delhi: Oxford University Press.

Kegan, R. (1994). *Over our heads: The mental demands of modern life.* Cambridge, MA: Harvard University Press.

Kim, Y., Butzel, J.S., & Ryan, R.M. (1998, June). *Interdependence and well-being: A function of culture and relatedness needs.* Paper presented at the International Society for the Study of Personal Relationships, Saratoga Spring, New York.

Kohn, M.L. (1969). *Class and conformity: A study in values.* New York: Dorsey.

Kornadt, H.J. (1987). The aggression motive and personality development: Japan and Germany. In F. Halish & J. Kuhl (Eds), *Motivation, intention and volition.* Berlin: Springer-Verlag.

Laboratory of Comparative Human Cognition. (1983). Culture and cognitive development. In W. Kessen (Ed.), *Handbook of child psychology* (4th ed., vol. 1, pp. 295–356). New York: Wiley.

Laosa, L.M. (1980). Maternal teaching strategies in Chicano and Anglo-American families: The influence of culture and education on maternal behavior. *Child Development, 51,* 759–765.

Laosa, L.M. (1982). Families as facilitators of children's intellectual development at 3 years of age. In L.M. Laosa & I.E. Sigel (Eds), *Families as learning environments for children* (pp. 1–45). New York: Plenum.

Laosa, L.M. (1984). Ethnic, socioeconomic, and home language influences upon early performance on measures of abilities. *Journal of Educational Psychology, 76,* 1178–1198.

Lerner, H.G. (1988). *Women in therapy.* Northvale, NJ: J. Aronson.

Leseman, P. (1993). How parents provide young children with access to literacy. In L. Eldering & P. Leseman (Eds), *Early intervention and culture* (pp. 149–172). The Hague: UNESCO/Netherlands Commission.

LeVine, R.A. (1989). Cultural environments in child development. In N. Damon (Ed.), *Child development today and tomorrow.* San Francisco: Jossey-Bass.

LeVine, R.A., & LeVine, B. (1966). *Nyansongo: A Gusii community in Kenya*. New York: Wiley.

Lin, C-Y.C., & Fu, V.R. (1990). A comparison of child-rearing practices among Chinese, immigrant Chinese, and Caucasian-American parents. *Child Development, 61*, 429–433.

Lombard, A. (1981). *Success begins at home*. Lexington, MA: Heath.

Markus, H.R., & Kitayama, S. (1991). Culture and the self: Implications for cognition, emotion, and motivation. *Psychological Review, 98*(2), 224–253.

McLoyd, V.C. (1990). The impact of economic hardship on Black families and children: Psychological distress, parenting, and socioemotional development. *Child Development, 61*, 311–346.

Mundy-Castle, A. (1974). Social and technological intelligence in Western and non-Western cultures. In S. Pilowsky (Ed.), *Cultures in collision*. Adelaide: Australian National Association of Mental Health.

Nunes, T. (1993). Psychology in Latin America: The case of Brazil. *Psychology and Developing Societies, 5*(2), 123–134.

Okagaki, L., & Sternberg, R.J. (1993). Parental beliefs and children's school performance. *Child Development, 64*, 36–56.

Phalet, K., & Schonpflug, U. (2001). Intergenerational transmission of collectivism and achievement values in two acculturation contexts: The case of Turkish families in Germany and Turkish and Moroccan families in the Netherlands. *Journal of Cross-Cultural Psychology, 32*, 186–201.

Ryan, R.M., & Lynch, J.H. (1989). Emotional autonomy versus detachment: Revisiting the vicissitudes of adolescence and young adulthood. *Child Development, 60*, 340–356.

Ryan, R.M., Stiller, J., & Lynch, J.H. (1994). Representations of relationships to teachers, parents, and friends as predictors of academic motivation and self-esteem. *Journal of Early Adolescence, 14*, 226–249.

Saal, C.D. (1987). Alternative forms of living and housing. In L. Shamgar-Handelman & R. Palomba (Eds), *Alternative patterns of family life in modern societies*. Rome: Collana Monografie.

Sameroff, A.J., & Fiese, B.H. (1992). Family representations of development. In I.E. Sigel, A.V. McGillicuddy-DeLisi, & J.J. Goodnow (Eds), *Parental belief systems* (pp. 347–369). Hillsdale NJ: Lawrence Erlbaum.

Saraswathi, T.S. (2001). Personal communication.

Savasir, I., & Sahin, N. (1988). *Weschler çocuk zeka ölcegi* (Wisc-R). Ankara: National Education Ministry Publications.

Savasir, I., Sezgin, N., & Erol, N. (1992). 0–6 Yas Çocuklari için gelişim tarama envanteri geliştirilmesi. (Devising development inventory for children aged 0–6). *Türk Psikiyatri Dergisi, 3*, 33–38.

Segall, M.H., Dasen, P.R., Berry, J.W., & Poortinga, Y.H. (1990). *Human behavior in global perspective*. New York: Pergamon Press.

Semin, R. (1975). *Failure in school*. Istanbul: Istanbul University Publication.

Serpell, R. (1977). Strategies for investigating intelligence in its cultural context. *Quarterly Newsletter, Institute for Comparative Human Development, 3*, 11–15.

Slaughter, D.T. (1988). Black children, schooling, and educational interventions. In D.T. Slaughter (Ed.), *Black children and poverty: A developmental perspective* (pp. 109–116). San Francisco: Jossey-Bass.

Smith, M.B. (1994). Selfhood at risk: Post-modern perils and the perils of postmodernism. *American Psychologist, 49,* 405–411.

Snow, C.E. (1991). The theoretical basis for relationships between language and literacy in development. *Journal of Research in Childhood Education, 6,* 5–10.

Snow, C.E. (1993). Linguistic development as related to literacy. In L. Eldering & P. Leseman (Eds), *Early intervention and culture* (pp. 133–148). The Hague, Netherlands: UNESCO.

Spence, J.T. (1985). Achievement American style. *American Psychologist, 12,* 1285–1295.

Stewart, S.M., Bond, M.H., Deeds, O., & Chung, S.F. (1999). Intergenerational patterns of values and autonomy expectations in cultures of relatedness and separateness. *Journal of Cross-Cultural Psychology, 30,* 575–593.

Teasdale, G.R., & Teasdale, J.I. (1992). Culture and curriculum: Dilemmas in the schooling of Australian aboriginal children. In S. Iwawaki, Y. Kashima, & K. Leung (Eds), *Innovations in cross-cultural psychology* (pp. 442–457). Lisse: Swets & Zeitlinger.

Turkish Family Research Institute. (1995). *Aielde çocuk eğitimi* (Child training in the family). Ankara: Bizim Buro.

Vannoy, D. (1991). Social differentiation, contemporary marriage, and human development. *Journal of Family Issues, 12,* 251–267.

Van Tuijl, C., Leseman, P.P.M., & Rispens, J. (2001). Efficacy of an intensive home-based educational intervention programme for 4–6 year-old ethnic minority children in the Netherlands. *International Journal of Behavioral Development, 25,* 148–159.

Wachs, T.D., & Gruen, G. (1982). *Early experience and human development.* New York: Wiley.

Wallach, M.A., & Wallach, L. (1990). *Rethinking goodness.* Albany: State University of New York Press.

Weil, S. (1987). Proximal households as alternatives to joint families in Israel. In L. Shamgar-Handelman & R. Palomba (Eds), *Alternative patterns of family life in modern societies.* Rome: Collana Monografie.

Young, N. (1992). Postmodern self-psychology mirrored in science and the arts. In S. Kvale (Ed.), *Psychology and postmodernism* (pp. 135–145). London: Sage.

෨ 6 ෬

Individualism in a Collectivist Culture:
A Case of Coexistence of Opposites

DURGANAND SINHA &
RAMA CHARAN TRIPATHI

The use of dichotomies is a heuristic device popular in the West, especially in psychological descriptions of individuals. A host of exclusive descriptive categories, such as extroversion versus introversion, tough-minded versus tender-minded, form-bound versus form-labile, have been used frequently in personality descriptions. Such dichotomous categories are also common in characterizations of nations and cultures. Though this device is convenient, it produces stereotypical and distorted pictures of complex social reality. When a whole culture or society is pigeonholed in dichotomous categories such as masculine/feminine, active/passive, or loose/tight, subtle differences and qualitative nuances that may be more characteristic of these social entities are glossed over. Such descriptive labels evoke unduly fixed and caricature

Uichol Kim, Harry C. Triandis, Cigdem Kagitcibasi, Sang-Chin Choi, & Gene Yoon (Eds), *Individualism and Collectivism: Theory, Method, and Applications*, Volume 18, Cross-Cultural Research and Methodology Series, pp. 123–136. Copyright © 1994 by Sage Publications, Inc. Reprinted by permission of Sage Publications Inc., 2455 Teller Road, Thousand Oaks, CA 91320, USA.

Professor Sinha was the first Nehru Chair Professor at the MS University of Baroda in 1992. This article on which one of his lectures was based is reprinted here as a tribute to his invaluable contributions to the thinking in the field of psychology in India.

like mental impressions of cultures or societies rather than representative pictures of their complexities. Also, when cultures are presented in black-or-white terms, not only does this cloud our understanding of them, but it inevitably leads to our making good/bad comparisons.

In this chapter we will argue that both individualist and collectivist orientations may coexist within individuals and cultures. How these orientations interact and the conditions under which they surface in the same culture are likely to provide us with far greater insights into that culture and its consequences than would categorizing the culture as either collectivist or individualist (see Kagitcibasi, 1994). To illustrate our point we will focus on the culture with which we are most familiar, that of India. Hofstede (1980) originally predicted that India would occupy a very low point on his Individualism Scale. In fact, India scored 48, compared with 91 for the United States and 12 for Venezuela. Yet Hofstede went on to characterize it as a collectivist culture. This categorization has some how gotten stuck to the Indian culture (Chinese Culture Connection, 1987; Sinha & Verma, 1987).

I/C as a descriptive category is inappropriate for designating Indian culture and social reality for two main reasons. First, the Indian psyche, which is a reflection of Indian social reality, is highly complex; contrasting values and basic propensities often coexist, and Indians display a high "tolerance of dissonance" (Chaudhuri, 1966; D. Sinha, 1979; 1988a). Second, as has been pointed out by Roland (1984), J.B.P. Sinha (1982), and Ramanujan (1990, p. 47), the Indian selfhood is so constituted that the typical way in which an Indian responds and reacts is "contextual". Though values occupy a high place in the cognitive–emotional structure of an average Indian, in actual practice they seem to be conditioned by the exigencies of the situation. We will elaborate both these points further in the discussion below.

In the Indian psyche, as well as in Indian modes of behaviour, juxtaposition of opposites has been frequently observed and commented upon by travellers, writers, social scientists, and historians. To some extent, historical circumstances have greatly contributed to this feature of the Indian psyche. Down the ages, instead of assimilation and integration of diverse cultural influences, what seems to have taken place in India has been a kind of coexistence of disparate elements without any synthesis. The country has been exposed to many cultural influences through invasions from its northwestern frontier. In most European countries, various cultural groups inhabiting the same territory for years have merged into homogeneous and cohesive systems, but nothing like this has occurred in India in spite of the unique capacity of Hinduism to incorporate often hostile elements into some kind of a unique sociocultural structure. In India, enormous numbers of dissimilar people with distinct cultures had to find a way of living together, and they have coexisted rather than merged. Neither a "melting pot" mechanism nor a "social blending machine" seems to have operated on the Indian scene.

The lack of homogenization in Indian culture and religion has been the result of a mechanism that can best be described as a process of "enfolding" or "engulfing" that has operated over centuries to deal with incoming diverse cultural elements. Hinduism did not absorb the influx of influences from outside into a unique and unified system, but it *engulfed them*, to use Schulberg's (1968, p. 17) expression. Groups coming into the country with their own customs, cultures, and lifestyles lived apart or amicably side by side with those who were already there. There occurred a kind of *cultural coexistence*. The process has also been described as *encompassing* (Dumont, 1970), in which seeming contradictions of thoughts and actions, instead of leading to confrontation, are tolerated, balanced, accommodated, and integrated (Marriot, 1976). The Indian strategy is not one of resolving conflict but of juxtaposing opposites, which is often perceived as synthesis. This is often reflected in the tolerance of dissonance (or contradictions) that appears to be a paradoxical characteristic of the Indian psyche and that has often been commented upon by observers. For example, Ramanujan (1990) remarks:

> When Indians learn, quite expertly, modern science, business, or technology, they "compartmentalize" these interests (Singer, 1972, p. 320ff); the new ways of thought and behavior do not replace, but live along with older "religious" ways. Computers and typewriters receive *ayudhapuja* (worship of weapons) as weapons of war did once. The modern, the context-free, becomes one more context, though it is not easy to contain (p. 57).

Coexistence of Contradictions

The coexistence of contradictions is reflected in various facets of Indian culture and behaviour, and historians, social scientists, and other writers have commented on it (for a fuller account of the coexistence model of the Indian psyche, see Sinha & Tripathi, 1990). Koestler (1960) remarks about Indian's basic predisposition of "indifference to contradictions" and "the peaceful coexistence of logical opposites." Mehta (1962) notes the simultaneous coexistence in Hinduism of "all gradations of beliefs, from the crudest to the most highly refined" (p. 130). Looking at all the degradation, squalor, and misery of slum life in Calcutta, Lapierre (1986, p. 75) has wondered how the people there can remain good humoured, with radiant expressions. Carl Jung (1978) made some perceptive comments after his visit to India:

> I have, so it seems to me, observed the peculiar fact that an Indian, in as much as he is really Indian, does not think, at least not what we call "think." He rather perceives the thought.... It is true that the logical processes of India are funny, and it is bewildering to see how fragments of Western science live peacefully side by side with what we, short-sightedly, would call superstitions. Indians do not mind seemingly intolerable contradictions. If they exist, they are a peculiarity of such thinking, and man is not responsible for them. He does not make them, since thoughts appear by themselves. The Indian does not fish out infinitesimal details from the Universe. His ambition is to have a vision of the whole. He does not yet know that you can screw the living world up tightly between two concepts (p. 101).

The historian Basham (1971, p. 3) in his famous book *The wonder that was India*, has talked about the Indian people's "love of ease and comfort" (*aram* culture), which has been inculcated by bounteous nature, as well as of a capacity for sustained effort and hard work that has produced gigantic temples, marvellous feats of architecture, and immense irrigation works. Contemporary Indian work behaviour is characterized by the attitude of *chalta hai* ("it goes on like this"): a virtual absence of work ethos and general inefficiency, casualness, and procrastination. On the other hand, the same people display the highest level of work culture when working abroad or when confronted with "big" tasks. Tripathi (1990) reports studies of Indian work organizations that were found to display a mixed set of values said to be characteristic of both Western and non-Western societies. Thus a belief in detachment was found to coexist with materialistic orientation, collectivism with individualism, and humanism with power orientation. Sinha and Sinha (1990) also have observed a "dissonance" in Indian work culture in which the highest ideal of work (as embodied in Indian scripture) stands side by side with lower examples of depravity in work behaviour. There is eulogization of the ideal along with tolerance of the profane. Two systems and two distinct concepts of work coexist and are exemplified in Indian work life.

There are contradictions galore when one looks at the mythological "heroes" and "models" portrayed in the two great Indian epics, the *Ramayana* and the *Mahabharat*. If one is looking for a model to emulate that is perfect in every respect, with no blemish, neither the *Mahabharat* nor even the *Ramayana* is able to furnish such a character. The greatest heroes in the two epics have their weaknesses. And, conversely, the villains possess many virtues worth emulating. Every character has compulsions, justifications, ambitions, virtues, and weaknesses. If these characters are reflective of the Indian psyche in any way, they indicate that in the Indian mind conflicting tendencies coexist and seldom are resolved. The actions of the characters reflect their inner contradictions: even in conflicts, the lines between friends and enemies are blurred. The heroes talk with and seek advice from their "enemies" during battle intervals. In contemporary times, Gandhi, through his technique of *satyagraha*, demonstrated very much the same—that there are no opposite sides in a conflict. For example, though Gandhi engineered and led the famous strike in the calico mills of Ahmedabad, the mill owner used to look after his comforts and welfare, and constantly sought his advice. Gandhi, on his part, praised the mill owner in the most laudatory terms (D. Sinha, 1987).

In philosophy and ethics, similar juxtapositions of contradictory elements are to be found where *dharma* (duty) and *moksha* (salvation) coexist with pursuit of wealth (*artha*) and sexual satisfaction (*kama*) as constituents of cardinal virtues. Material wealth and worldly pleasures are considered illusory (*maya*), and spiritual values and other worldliness are emphasized. At the same time, how much sexual pleasure is cherished can be gauged from the most elaborate treatise on the art of love that the ancient seer has given to posterity, the *Kama Sutra*.

Even the conceptualization of well-being in ancient Indian treatises on medicine reflects the same point. In the context of health and well-being of the individual, the balancing of opposite tendencies and elements is emphasized (D. Sinha, 1990). Imbalance (*asantulan*) is the cause of illness, and avoidance of extremes is vital to humans' well-being. According to Caraka, the preponderance of *gunas* or the humors called *vayu* (wind), *pitta* (bile), or *kapha* (phlegm), the imbalance of which results in disease, are variable conditions, and cure or healing requires restoration of normal conditions of the body or the mind. Both positive and negative elements are present at the same time. The factor of *sama*, or having elements in right or natural quantities, is considered essential for health. All along, the adoption of a middle path (*madhyama*) has been emphasized. Thus a healthy being is equipoised both in pleasure and in pain, in success and in failure. What is significant for functioning is not the extremes, but the middle range. It is the ambiguous middle area, and not the extremes or the dichotomies, that is vital. To give an analogy from music, the beauty of playing the sitar lies not so much in producing the true notes, but in *mirh* (i.e., the delicate nuances between the two adjacent notes). It appears that the Indian has the propensity to function in the "gray area", or between the opposites.

It is this coexistence of opposites all through Indians' lives and culture that is considered to be the cultural and psychological root of their anxiety. An average Indian is "caught in a chaos of conflicting patterns, none of them wholly condemned but no one of them clearly approved and free from confusion" (D. Sinha, 1962, p. 34). Such contradictions and odd paradoxes are in evidence in the sociopolitical plane, where, to give a few examples, Gandhian *sarvodaya* goes hand in hand with building of highly complex technoindustrial society, cottage industry with mass production, and *ahimsa* (nonviolence) with the worst kind of social violence (D. Sinha, 1962, p. 35).

Instances of coexistence of contradictions in Indian life and psyche have led Chaudhuri (1966), a sharp observer and critic of Indian character, to designate Indians as "Janus Multifrons," torn by internal psychological struggles. He refers to the creation of double consciousness, each complete and coherent, but capable of shutting out the other when one is dominant. He talks of the "terrible dichotomy" of the Hindu personality, where a large number of antithetical though connected traits that shape behaviour coexist: a sense of solidarity with an uncontrollable tendency toward diversity, collective megalomania with self-abasement, extreme xenophobia with abject xenolatry, authoritarianism with anarchic individualism, violence with nonviolence, militarism with pacifism, possessiveness with carelessness about property owned, courage with cowardice, cleverness with stupidity. As Kapp (1963) points out, there remains "an unresolved dualism within the present human situation which explains the paradoxical coexistence in one culture system of contradictory value orientations and actual behavior pattern" (p. 18).

In view of the above, it is not surprising that various analysts of Indian behaviour and child rearing have often emphasized features that are contradictory. Whereas one refers to indifference and less affection between parents and children than in the West (Carstairs, 1957, p. 168), others stress closeness and high participation in adult life by children (Minturn & Hitchcock, 1966; W.S. Taylor, 1948). Weaning has been found to be a very traumatic experience for Indian children (Carstairs, 1957, p. 158) as well as a transition accompanied by no signs of emotional upset (Minturn & Hitchcock, 1966, p. 321). D. Sinha (1962) has highlighted many contradictory practices in Indian child rearing and socialization. These conflicting behaviour patterns do not represent mere errors of judgement on the part of observers, but evidence of the paradoxical nature of the reality itself. It is therefore not surprising that Western scholars, used to thinking in terms of logically exclusive categories and disjunctures, fail to understand and appreciate the Indian social reality.

Contextual Nature of Values and Behaviour

A second, but related, aspect of the Indian psyche is that values and reactions are *contextual* rather than *textual*. Indians switch gears constantly according to the situation, thereby displaying many frequently contradictory facades. This is true not only on the political plane—where practical and pragmatic considerations are bound to be dominant, often producing bizarre "compromises"—but also in spheres where purely moral and ethical issues are involved. Moral values occupy a very high place in Indian life, but in their actual behaviour, Indians do not appear to operate in abstract and absolute ethical terms; rather, actions are conditioned by the exigencies of the situation. Though truth has a very high place in the Indian moral code, its practice is bound by context. Thus, as one popular Indian adage goes, "One should speak the truth; one should speak what is pleasant; and one should *not* speak the truth if it happens to be unpleasant."

Similar is the case relating to the social code prescribed for taking food or drink that has been "polluted" by being touched by persons of low caste. According to tradition, high caste individuals are enjoined not to drink water or partake of food touched by those of low caste. But exceptions to this "prohibition" are straightaway provided; for example, one may have such food or drink when one is on a journey or travelling in a conveyance such as a boat or a cart (*apaddharma*). "Rightness" and "wrongness" appear to be determined by the context in which the behaviour takes place. Here, unlike in the Western tradition, which concentrates on the textual and the individual, the entire emphasis is on the contextual and the relational. The action or behaviour by itself is not to be judged; it is the context in which it is made that determines the ethical meaning. As Roland (1984) remarks, "Correct behavior is much more oriented towards what is expected in specific contexts of a variety of roles and relationships, rather than any unchanging norm for all situations" (p. 174). In this context, Ramanujan's (1990) observation is very pertinent:

I think cultures [may be said to] have overall tendencies (for whatever complex reasons)—tendencies to *idealize*, and think in terms of, either the context-free or the context-sensitive kind of rules.... In cultures like India's, the context-sensitive kind of rule is the preferred formulation. Manu explicitly says: [A king] who knows the sacred law, must imagine into the laws of caste (jati), of districts, of guilds, and of families, and [thus] settle the peculiar law of each (p. 47).

In fact, as J.B.P. Sinha (1990a) points out, two opposite sets of values coexist, one pertaining to one's own group and the other for the eyes of others. In interpersonal relationships, the norms and values for ingroup members are different from and sometimes opposite to the norms for outsiders. Ingroup behaviour is characterized by shared needs, beliefs, values, and goals. The members cooperate, make sacrifices, and protect each other's interests, and show what Roland (1984) has called "affective reciprocity." J.B.P. Sinha (1990a) notes that "the interaction patterns with the outside members, however, are strikingly different," and "the ingroup members compete with the outside members rather than cooperate, exploit rather than sacrifice, manipulate rather than help, fight rather than accommodate" (p. 37).

Ambiguity of role models and values among Indian youth (D. Sinha, 1979) is evidenced not only in the high degree of diversity in their choices of role models and "heroes" to be emulated, but also in the fact that they give a high proportion of "uncertain" and "undecided" responses when confronted with questions about situations of social–moral transgression. These are considered to exemplify the dichotomies inherent in the Indian personality and situation, being instances of the "compartmentalization" (Singer, 1972) that characterizes a society in a state of transition (Dawson, 1963).

In a study that examined the dynamics of interrelationships at the intergroup level in a rural setting and focused on the modes of interconnection between cooperation and competition, Jha, Sinha, Gopal, and Tiwary (1985) observed the coexistence of the two that was crucial for the occurrence of events at any level of social structure. The primacy of one over the other depended upon the sociohistorical and cultural context. Not only did the two opposite processes, cooperation and competition, operate together, their primacy was governed by situational factors. This complex operation may appear paradoxical and bizarre to outsiders, but it is a characteristic way of functioning at the group level so far as the Indian setting goes.

I/C and the Indian Culture

The aspect of the coexistence of opposites so characteristic of the Indian psyche is amply evident with respect to I/C. Before detailing the same, we should note that Caraka, the famous ancient *guru* of the Ayurveda system of medicine, recognized individualist and collectivist orientations in conceptualizing personality topology. Based on the preponderance of the three *gunas* (qualities) of *sattva*, *rajas*, and *tamas*, Caraka suggested 16 classifications of human nature. Of the seven types in which *sattva* predominates, two are indicative, respectively, of individualist and collectivist orientations. The *aindrasattva* type is energetic, powerful, unfatigued by activities, and given to religious, economic, and pleasure-giving activities. The *kaubera-sattva* type is fond of family life, given to performance of religious and secular duties, and favours and chastises fellow beings according to their merits and demerits.

Two important factors constituting collectivism are family integrity and interdependence. It is said that Indians are collectivists so far as orientation to family is concerned. In support of this claim, existence of extended family and the important role played by family and kinship ties are cited. However, research concerning valence and psychological proximity to family among older and younger generations has revealed that there is a mix of both individualist and collectivist orientations in family life. From the empirical evidence that is available in this context (D. Sinha, 1979), it is clear that, unlike the older generation, who regard "near" and "other" relations also as parts of the family, among the young there is a distinct trend toward nuclearization, that is, greater individualist orientation. The young tend to define the family in narrower and more restricted terms than do their elders. A mix, however, is there, because the "joint" family is still perceived as fulfilling many needs of the individual. Many of the younger generation are not prepared psychologically to break away completely from the advantages of extended family.

Attitudinally, at least, the individual is going nuclear, but without losing the benefits of kinship and extended family living (D. Sinha, 1988b). The individualism of nuclear family structure is juxtaposed with the collective advantages of extended family ties.

In religion and ethics, some essential features of Hindu religious practices and ethical tenets indicate clearly the strong individualist strand present in them. There are infinite varieties of religious tenets and forms of worship permitted in Hinduism; most are based on the individual. Unlike in Semitic religions, there is no central revelation of God, no one messenger of that revelation; no one central religious book is considered the ultimate authority in all religious matters, and no single code of commandments or laws exists for regulating behaviour. There is enormous heterogeneity of beliefs and practices, ranging all the way from strict monism to monotheism, to dualism, pantheism, and near-paganism, and even atheism. Regulation of behaviour through conformity to group or social norms, which is an important aspect of collectivist orientation, is all but absent. At least the pressure for conformity is much less than what obtains in Islam, Judaism, or Christianity. The individual has the widest range of choices, making any kind of collectivist conformity meaningless. One can believe in an absolute reality, or in many gods, or be an atheist, and still remain a Hindu. Individuals are permitted to follow whatever forms suit them, according to their *samskara* (basic predisposition), *karma* (past actions), and inclinations. The variety is so great and individuals' choices so unlimited that it almost seems there is no such religion as Hinduism. Worship, again, is entirely a matter of individual preference. An entire range of choices is available among the innumerable forms that the gods and goddesses are said to have assumed. As it has been put in Bengali, worship is to be done in a corner, in one's mind, and in the forest (*kone, mane,* and *vane*). Congregational worship is not particularly important, and collectivist forms such as *kirtan* and mass prayers are of recent origin. As far as Indian religion goes, the feature that stands out is strong individualism.

The same is true of Hindu ethics. The importance of individuals' own conduct and behaviour has been emphasized. The law of *karma*—that is, the doctrine of "As you sow, so shall you reap"— which still pervades the belief system of Indians, is all-powerful. *Karma* is a force generated by one's actions; it is accumulated and stored by the individual in his or her past lives (*sanchita*), and it is already bearing fruit owing to the individual's actions in the past (*praradha*). It is constantly being acquired and accumulated as a result of actions during the individual's present life (*sanchiyamana*). Thus the individual is the master of his or her own destiny. Any present evil and suffering are consequences of one's own past actions. There is rarely any idea of collective sin for which the entire community is responsible and has to suffer, as found in Judeo-Christian religions (e.g., biblical stories of punishment by famine and pestilence). There is hope for a better future for the individual if he or she adopts the rightful path. There is room for individual effort and personal endeavour (*purusartha*).

In Hindu culture there is a belief that the root cause of bondage is an individual's own ignorance, and he or she can achieve liberation from the world by acquiring true knowledge of reality. Attainment of *vivekajnana* (discriminative knowledge) is an essential condition for liberation. The discipline that is considered essential and prescribed for its attainment is, again, based in the individual. Among other things, it consists of a life of self-control and meditation. Thus, whether one takes Jainism, Buddhism, or the orthodox Hindu system of thought, one has the central place in the entire scheme of religion and ethics. In collectivist cultures, group goals are said to have primacy over individual goals, whereas in individualist cultures personal goals have primacy over ingroup goals. As far as the Indian ethical goal of liberation is concerned, though it is the *summum bonum* (the ultimate goal to be shared by all), it is one that is attainable through personal effort. That is, liberation is the goal for everyone, but it is individualistic in the sense that it is attainable only through personal endeavour. Everyone can achieve the ultimate goal for and by him- or herself. The two strands coalesce. Strong emphasis is put on the realization of the self, although one is also told to transcend the self in the interest of larger social good.

A series of studies done on competition versus cooperation have found Indians to score high on the former and low on the latter. When asked to make wagers on their own behalf and on behalf of partners, US subjects were found to do better when they bet on behalf of their partners, whereas Indian subjects did better when they bet on their own behalf and were allowed to keep the money (L' Armand & Pepitone, 1975). They also did better when they bet on behalf of their caste group members. In another study that examined bargaining behaviour in India, the United States and Argentina, competition motivation was found highest among Indians (Druckman, Benton, Ali, & Berger, 1974). Similarly, in a maximizing differences game, Indians were found to be more competitive than Canadians (Carment, 1974). Indians have also been found to be more competitive when they are in the "top-dog" position than when they are in the "underdog" position (Alcock, 1975). As Tripathi (1988, p. 226) has observed, the form of collectivism found in Indian society is a mix of individualism and collectivism that is conditioned by many values and contingencies.

A Study of the Coexistence Model

In developing the questionnaire used in the study reported below, we adopted a different strategy.[1] Instead of giving only individualist and collectivist statements, we provided three alternative statements pertaining to the situation given in each item. One was how an individualist would respond, the second was a collectivist's response, and the third was a mix of the two. In the third alternative, individualist and collectivist elements were blended where the juxtaposition consisted of contradictory elements. In other words, the mix provided a position in which the subject could have something of both the orientations at the same time, but the natures of the two elements were often conflicting, so that one could not always have both at the same time. The third alternative was in consonance with the coexistence model we have proposed above for the Indian psyche and cultural system.

We constructed 22 items centring on some of the factors that have been identified with I/C syndrome, including family integrity and orientation, interdependence, self-reliance, personal achievement and group consideration, and cooperation and competition. We used a variety of social and personal situations that an individual is likely to face in day-to-day life to prepare the three alternatives that were offered on each item. The situations pertained to decision making on various matters, work behaviour, facing

[1] We are grateful to Ms Anshu Mehra, junior research fellow, Department of Psychology, Allahabad University, for her assistance in the preparation of the questionnaire.

personal problems, the value of friendship, family interrelationships, personal freedom, ability, achievements, personal happiness, concern for others, and the like.

We administered the questionnaire, at three sessions, to a total of 82 English medium undergraduates of a university in north India. We then conducted a qualitative analysis of the responses based mainly on the frequencies of choices made by the subjects among the three sets of alternatives indicating individualist, collectivist, and mixed orientations. Each subject was designated as displaying one of the three orientations, depending on most frequent choices among the three alternatives on the 22 items.

The results of the study support our contention that Indian culture contains the coexistence of opposites: Mixed orientations were overwhelmingly found. A total of 86.6 per cent of subjects displayed mixed orientations; 12.2 per cent were individualists and only 1.2 per cent showed collectivist orientations. In their second choices, 64.5 per cent subjects showed individualist orientations, followed by 23.2 per cent collectivist and 12.3 per cent mixed.

Itemwise analysis of the frequencies of choices made also support the above findings (see Table 6.1). On 17 of the 23 items, the highest frequency was always of the mixed type. Individualist orientation was most frequent on only 5 items, and there was only 1 instance of collectivist orientation being most frequent. Looking into the items on which there were higher frequencies for individualist choices, we found that they pertained to situations concerning personal problems, achievement, and basis of choice in voting (one question asked whether the respondent would vote on the basis of the candidate's ability or personal relationship or both, and another asked about voting on the basis of the candidate's ability or caste or both; in both cases, the majority of respondents opted for ability as the basis for voting). Similarly, when asked what motivated them more to work, 45 out of 82 respondents chose competition and personal achievement, compared with 6 who opted for cooperation and sharing. However, a sizeable proportion (31 of 82 respondents) said that a mix of both the factors would motivate them to work. The only item on which collectivist orientation appeared to be prominent concerned a purely personal relationship issue: reaction to a person who was once close becoming distant.

Table 6.1
Distribution of the Three Modes of Responses on Individual Items

Theme of the Item	Individualist	Collectivist	Mixed
1. Health and disease: consult a doctor versus members of family	12	2	68
2. Voting: own concern versus family solidarity	25	4	58
3. Career: own inclination versus advice of parents/friends	13	1	68
4. Vital matters: decide oneself versus discuss with friends	39	6	37
5. Staying with parents: loss of personal freedom versus would not mind it	2	12	68
6. Voting: ability versus friendship	47	2	33
7. Guests: avoid versus would not mind	4	19	59
8. Interest in problems of others: perceived as interference versus social support	4	15	63
9. Personal problems: struggle on my own versus discussing with others	53	6	23
10. Own happiness versus others' happiness	22	4	56
11. Feeling of loneliness: if family not around versus no such feeling	13	16	53
12. Skill/ability versus congenial coworker	16	1	65
13. Being successful versus being helpful	11	4	67
14. Cooperation versus competition	6	8	68
15. Loss of affective closeness	10	39	33
16. Independence versus dependence	16	2	64
17. To get work done: importance of procedure versus knowing people	18	7	57
18. Concern about opinions of others	22	18	42
19. Solving problem on own versus looking for guidance and support	20	10	52
20. Cooperation versus personal achievement	45	6	31
21. Work: done at any cost versus not at the cost of friendship	11	15	56
22. Voting: ability versus caste	68	3	11

Discussion

As the above account of the Indian psyche indicates, Indian behaviour is highly complex. Contradictions often coexist, and the stances individuals take are not usually the result of value

considerations in absolute terms; rather, reactions are often conflicting and contextual, and situational contingencies operate in a
powerful manner. Individualism and collectivism often coexist in
individuals' behaviour, and, as we have observed, the cultural
system reflects both these elements as well.

The Indian form of collectivism contains strands of individualism. Tripathi (1988) explains at some length this apparent paradox that characterizes the Indian orientation:

> He is revengeful yet forgiving. He acts to protect family honor,
> yet does not mind killing his own kith and kin if called upon by
> his *dhurma*. He is called upon to engage in *karma* but not seek
> fruit of it. However, these apparently contradictory values and
> attitudes are integrated in one scheme by him on the basis of
> some higher moral principle. An Indian is, therefore, not sur-
> prised or shocked by the coexistence of things which are mu-
> tually contradictory, either in his own mind or in reality (p. 321).

The most important distinction between Indian and Western
minds, Tripathi (1988, p. 322) points out, lies in the ways boundaries are laid down that define mental structures. In the Western
mind, boundaries appear to be more stable and fixed—self and
environment, mind and matter, subjective and objective, material
and spiritual, secular and religious, and so on. The Indian mind,
on the other hand, is governed by boundaries that are constantly
shifting and variable. The self sometimes expands to fuse with the
cosmos, but at another moment it may completely withdraw itself
from it. The self and ingroup have variable boundaries. The self
does not relate to the ingroup but is included in it. In the Western
mind, such dichotomies are complete. The self and ingroup are
taken as two different entities, each having its own boundaries.
The self is then related to its ingroup by forging links with the
group. Thus, as Tripathi (1988) points out, "In the Indian society,
I/C act like figure and ground. Depending on the situation, one
rises to form the figure while the other recedes into the background" (p. 324).

The Indian culture and psyche are neither predominantly collectivist nor individualist in orientation. Their distinguishing feature
is that they incorporate elements of both orientations. Though these
elements often conflict with one another and appear mutually

exclusive, Indians endeavour to incorporate both orientations in their preferred modes of behaviour. They try to have the best of both and frequently display a mixture of collectivist and individualist modes at the same time. Therefore, it is erroneous to label the Indian cultural system as collectivist; if it is collectivist at all, there is still plenty of individualism to be found there.

References

Alcock, J. (1975). Motivation in an asymmetric bargaining situation: A cross-cultural study. *International Journal of Psychology, 10,* 69–81.
Basham, A.L. (1971). *That wonder that was India.* Calcutta: Rupa.
Carment, D.W. (1974). Indian and Canadian choice behaviour in a maximizing difference game and in a game of chicken. *International Journal of Psychology, 9,* 213–221.
Carstairs, G.M. (1957). *The twice-born: A study of the community of high caste Hindu.* London: Hogarth.
Chaudhuri, N.C. (1966). *The continent of Circe.* Bombay: Jaico.
Chinese Culture Connection. (1987). Chinese values and the search for culture-free dimensions of culture. *Journal of Cross-Cultural Psychology, 18,* 143–164.
Dawson, J.L.M. (1963). Traditional values and work efficiency in West African mine labour force. *Occupational Psychology, 37,* 209–218.
Druckman, D., Benton, A.A., Ali, F., & Berger, J.S. (1974). Cultural differences in bargaining behavior: India, Argentina, and the United States. *Journal of Conflict Resolution, 20,* 413–452.
Dumont, L. (1970). *Homo hierarchicus: The caste system and its implications.* Chicago: University of Chicago Press.
Hofstede, G. (1980). *Culture's consequences: International differences in work-related values.* Beverly Hills, CA: Sage.
Jha, H., Sinha, J.B.P., Gopal, S., & Tiwary, K.M. (1985). *Social structures and alignments: A study of rural Bihar.* New Delhi: Usha.
Jung, C.G. (1978). *Psychology and the East.* Princeton, NJ: Princeton University Press.
Kagitcibasi, Cigdem. (1994). A critical appraisal of individualism and collectivism: Toward a new formulation. In U. Kim, H.C. Triandis, C. Kagitcibasi, Sang-Chin Choi, & Gene Yoon (Eds), *Individualism and collectivism: Theory, method, and applications* (pp. 52–65). Thousand Oaks, CA: Sage.
Kapp, W.K. (1963). *Hindu culture, economic development and economic planning in India.* Bombay: Asian Publishing House.
Koestler, A. (1960). *The lotus and the robot.* New York: Harper & Row.
L'Armand, K., & Pepitone, A. (1975). Helping to reward another person: A cross-cultural analysis. *Journal of Personality and Social Psychology, 31,* 189–198.
Lapierre, D. (1986). *The city of joy.* London: Arrow.

Marriot, M. (1976). Hindu transactions: Diversity without dualism. In B. Kapferer (Ed.), *Transaction and meaning* (pp. 109–142). Philadelphia: Institute for the Study of Human Issues.

Mehta, V. (1962). *Portrait of India*. New York: Penguin.

Minturn, L., & Hitchcock, J.T. (1966). *The Rajputs of Khalapur, India*. New York: John Wiley.

Ramanujan, A.K. (1990). Is there an Indian way of thinking? An informal essay. In M. Marriot (Ed.), *India through Hindu categories* (pp. 41–58). New Delhi: Sage.

Roland, A. (1984). The self in India and America: Toward a psychoanalysis of social and cultural contexts. In V. Kovolis (Ed.), *Designs of selfhood* (pp. 123–130). Cranbuy, NJ: Associated University Presses.

Schulberg, L. (1968). *Historic India*. Nederland, NV: Time-Life International.

Singer, M. (1972). *When a great tradition modernizes*. New York: Praeger.

Sinha, D. (1962). Cultural factors in the emergence of anxiety. *Eastern Anthropologist, 15*(1), 21–37.

Sinha, D. (1979). The young and the old: Ambiguity of role models and values among Indian youth. In S. Kakar (Ed.), *Identity and adulthood*. New Delhi: Oxford University Press.

Sinha, D. (1987, January). *Ahimsa as conflict resolution technique and instrument of peace: A psychological appraisal*. Paper presented at the seminar on Peace and Conflict Resolution in the World Community, Nehru Memorial Museum Library, New Delhi.

Sinha, D. (1988a). Basic Indian values and behaviour disposition in the context of national development: The case of India. In D. Sinha & H.S.R. Kao (Eds), *Social values and development: Asian perspectives*. New Delhi: Sage.

Sinha, D. (1988b). Family scenario in a developing country and its implication for mental health: The case of India. In P.R. Dasen, J.W. Berry, & N. Sartorius (Eds), *Health and cross-cultural psychology: Toward applications*. Newbury Park, CA: Sage.

Sinha, D. (1990). Concept of psychological well-being: Western and Indian perspective. *NIMHANS Journal, 8*(10), 1–11.

Sinha, D., & Sinha, M. (1990). Dissonance in work culture in India. In A.D. Moddie (Ed.), *The concept of work in Indian society*. Shimla: Indian Institute of Advanced Study.

Sinha, D., & Tripathi, R.C. (1990, July). *Individualism in a collective culture: A case of coexistence of dichotomies*. Paper presented at the International Conference on Individualism and Collectivism: Psychocultural Perspectives from East and West, Seoul.

Sinha, J.B.P. (1982). The Hindu (Indian) identity. *Dynamic Psychiatry, 3/4*, 148–160.

Sinha, J.B.P. (1990a, October). *Inner transformation of Hindu identity*. Paper presented at the 8th Congress of the World Association for Dynamic Psychiatry, Berlin.

Sinha, J.B.P., & Verma, J. (1987). Structure of collectivism. In C. Kagitcibasi (Ed.), *Growth and progress in cross-cultural psychology*. Lisse, Netherlands: Swets & Zeitlinger.

Taylor, W.S. (1948). Basic personality in orthodox Hindu culture patterns. *Journal of Abnormal and Social Psychology*, 43, 3–12.

Tripathi, R.C. (1988). Aligning development to values in India. In D. Sinha & H.S.R. Kao (Eds), *Social values and development: Asian perspectives*. New Delhi: Sage.

Tripathi, R.C. (1990). Interplay of values in the functioning of Indian organizations. *International Journal of Psychology*, 25, 715–734.

ಋ Part 2 ಜ

Research and Applications

๑ 7 ๗

Conceptualizing Human Development and Education in Sub-Saharan Africa at the Interface of Indigenous and Exogenous Influences

A. BAME NSAMENANG

Sub-Saharan Africa is immense, not only in terms of its size, but more so with respect to the cultural, linguistic, and ethnic diversity that characterize the over 500 million inhabitants of its numerous countries. As Olaniyan (1982, p. 1) observed, "With almost a thousand separate language groups, a variety of climatic regions and greatly different levels of social and economic development... Africa is a continent of bewildering diversity and extraordinary dynamism." This dynamism perhaps reflects the youthfulness of the continent's population. Over 60 per cent of Africa's population comprise children and youth, and in many countries, females outnumber the other demographic cohorts. Age structure determines national needs, particularly access to wholesome education, and patterns of public and personal expenditure. As elsewhere in the world, though much more so for sub-Saharan Africa, the continent's future hope lies in its youth, especially the girl child, who, compared to the boy child, has limited opportunities but performs the bulk of family subsistence work. Today's children are the bridges to the future, a point that calls for critical examination of Africa's apparent difficulty or faltering efforts at providing a headstart for proper development and utilizing the potential of its youth fully as a productive resource for personal progress and national development. In order to view this problem in context, it is instructive to first understand how Africa fares in societal development and other indicators of quality of life.

Vital statistics and development indicators overwhelmingly point to the failure of educational and development efforts in sub-Saharan Africa. The failure is partly attributed to educational curricula that are externally rather than locally-oriented. For example, Africa inherited systems of education and development planning from colonial Europe, but they have neither genuinely incorporated African views on personhood and child rearing nor addressed indigenous African social thought and modes of constructing knowledge.

African cultural communities have a rich heritage of education and, like all cultures, seek to pass on what they know and have learned to the next generation. This ensures not only their inclusive fitness, but their cultural continuity as well. However, the history of education as it is now conceived and taught, focuses almost exclusively on the ways in which Western educational traditions emerged, evolved and became consolidated, to the unfortunate neglect of non-Western educational heritages. In this way educational curricula and development programmes fail because they largely ignore or undermine African patterns of child development, economic life, and participatory education (Nsamenang, 1992).

This paper aims to draw attention to some theoretical and practical issues that pertain to conceptualizing human development and education in sub-Saharan Africa at the interface of competing indigenous and imported psychologies. It is framed by the fact that contemporary Africa has a hybrid cultural character that is the product of local and alien mentalities and lifestyles living together in the same communities and individuals. The cultural braid this duality engenders is, theoretically speaking, a more complex lived reality than has hitherto been articulated (Nsamenang, 2001). This paper begins with an explication of an indigenous African worldview and conceptions of human development and education. It proceeds to examine the relationship between human development and education and ends with a discussion of the implications of an Afrocentric perspective for human development research in the context of school education and the issues emerging therefrom.

Indigenous African Views on Personhood and Human Development

Keller and Greenfield (2000) submitted that the human disposition to benefit from experience is based on evolved, maturational capacities for the co-construction of language, tools, social interaction, etc. Indeed, between a universal humanity and specific individuality lies the large cultural zone in every human being created by a particular culture (Maquet, 1972) that inspires a specific view of life and the world. A set of ecological and demographic realities, cultural traditions, and existential imperatives marks out an indigenous African worldview. In fact, LeVine and colleagues (LeVine, Dixon, LeVine, & Richman, 1994) asserted that sub-Saharan Africa includes meaningfully different human populations and interactional networks within which specific patterns of mating and other communicative processes tend to be concentrated. For instance, sub-Saharan Africans share a "natural" ecology, symbol systems for encoding that ecology, and such social institutions as marriage and family and cultural rule systems for adapting to them. This presupposes the existence of peculiarly African ideas, practices, and issues that in the opinion of Serpell (1992) stand in sharp contrast to the group of cultures loosely known as Western. African views of the world and the human person, for example, ordain a developmental path that differs from those that inform contemporary developmental psychology and the processes of education (Serpell, 1993; 1994).

African Worldview and Conception of Personhood

Every cultural community has a worldview that includes an image of the human being and his or her ontogenesis. A worldview is a shared frame of reference or psychosocial outlook by which members of a particular culture perceive or make sense of the universe and the place of the human being in it (Nsamenang, 1992). It implicates the social representations with which a given culture makes sense of human existence. Social representations shape social interactions and impose an imperative obligation on members to adopt a culturally appropriate gender identity and pattern of social thought. It inspires a specific image of the human being and the life course. Essentially, a worldview conceives of the child as a cultural agent to which the future hopes of society and survival of its culture is entrusted (Reagan, 1996). Bruner (1996) used notions of folk psychology and folk pedagogy to drive home the point that each society develops ethnotheories about why people behave the way they do and how children grow up and become adults. Indeed, throughout human history, people have socialized and educated their offspring to maturity and responsibility.

A worldview is psychologically salient because its central concern is the fate of the individual. But African notions of individuality and autonomy are basically relational and interdependent rather than individualistic and self-contained. In this sense, a frame of reference that focuses on the individual does not come to the African easily, because the individual gains significance from and through his relatedness with others (Ellis, 1978). Thus, like the Japanese (Lebra, 1976), Africans are most fully human in the context of others, hence the developmental value of the environing community. The community of other humans is so essential that African social thought prescribes rites of social incorporation at various ontogenetic points of life like birth, puberty, marriage, and death.

An African metaphor that addresses a gradual ontogenetic progress to maturity, relatedness, and competence is *seed*. The seed is typically nursed into maturity and responsibility in a sociological field in which roles are shared among the young and the old (Nsamenang, in press). The West African conception of person centres on the image of the "unfinished child" (D'Alessio, 1990). Thus, the African worldview visualizes the infant in terms of its "becoming" (Erny, 1968) more and more humane through enculturation, socialization, and education. Becoming fully a human person is thus a matter of incremental maturation throughout ontogeny (Nsamenang, 2000b). The African concept of being is dynamic and rooted in the belief that personhood is attained not only as one grows old, but also in direct proportion to the enactment of one's status roles and social insertion in the community (Nsamenang, 1992). The structure of the self that emerges from the African social ontogenesis is reflected in Mead's (1934/1972) submission that "The self has a character which is different from the physiological organism. The self is something which has a development; it is not initially there at birth but arises in the process of social experience and activity" (p. 154). In their assent to adult maturity and responsibility, children construct and modify their social identities through successive interpersonal encounters and autobiographical experiences that make up their ontogenetic history. For example, adolescents are obliged to construct a gender and ethnic identity consistent with the cultural scripts and gender demands of their worldviews. Within this worldview, socialization and education are organized to gradually integrate children from an early age into responsible roles through guided participation in valued cultural and economic activities at different stages of life. It is modulated to mesh with children's emerging abilities. The desired end state is not cognitive competence, per se, but responsible social development or cognition in service of social ends.

Applied to the African context, the concept of social ontogeny draws on African life journeys (Serpell, 1993) to posit three phases of the human life cycle: spiritual selfhood, social selfhood, and ancestral selfhood (Nsamenang, 1992). The experiential or social selfhood begins at birth (or more accurately from the ritual naming of the child) and extends to death. West Africans regard the human neonate as a framework that shelters a spiritual selfhood on to which a social selfhood begins ontogenetic development on the conferment of a name. Children are not thought to belong to this world until they have been incorporated into the community of the living through naming. Ancestral selfhood follows biological death and extends to the ritual initiation of the ancestral spirit into the spiritual realm. Spiritual selfhood begins from the ritual incorporation of the ancestral spirit into the world of spirits and ends with birth (through reincarnation), or more accurately with the naming ritual. Although this viewpoint extends the human life course to an afterlife, developmental psychology has so far concentrated on the experiential self. Social selfhood is divided into seven stages: the newborn, social priming, social apprenticing, social entrée, social interment, adulthood, and old age (Nsamenang, 1992). Each of these stages is characterized by a distinct developmental task that derives from important transitions between patterns of social participation that define the culture's perceptions of the family, children and their welfare.

An Afrocentric perspective on human development may begin to inform the field of how current theorizing and assumptions ignore or undermine alternative developmental pathways. Thus, a training programme or research agenda based on alternative viewpoints will introduce important inputs against which to gauge the extent to which some normative elements of human development constructed within Euro-American worldviews, for instance, may be inappropriate for Africans and the global nature of human development (Nsamenang, in press). A modest contribution in this direction is perhaps my (Nsamenang, 1992) characterization of African social ontogeny as a cumulative process of social integration into the family and community that Serpell (1994) claimed differs in theoretical focus from the more individualistic perspectives on ontogenesis that dominate Western paradigms.

Students and scholars will gain from this perspective because an Afrocentric view on human development is ordained by a worldview that differs from that of Europe and its diaspora on which contemporary developmental psychology has evolved. Thus, an African view of human ontogenesis can enrich the discipline, informing it about some of what are, or are not, universal aspects of the human life path (Nsamenang, 1999). More specifically, it invites Euro-American social scientists and Western trained social scientists of all nations to critically question their motives for neglecting sub-Saharan African or similar views on human development (Holdstock, 2000).

How Culture Influences Human Development

Although the need to integrate biology into the social sciences seems obvious, it has not received the attention it deserves. However, the pitting of biology against culture is gradually leading to the recognition that social ontogeny interfaces human biology and culture (Keller, 2000). For example, the human capacity to be educated, or more accurately, to acquire culture, is provided by biological heritage or genetic endowment. The human being as a biological organism fuses with the developmental context as an ecosystem and culture because what matures in human organisms are the abilities to learn various elements of culture (Keller & Greenfield, 2000). The interface is the *zone of developmental change* requiring exploration (Nsamenang, 2000a). A developmental approach to social ontogeny provides the framework within which to explore the interplay of biological and cultural influences as different developmental tasks (Keller & Greenfield, 2000). To understand the ontogeny of human culture calls for a consideration of both universal processes of human development and the specificity of cultural differentiation during ontogeny. In order to accurately capture this interplay, it seems advisable to critically review the distinction between expected and actual life experiences (Greenough, Black, & Wallace, 1987/1993). The plausibility of this advice derives from the fact that, so far, the primary focus of developmental research has been more on conceptualized attributes rather than on lived experiences that social ontogeny inspires.

The foregoing discussion cautions us against the thinking that because a behavioural phenomenon has a biological foundation, it is immune to cultural or environmental influences. The interaction between symbolic culture and biology is a key determinant of the development of behaviour, emotion, and mentality that equally deserves attention. This calls for the focus of research on cultural learning, as characterized by the processes, outcomes, and biological foundations that make possible language, tools, thought, and patterns of social thought and interaction.

Approaches to incorporating culture into developmental research should be grounded on the realization that, although the developmental impact of culture is at the individual level, it has generally been operationalized as a macro level construct. It is obvious that every human mind develops in a cultural context. The mind grows by assimilating the culture and adapting to it; the mind weaves a new culture around and inside it (Azuma, 2000). This "personal culture" is fed back to the wider culture (Kitayama, 1997). We should further note that all human beings operate in their worlds as individual agents of culture, bringing their implicit, underlying psychological culture to every context, situation, and interaction (Matsumoto, 1996). For example, children carry their culture to school, whereas parents take theirs to work and to all social encounters. Since culture fulfils a fundamental role, it is a basic part of every human being. As it plays a key role in shaping our sense of self and identity, it has a pervasive influence on all our behaviours across all contexts (Matsumoto, 1996). The processes of cultural learning both depend on and affect human development (Tomasello, Kruger, & Ratner, 1993).

Culture influences human development by not only ensuring the physical survival of children (LeVine, 1974), but also by ensuring that children acquire the survival skills and strategies of their group or people (Ogbu, 1988). Culture equally influences development by ensuring that children acquire appropriate cognitive, communicative, motivational, and social–emotional or affective and spiritual attributes, as well as practical skills that will make them competent adults who will contribute to their own survival and progress and that of their people and society. Finally, culture influences development by providing the formulas by which competencies are transmitted and acquired by children. These are the processes of cultural learning, and these vary over both ontogenetic time (different points in the life cycle) and cultural domains (such as cognition, affect, and social responsibility).

Therefore, human development is a cultural process, albeit a dynamic one. In every society children learn a cultural, not a universal, curriculum. They are obliged to adapt to the accumulated cultural heritage of their people or adjust to that of the dominant culture, but often they adapt selectively to both. Cultural learning usually takes place, not in a homogenous society, but in a culturally diverse one, where competing sets of norms and values interplay. The vast majority of human beings acquire culture in multicultural contexts, hence the need to understand how multiculturalism shapes psychological development. According to Azuma (2000), every known culture is hybrid; any mind develops through interacting with a multiplicity of cultures. The mentality of the contemporary Africans, for instance, is shaped by the interplay of indigenous and alien cultural forces and images of personhood that coexist in what Mazrui (1986) termed a triple heritage. This triple inheritance pertains to the extent to which imported Eastern and Western images and conceptions of childhood and child life now coexist, collide and have transformed or stagnated indigenous

African views on children and their development. Although the word indigenous connotes circumscribed, fixed and being solid and stable, in reality, any culture involves some fluidity (Azuma, 2000). Thus, even in traditional Africa, cultural as well as developmental norms are not static; they are socially contested and rapidly changing in response to contact with other cultures, ecological shifts, and existential dynamics. This creates a dialectical process that implicates cross-cultural value conflict. An innovative cross cultural research programme may focus on the psychological effects of value conflict on the development of school children in the hybrid societies of Africa and their implications for curricular reforms and development assistance.

Search for Relevant Educational Curricula for Sub-Saharan Africa

Most books and study programmes that deal with the history and philosophy of education and human development include few, if any, references to indigenous educational ideas and practices in Africa. Although there have recently been calls for the consideration of African perspectives (Holdstock, 2000), most such efforts, whenever they have been attempted, have often entailed little more than the addition of vignettes or footnotes pointing to African contributions to Western databases. In fact, whenever Western scholars elect to listen, say, to African social thought, the tendency has been to decide *a priori* what they wanted to hear or see and how it should be said or seen (Tangwa, 1996). Even African scholars are constrained by Eurocentric rules of the game to address the international audience, that is, North Americans and Western Europeans, rather than speak to their own people in their own terms (Nsamenang, 1999).

In this section, we first present some salient features of African educational traditions. Then, we proceed to examine the current state of formal education or schooling in Africa in juxtaposition to indigenous African educational thought and practice. In the process, we explore some of the key reasons for the failure of education to satisfy sub-Saharan Africa.

INDIGENOUS AFRICAN EDUCATIONAL
THOUGHT AND PRACTICE

Education, as deliberate teaching or training of the young, is a specific form of enculturation and socialization, widely referred to as schooling (Nsamenang, in press). Tomasello, Kruger, and Ratner (1993) characterized it as instructed learning. Others have referred to it variously as school learning, formal, formalized or institutional education, usually in contrast to participatory or societal learning, home training and nonformalized or nonformal education. It is important to note, however, that teaching and learning are not the monopoly of schools; they occur in and out of school (Desforges, 1995). In some cultures, children's learning is organized primarily through didactic instruction and extensive cognitive stimulation in institutions. In African family traditions, children are guided and encouraged, with little or no instruction, to observe and participate in the ongoing cultural and economic life of the family and community.

The aim of indigenous African education is to socialize responsible participation in acceptable and valued social and economic activities—a highly cherished moral quality that is relatively ignored in the curricula of most schools in Africa (Serpell, 1993). Most productive and moral lessons imparted to children are tacitly woven into the texture of daily life activities. Through them, children are apprenticed not only to imbibe useful economic skills but also to acquire prosocial attitudes and values of generosity, sharing, and caring. For example, children perform chores and take care of younger siblings to reflect the principle of sharing family responsibility (Serpell, 1992) and the priming process of learning the caretaker role from an early age (Nsamenang, 1992). Unfortunately, school curricula in Africa continue to ignore these forms of responsibility training and cognitive functioning.

The role of parents and other mentors in this type of education is (Nsamenang, in press):

1. To guide children to accept and understand the appropriate adult identity and models toward which they are being prepared.
2. To communicate standards of valued behaviour and virtue.
3. To prime and ensure their acquisition.

The input of the peer group at all ages is significant because from toddlerhood, children spend more time and interact more within the peer culture than in adult–child dyads (Jahoda, 1982). For example, when children play, share, challenge one another, and engage in and resolve conflicts within the free spirit of the peer culture or interact with significant others, the social identities asserted therein and the values deployed evoke social representations and locate children and their interlocutors as important social partners.

Whereas international advocacy tends to condemn the participatory role of the African child as exploitative child labour, it is important to realize that in the subsistence economies of Africa, such "labour" is legitimately interpreted as "an indigenous educational strategy that keeps children in contact with existential realities and the activities of daily life" (Nsamenang, 1992). By deriving its contents from the local environment, being integrated with productive work, and by addressing the needs of society, traditional education appears more salient than schooling (Segall, Dasen, Berry, & Poortinga, 1999), at least in the context of sub-Saharan Africa. Incidentally, it is schooling that separates and distances children from these activities. This shortcoming of the school in Africa is reflected in Bruner's (1996) cogent remark that "schooling may even be at odds with a culture's other ways of inducting the young into the requirements of communal living" (p. ix).

DEVELOPMENT AND DECLINE IN EDUCATION IN SUB-SAHARAN AFRICA

As soon as schooling was introduced in Africa, it began to spiral out of control, as schools began to churn out unemployed youth who could read and write, but could not interpret, construct, or use knowledge from their own environments (Hoppers, 1981). This state of affairs was perhaps due to the fact that Western-type of education was introduced in Africa as a "modernization" tool to assist Africa to catch up with "progress" and civilization. Education was not designed to help Africans understand themselves and their world. The imported systems of education did not incorporate African cultural and economic realities, social thought, and modes of constructing knowledge, among other exclusions.

Thus, while most African families continue to rely on indigenous forms of participatory learning, African countries have put in place imported education systems in which children receive didactic instruction from adults outside the context of skilled activity. The imported systems only intermittently and uncommittedly attempt to gain from the social intelligence and responsibility training inherent in African educational traditions. Thus, the education so far imparted by schools in sub-Saharan Africa has somehow been inadequate as schooling denies African children the constructs that form the building blocks of their daily life and identity. That is, the education of African children has failed to connect appropriately with their everyday cognition and life journeys (Serpell, 1993).

Instead, the school led to the impression that African culture is an obstacle to development and modernity (Serpell, 1993) and that African homes are culturally deficient dungeons to escape. Consequently, the role of the school has been to help Africans overcome their backwardness. This explains why deficit models have been applied in Africa. Such models continue to be applied, failing to acknowledge that the education imparted so far has been of limited value and little relevance to Africans. Our estimation is that the present systems of schooling instead help to alienate and decontextualize their African learners because they fail to mesh with local realities. They have, for instance, taken education away from parents, thereby reducing parent–child relations and separating them from the daily activities of personal and family life. Thus, the massive and expensive expansion of inherited colonial systems of education is not entirely suitable for contemporary African realities and needs (Basu, 1987).

The Current State of the Field

The evolution of schooling shows some disparities such as differences in enrolment, literacy rates, and the gendered profile of literacy. In Cameroon (Republic of Cameroon, 1993), for instance, 44.9 per cent boys as compared to 37.3 per cent girls received primary education and 14.6 per cent boys as against

8.9 per cent girls were enrolled in secondary education. The general pattern is similar for sub-Saharan Africa. Although educational opportunities for girls have shown signs of improvement, Africa still has the lowest female literacy rate in the world. In 1993, 26 million African girls were out of school, most of them in rural areas. This figure was estimated to rise to 36 million by the year 2000 (The Ouagadougou Declaration, 1993). This disparity may be due to the fact that the girl child carries the double burden of household chores and childcare.

Some Liberian adolescents perceived the school as a "golden key of our New World" (Fricke, 1979). The view of the school as a source of enlightenment and expansion of horizons carries the potential to transcend the shortcomings of the forms in which schooling is packaged (Serpell, 1996). This positivist outlook should be viewed vis-à-vis Freitag's (1996) caution that the school is neither a panacea for all societal ills nor an all-powerful poison that destroys society. Although schooling is fundamentally about individual experience (Serpell, 1993), the intellectual empowerment the school confers instead serves to alienate its African converts to their traditions and stark realities. The cognitive systems and lifestyles the school inspires have not really suited the requirements of Africa's agrarian economies.

Not only does schooling distance children from parents, thereby increasing peer influence and the generation gap, but it also limits children's availability and contribution to the family economy. Faced with the conflict of interests between family subsistence and the demands of school (Serpell, 1993), some parents allow their children to continue in school but use their services intermittently for economic activities, while others withdraw them and involve them in economic activities. In urban areas in Africa, teenage school children are active in the street economy, as a full-time or part-time after school activity that may fetch the only income for the family (Bekombo, 1981). Other factors that stifle educational progress include modern information and communication technologies that are conspicuous by their non-existence. The diploma syndrome and rote learning dominate the pedagogical system. There are innumerable unemployed school leavers and graduates whose education is unsuited to the needs of Africa's largely agrarian job market. For example, school curricula have little or no relationship with the life of Africans and the environment they are familiar with. These are only some of the factors that make school dismal and evoke limited flickers of interest in learners. This precipitates a high rate of school dropout. These constraints compromise the potential contribution of the school in sub-Saharan Africa.

The disjunction between school and daily life is a cause for concern for African nations—whether their youths are acquiring the skills and responsible values to catch up with the technological developments of the twenty-first century and satisfy the demands of an acceptable human growth index. The core issue is how to design and implement relevant educational curricula; how to use youth, school leavers and graduates as a potential resource rather than as problematic cohorts. Whereas indigenous African educational traditions endeavour to connect children to their local contexts and daily life activities, the school tends to isolate and distance them.

The crucial value of the school is not being disputed or questioned here. However, efforts to evolve relevant and appropriate educational curricula for Africa need to take cognizance of the fact that "schooling is only one small part of how a culture inducts the young into its canonical ways" (Bruner, 1996, p. ix). In spite of the current emphasis on formal education, schooling represents only one of the resources that contribute to the wholesome development of learners. Formal educational provisions need to be integrated with other resources. More appropriate school curricula are, therefore, better designed and organized to handle school children in the "school of life" (Moumouni, 1968).

An understanding of these factors necessarily entails not only a theoretical framework, but also the relationship between education and human development.

How are Human Development and Education Related?

Throughout human history, every culture has taught its young, and has made great effort to train and prepare the next generation. The primary focus of basic education is on the developing person. The human disposition to learn from experience derives from biological integrity and maturational capacity.

Indeed, developing and learning constitute the essence of human life, which, as we stressed earlier, become more meaningful within the framework of a given cultural context. Cultures recognize, define, and assign different developmental tasks to biological development, therein infusing cultural curricula into human biological ontogeny (Nsamenang, 1992). In reality, human cultures seek to pass on from one generation to the next what they know and have learned, hoping to ensure not merely the survival and progress of their offspring, but that of their cultures as well (Reagan, 1996).

All forms of education appear to target developing persons at critical points and different stages of life. Traditional African education, for example, progresses gradually in conformity with the successive stages of physical, emotional, and mental maturation of the child (Moumouni, 1968). It interweaves social, economic, political, cultural, and existential strands of life into a common tapestry. The graduated nature of African educational thought and practice follows from the principle that, since one cannot teach or learn everything at once, the tasks and activities to be taught and learned have to be sequenced within the curriculum as well as across ontogenetic stages. They should be fitted to children's emerging minds and capacities. The schooling system, too, has been organized to correspond to the human maturational trajectory. Thus, school curricula tend to be organized to fit teaching and learning to what is perceived as the "blueprint" of biological development. Given that children learn a cultural curriculum as they develop, the cultural opportunities provided to them in, say, sub-Saharan Africa may not exactly correspond to the image of childhood and child life portrayed in the extant developmental literature. The implication is that the existing literature on human development and educational thought and practice does not reflect their nature in a global perspective.

A developmental perspective on how children make progress in understanding the world is more complex than the accumulated episodes of their learning. Human knowledge accrues from learning, albeit learning as predicated on the pace and quality of biological maturation and the existing repertoire of the child's knowledge (Fox, 1995). Other factors include the ability to manage and apply the knowledge already acquired and the extent of involvement in creative and participative learning. Often, children are active in the business of learning; they spontaneously work out their understanding of the world rather than having to be prodded into learning through external pressure. With partici- patory learning, development becomes a self-regulating process, increasingly under the child's own control, and is contrasted with a view of children as passive learners, who are shaped by the learn- ing environment (Fox, 1995). For example, when children en- counter difficulties in everyday life or in school learning, they typically respond by drawing on their existing repertoire of knowledge and skills, which includes what they understand the problem to be, how important they rate its solution, what help they think is available, and whether or not they feel confident of finding a solution. This invokes the concept of readiness and high- lights the futility of teaching or rushing the learning of contents for which children are not yet biologically or psychologically ready (Fox, 1995). Perhaps, it would be more productive to view read- iness in terms of a gradient of difficulty with respect to a problem, necessitating the presentation of simpler forms of the problem in familiar contexts as a prerequisite for presenting more complex ones in unfamiliar environments. The family is the most familiar milieu in which children begin to acquire their knowledge.

THEORETICAL AND METHODOLOGICAL PERSPECTIVES

Human infants are born into a social world constructed in terms of the social representations of adults, particularly parents. Children's search for understanding, relatedness, and competence begins in the family, with their parents, long before they start schooling. However, in many African families, participatory learn- ing proceeds alongside didactic school learning, an existential reality that diverges from what has typically been theorized and researched. The family and the school are the key agents of social- ization. Unfortunately, both these institutions are facing an acute crisis. Dedy and Tape (1991) described how musicians, novelists, and scriptwriters in Cote d'Ivoire have taken up the crisis as the central theme of their work. In tracing the evolution of the forces disabling the family and the educational constraints that have led to a crisis in the two institutions, the authors highlighted the difficulty, if not the failure, of the family and the school to play the pivotal role of ensuring the proper socialization and education of the next generation.

The Social and Cultural Context of Human Development and Education

From a social psychological perspective, social norms, status positions and role relationships as well as the contingencies embedded in cultural institutions like the family are the primary forces that instil and shape the norms and values that regulate behaviour, and that set limits on the developing person. The development of behavioural regulation is not a process of mere accretion but an active process of increasingly internalizing and integrating external values, particularly parental injunctions, into a regulatory experience. From an evolutionary perspective, human culture permeates human adaptability to its varied ecological and cultural niches (Keller, 2000), hence the notion of contextual situativity of human behaviour. Children's recognition of social relationships and the development of the competencies to participate and become socially integrated members of the family and community implies that they have access to and can acquire the norms and values inherent therein. Indeed, human offspring possess an innate ability to acquire, create, and share culture (Trevarthen, 1980).

The family is the interactional unit that initiates and sustains children's learning and acquisition of societal values, social norms, and other interactive and communicative skills. As primary socialization agents, parents serve as the first educators of their children; they deploy socialization techniques that provide children with introductory experiences of their physical, interactive, affective, and cognitive world. Through parents, children become acquainted with the linguistic, cognitive, social, and other rule systems of the family and culture. Parents are natural teachers who first orient children to culture specific notions of individuality, relatedness, autonomy, and competence. Indeed, parents have an imperative obligation to ensure their children's acquisition of appropriate gender roles and orientation to the status positions available in their culture. In African family traditions, such parenting behaviours are embedded in a social matrix that includes siblings, extended family members, other mentors and even neighbours. The family, the child, and the context constantly interact, thereby influencing each other.

Learning, whether in or out of school, is an active process that requires inner motivation. Development itself is an internal process in which children autonomously exercise, elaborate, and organize their capacities. Children's activities within the peer culture are illustrative of self-motivated learning. The participatory mode of indigenous African education is based on the assumption that children have innate tendencies toward being competent, affiliative, and self-regulated.

The emergence and development of the *self* is an important dimension of autonomy and relatedness. As the child elaborates a sense of *self* within the family, ideas begin to emerge and consolidate about "that which is me" and "that which is not I" (Lonner & Malpass, 1994). A child's active abstraction of a sense of identity as well as the social, affective, and cognitive rules of the culture through socialization and enculturation is a cognitive process that allows the child to progressively individuate into whom he or she is and where he or she belongs (Lewis, 1990). While this way of thinking appropriately focuses on individual agency in developmental processes, it must be emphasized that development occurs within the imperatives of a definite ecological and cultural context. The developmental context of contemporary African children is neither entirely traditional nor entirely modern, because "the old traditional ways have continuing relevance, along with the new" (Ellis, 1978, p. 7). The forces of traditionalism, modernity, and globalization thus coexist and interplay, thereby precipitating uncertainty and the attendant apprehension and anxiety.

Consequently, contemporary African societies have evolved a hybrid cultural character that is a product of the coexistence of indigenous and modern factors in the same communities and individuals. Social reality and the economic motive lie at the interface of endogenous and alien norms and value systems. In other words, human development and education are shaped by the acculturative forces and behavioural shifts incidental to Africa's triple heritage (Mazrui, 1986). This is confusing Africans, as they grope for a meaningful future and answers to the ambivalences and contradictions of their marginal existence. A conceptualization that ignores or trivializes how various strands of Africa's rich sociocultural heritage mesh to shape and sharpen lifestyles and educational efforts portrays only a partial image.

THEORETICAL CONSIDERATIONS AT THE INTERFACE OF TRADITIONALISM AND GLOBALIZATION

The forces of globalization, which is essentially Eurocentric in content and deliberate effort, are irreversibly affecting Africa's indigenous identity. The interpretation of globalization as the extent to which Western civilization changes humanity ignores or trivializes the contributions of non-Western peoples. Africans, for example, have been at the centre stage of global forces over the course of human history. A cohort on whom the future of Africa hangs, youths, are key players in the global supply of migrant labour, addictive drugs, and are used as guinea pigs for commodities of the international marketplace like cigarettes, alcohol, and sports. Their role in globalizing technologies like the Internet and the media, especially Hollywood scripts, which are simulations that place adolescent hopes and desires on edge, is also quite significant (Nsamenang, in press). The acknowledgement of such contributions per se can be empowering.

An understanding of the processes of education and the development of children in Africa today is necessarily constructivist and best undertaken within the discourse of traditionalism and postmodernism. Contemporary Africans daily navigate between the value demands and lifestyles of traditionalism and globalization. A plausible and realistic conceptual approach to this hybrid is not to pit "traditionalism" against "modernity", but to create the value on which to abstract an appropriate content from the interface of multiple images that sometimes conflict and transgress each other. This value is best crafted from the positive elements of each system. In so doing and given Africa's participatory education and agrarian economies, it is essential to understand how learners can be brought to the centre of the development process by allowing them meaningful roles in the family, society and the nation, as well as prepare them to cope and make progress with globalization.

Regardless of the persistent nostalgia for tradition or the overwhelming allure of globalization, we must resist seeing one image as the *right* one. This calls for bringing into sharp focus stark local realities as they confront the intrusive encroachments of globalization. Educational curricula should be developed on the imperatives of both localization and globalization, necessitating global thought but localized action. The best way to understand and tackle curricular issues is to know how the young we endeavour to educate perceive and understand their circumstances and futures, and attempt to cope with their multiple and sometimes conflicting demands and role obligations.

Concluding Comments

Given that human development and education interface several disciplines of the behavioural and social sciences, education and research are best conceptualized within a multidisciplinary framework that permits several disciplines to cross-fertilize and enrich theory, method, and practice (Nsamenang, 1999). What is needed are curricula and research agendas that are grounded in our best understanding of the processes of developing and learning in context. What is lacking in curricula and research in psychology is knowledge of the methods and concepts of multiple disciplines that have a bearing on understanding human beings as organisms that acquire and use culture. Accordingly, it would be useful if methodological approaches are sensitive to how developing persons are increasingly rendered cultural agents during ontogeny.

Our theoretical position in this paper is that different cultures value and socialize diverse pathways to the human life course. This requires sensitizing educationists and social scientists to the diversity that exists to be discovered. Our concern is to train scholars in the field of culture, education and human development that are problem driven, not discipline driven, but who, nonetheless, are fortified to contribute to and advance theory and methods. The vision is to develop researchers and practitioners who understand that to become human is to acquire and create culture, and to ground them in context relevant theories and methodological techniques to actualize this vision in empirical research that utilizes both quantitative and qualitative methodologies in an interdisciplinary framework. Sensitivity to the power of participation compels the incorporation of the voices of learners and their cultures into the discourse.

This theoretical orientation calls for the incorporation of biology in a research programme on culture and development and carries the potential of enriching both the research process and the outcome.

The foregoing discussion poignantly reinforces the need to explore African views, not so that the extant knowledge is necessarily displaced, but that we may arrive at a broader and more comprehensive understanding (Wright, 1984) of human developmental paths and educational traditions. Even if we learn that they are worthless, at least we have learned something worthwhile.

References

Azuma, H. (2000). Commentary. Indigenous to what? *ISSBD Newsletter*, 1(37), 9–10.

Basu, A. (1987). Re-thinking education in the Third World. *Africa Quarterly, 27*, 89–95.

Bekombo, M. (1981). The child in Africa: Socialization, education and work. In G. Rodgers & G. Standing (Eds), *Child work, poverty, and underdevelopment* (pp. 113–129). Geneva: International Labor Organization.

Bruner, J. (1996). *The culture of education*. Cambridge, MA: Harvard University Press.

D'Alessio, M. (1990). Social representations of children: An implicit theory of development. In G. Duveen & B. Lloyd (Eds), *Social representations and the development of knowledge* (Introduction, pp. 70–90). Cambridge: Cambridge University Press.

Dedy, F.S., & Tape, A.G. (1991). *Famille et Education en Cote d'Ivoire*. Abidjan, Cote d'Ivoire: Institut d'Ethnosociologie.

Desforges, C. (1995). Learning out of school. In C. Desforges (Ed.), *Introduction to teaching: Psychological perspectives*. Oxford, UK: Blackwell.

Ellis, J. (1978). *West African families in Britain*. London: Routledge & Kegan Paul.

Erny, P. (1968). *L'Enfant dans la pensees traditionelle de l'Afrique Noire (The child in traditional African social thought)*. Paris: Le livre africain.

Fox, R. (1995). Development and learning. In C. Desforges (Ed.), *Introduction to teaching: Psychological perspectives* (pp. 55–71). Oxford, UK: Blackwell.

Freitag, B. (1996). The role of the school in child development. *ISSBD Newsletter*, 1(29), 1–3.

Fricke, R. (1979). Orientation towards the future by Liberian schoolchildren: A contribution to the understanding of young West Africans. *Human Development, 22*, 113–126.

234   ᎧᎭ   *A. Bame Nsamenang*

Greenough, W.T., Black, J.E., & Wallace, C.S. (1987/1993). Experience and brain development. *Child Development, 58,* 539–559. In M.H. Johnson (Ed.), *Brain development and cognition: A reader* (pp. 290–319). Oxford: Blackwell.

Holdstock, T.L. (2000). *Re-examining psychology: Critical perspectives and African insights.* Hampshire: Routledge.

Hoppers, W.H.L.M. (1981). *Education in a rural society: Primary pupils and school leavers in Mwinilunga, Zambia.* The Hague: Nuffic.

Jahoda, G. (1982). *Psychology and anthropology.* London: Academic Press.

Keller, H. (2000). Parent-child relationships from an evolutionary perspective. *American Behavioral Scientist,* Special issue on Evolutionary psychology: Potential and limits of a Darwinian framework for the behavioral sciences, 43(6), 957–969.

Keller, H., & Greenfield, P.M. (2000). History and future of development in cross-cultural psychology. *Journal of Cross-Cultural Psychology, 31*(1), 52–62.

Kitayama, S. (1997). Bunka-shinrigaku towa nanika (What is cultural psychology?). In K. Kashiwagi, S. Kitayama, & H. Azuma (Eds), *Bunka-shinrigaku: Sono rironin to jisshou (Cultural psychology: Theories and facts)* (pp. 17–43). Tokyo: University of Tokyo Press.

Lebra, T.S. (1976). *Japanese patterns of behavior.* Honolulu: University of Hawaii Press.

LeVine, R. (1974). Child rearing as cultural adaptation. *Teachers College Record, 76*(2), 226–239.

LeVine, R.A., Dixon, S., LeVine, S., & Richman, A. (1994). *Child care and culture: Lessons from Africa.* Cambridge: Cambridge University Press.

Lewis, M. (1990). Social knowledge and social development. *Merrill-Palmer Quarterly, 36,* 93–116.

Lonner, J.W., & Malpass, R. (1994). *Psychology and culture.* Boston: Allyn & Bacon.

Maquet, J. (1972). *Africanity.* New York: Oxford University Press.

Matsumoto, D. (1996). *Culture and psychology.* Pacific Grove, CA: Brooks/Cole.

Mazrui, A.A. (1986). *The Africans.* New York: Praeger.

Mead, G.H. (1934/1972). *Mind, self, and society.* Chicago: University of Chicago Press.

Moumouni, A. (1968). *Education in Africa.* New York: Praeger.

Nsamenang, A.B. (1992). *Human development in cultural context: A third world perspective.* Newbury Park, CA: Sage.

Nsamenang, A.B. (1999). Eurocentric image of childhood in the context of the world's cultures: Essay review of *Images of childhood,* edited by Philip C. Hwang, Michael E. Lamb, and Irving E. Sigel. *Human Development, 28,* 159–168.

Nsamenang, A.B. (2000a). Issues in indigenous approaches to developmental research in sub-Saharan Africa. *ISSBD Newsletter, 1*(37), 1–4.

Nsamenang, A.B. (2000b, September). *African view on social development: Implications for cross-cultural developmental research.* Paper presented at the 5th ISSBD African Regional Workshop, Kampala, Uganda.

Nsamenang, A.B. (2001). Indigenous view on human development: A West African perspective. In N.J. Smelser & P.B. Baltes (Eds), *International encyclopedia of the social and behavioral sciences* (vol. 3–14, article 23, pp. 7297–7299). Oxford: Elsevier.

Nsamenang, A.B. (in press). Adolescence in sub-Saharan Africa: An image constructed from Africa's triple inheritance. In B.B. Brown, R.W. Reed, & T.S. Saraswathi (Eds), *The world's youth: Adolescence in eight regions of the globe.* Cambridge: Cambridge University Press.

Ogbu, J.U. (1988). Cultural diversity and human development. In D.T. Slaughter (Ed.), *Black children and poverty: A developmental perspective* (pp. 121–170). San Francisco, CA: Jossey-Bass.

Olaniyan, R. (1982). African history and culture: An overview. In R. Olaniyan (Ed.), *African history and culture* (pp. 1–15). Lagos, Nigeria: Longman.

Reagan, T. (1996). *Non-western educational traditions: Alternative approaches to educational thought and practice.* Mahwah, NJ: Erlbaum.

Republic of Cameroon. (1993). *Indicateurs demographique sur le Cameroun.* Yaounde: Republic of Cameroon.

Segall, M.H., Dasen, P.R., Berry, J.W., & Poortinga, Y.H. (1999). *Human behavior in global perspective.* Boston: Allyn & Bacon.

Serpell, R. (1992, April). *Afrocentrism: What contribution to science of developmental psychology.* Paper presented at the Ist ISSBD Regional Workshop on Child Development and National Development in Africa, Yaounde, Cameroon.

Serpell, R. (1993). *The significance of schooling: Life-journeys in an African society.* Cambridge: Cambridge University Press.

Serpell, R. (1994). An African social ontogeny: Review of A. Bame Nsamenang (1992): Human development in cultural context. *Cross-Cultural Psychology Bulletin, 28*(1), 17–21.

Serpell, R. (1996). Commentary on Freitag's lead article: The role of the school in child development. *ISSBD Newsletter, 1*(29), 5.

Tangwa, G.F. (1996). Bioethics: An African perspective. *Bioethics, 10*(3), 183–200.

The Ouagadougou Declaration. (1993). *Ouagadougou declaration on the education of the girl child.* Ouagadougou: UNESCO.

Tomasello, M., Kruger, A.C., & Ratner, H.H. (1993). Cultural learning. *Behavioral and Brain Sciences, 16,* 405–552.

Trevarthen, C. (1980). The foundation of intersubjectivity: Development of interpersonal and cooperative understanding in infants. In D.R. Olsen (Ed.), *The social foundations of language and thought* (pp. 316–342). New York: Wiley.

Wright, R.A. (1984). Preface to the first edition. In R.A. Wright (Ed.), *African philosophy* (pp. i–xvi). Lanham, MD: University Press of America.

ട 8 ൞

Modernization and Changes in Adolescent Social Life

ALICE SCHLEGEL

The Question

Adolescence is a period when the young prepare for their future lives as adults. Modern and developing nations invest heavily in the cognitive training of adolescents, teaching them the knowledge and skills that the educational establishment believes they need to know. This teaching is imparted in schools, in which a few adults instruct a fairly large number of students and guide them through the comprehension and production of written materials. During school hours, adolescents are in peer centred settings, away from the adult centred settings of the family and community. For many adolescents in industrial nations, their after school hours are spent either alone, studying or listening to music or both at the same time, or with friends, that is, in another peer centred setting. The extension of schooling along with other changes in social arrangements have resulted in a shift of adolescents away from participation with adults to increased time in the company of peers.

Is this segregation of adolescents and adults a matter of concern? That was one question that Herbert Barry and I addressed in our book *Adolescence: An anthropological inquiry*, an investigation of how adolescents behave and are treated in preindustrial societies (Schlegel & Barry, 1991). Our data were obtained from the histories and ethnographies of cultures in the Standard Cross-Cultural

Sample, a sample of 186 tribal and traditional societies. While this sample is not random, it is representative of preindustrial societies in all regions of the world.

The Cross-Cultural Method

The method we used is known as the cross-cultural method, in which cultures are the units of analysis. The cross-cultural method tests theory by establishing statistically significant associations between and among variables such that one could be said to cause the other, or all could be the result of a common cause. The method was originally developed on the premise that social facts are knowable and can be explained, that is, the social world follows "laws" as does the natural world. Over the years, users of the method have talked less of social laws and more about tendencies, and students are warned from the beginning that correlations do not prove the cause. The expectations of the early developers of the method to establish a science of society comparable to the natural sciences have been somewhat modified; nevertheless, comparisons of various types are the closest methods anthropology has to experimentation in the natural sciences. The cross-cultural method allows for the large array of naturally occurring cases, individual cultures, to be utilized. There is a huge body of literature on this method (for basic instruction, see Naroll, Michik, & Naroll, 1976).

The problem to be studied has to be amenable to reduction into operationalized terms. The cultural variables to be tested are measures of the social or psychological aspects of interest. For example, one may be interested in studying whether poor maternal care is an antecedent of fear of female ghosts. "Poor maternal care" may be operationalized as harsh weaning practices, physical punishment either through fear or physical means, lack of attention to a child's needs, or any number of other measures. Of all possible measures, the ones chosen should be those that are mentioned in ethnographies; otherwise, there will be very few cases of cultures with information to allow for testing.

There is no perfect sample of cultures, as the parameters of the universe from which the sample is drawn—all human cultures— are unknown and unknowable. Even if one were to take the universe of all human cultures at one point in time, say, 1600, the cultures on which information is available would be incomplete and probably unrepresentative of the total universe. Limiting the universe to preindustrial cultures on which adequate information is available presents a daunting task. The comparativist, therefore, has to rely on a sample.

The purpose of a sample is to be representative of the universe to which the results of the study apply. Statistical purists insist that a sample be random, on the grounds that statistical tests of significance are not suitable for other kinds of samples. However, cultures are not independent units; because of diffusion or common origin, neighbouring cultures are in general more like one another than they are like cultures at great distances. Therefore, random samples will probably include similar cultures, biasing the results. The solution Murdock (1966) suggested, and the one he had applied in constructing the World Ethnographic Sample of 565 cultures, is to stratify the sample by geographic area. In this way, the researcher avoids selecting close neighbours and also ensures that all world regions are equally represented. A later and more feasible version of this, the Standard Cross-cultural Sample of 186 cultures (Murdock & White, 1980/1969) has been widely used in the preparation of codes and for testing hypotheses.

If the variables to be tested have been adequately operationalized, it would seem that coding from ethnographic literature should be a fairly mechanical process. This is almost never the case. First, the operationalized variables themselves have to be carefully defined; thus the variable "harsh weaning practices" includes a range of behaviours like threats, punishment, unpleasant substances, neglect by the mother, or anything else that frightens or discomfits the infant. A coder should test the code; and if there is more than one coder, they have to work together to arrive at common understandings of the code. Codes that measure personality traits or dispositions through variables such as behaviours or socialization pressures are among the most complex and call for the greatest degree of coder training (Barry, Josephson, Lauer, & Marshall, 1980).

Statistical testing procedures depend on the quantity and type of data, whether nominal, ordinal, or interval. Much of the analysis is bivariate; multivariate and linear regression analyses are often impossible because of the small number of societies with information on the selected variable. For example, a researcher may be interested in the relationship among variables X, Y, and Z, but one-third of the sample may have information on X and Y, one-third on Y and Z, and one-third on X and Z.

The conscientious cross-cultural researcher understands that results, even those that support a hypothesis, can be interpreted in various ways, and that it is necessary to consider alternative explanations for positive (or negative) results. The analysis of deviant cases, those that do not conform to the pattern of association, is often illuminating and may allow the researcher to refine the hypothesis.

Social scientists often advocate triangulation, or the replication of the study by another method, as a means for checking results. The cross-cultural method is useful for testing hypotheses generated by or tested in single case studies. Similarly, field based studies are useful for checking and developing further the investigations of cross-cultural research. Another validation procedure is "subsystem validation", the within-culture test comparing different populations like age cohorts or social classes, within the same culture. Triangulation often occurs spontaneously when researchers using different research methods, even scholars from different disciplines, work on similar or related problems.

Cross-cultural studies have been conducted on a number of topics that are directly related to human development such as adolescent initiation ceremonies, father absence, sleeping arrangements, taboos related to reproduction (for example, menstrual, pregnancy, and postpartum taboos), taboos concerned with the ingestion of food or other substances, and other kinds of taboos (cf. Levinson & Malone, 1980).

The Social Organization of Adolescence

To begin our study of adolescence, the first question we asked was whether all cultures recognize adolescence, a social stage intervening between childhood and adulthood. We found this stage in all the cases in the sample. There is no society, that I know of either in or outside the Standard Sample, that forces children directly into adulthood. The content of this stage, however, may vary greatly from one culture to another. In some cultures, adolescence is believed to be a period of emotional turbulence and rebellion, a familiar but largely untrue stereotype of adolescence in Western nations, in others, like the Japanese aristocracy before the Second World War, adolescents may be docile and placid (Lebra, 1990). Within a single culture, adolescent attitudes and behaviour may differ in accordance with the social class or the social setting (for a comparison of two Ijo villages in Nigeria, see Leis & Hollos, 1995).

In a number of societies, including some tribal and traditional groups as well as modern industrial nations, there is a second stage preceding adulthood, which I have labelled as *youth*. In cultures which have a youth stage, youths engage in more adult-like activities as compared to their adolescent sisters and brothers, such as working more independently, preparing seriously for marriage, or going to war. The line between adolescence and youth may be blurred, although there are observable changes in the way young people are treated and in what is expected of them as they enter into their late teens and early 20s. A youth stage is usually recognized in cultures that delay marriage for at least one sex, since in most societies marriage marks the entry of a person into social adulthood. For example, among the Maasai, as in some other cattle keeping tribes of East Africa, girls married shortly after puberty and their adolescence was short. For boys, however, marriage was delayed several years while they were warriors who defended their herds and raided those of other villages. These *moran*, adolescents and youths in the age group of 15 to the mid-20s, were the embodiment of Maasai masculinity (see Llewellyn-Davies, 1981). (For a discussion of American "emerging adults" as he calls them, see Arnett, 2000).

Unlike younger children, adolescents in tribal and traditional societies may be active participants in public life. They have to be involved in any discussion of the social organization of a community. To show how adolescents fit into the general pattern of social organization, I have constructed a model of what I call the elementary structure of human society (see Figure 8.1). This model depicts the fundamental social groups that are found everywhere: adult women, adult men, adolescent girls, adolescent boys, and the family and kinship group, these comprising both sexes and different generations. The model is based on data from both the cross-cultural study of adolescence (Schlegel & Barry, 1991) as well as a broad survey of ethnographic and historical studies.

Figure 8.1
The Elementary Structure of Human Society

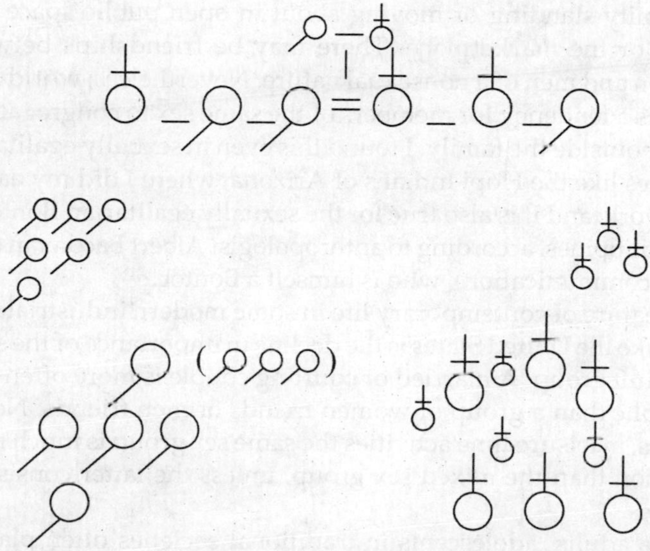

Note: The Venus figures represent females, the Mars figures represent males. The small figures represent adolescents. The distribution indicates that while both sexes have their peer groups, girls are also incorporated into groups of women whereas boys are on the spatial and social periphery of men's groups. The family is represented as a small nuclear unit only for purposes of convenience.

At the centre of the model is the family and kin group. Family types range from the nuclear family, a two-generation unit with the married or otherwise bonded couple at its centre, to the extended or joint family that includes several related married pairs and their unmarried children. Even where the nuclear family is the norm, the young couple in most societies until recently typically lived near the parents of at least one of the partners, and there was reciprocal aid between the households. Thus, adolescents in most societies have a range of adult kin other than parents with whom they are in constant or frequent contact.

Outside of these kin based structures, adults tend to divide into single sex groups during leisure time or when the activities do not require the participation of both sexes. There are, of course, occasions in many societies for women and men to mingle freely, such as feasts or other festivities. Men and women may also be in close proximity standing or moving about in open public space as a street or the marketplace. There may be friendships between women and men of a nonsexual nature. Nevertheless, worldwide there is a tendency for members of the same sex to congregate together outside the family. I found this even in sexually egalitarian cultures like the Hopi Indians of Arizona, where I did my earlier fieldwork; and it is also true for the sexually egalitarian Bontoc of the Philippines, according to anthropologist Albert Bacdayan (personal communication), who is himself a Bontoc.

A feature of contemporary life in some modern industrial societies like the United States is the decline in importance of the same sex adult group. A married or courting couple is more often seen in public than a group of women friends or men friends. Nevertheless, in leisure time activities the same sex group is much more common than the mixed sex group, unless the latter consists of couples.

Like adults, adolescents in traditional societies often play an active role in the public sphere as workers or participants in community activities. Children, of course, are visible in public places, but they have little social importance except as consumers of public resources in nations that provide services like schools, parks, and medical facilities for them. It is expected that children are firmly embedded in their families, which explains the special concern for young orphans and street children who do not, or do not seem to, have families to protect and shelter them. In contrast, adolescents are expected to show greater responsibility and to be able to interact with adults in a more mature way, even though equality is denied them until they reach social adulthood.

Although gender differences are evident even among young children, they become marked at adolescence. These differences are manifest in the position of adolescent girls and boys in both the family and the larger society.

One feature that affects how girls and boys relate to other family members is the residence pattern of married couples. If one person leaves the family at marriage but the other stays, the transferring person and his or her family prepare for the move by attenuation of family ties during adolescence. Where only girls move out at marriage, they retain strong ties of affection for parents, but their brothers may be more significant figures in their adult lives than their sisters, who have transferred their attention to their husbands' families.

Where boys move out at marriage, the reverse is seen. For example, among the formerly matrilocal Hopi, a man's primary economic responsibilities were to his wife and children, but his sisters and their children were not far behind. In addition, he acted as an authority figure to his sisters' children rather than to his own. Parents in patrilocal societies often indulge young daughters, just as Hopi parents would indulge young sons, as compensation for the difficulties they would face as young brides or grooms in the homes of their in-laws. In cultures with nuclear family households, both sons and daughters have to be socialized for some measure of independence from the family of birth. In spite of some cultural variations, worldwide patterns show gender differences.

Adolescent girls and boys in all cultures are firmly attached to their families. In most tribal and traditional cultures, adolescents work alongside the parent of the same sex on the family's productive tasks. There are exceptions, however; in hunting bands, adolescent boys may not have the strength or skill to keep up with adult men on the hunt; and in pastoral economies, adolescents are likely to be herders who take their families' cattle or sheep away from the village for the day.

Nevertheless, the involvement of girls in their families is greater than that of boys. By that I mean that when they are not working on a specific task, girls spend more time with female family members, including their mothers, than boys spend with their fathers or other male kin. Girls are also more intimate, i.e., confiding and close, with mothers than boys are with parents of either sex. These features are presented in Table 8.1. This is true even of cultures which value sons more than daughters, as in Japan or India.

Girls accompany their mothers and other adult relatives to gatherings of women. Mixed age groups of adolescent girls and

Table 8.1
Contact and Intimacy with Parents

	Boys' Mean Score		Girls' Mean Score	
	Contact	Intimacy	Contact	Intimacy
Mother	2.4 (126)	5.3 (92)	7.1 (133)	6.4 (51)
Father	5.3 (134)	4.8 (56)	2.5 (122)	4.1 (47)

Source: Schlegel and Barry, 1991, p. 46. Numbers in parentheses indicate number
of societies in the sample for which data are available.

women are common in preindustrial societies, from the pottery-
making sessions of the Hopi to the gathering parties of the !Kung
Bushmen to the groups of Sicilian women neighbours, sitting
together as they embroider and discuss matters of common interest. This free mixing of females of all ages is depicted in Figure 8.1.

The model reveals that girls also have peer groups, apart from
their associations with adult women. However, these groups are
not as large or as structured as those of boys, nor do girls spend as
much time exclusively with peers as boys do.

When boys are not engaged in some task with adult men, they
are likely to be congregating with other boys. At times a boys'
peer group may be in the proximity of, but beyond the visual proximity of adult men; at other times they hang around the periphery
of a group of adult men. Boys have to wait to be accepted into the
adult male group until they get married or have experienced whatever else it is that marks the transition to adulthood. Unlike girls,
who are incorporated into all-female groups, boys remain both
physically and socially on the periphery.

I want to emphasize that although there are gender differences,
the general pattern is that adolescents have much contact with
adults, particularly adults of the same sex. Girls and boys who
work away from the home and kin are supervised by persons
of the same sex. In many parts of Eurasia, adolescent boys and
girls are sent to custodial institutions such as boarding schools or
monasteries and convents which have till recently been sexually
segregated.

Deviating from the worldwide tendency of adolescents to have
considerable contact with adults of the same sex, there are some
cases in the sample in which boys (but not girls) do spend considerable time with peers. This variation among boys is associated
with differences in attitudes toward anti-social behaviour: in those

cultures that are rated below the mean for boys' contact with adult men, boys are more likely to commit anti-social acts (see Table 8.2). In other words, most cultures treat adolescents in ways that are conducive to conformity to cultural norms by including them in adult activities and monitoring their actions.

Table 8.2
Boys' Relations to Adults and Their Expected Antisocial Behaviour

	N	r	p
Adult men are principal companions	50	-.36	.024
Adult men are principal companions outside the home	42	-.43	014

Source: Schlegel and Barry, 1991, p. 137.

Ensuring that adolescents are included in the company of adults promotes compliant behaviour for two reasons. First, children do not usually misbehave in adult centred settings because they know that punishment is swift and sure. Second, children who are actively engaged with adults in positive, non-exploitive ways wish to please them and win their approval and respect. They learn to control their impulses in order to achieve this goal. This extends to times when children are not being supervised directly.

Another feature of adolescent life in many tribal and traditional societies that strikes the modern observer is the degree of participation in community activities, especially of boys. The energy of adolescents is often harnassed by the local community for civic welfare; the peer group, often but not always under the supervision of adult men, is assigned the task of cleaning the streets or other such work. In Europe and some parts of Asia there was a long tradition of adolescents and youths organizing festivities on public holidays, like dances at Christmas in Hungary (Kresz, 1976) or public displays at Ramadan in Malaysia (Khadijah Muhamed, personal communication).

The Exclusion of Adolescents from Adult Life

The isolation of most American teenagers—middle and high school students—from adult life is so commonplace that

Americans take it for granted. When problems of teenagers attract public notice, one of the first responses is to "do something for the kids" by providing places like youth centres where they can congregate after school, or by organizing teen focused activities like age segregated festivities. It never occurs to anyone that perhaps "the kids" need more time with adults instead of each other.

The isolation of adolescents from adult company and activities has been documented in a study of middle class American high school students by Csikzentmihalyi and Larson (1984). They found that subjects spent only 13.3 per cent of their time with their parents and other adult kin and only 2 per cent with other adults. This was almost the same amount of time they spent with same sex friends apart from the classroom, and much less time than they spent with their classmates (23 per cent) or alone (27 per cent). Time spent with all family members and relatives, of any age, was 19 per cent.

From these figures, we can see that one factor in the segregation of American adolescents is the school, which keeps them in peer centred settings for much of the day. Since school is over by about 3 o'clock in the afternoon, how do they spend the rest of the day?

Many adolescents work after school hours and on weekends. They may work in adult centred settings like dry-cleaning establishments or small shops, but often they work in places where they are either alone—such as stacking boxes at the back of a grocery store—or in the company of other adolescent workers, as in most fast food restaurants (Greenberger & Steinberg, 1986). Rarely do they work in close association with adults who monitor their performance and teach them physical or cognitive skills that they would draw on when they attain adulthood.

Adults generally believe and state that adolescents prefer to be with their peers rather than with adults. It is true that at this stage of life, relations with parents can become somewhat strained and adolescents may seek refuge from parental company. This may be particularly true of nuclear families, where both boys and girls are preparing for independence at the same time that they are subordinate within their parents' home. Although some reorientation of family relations is probably inevitable in all cultures as people move out of childhood and want to assume some control over their own lives, very few cultures expect adolescence to be a time of turbulence or rebellion. Even in those cultures where some tension is expected between parents and adolescent children, these tensions do not necessarily spill over into relations with other relatives or with adult neighbours and friends. If anything, adolescents hunger for recognition and respect from adults whom they like and look up to. When there are difficulties at home, the opportunity to turn to friendly adults outside the home becomes a great source of comfort and reassurance.

However, where can American adolescents find such adults with whom they can share close and sustained personal relationships? Teachers, scout leaders, and others who work with adolescents are often sympathetic, but they do not necessarily have the time or interest to maintain close sustained contacts with the young under their charge. If a young person is lucky, a grandparent or a neighbour or a family friend is available. But this is hit or miss. With most Americans working, no adults are available in the afternoons, when young people would be most likely to visit neighbours or to come under their surveillance. More importantly, there are very few institutions in America that provide settings where adults and adolescents have close and sustained contact outside the home. Even churches and other religious institutions, for all their emphasis on family and community, segregate the social activities of their congregations by age and status into adult groups separate from youth groups. Thus, the church simply replicates the peer centred settings of the school.

The desire for adult contact and recognition was brought home to me when I interviewed a group of teenage participants in an apprenticeship programme initiated by the state government of Wisconsin (Schlegel, 1996). For all of them, good relations with adult co-workers were very important, and they were proud to be accepted and taken seriously by those with whom they worked. Several of them made special mention of having been invited to parties given by co-workers to celebrate a baby's christening or a new house.

Not all American adolescents lack significant adult contacts outside the home. Many of them have close and sustained relations with adults and try to act in ways that will win their approval. Even when deprived of these contacts they thrive, because they are focused on activities that absorb their attention. However, many adolescents who do not have close adult contacts may do well or adequately in school and stay out of trouble, but they do not learn the behaviours and social skills that would ensure their smooth transition to adult society. Consequently, they are ill prepared for adult responsibilities like full-time work and participation in civic life.

Are Adolescents Inevitably Isolated in Industrially Developed Societies?

We have seen two patterns. One is the traditional pattern, no longer applicable in most parts of the developed or developing world as family enterprises decline and schooling for adolescents extends over the greater part of the day. The other is the extreme form of isolation that exists in America. The question is: Can adults and adolescents be brought together in meaningful ways that fit into a modern industrial, economic and social structure? I shall examine two modern societies where I have done field research.

GERMANY

From 1994 to 1997, I directed a field project in Frankfurt, studying adolescent industrial apprentices. The field sites were two large factory based training centres, which were run as in-house schools although they included actual work experience on the factory floors, and several small craft shops. Alongwith two German researchers, I observed these apprentices in their workplace settings and in the special vocational schools that they had to attend 1½ days per week. We interviewed each apprentice along with the training personnel and some of the school teachers and directors. My interest was not in vocational education per se but rather whether adolescents who are in an adult centred setting (the small shops) differ in measurable ways from adolescents who are in a peer centred setting (the factory schools). It became apparent from the interviews as well as from conversations with the apprentices and others that adolescents in Germany were far more integrated into adult activities than American adolescents. This may be particularly true for working and middle class adolescents and those living in villages and small towns (which accounts for a majority of the population).

One of the mechanisms for this integration is the kin network. Employers believe that workers would rather be jobless than move to find a job, and the generous German welfare system makes this possible. Reluctance to move is not simply irrational sentiment: as the interviews revealed, dense webs of mutual aid existed among kin and also among old friends, especially those who grew up together. These connections were maintained through family visits and frequent family gatherings. Several of the apprentices mentioned birthdays of grandparents and others and how these were occasions for them to meet all their relatives. Adult siblings, in-laws, cousins, and other kin supported one another in household projects, and provided each other appliances and other goods that they were able to buy at a steep discount from the factories or stores where they worked. It would be irrational to give up this aid, and the possibility of a job obtained in the future through personal connections, for a present job at some distance.

Kinship and close neighbourhood ties brought together people of different ages into groups with similar interests. One apprentice, for example, spoke of being constantly in the company of his older male cousins, in their mid-20s, who left the group one by one as they got married and associated more with other married couples. (I assume that the married ones met as couples, and that wives were incorporated into their husbands' friendship circles as husbands were incorporated into their wives' unless their circles were the same, which was not unusual.) Boys who accompanied their fathers in outdoor activities—one of them mentioned surfing trips—also associated with their fathers' adult male companions. Within the neighbourhood, it was impossible not to maintain contact with adults who had known and observed a person ever since his or her birth.

Apprenticeship is, of course, a formal occupational institution that brings together adults and adolescents and about two-thirds of all young Germans enter an apprenticeship sometime between the ages of about 15 and 17, when they leave full-time school. This means that adolescents work alongside adults for most of the day in factories, shops, and business offices. Even though they attended vocational school part-time, the apprentices in the study made it clear that they wanted to be called workers rather than students.

There are other formal institutions, in the sense of structured organizations, that bring adolescents and adults together. These are civil institutions designed for public benefit and recognized as a vital part of community life. One such institution in German towns is the voluntary firefighters association. There are relatively few professional firefighting units in Germany, the others draw on members from the community. Until recently, these units were composed only of men, but now they include women and girls as well. Although the associations are split into senior and junior divisions, the latter for young people between the ages of 14 and 18 years, the older members train the younger ones, and all members get together after practice sessions. If there is an occasion to celebrate such as a member's birthday, beer is served and the older adolescents drink with their elders. Nearly half of the apprentices were members of such an association.

Political socialization is taken seriously in Germany. Each political party has a youth branch organized at the state, county, and local levels. Adolescents join these at the age of about 16, and by the time they are 18, i.e., legal voting age, they can run for offices within them. The upper age limit is around 25 years. The purpose of these organizations is not to provide unskilled labour for political campaigns, as the Young Republicans and Young Democrats wings of American political parties, but rather to give the young a say in national politics. At the local level, members discuss local problems like the need for traffic lights, and they may undertake such civic activities as removing trash from a stream. At the county and state levels, representatives discuss larger issues and declare their positions on them that are conveyed to the national party, where they are discussed. The positions taken by the youth branch are not necessarily in concordance with those of the political party. On the issue of abortion, for example, a local youth branch defied the national party by taking a public stand in favour of women's right to choose abortion. Although they were reprimanded by the party headquarters for their defiance, they stood their ground and there was nothing the headquarters could do about it.

An important part of social life is the *Verein*, or a registered special purpose association. There is a *Verein* for every imaginable hobby or interest: instrumental and choral music-making, gardening, hunting, etc. A popular one, especially with boys and men, is the local *Sportverein*. Sports training and competitive matches are organized through these associations, and people join teams on the basis of ability rather than age. Older, more competent members train the younger ones, so that often adolescents train children and young adults train adolescents. Almost all adolescent boys, and even many girls, are members of these clubs.

A special type of *Verein* found in Catholic villages and towns is the *Karnevalsverein*, or the association that is involved in year-round planning and preparing for *Fasching*, the Carnival season. This is the period before Lent, when Christians prepare themselves spiritually for the commemoration of Christ's death by reflecting on their sins and repenting for them. The Carnival is the last phase of merrymaking before Lent, and it is enthusiastically celebrated in Catholic countries and towns. In German Catholic villages, preparations for the next year's Carnival begin as early as immediately after Easter. Along with this association, these towns also support various religious brotherhoods and sisterhoods that draw adolescents into church related activities. Some adolescents in the sample were active participants in a *Karnevalsverein*.

In addition to the *Vereine*, which are legally registered for insurance and other purposes, there are innumerable informal clubs. Adolescents also form ad hoc associations with adults: one of the apprentices, living in Frankfurt, visited the park whenever the weather was fine, where he played chess or cards with a group of men of all ages who used this as their social centre. He made friends with a couple of these men, who helped him in various ways. This was neither odd nor unusual.

It may seem strange to regard a drinking establishment as an informal civil institution, but the *Kneipe*, or local pub, serves as a meeting point for neighbours and friends. Though the legal age of drinking is 16 years, younger adolescents are served if they behave themselves and particularly if they are acquainted with the bartender. While they may not be sharing a table with adults, they are under the surveillance of people who are their relatives and neighbours. There they learn how to conduct themselves in public places.

Most German adolescents are involved with adults through kinship and neighbourhood circles and through membership of civil associations. In addition, nearly two-thirds are enrolled in white-collar or blue-collar apprenticeship programmes, through which they work alongside adults as they learn their job. While the German apprenticeship system is probably the best known, similar systems exist in Austria and Switzerland, particularly in German-speaking Switzerland. There are apprenticeship programmes in other European countries also, but either they are not as extensive as the ones in Germany or they have not been as well reported.

NORTHERN ITALY

Participation in economic and voluntary social institutions is not the only way of integrating adolescents and adults. Following my investigations in Germany, I conducted research over two summers in Siena, in the province of Tuscany, which has another form of civil institution that calls for intergenerational participation. This is the *contrada*, a structure that developed during the Middle Ages (by about the fourteenth century) and has been retained in that former city state, albeit in a modified form (for a history of the *contrada*, see Dundes & Falassi, 1975).

Contrade are the districts into which intramural Siena is divided, 17 in all. Today Siena has expanded to include areas outside the ancient city walls, but many people who live in these areas retain *contrada* membership acquired through their parents or from having once lived in the old historic city. Traditionally, a person belongs to the *contrada* in which he or she was born; it is possible to become a member of the *contrada* by moving into the district, although a native Sienese would not change *contrada* affiliation even though he or she has shifted to another district.

This suggests that there is more to *contrada* membership than simply being a resident of a city district. *Contrada*, in fact, has two meanings: the district itself, and the association of that district, into which one is initiated during infancy or later through a *contrada* "baptism", as it is called, administered by the current *priori* or president of that *contrada*. For most Sienese, these two meanings are conflated. The *contrada* association is the most active civil institution in the city, superseding the Church not only in the organization of societal events, but also in the intensity of participation. Participation begins during childhood in outings and other activities organized by *contrada* women, and becomes greater during adolescence.

Each *contrada* (as an association) owns a *contrada* hall which has meeting facilities, a chapel, a museum for housing trophies and other *contrada* valuables, and a *circolo* or club where members (primarily but not exclusively men and boys) meet and can invite their friends. *Contrade* also own property like apartment buildings, purchased with funds donated by the members. To have a say in *contrada* affairs, members are expected to be involved: poorer members and adolescents often organize *contrada* events, while richer members donate large sums of money. *Contrada* events include public dinners for which tickets are sold, outings to various tourist spots, parades of *contrada* men and boys dressed in medieval costumes through the streets of old Siena, and the Palio.

One cannot understand the intensity of *contrada* loyalty and passion without an understanding of the Palio. This is the famous horse race in Siena's Piazza Publico held twice a year, in July and August. Ten *contrade* participate in each race, with rules specifying which ones can enter horses each time. A complete description of the Palio is not warranted here; suffice it to say that rivalry is intense and the entire Palio period is marked by much tension and enjoyment.

Adolescents play a very active role in *contrada* life, as by the age of 16 or so they are expected to serve the *contrada*. Teenage boys often serve as bartenders at the *circolo* bars, where coffee and soft drinks are served (although there are no laws or norms against adolescents drinking or selling wine and beer). Girls assist adult women in preparing food for *contrada* dinners and both boys and girls are assigned duties like setting up tables, serving the food, and cleaning up.

An important function of adolescent boys and slightly older youths is to march in *contrada* parades carrying the *contrada* banners. The parade halts at various places along the way; the flag-bearers toss these heavy banners high into the air so that they unfurl and then catch them before they hit the ground. These young men in their early and mid-20s train adolescent boys in this highly prized skill. These adolescents, in turn, train younger boys of 8 or so to beat the drums that accompany the parade.

Palio period is marked by intense rivalries between *contrade*. Every *contrada* is on friendly terms with two or three other *contrade*, and has the same number of rivals. When horses of enemy *contrade* run in the same Palio, the rivalry that is at other times somewhat playful becomes serious. Gangs of teenage boys and young men from enemy *contrade* challenge each other and fights break out, although the rules of fighting preclude serious injury in most cases. Troops of teenage girls march through the streets and piazzas singing offensive songs about enemy *contrade*, their songs portray the men as weaklings and the girls and women as sluts. All this rivalry intensifies the loyalty of the young to their *contrada* and reinforces their devotion to *contrada* members and *contrada* pursuits.

This brief introduction to the *contrada* shows that adolescent integration into adult centred activities can take the form of contributing to civic life in ways different from those of Germany. Siena is not only a centre of art and history as a United Nations World Heritage City; but is also a venue for banking and has a flourishing tourist industry. This socially progressive city has managed to preserve in a modified form those ancient traditions that bring the young and the old together in ways that prevent the emergence of a generation gap.

Siena is unique in the degree to which district loyalties pervade civic life, but other Italian cities may also have their district traditions. Villages in Tuscany, too small for distinct districts, also bring the young and the old together in rather different ways. For instance, adolescents and adults of the village gather in the central piazza to chat, drink coffee or wine, play cards, and dance if there is music. Integration across the generations is possible even in the most modern industrial centres, if various types of social structures are designed in a way that bring adolescents and adults together.

Is There a Lesson for India Here?

Germany and Italy are relatively homogeneous countries. Both are Christian, although Germany has been divided between Protestant and Catholic communities since the seventeenth century. The small ethnic and religious minorities in each nation do not play any important role in political or social life. Late twentieth century prosperity and progressive laws regarding employment and welfare have removed the distinctions between rich and poor, and education is provided to all by the state.

In contrast, India is the most heterogeneous nation in the world, marked by ethnic, religious, caste, and regional differences. The wide differences in wealth and opportunity are captured by the title of Verma and Saraswathi's (2002) paper, "Adolescence in India: Street urchins or Silicon Valley millionaires?". With all its diversity, do the lessons of Europe, where age integration has been preserved, and the United States, where it has been lost, have something to offer India?

The one commonality that almost all Indians share is the tradition of the joint family system.[1] Whether in a village or an old established urban area, the patriarchal household consisting of three generations—parents, unmarried children, and one or more married sons along with their wives and children—is known throughout the land. Furthermore, the traditional joint family is embedded in close circles of kinship and neighbourhood. If the family farms or runs a small productive or mercantile enterprise, adolescent boys (and even girls) assist in the family business, full-time in poorer families, part-time in those families that can afford to keep their adolescent children in school. Adolescents from the middle to upper classes use their free time for leisure and personal development.

Among the lowest one-third of the population, children and adolescents are likely to be engaged in full-time employment. Many of them work for wages. Unlike the apprentices in Germany, there is no career ladder for these children. Their future as adults is characterized by unemployment and low paid work, and exploitation. Those at the bottom of the economic scale often come from broken and abusive families; and adolescents and younger children from these families may flee and lead precarious lives on the streets.

Regardless of the personal circumstances of adolescents in traditional cultures, majority of them are fully integrated into adult based settings of kin and neighbourhood groups and, for those who work outside the family, places of employment. But for some that is changing.

Like other developing nations, India has modern urban sectors that have emerged from its traditional village and small city base. In my discussions with people who belong to this modern sector, largely middle class educated women and men, it is clear that the changes taking place in family and social life not only affect adolescents, but also how they are socialized.

---

[1] Unless otherwise indicated, the information on Indian adolescents comes from Verma and Saraswathi, 2002.

One such change is the decline in family size. This means that the kin network is already small for some people, and it will be far more in the next generation. Another change is the increasing mobility of families of professionals and employees of large corporations, with the result that adolescents cannot easily maintain regular daily or even weekly contact with their kin. With occupational and geographical mobility, neighbourhood relations are attenuated as well. There is no guarantee that the old neighbours who watched the child grow will be available when the child reaches adolescence. Neighbourhood relations may be cordial, but neighbours are not likely to have a close, confiding relationship with, or even care much about, someone they hardly know.

Most young Indians today, as in the past, are socialized primarily by their family, the kin network, and to some extent by the neighbourhood and caste (*jati*). As mobility removes people from these localized structures, what will replace them? It is unrealistic to expect schools alone to successfully prepare adolescents for the adult world, for the school is itself a peer based setting. Young people need daily contact with adults from whom they can learn informally, by observation and imitation as well as instruction. They need to hear tales of caution, the informal remarks of approval or disapproval of their own actions and those of others, to learn what the boundaries are and what directions to take. The school cannot provide this. Parents, of course, have primary importance; but as young people step out into the world as adolescents, they need close association with other adults and the sense of becoming a part of the larger community.

More and more middle class Indian youths, and those of other classes who also live in families isolated from familiar networks, will be focused on peers: indeed, there is already evidence of a distinct peer culture among upper middle and upper class adolescents (Verma & Saraswathi, 2002). Will they become like American teenagers, excluded from significant participation in the life of the community? Or, can Indian occupational and civil institutions include adolescents, replacing kinship, caste, and neighbourhood structures that are weakening with other structures?

References

Arnett, J.J. (2000). Emerging adulthood: A theory of development from the late teens through the twenties. *American Psychologist, 55*, 469–480.

Barry, H. III, Josephson, L., Lauer, E., & Marshall, C. (1980). Infancy and early childhood: Cross-cultural codes 2. In H. Barry & A. Schlegel (Eds), *Cross-cultural samples and codes* (pp. 205–236). Pittsburgh: University of Pittsburgh Press.

Csikszentmihalyi, M., & Larson, R. (1984). *Being adolescent: Conflict and growth in the teenage years.* New York: Basic Books.

Dundes, A., & Falassi, A. (1975). *La terra in Piazza: An interpretation of the Palio of Siena.* Berkeley, CA: University of California Press.

Greenberger, E., & Steinberg, L. (1986). *When teenagers work: The psychological and social costs of adolescent employment.* New York: Basic Books.

Kresz, M. (1976). The community of young people in a Transylvanian village. In Estelle Fuchs (Ed.), *Youth in a changing world: Cross-cultural perspectives on adolescence* (pp. 207–212). The Hague: Mouton.

Lebra, T.S. (1990). The socialization of aristocratic children by commoners: Recalled experiences of the hereditary elite in modern Japan. *Cultural Anthropology, 5*, 78–100.

Leis, P.E., & Hollos, M. (1995). Intergenerational discontinuity in Nigeria. *Ethos, 23*, 103–118.

Levinson, D., & Malone, M.J. (1980). *Toward explaining human culture: A critical review of the findings of worldwide cross-cultural research.* New Haven: HRAF Press.

Llewellyn-Davies, M. (1981). Women, warriors, and patriarchs. In S.B. Ortner & H. Whitehead (Eds), *Sexual meanings: The cultural construction of gender and sexuality* (pp. 330–358). Cambridge: Cambridge University Press.

Murdock, G.P. (1966). Cross-cultural sampling. *Ethnology, 5*, 96–114.

Murdock, G.P., & White, D.R. (1980/1969). Standard cross-cultural sample. In H. Barry & A. Schlegel (Eds), *Cross-cultural samples and codes* (pp. 3–42). Pittsburgh: University of Pittsburgh Press.

Naroll, R., Michik, G.L., & Naroll, F. (1976). *Worldwide theory testing.* New Haven: HRAF Press.

Schlegel, A. (1996). *The Fox Valley apprenticeship program.* Report for the Menasha Corporation Foundation and the Fox Cities Chamber of Commerce. Unpublished manuscript, Arizona State University, Tucson.

Schlegel, A., & Barry, H. III. (1991). *Adolescence: An anthropological inquiry.* New York: Free Press.

Verma, S., & Saraswathi, T.S. (2002). Adolescence in India: Street urchins or Silicon Valley millionaires? In B. Brown, R. Larson, & T.S. Saraswathi (Eds), *World's youth. Adolescence in eight regions of the globe* (pp. 105–140). New York: Cambridge University Press.

ಌ 9 ಛ

Adolescence without Family Disengagement: The Daily Family Lives of Indian Middle Class Teenagers

REED LARSON, SUMAN VERMA*
& JODI DWORKIN*

Compared to other cultures, the Indian family is viewed as strong and cohesive (Bharat, 1997). India is often identified as the prime example of a collectivist (as opposed to individualistic) culture, with these collectivist values, more than anything else, embodied in strong family ties (Sinha, 1988; 1994). What does this mean in terms of Indian adolescents' family experience? Many Western people have difficulty in understanding that the adolescents' family experience in another culture could be any different than the ambivalence—the combination of distancing, individuation, and renegotiation—that characterizes parent–adolescent relationships in the West. This paper describes Indian adolescence in its own right, but also addresses this incredulity: Do Indian adolescents have a fundamentally different kind of experience with their families than adolescents in individualistic Western societies?

To address these concerns, we focus on the daily, hour-to-hour family experience reported by a sample of Indian middle class adolescents. How much time do teenagers in a collectivist culture

* The co-authors were coopted by Professor Larson for the preparation of this paper. Professor Larson was in Baroda as Visiting Fulbright Professor in December 1999.

such as this spend with their families, and in what types of situations? Do Indian adolescents experience positive emotions during this family time, or do they feel an undercurrent of unhappiness, irritability, and anger? Might time spent with their families provide richer developmental experiences? Unlike research on the abstract traits of adolescent–parent relationships, such as emotional autonomy and attachment, we are interested in what happens on the ground in daily life. What is the lived experience of this cultural group?

We approach our topic with a posture of critical inquiry. Our data show that middle class Indian adolescents spend most of their waking hours with their families, but we do not automatically assume that this is a positive experience. Is it possible that the traditional hierarchical nature of Indian families or tensions between spouses or in-laws make family members, though physically present, emotionally unresponsive to children? How much time do Indian adolescents actually spend talking to other family members? Do they experience other family members as responsive and friendly or as authoritarian? We also ask whether the ongoing socioeconomic changes in India tending towards both parents being employed and nuclear (as opposed to extended) households are related to changes in adolescents' family experience.

This paper by two Americans and an Indian attempts to build from our different cultural perspectives on adolescence. We have chosen to focus on the family experience of a sample of urban middle class Indian adolescents, a group that is experiencing (and initiating) dramatic cultural change. In some ways, this group is influenced by Western culture, particularly in their material acquisitions and lifestyle (such as drinking Coke and wearing Levis). However, there is much evidence to suggest that adolescence in India is not converging with Western adolescence (Verma & Saraswathi, 2002). Rather, we see the evolution of an alternate conception of this life period, particularly in its orientation toward the family.

Culture and Family Experience

In the West, individuation from family is seen as a developmental task of adolescence (Havighurst, 1953), and the process of distancing or "breaking away" from the family is endorsed by the cultural scripts of literature and films (Considine, 1985; Kiell, 1959). This does not necessarily mean rebellion and it certainly does not mean renouncing the family, but it does mean a mutual renegotiation of relationships with parents that grants adolescents more individual autonomy and leads them toward becoming independent adults who have a more peer-like relationship with their parents (Grotevant & Cooper, 1986; Hauser with Powers, & Noam, 1991; Hill & Holmbeck, 1987). In contrast to India, American culture places a high priority on adolescents' development of self-reliance and fulfilment of each individual's distinct potentials (Saraswathi & Ganapathy, 2002).

In terms of everyday family interactions, this process of change takes the form of diminishing daily contact. In a longitudinal study of 220 middle class European American youth, we found that as they moved into adolescence they spent less time at the kitchen table or on the living room floor and more time in the seclusion of their bedrooms. As they entered middle adolescence, they gained access to cars, and were given more freedom of movement by their parents, they spent less time at home and more time with their friends. The outcome was that time spent with family decreased from an average of 35 per cent of waking hours at age 10 to 14 per cent by the last year of high school (age 18). This disengagement from daily interaction with the family occurs at an age when American adolescents are experiencing new developmental challenges and could benefit from family support, thus we have questioned whether it occurs too soon for their good. Rutter and Smith (1995) questioned whether the insulation experienced by Western adolescents from adults, particularly their parents, may not be a contributing factor to psychosocial disorders. It should be noted, however, that while total family time decreased dramatically with age, the amount of time that these American adolescents spent alone with their mother, alone with their father, and talking with the family did not diminish over the junior and senior high school periods. This indicates that most American adolescents maintained an open channel of communication with their families, at the same time they became more behaviourally autonomous (Larson & Richards, 1991; Larson, Richards, Moneta, Holmbeck, & Duckett, 1996).

Across this same developmental period, we found that the average emotions experienced by these American adolescents when with their families dipped in early adolescence—they became more dysphoric—but the average rose again in late adolescence, indicating an improvement in the quality of experience in this later period (Larson et al., 1996). This trough in American adolescents' family experience has been noted by other researchers as well (Arnett, 1999; Laursen, Coy, & Collins, 1998). In our data, it took the form of less enjoyment of family time, and more experience of unhappiness, irritability, and anger, feelings that may be perceived as disassociative. This emotional trough suggests that American adolescents' time with their families is often not "quality time", at least for many youth. It may also be seen as intrinsic to the process of distancing and renegotiation in adolescent–parent relationships. In general, American adolescents experience time spent with their families as boring and unexciting, especially in comparison to time spent with friends, although it is also a context in which they feel more relaxed, comfortable, and safe—the family provides a secure base for the project of self-discovery and individuation (Csikszentmihalyi & Larson, 1984; Larson & Richards, 1994).

This scenario of distancing and renegotiation of relationships with the family is, of course, a modal path, and there is much variation among American adolescents. Across different teenagers, one sees a range in the degree of negative emotion and conflict. Furthermore, patterns differ across ethnic groups. A sample of African American adolescents of Grades 5–8 whom we studied did not show a decline with age in the amount of time spent with family, nor age related change in emotions experienced when with the family (Larson, Richards, Sims, & Dworkin, 2001). For European American adolescents, however, this process of distancing, with an ambivalent range of emotional experiences, is the normative pattern.

In India, there is much reason to expect that the normative adolescent scenario will be different. We have already mentioned collectivist values that place the family at the centre of people's lives (Bharat, 1997; Sinha, 1994). Far from romanticizing "breaking away", celebrated Indian epics, such as the Ramayana and the Mahabharata, provide scripts of lifelong devotion to parents; and traditional Indian values stress continuity rather than discontinuity

in family ties from childhood to adulthood (Kumar, 1993). In traditional Indian values, subordinating one's own individual needs
to the interests of the kinship group is perceived as a virtue (Saraswathi, 1999). Respect, trust, and deference to elders is taught to
children from an early age and "behavior that threatens the cooperative spirit and unity [of the family] is discouraged from surfacing"
(Bharat, 1997, p. 204). Hence, Ramanujam (1978) noted that independence is not valued in Indian families and is equated with dis-
obedience. The pursuit of individual autonomy occurs only among
older adults (Mines, 1988).

Within the growing Indian urban middle and upper class there
is greater differentiation of a distinct adolescent stage, but many
of the values toward family remain similar (Saraswathi, 1999). With
smaller families and less economic press, urban middle class parents are becoming less authoritarian, more child centred, and more
responsive to children (Kashyap, 1993; Saraswathi & Ganapathy,
2002). As compared to traditional rural families, these parents give
more weight to the psychological rather than economic value of
children; they value children as a source of love and personal
fulfilment (Kapadia & Shah, 1998; Srivastava, 1997). These changes,
however, have not altered the strong Indian value of family cohesiveness and the continuity of family connections into adulthood.
Parents often choose careers for their children, and, in the great
majority of cases, select their spouses (Ramu, 1988; Uplaonkar,
1995). Adolescents and young adults, irrespective of educational
level, generally accept that "parents know best" (Saraswathi, 1999).
Sudhir Kakar (1978) observed that strong ties to the family persist
into adulthood, with continued emotional dependence on the
family, particularly on mothers.

What does this mean in terms of the daily family experience of
Indian middle class adolescents? The data from Indian youth that
we consider in this paper do not allow us to evaluate age trends
as all the Indian subjects in our study were Grade 8 students. But
they do allow us to see what Indian adolescents' family experience
is like at an age that falls in the middle of American adolescents'
renegotiation and the middle of their emotional trough. How much
time do they spend with their families, and do they feel negative,
disassociative emotions even if they are enacting the cultural role
of being the filial child?

We also used these data to examine differences in the family
experience of Indian boys and girls. In traditional families, both

mothers and fathers have been described as showing a preference for sons (Bharat, 1997; Dube, 1998; Srivastava, 1997). However, increasing attention to the subjugated status of girls may lead to greater gender equality among children in some families, at least in the urban middle class (Datar, 1995; Saraswathi & Pai, 1997; also see Jain, 1994; Veeraraghawan & Srivastava, 1994). Do girls' and boys' daily patterns of family engagement and emotional involvement show convergence?

A Study of Indian Adolescents' Daily Lives

The sample for this study included 100 middle class Grade 8 students from Chandigarh and its satellite towns. This metropolitan area has a population of about 1.2 million and is described as comparatively affluent, modern, offering a more comfortable style of life than other Indian cities. The median family income of the subjects was between Rs 1,50,000 and Rs 2,00,000 per year (US $3,600–4,800). Their parents were well educated: 52 fathers and 49 mothers had graduate degrees. The sample comprised 51 girls and 49 boys, with a mean age of 13.2 years. All these adolescents came from two-parent families. Their parents also participated in the study, although we do not report those data here. Of the total sample, 40 adolescents lived in households that included the extended family; the remaining 60 belonged to nuclear households. Mothers of 40 adolescents were employed. Seventy of these families were Hindu and 30 were Sikh.

To study daily experience, we employed a procedure known as the Experience Sampling Method (ESM) (Csikszentmihalyi & Larson, 1984). All subjects carried alarm watches for a week and completed a self-report on their experience each time the alarm went off. Eight signals were sent at random times each day between 7:30 am and 9:30 pm. The subjects responded to an average of 86 per cent of the signals, providing a total of 4,764 self-reports.

At the time of each ESM signal, subjects reported on their experience at that moment. They first reported on their objective situation: where they were, whom they were with, and what they were doing. Responses to these questions were coded into mutually exclusive categories so that we may determine how often each adolescent reported being in each type of situation. Time with family was identified in terms of responses to a fixed-response item—whom they were with. Following rules we have used earlier, the short period of time that they indicated being with both friends and siblings was coded as being with friends; and the short period of time with both parents and friends was coded as family.

In addition, respondents rated their subjective states at the time of each signal on a series of rating scales which covered their emotional experience, cognitive and motivational state, the social climate they experienced at the moment, and whom they perceived to be the leader of the current interaction. For most analyses, we have used values for these scales that were standardized to z-scores within person. Raw values were adjusted according to the person's mean for that scale and divided by the person's standard deviation. These z-values reflected scores relative to each person's average rating on that scale, with negative values indicating responses below the person's norm and positive values indicating responses above the norm.

To make cross-cultural contrasts, for several of the analyses, we reported data from a sample of 84 American middle class Grade 8 pupils who were examined using the same procedures. This sample comprised 41 boys and 43 girls, having a mean age of 13.2 years. They were studied during the school year and completed self-reports for the time period between 7:30 am and 9:30 pm. As in the case of the Indian sample, their average rate of responding to the random signals was 86 per cent. (For a complete description of this American sample and study see Larson & Richards, 1989.)

We will first examine the quantity of time Indian adolescents spent with their families, and how they spent this time, then we will look at how they experienced this time, its subjective qualities.

Quantities of Family Time

WITH WHOM DO INDIAN ADOLESCENTS SPEND THEIR TIME?

Because the ESM signals occurred at random times, they provided a representative sample of how these Indian adolescents spent their waking hours. A pie chart of how often these Grade 8 students reported being with different categories of companions is presented in Figure 9.1. For comparison purposes, we have included a similar pie chart for American Grade 8 students. Since both groups of youth were studied for approximately 100 hours across the week, 1 per cent of their self-reports was equivalent to approximately 1 hour per week.

Figure 9.1
Whom Adolescents Spend Time With

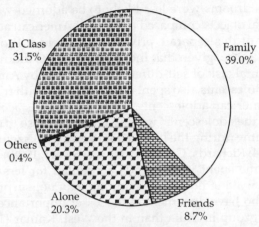

Indian 8th Graders

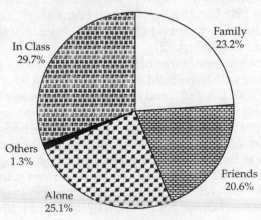

US 8th Graders

To begin with, we can see that the two cultural groups spent similar amounts of time with classmates (in class) and Indian adolescents spent somewhat less time alone. Larson (1990; 1997) demonstrated that time alone for American adolescents serves an important function, as a sanctuary for the development of a private autonomous self. However, similar analyses with Indian adolescents did not yield any evidence of such a function. Unlike American teenagers, Indian adolescents who spent intermediate amounts of time alone were not better adjusted than those who were rarely alone. We also found in our interviews with Indian adolescents that their bedrooms were less likely to be adorned with posters and personal objects compared to those of American adolescents, as symbols of this separate private self (Steele & Brown, 1995). This makes sense, given that Indian adolescents did not face the developmental task of self-differentiation faced by Americans.

Indian adolescents also spent much less time with friends compared to American adolescents. In the US, friends accounted for one-fifth of the adolescents' waking hours and rose to one-fourth of waking time during the high school years (Csikszentmihalyi & Larson, 1984; Richards, Crowe, Larson, & Swarr, 1998). For Indian students, time spent with friends accounted for less than one-eleventh of waking hours. This finding may not surprise Indian scholars, who have documented the lesser importance accorded to the peer group in India than in the West. Kumar (1993) commented that in a traditional society, youth were "so warmly accepted and comfortably seated in the adult world that they had little need for peer bonding" (p. 69), and even today, "The absence of peer-group activity seems to be a critical feature of the culture of childhood in India" (p. 72).

This is, however, more true of girls than boys. Indian girls spent much less time with friends (M = 6.0 per cent) than boys (M = 11.0 per cent, t = 3.37, p < .001), and this difference was attributable to girls spending less time with friends in public locations (2.8 per cent of all reports) than boys (7.4 per cent). In India, boys are given more freedom of movement; it is less acceptable for girls to be on their own away from home, family, and adult chaperonage (Bharat, 1997; Verma & Saraswathi, 2002). In the American sample, there was no gender difference in the amount of time spent with friends. Further, American Grade 8 girls spent twice as much time talking to friends as American boys, often on phone (Raffaelli & Duckett,

1989); in India, the amount of time spent talking to friends was the same (1.6 per cent of waking hours) for both sexes.

While spending less time alone and with friends, Indian Grade 8 students reported spending much more time with their families. Their family time—accounting for nearly 40 per cent of their waking hours—was two-thirds more than that of their American counterparts. Time budget data obtained from older Indian adolescents revealed that the amount of time did not diminish with age (Verma, 1995; Verma & Saraswathi, 1992). Indian girls in our sample spent more time with their family (M = 44.1 per cent) than boys (M = 34.9 per cent; t = 3.03, p < .01), while there was no gender difference for Americans. For Indian boys and girls, family was a prominent part of their daily life. They were not breaking away; they were not disengaging from daily interaction with their families.

What impressed us most was the responses of these Indian adolescents to a question in our follow-up questionnaire—whom they would rather spend time with. In the US, by Grade 8, this type of question almost always elicits an answer in favour of peers (Bowerman & Kinch, 1959). In contrast, 43 of our Indian adolescents named family members as their preference, and only 29 mentioned peers, 9 said alone, and 19 mentioned family *and* friends. This clearly indicated that the large amount of time they spent with their families was not simply a result of parental constraints. Family appeared to be a high priority for many of these teenagers. They had internalized cultural values that placed the family at the centre of Indian life.

WHAT HAPPENS DURING INDIAN ADOLESCENTS' FAMILY TIME?

Does the large amount of time that Indian youth spend with their families provide rich experiences? Is it a developmental asset? As a first step toward approaching this question we asked: where was this family time spent, who was present, and what activities occurred. Developmental scholars have stressed the importance of identifying the specific daily contexts and interactions that constitute the daily lives of children and adolescents (Super &

Harkness, 1997; Whiting & Edwards, 1988). So this was our starting point.

We first determined that a large part of family time was spent at home: 86 per cent (vs 78 per cent for American Grade 8 students). As in the case of East Asian adolescents, schoolwork and preparation for competitive examinations was a very high priority for these youth (Verma, Sharma, & Larson, 2002), and parents often gave that as an explanation for organizing few family outings. Compared to American parents, Indian parents spent far less time in transportation, driving their Grade 8 children from one place to another, from one activity to another. Indian families were also less likely to eat out. In short, the family experience of Indian adolescents was less extended into external environments. Csikszentmihalyi and Larson (1984) observed that American adolescents often had their closest interactions with their families when they were away from home. In India, home is clearly the dominant site of family life.

We next looked at which family members or groups of family members these Indian adolescents were with during the ESM signals. We found that nuclear family members accounted for a large proportion of family time (Table 9.1). Despite the importance attached to the extended family in India (Biswas, 1992), the amount of time adolescents spent with their extended family was comparatively less: 3.8 per cent of all time (10 per cent of family time). Of course, total time spent with the extended family was greater for adolescents living in extended households (extended: 7.5 per cent of all time, nuclear: 2.3 per cent, t = 3.65, p < .001). Even for these adolescents this amount of time was notably short—about an hour a day—suggesting that for these middle class youth the nuclear family was predominate.

Consistent with traditional family roles, Indian adolescents spent most of the time with their mothers and siblings. Daily contact with fathers was less. The amount of time spent alone with the mother (including time with the mother and siblings) was nearly twice the amount of time spent alone with the father. The longest period of time spent with the father occurred in family groups in which the mother was also present. This lesser contact with fathers than mothers is common across most societies that have been studied (Collins & Russell, 1991; UNICEF, 1995), including in our European American and African American data (Larson, 1993;

Table 9.1
Division of Adolescents' Time with Family

	Total	Girls	Boys
Mother	**21.6**	**22.6**	**20.2**
Mother only	12.6	14.2	10.4
Mother and siblings	9.0	8.4	9.8
Father	**9.8**	**10.2**	**9.1**
Father only	6.1	6.1	6.0
Father and siblings	3.7	4.1	3.1
Mother and father	**34.1**	**33.8**	**34.7**
Parents only	8.2	9.0	7.2
Parents and siblings	23.4	22.6	24.5
Parents and others	2.5	2.2	3.0
Siblings	**24.4**	**22.5**	**27.0**
Siblings only	24.4	22.5	27.0
Extended relatives	**10.2**	**11.0**	**9.1**
Uncles, aunts, and cousins	5.2	5.9	4.2
Grandparents	2.6	2.3	3.0
Grandparents and other relatives	2.4	2.8	1.9
	100.0	100.0	100.0

Note: The comparison between girls and boys is significant, $\chi^2 (10, N = 1843) = 19.7$, $p = .032$.

Larson, Richards, Sims, & Dworkin, 2001). Unlike in many groups, however, we found that the proportion of family time adolescents spent with mothers versus fathers did not differ markedly by gender of the child. While Western studies have reported a tendency among the youth to spend more time with their same sex parent (Collins & Russell, 1991; Youniss & Smollar, 1987), there was no evidence for this in the case of Indian adolescents.

Lastly, we looked at what activities occurred during family time (Table 9.2). We were particularly interested in how much time was spent talking with the family, because this activity represents the most direct interaction. We found that the most frequent activities with the family were watching TV (21.0 per cent of family time), homework (19.0 per cent), and eating (16.9 per cent), with few sex differences. Talking was the fourth most frequent activity, accounting for 12.5 per cent of family time. Around the same percentage was obtained in the case of our American Grade 8 students (11.1 per cent). Given that Indian Grade 8 students spent much

Table 9.2
Activities during Family Time

	Total	Gender[1] Girls	Boys	Mother	Father	Who with[2] Parents	Siblings	Extended Relatives
N	1843	1064	779	397	180	629	449	188
Eating	16.9	15.0	19.5	14.9	12.2	25.4	5.8	23.9
Personal care	6.3	6.1	6.5	7.6	3.3	6.4	5.8	7.4
Chores	4.2	4.1	4.2	6.8	9.4	3.0	1.8	3.2
Transportation	4.5	4.2	4.9	3.8	9.4	3.0	4.5	6.4
Resting	6.2	6.0	6.4	5.3	3.3	4.5	11.1	4.8
Media	21.0	19.9	22.5	16.4	22.2	22.6	23.8	17.6
Hobbies	3.2	4.0	2.1	3.8	1.1	2.9	3.6	4.3
Talking	12.4	13.3	11.3	14.4	12.2	11.6	10.0	17.0
Sports and games	3.2	3.1	3.3	0.5	1.7	2.2	7.6	3.2
Idling	3.1	3.2	3.0	2.0	6.1	2.9	2.7	4.3
Homework	19.0	21.0	16.3	24.7	18.9	15.6	23.4	8.0
	100.0	100.0	100.0	100.0	100.0	100.0	100.0	100.0

Notes: [1] When comparing boys versus girls $\chi^2 (10, N = 1843) = 19.6, p = .033$.
[2] When comparing other five categories $\chi^2 (40, N = 1843) = 231.6, p < .001$.

more time with their families, the net amount of time spent talking with the family was substantially higher (4.9 per cent vs 2.6 per cent of waking hours). Talking with the family took up twice as much of an Indian than an American adolescent's day.

Although Indian girls and boys had similar high rates of talking to the family, they differed with respect to which family members they talked with. Rates of family time spent talking did not differ by gender, but girls were more likely to talk when with their mothers, with their fathers, and with their siblings, whereas boys were more likely to talk in larger groups: mother and father and extended relatives (Figure 9.2). Girls talked more in one-on-one situations, while boys talked more in larger family groups, including those with grandparents, uncles, and aunts. We suspect these larger groups are more influenced by traditional roles and, given the greater prestige of boys in traditional families, boys feel freer to participate in the conversation in these contexts.

Perhaps, the most notable finding was related to how frequently fathers were conversational partners. In European American families, fathers were less frequent companions in conversation than mothers, especially for adolescent daughters (Larson et al., 1996;

Figure 9.2
Rates of Talking When with Family Members

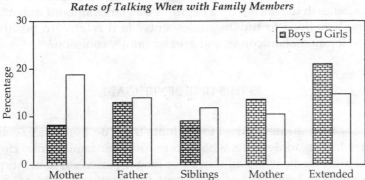

Youniss & Smollar, 1987). In the case of the Indian sample, the rate of talking did not vary greatly between the time when they were with mothers (14.4 per cent) and with fathers (12.2 per cent). Indian adolescents did not become silent when the father was present. Furthermore, as we saw (Figure 9.2), girls talked as much if not more with their fathers than boys. In our interview, one girl said, "I talk about everything with my father: politics, games, movies, friends, day's activities at school." Another girl said, "I talk about everything with my father, even about good looking guys." This is consistent with the data we obtained from the ESM reports of these fathers (Larson, Verma, & Dworkin, 2001) and with those of another study in which middle class Indian fathers reported equality in their treatment of sons and daughters (Srivastava, 1997). Indian fathers fared better than American fathers in engaging their children in conversation. Although the traditional Indian father has been portrayed as being on the periphery of the family (Kakar, 1978), these middle class fathers appeared to be comparatively involved in the lives of their adolescent children, boys and girls.

To summarize, we found that the large amount of time that Indian middle class adolescents spent with their families was mainly at home, in the company of nuclear family members, and involved a range of routine activities from watching TV to homework to conversation. While fathers were less frequently present during these interactions than mothers, rates of conversation with fathers, including by daughters, were comparatively high. These are the daily motions that Indian families go through, but what lies beneath the surface? To begin, is this large amount of family time beneficial to Indian adolescents? Is it related to positive developmental outcomes and greater family cohesion?

IS THIS TIME BENEFICIAL?

One means we had to evaluate this question was to compare Indian adolescents who differed in their family time. How did individuals who had shorter or longer periods of family time compare on indicators of adolescent and family adjustment? We tested whether differences in total family time and time spent talking to the family were correlated with scores on the CESD Depression Inventory (Radloff, 1977), scores for internalizing and externalizing symptoms on the CBCL (Achenbach, 1991), and adolescents', mothers' and fathers' rating of family cohesiveness on the Family Environment Scale (FES) (Moos & Moos, 1986). We found that per cent time with family was significantly correlated with less adolescent depression ($r = -.32$, $p < .001$), and fathers' ratings of family cohesion ($r = .22$, $p < .05$), but not with the other variables. Also, rate of talking with the family was significantly correlated only with the adolescents' ratings of family cohesiveness ($r = .22$, $p < .05$). These patterns did not differ markedly by gender of the adolescent.

These correlations provided modest support for the thesis that Indian adolescents benefited from their large amount of family time. Adolescents who had more interactions with their families were clearly not handicapped in any way, and time spent talking with the family was related to being less depressed. Since these findings are correlational, caution is needed in interpreting them to mean that greater family time *leads to* positive outcomes. It is possible, for example, that an adolescent's depression leads to reduced family time, or that the relationship between depression and family time is reciprocal.

Another means we had to evaluate whether Indian adolescents' family time was an asset was to examine the subjective qualities of their experience during this time—were they happy, attentive, and did they experience family members as helpful and responsive?

Qualities of Family Time

ADOLESCENTS' EMOTIONAL STATES ACROSS CONTEXTS

Large amounts of family time may be meaningless or even detrimental if, beneath the surface, adolescents are filled with anger, worry, or unhappiness. Emotions reflect a person's ongoing state of "being-in-the-world"—whether they are engaged and responsive to others or disengaged and disassociated from others. What did Indian adolescents feel during this large proportion of family time? Beneath their filial role of being a good child, were there undercurrents of negative feeling?

To begin, we looked at responses to a general index of emotional states. Subjects in both the Indian and US samples rated their emotions or "affect" at each ESM signal on a scale summing responses to three semantic differential items (happy–unhappy, cheerful–irritable, friendly–angry) that represented how positive to negative their state was on a scale from +9 to –9. Both groups reported a wide range of mostly positive but not infrequent negative states; in fact, we were surprised to find that the distribution of hour-to-hour emotions on this scale was virtually identical for these middle class adolescents living on opposite sides of the globe. They differed, however, in where they most often experienced these positive and negative states.

In the two contexts, there was no cultural difference. When they were in class and alone, Indian and American youth reported remarkably similar states. Averages for values that have been z-scored within each person are presented in Figure 9.3. Being in class was associated with average affect that was slightly above each person's mean in both countries. Being alone was associated with average affect that was markedly below each person's mean.

The largest differences between Indians and Americans were related to their emotional experience with friends and with family. Both groups reported favourable affect with their friends: this was the happiest part of their daily lives. Indian adolescents, however, reported feeling somewhat less happy on average during this time. Compared to Americans, they were at the extreme positive end of the scale on fewer occasions (on the raw, non-z-scored scale, they

Figure 9.3
Affect by Whom Adolescents are With

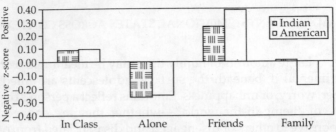

were above +7 for 20 per cent of their reports with friends vs 26 per cent for Americans); and they experienced negative emotions on a few more occasions (7 per cent vs 5 per cent for Americans). As we have discussed, friends occupy a central place in American adolescents' lives, and this may explain why this is a context of such exuberant emotions for them. American adolescents also have more freedom with friends as by this age they spend more time with friends away from home and parental supervision (Larson & Richards, 1991; 1998), which may facilitate a particular type of enjoyable positive feedback interaction (Larson, 1983).

Indian adolescents, in contrast, reported feeling happier than Americans during time with their families. Affect was below average for Americans during time with family, whereas for Indians it was average. The main reason for this is that there were fewer occasions when Indian adolescents experienced negative emotions during time with family. They reported feeling irritable for 12 per cent of these times, as compared to 20 per cent for Americans; and they reported feeling unhappy 10 per cent of the times (15 per cent for Americans). We may recall that Grade 8 is the trough period for American adolescents' experience with families, as is evident from their more frequent negative emotions. It cannot be said that Indians did not experience negative and disassociative feelings in the presence of their families. One girl said, "When there is an argument, we all get involved. We shout, walk out and then come back." However, these kinds of feelings were experienced less often, and in fewer families. Another Indian girl said, ·"Anything that happens in the family makes me feel good; I know that someone cares."

SUBJECTIVE EXPERIENCE DURING TIME WITH FAMILY

We can obtain a fuller picture of Indian adolescents' family experience by examining a broader range of subjective dimensions. On the ESM form, we had the Indian youth report on diverse aspects of their subjective experience at the moment of each report: How well were they paying attention? Did they experience choice over their activities? Did they find family members to be friendly? Whom did they experience as being the leader? All these items were continuous, with the exception of the item on who the leader was. For these continuous items, we converted the raw values for each of these dimensions to z-scores and computed average z-values for time with family, which are plotted in Figure 9.4.

On most dimensions, Indian adolescents experienced time with family as somewhat more positive, on average, than the norm for the rest of their lives. They reported lower levels of attention and challenge than in other parts of their daily lives (schoolwork was the context in which these were high)—family time was not typically an occasion of deep mental engagement. They also reported feeling more choice over their activities than in other settings; they experienced less loneliness and worry than at other times; and they felt more calm, safe, and relaxed. This combination of lower engagement and feeling relaxed and secure was similar to what we have often found among American adolescents (Csikszentmihalyi & Larson, 1984; Larson & Richards, 1994), however, the values were generally more positive for Indian adolescents, especially for the Grade 8 period.

Indian adolescents rated the social climate when they with their family as responsive and favourably disposed towards them. On each ESM report, they rated whether they perceived the people they were with as helpful (vs unhelpful) and friendly (vs unfriendly), which we summed to develop the social climate scale. For American Grade 8 students, mean z-scores for these items were negative during family time; for Indians they were significantly positive. Indian adolescents reported family members to be very friendly 52 per cent of the time and unfriendly 2 per cent of the time; the corresponding figures for Americans were 40 per cent and 6 per cent of the time, respectively.

Therefore, family experience was generally positive for these Indian youth. However, we found this to be somewhat more true

Figure 9.4

Adolescents' Subjective States When with Their Families

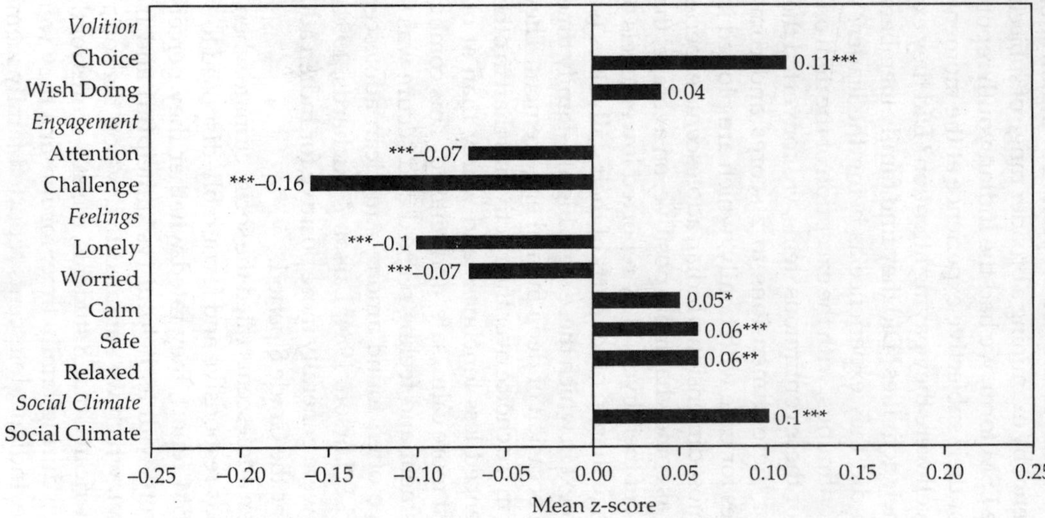

Volition

Choice 0.11***

Wish Doing 0.04

Engagement

Attention −0.07***

Challenge −0.16***

Feelings

Lonely −0.1***

Worried −0.07***

Calm 0.05*

Safe 0.06***

Relaxed 0.06**

Social Climate

Social Climate 0.1***

Mean z-score

−0.25 −0.20 −0.15 −0.10 −0.05 0.00 0.05 0.10 0.15 0.20 0.25

for Indian boys than girls. Boys and girls did not differ in the average affect states they reported when they were with their family. However, boys felt less lonely than girls when with their families ($t = 2.41$, $p < .05$) (although loneliness was uncommon for both sexes); and boys experienced the social climate as more favourable ($t = 2.13$, $p < .05$). Further analyses revealed that this gender difference was maximum when they were with extended family members. Girls were less happy and experienced a less positive social climate when they were with extended relatives. As we mentioned earlier, this may be a context in which traditional values that accord greater preference to boys were more in force. We also found that boys experienced a more favourable social climate during conversation across all types of family groups. When talking with family members, boys experienced them as somewhat more friendly and helpful than girls did.

Lastly, we examined whom adolescents identified as the leader during these interactions. The traditional Indian family is described as having a clear hierarchy of authority based on age and gender (Seymour, 1999). If this is true for these middle class families, we would expect adolescents to experience their parents, especially their fathers, as being the leader for most of the time. In fact, the adolescents reported that there was no leader for a mean of 72 per cent of the times they were signalled when with family members. This was close to the rate reported by Americans (62 per cent). Indian adolescents reported that their parents or someone else was the leader for a mean of 25 per cent of the times; and they added that they were the leader only 2 per cent of the times. This rate of self being the leader was substantially below that reported by Americans (8 per cent). Nevertheless, these rates indicated that Indian middle class adolescents' experience of the family was anything but authoritarian.

However, this was more true for Indian boys than girls. Boys reported others to be the leader less often than girls (20 per cent vs 34 per cent). This was particularly evident during family conversations (girls: 44 per cent, boys: 25 per cent, chi square [1, N = 200] = 7.55, $p < .01$). The gender of the parent, however, made little difference. Boys and girls were equally likely to report that there was no leader when with mother versus father. Fathers were not experienced as a remote authority figure. One boy said, "My father opens his mind in front of me. The emotional quality of these conversations is intimate. If I lose my temper, he consoles me." A girl reported that in interactions with her father, "We joke, we are equals in it. But I talk more than him."

EVALUATING QUALITY TIME

We found that in addition to spending long hours with their families, Indian adolescents had in general a positive experience in this context. Their affect was at the mean for the rest of their daily experience—which was much more favourable than what American adolescents experienced with their families. While experiencing low levels of challenge and attention when with their families, Indian adolescents felt relaxed, less worried, and perceived others as friendly and helpful. One caveat being that for some dimensions family experience was more favourable for boys than for girls, which may be a reflection of the unequal treatment of girls in Indian middle class families (Dube, 1998; Jain, 1994; Veeraraghawan & Srivastava, 1994).

Are these dimensions of subjective experience important? Do they indicate that Indian adolescents gain more from family experience? As a step towards answering this question, we evaluated whether individual Indian adolescents' affect and reported social climate during family time were correlated with measures of their well-being and perceptions of family cohesion (see Table 9.3). Affect with family was associated with less internalizing and externalizing on the CBCL, and less depression. It was also associated with family cohesion as rated by all family members. Social climate was inversely related to depression and positively to mother's rating of family cohesion. These correlations were significant with statistical controls for gender, although separate analyses by gender revealed that they may be stronger for boys. Of course, the conclusions we can draw from these cross-sectional correlations are limited as they deal with only a small set of variables, and they do not establish causality. Nevertheless, these correlations indicated that the positive experience of Indian adolescents with their families was related to positive mental health and family cohesion. They suggest that the warm family climate they experienced served them well.

Table 9.3
Correlations of Subjective Experience during Family Time

	Affect	Social Climate
Internalizing behaviours	−.262**	−.156
Externalizing behaviours	−.212*	−.140
Depression	−.235*	−.233*
Child cohesion (FES)	.233*	.130
Mother cohesion (FES)	.216*	.209*
Father cohesion (FES)	.278**	.150

Notes: *p < .05; **p < .01.

Cultural Differences and Cultural Change

CULTURAL CHANGE

While our findings present a positive picture of Indian adolescents' family experience, several Indian scholars have expressed concern about the possibility that changes in the family may be pushing India toward an American-like pattern in which adolescents spend less time with their families, experience less adult control, and manifest more problem behaviours. Biswas (1992) noted that traditional affectional, economic, and religious bonds that create family cohesion were weakening. A common lament is that adolescents in nuclear households are deprived of the benefits of the rich social support system provided by multiple adults in traditional joint households. "Nucleation has depleted the emotional surround of individuals" and the "emotional support structure is weakening", observed Bharat (1997, p. 312). Concerns about the effects of mothers' employment have also been voiced. As in other parts of the world, every time a crime is committed by an adolescent or young adult, it leads to profuse public soul searching about the state of Indian middle class families (Thapa, Raval, & Chakravarty, 1999).

To evaluate these concerns, we examined whether the distinct patterns of Indian adolescents' family relationships varied as a function of indicators of cultural change. Is time with family and affect with family less in nuclear households? Or, in families where mothers are employed? Or, in families where parents have higher education and income? An evaluation of these comparisons did not indicate any weakening of the family related to these variables. Adolescents in nuclear families did *not* spend significantly less time with their families than those in extended households (nuclear: 39.8 per cent, extended: 39.1 per cent); mothers' employment was also not significantly related to less family time (employed: 37.6 per cent, nonemployed: 41.0 per cent). We also found no significant difference by either of these variables in the amount of talk with the family, average affect with the family, perceived social environment, or perceived leadership. We found less family time as a function of mothers' education ($r = -.26$, $p < .01$). Further analyses, however, revealed that this was not a cause for alarm. Mothers' education was not related to the amount of time talking with the child or the child's experience of affect and social climate when with the family; nor was fathers' education or family income related to any of these variables. We found that adolescents perceived there to be no leader more often in families with higher incomes ($r = .22$, $p < .05$). They perceived parents to be the leader less often if the mother was more educated ($r = -.25$, $p < .05$). We did not view these latter two findings as signs of a weakening of the family but rather of family democratization.

Thus, changes within the family did not appear to be related to compromises in adolescents' family experiences. They did, however, appear to benefit girls. In most cases, the associations we reported showed little difference by gender, but there were two differences. First, boys spent more time with their families when they lived in a joint rather than a nuclear household ($r = .26$, $p < .10$), whereas the opposite trend was seen in the case of girls ($r = -.24$, $p < .10$). This is only an isolated finding, but it suggests that girls may have a more favourable family experience in nuclear households. Second, mothers' education was related to less favourable affect with family for boys ($r = -.37$, $p < .01$), but the trend was opposite in the case of girls ($r = .20$, n.s.). More educated mothers possibly exhibited less of the traditional favouritism toward boys.

These analyses dealt with variables that may be perceived as superficial. Amount of time and emotional experience may not be the best indicators of alienation and loss of family control, nor have our analyses directly examined historical change. It seems possible that the negative effects of cultural change are manifest for only a small fringe subset of society, and thus would not be evident for these mainstream families. Keeping in mind these quali-fications, our findings do not support alarm about the average Indian middle class family. Indian adolescents' rich experience of high quantity and quality of time with their families does not appear to be threatened by changes in the family.

Conclusion

Indian adolescents' experience with their families, we conclude, is quite positive. They spend much more time with their families than European American adolescents and they generally feel positive about this time. They do have negative experiences, for example, at one signal, a youth reported feeling: "bored, my father was giving me a lecture." Another reported feeling lonely because "nobody loves me as they always criticize me." Neverthe-less, they reported many more positive experiences, for example, "Excited, my uncle was coming to visit us this evening." "Happy, we started the Ganesh Pooja." "Very happy, we just bought a gift for papa for his birthday."

What came as a surprise to the American authors (but not to the Indian author) was that we found little undercurrent of rebellion or distrust. During the interviews, very few of these adolescents reported any significant conflict or difference of opinion with their parents. They genuinely liked being with their families. They did not feel a cultural imperative to break away. One father reported that his daughter had asked him to memorize facts about each of her friends, including their likes and dislikes, a request that would be unheard of in the US, especially between a daughter and father. The American phenomenon in which adolescents do not want to be seen in public with their families would, in turn, be very anom-alous in India.

The large amount of time that Indian adolescents spend with their families may well be a developmental asset. The amount of time children and adolescents spend in a context can be viewed as an indicator of the degree of exposure of these groups to the infor-mation and socialization experiences of that context, the extent to which they participate in the rules, scripts, and emotional messages of that milieu (Larson & Verma, 1999). The family is typically a context that reinforces adult values, promotes school success, and supports emotional security (Larson & Richards, 1991). In the case of Indian adolescents, in addition to more time in the family's presence, they spent nearly twice as much time as Americans talking to their families, with much more time talking to their fathers. We believe that this greater degree of family interaction, especially given that it is experienced positively, is developmentally beneficial.

The Indian middle class family is changing no doubt, but we should not assume that it is becoming Western. The hierarchical relationships characteristic of the traditional Indian family were not evident in this study as the subjects reported that there was no leader during family interactions most of the time. Fathers were not feared. These findings are consistent with others' findings that patriarchal hierarchies are being relaxed in the educated Indian middle class (Verma & Saraswathi, 2002).

Vestiges of the traditional hierarchical Indian family were most evident in our scattered finding of differences between girls and boys. We found that girls spent more time with the family and had a somewhat less favourable experience. They were less likely to participate in conversation in family groups and with extended relatives. They experienced other family members as the leader more often than boys. Despite cultural changes, Indian middle class girls are expected to direct their personal aspirations toward the goals of marriage and service to the family into which they will marry (Saraswathi, 1999). Our data indicated that girls had a more favourable family experience when their mothers were educated and the family was nuclear.

Students of cultural values have repeatedly reached the conclusion that the cluster of societal changes sometimes referred to as "modernization" does not inevitably mean adoption of individualism (Kagitcibasi, 1997; Malik, 1981; Smith & Schwartz, 1997). Many collectivist societies, such as Japan, have undergone social and technological modernization without discarding family interdependency, without absorbing Western individualism. Middle class families in these societies are becoming more materially independent, but emotional interdependence persists (Mistry & Saraswathi, 2003). We found that Indian adolescents from more "modern" families—nuclear families and families where mothers were employed—neither spent less time with their family members nor reported less positive experiences.

Seymour (1999) concluded that the self in Indian society is defined, not through differentiation from others, but through connection to them, through cultivation of a "we-self". As such the developmental task of Indian adolescents is not to become separate but to *break down* forms of separation—to strive to reduce impulses that might set one apart and to strengthen emotional bonds. The large amount of time and positive feelings reported by Indian adolescents with their families indicate that they are earnestly engaged in this developmental task.

References

Achenbach, T. (1991). *Manual for the Child Behavior Checklist/4–18*. Burlington: University of Vermont, Department of Psychiatry.

Arnett, J.J. (1999). Adolescent storm and stress, reconsidered. *American Psychologist*, 54(5), 317–326.

Bharat, S. (1997). Family socialization of the Indian child. *Trends in Social Science Research*, 4(1), 201–216.

Biswas, P.C. (1992). Perception of parental behaviour and adolescents' frustration. *The Indian Journal of Social Work*, LIII(4), 669–678.

Bowerman, C.E., & Kinch, J.W. (1959). Changes in family and peer orientation of children between the fourth and tenth grades. *Social Forces*, 37, 206–211.

Collins, W.A., & Russell, G. (1991). Mother-child and father-child relationships in middle childhood and adolescence: A developmental analysis. *Developmental Review*, 11, 99–136.

Considine, D.M. (1985). *The cinema of adolescence*. Jefferson, NC: McFarland.

Csikszentmihalyi, M., & Larson, R. (1984). *Being adolescent: Conflict and growth in the teenage years*. New York: Basic Books.

Datar, C. (1995). Democratizing the family. *The Indian Journal of Social Work*, LVI(2), 211–224.

Dube, L. (1998). On the construction of gender: Hindu girls in patrilineal India. In K. Chanana (Ed.), *Socialization, education and women: Explorations in gender identity*. New Delhi: Orient Longman.

Grotevant, H.D., & Cooper, C.R. (1986). Individuation in family relationships: A perspective on individual differences in the development of identity and role-taking skill in adolescence. *Human Development*, 29, 82–100.

Hauser, S.T. (with Powers, S.I., & Noam, G.G.). (1991). *Adolescents and their families: Paths of ego development*. New York: Free Press.

Havighurst, R.J. (1953). *Human development and education.* New York: McKay.

Hill, J., & Holmbeck, G.N. (1987). Familial adaptation to biological change during adolescence. In R.M. Lerner & T.T. Foch (Eds), *Biological-psychosocial interactions in early adolescence* (pp. 207–223). Hillsdale, NJ: Erlbaum.

Jain, S. (1994). Study of anxiety, tension and depression as related to gender discrimination perceived by girls. In V.R. Dhoundiyal, N.C. Dhoundiyal, & A. Shukla (Eds), *The Indian girls* (pp. 105–115). Almora, UP: Shri Almora Book Depot.

Kagitcibasi, C. (1997). Individualism and collectivism. In J.W. Berry, M.H. Segall, & C. Kagitcibasi (Eds), *Handbook of cross-cultural psychology: Social behavior and applications* (2nd ed., vol. 3, pp. 1–49). Boston: Allyn & Bacon.

Kakar, S. (1978). *The inner world: A psycho-analytic study of childhood and society in India.* Oxford, NY: Oxford University Press.

Kashyap, L.D. (1993). Adolescent/youth and family dynamics and development programmes. *The Indian Journal of Social Work, LIV,* 94–107.

Kiell, N. (1959). *The adolescent through fiction.* New York: International Universities Press.

Kumar, K. (1993). *Political agenda of education: A study of colonialist and nationalist ideas.* New Delhi: Sage.

Larson, R. (1983). Adolescents' daily experience with family and friends: Contrasting opportunity systems. *Journal of Marriage and the Family, 45*(4), 739–750.

Larson, R. (1990). The solitary side of life: An examination of the time people spend alone from childhood to old age. *Developmental Review, 10,* 155–183.

Larson, R. (1993). Finding time for fatherhood: The emotional ecology of adolescent-father interactions. In S. Shulman & W.A. Collins (Eds), *Father-adolescent relationships. New directions for child development.* No. 62 (pp. 7–18). San Francisco: Jossey-Bass.

Larson, R. (1997). The emergence of solitude as a constructive domain of experience in early adolescence. *Child Development, 68*(1), 80–93.

Larson, R., & Richards, M. (Eds). (1989). The changing life space of early adolescence. *Journal of Youth and Adolescence,* Special issue, *18*(6), 501–626.

Larson, R., & Richards, M. (1994). *Divergent realities: The emotional lives of mothers, fathers, and adolescents.* New York: Basic Books.

Larson, R., & Richards, M. (1998). Waiting for the weekend: Friday and Saturday nights as the emotional climax of the week. In R.W. Larson & A.C. Crouter (Eds), *Temporal rhythms in the lives of adolescents: Themes and variations* (pp. 37–54). San Francisco: Jossey-Bass.

Larson, R., & Richards, M.H. (1991). Daily companionship in childhood and adolescence: Changing developmental contexts. *Child Development, 62*(2), 284–300.

Larson, R.W., Richards, M.H., Moneta, G., Holmbeck, G., & Duckett, E. (1996). Changes in adolescents' daily interactions with their families from ages 10 to 18: Disengagement and transformation. *Developmental Psychology, 32*(4), 744–754.

Larson, R., Richards, M.H., Sims, B., & Dworkin, J. (2001). How urban African American young adolescents spend their time: Time budgets for locations, activities, and companionship. *Journal of Community Psychology, 29,* 565–597.

Larson, R., & Verma, S. (1999). How children and adolescents around the world spend time: Work, play, and developmental opportunities. *Psychological Bulletin, 125*(6), 701–736.

Larson, R., Verma, S., & Dworkin, J. (2001). Men's work and family lives in India: The daily organization of time and emotion. *Journal of Family Psychology, 15*(2), 206–224.

Laursen, B., Coy, K.C., & Collins, W.A. (1998). Reconsidering changes in parent-child conflict across adolescence: A meta-analysis. *Child Development, 69,* 817–832.

Malik, S.M. (1981). *Psychological modernity: A comparative study of some African and American graduate students.* Unpublished doctoral dissertation, University of Chicago, Chicago.

Mines, M. (1988). Conceptualizing the person: Hierarchical society and individual autonomy in India. *American Anthropologist, 90,* 568–579.

Mistry, J., & Saraswathi, T.S. (2003). The cultural context of child development. In I. Weiner (Series Ed.), *Handbook of psychology, Vol. 6. Developmental psychology* (R.L. Lerner, A. Easterbrooks, & J. Mistry, Eds, pp. 267–291). New York: Wiley.

Moos, R.H., & Moos, B.S. (1986). *Family Environment Scales Manual* (2nd ed.). Palo Alto, CA: Consulting Psychologists Press.

Radloff, L.S. (1977). The CES-D Scale: A self-report depression scale for research in the general population. *Applied Psychological Measurement, 1,* 385–401.

Raffaelli, M., & Duckett, E. (1989). "We were just talking...": Conversations in early adolescence. *Journal of Youth and Adolescence, 18,* 567–582.

Ramanujam, B.K. (1978). The Ahmedabad discussions on change: An Indian viewpoint. In. E.J. Anthony & C. Chiland (Eds), *The child in his family* (pp. 415–419). New York: John Wiley. •

Ramu, G.N. (1988). *Family structure and fertility.* New Delhi: Sage.

Richards, M., Crowe, P., Larson, R., & Swarr, A. (1998). Developmental patterns and gender differences in the experience of peer companionship during adolescence. *Child Development, 69,* 154–163.

Rutter, M., & Smith, D. (1995). Towards causal explanations of time trend in psychological disorders in young people. In M. Rutter & D. Smith (Eds), *Psychological disorders in young people: Time trends and their causes* (pp. 782–808). New York: John Wiley.

Saraswathi, T.S. (1999). Adult-child continuity in India: Is adolescence a myth or an emerging reality? In T.S. Saraswathi (Ed.), *Culture, socialization and human development: Theory, research and applications in India* (pp. 213–232). New Delhi: Sage.

Saraswathi, T.S., & Ganapathy, H. (2002). Indian parents' ethnotheories as reflections of the Hindu scheme of child and human development. In H. Keller, Y.H. Poortinga, & A. Scholmerich (Eds), *Between culture and biology: Perspectives on ontogenetic development* (pp. 79–88). Cambridge, UK: Cambridge University Press.

Saraswathi, T.S., & Pai, S. (1997). Socialization in the Indian context. In H.S.R. Kao & D. Sinha (Eds), *Asian perspectives on psychology* (pp. 74–92). New Delhi: Sage.

Seymour, S.C. (1999). *Women, family, and child care in India.* Cambridge: Cambridge University Press.

Sinha, D. (1988). Basic Indian values and behaviour dispositions in the context of national development: An appraisal. In D. Sinha & H.S.R. Kao (Eds), *Social values and development: Asian perspectives* (pp. 31–55). New Delhi: Sage.

Sinha, D. (1994). The joint family in tradition. *Seminar, 424,* 20–23.

Smith, P.B., & Schwartz, S.H. (1997). Values. In J.W. Berry, M.H. Segall, & C. Kagitcibasi (Eds), *Handbook of cross-cultural psychology: Social behavior and applications* (2nd ed., vol. 3, pp. 77–118). Boston: Allyn & Bacon.

Srivastava, A.K. (1997). The changing place of child in Indian families: A cross-generational study. *Trends in Social Science Research, 4,* 191–200.

Steele, J.R., & Brown, J.D. (1995). Adolescent room culture: Studying media in the context of everyday life. *Journal of Youth and Adolescence, 24,* 551–576.

Super, C.M., & Harkness, S. (1997). The cultural structuring of child development. In J.W. Berry, P.R. Dasen, & T.S. Saraswathi (Eds), *Handbook of cross-cultural psychology: Basic processes and human development* (vol. 2, pp. 3–39). Boston: Allyn & Bacon.

Thapa, V.J., Raval, S., & Chakravarty, S. (1999, January 18). Young men. *India Today,* 52–58.

UNICEF. (1995). *Achieving gender equity in families: The role of males.* Florence, Italy: Author.

Uplaonkar, A.T. (1995). The emerging rural youth: A study of their changing values towards marriage. *The Indian Journal of Social Work, 56*(4), 415–423.

Veeraraghawan, U., & Srivastava, C. (1994). Attitudes toward women: A study on the cross-section of Delhi population. In V.R. Dhoundiyal, N.C. Dhoundiyal, & A. Shukla (Eds), *The Indian girls* (pp. 207–234). Almora, UP: Shri Almora Book Depot.

Verma, S. (1995). *Expanding time awareness: A longitudinal intervention study on time sensitization in the Indian youth.* Zurich: The Johann Jacobs Foundation.

Verma, S., & Saraswathi, T.S. (1992). *At the crossroads: Time use by university students.* A report submitted to the International Development Research Centre. New Delhi: International Development Research Centre.

Verma, S., & Saraswathi, T.S. (2002). Adolescence in India: Street urchins or Silicon Valley millionaires? In B. Brown, R. Larson, & T.S. Saraswathi (Eds), *The world's youth: Adolescence in eight regions of the globe.* New York: Cambridge University Press.

Verma, S., Sharma, D., & Larson, R. (2002). School stress in India: Effects on time and daily emotions. *International Journal of Behavioral Development, 26*(6), 500–508.

Whiting, B., & Edwards, C. (1988). *Children of different worlds: The formation of social behavior.* Cambridge, MA: Harvard University Press.

Youniss, J., & Smollar, J. (1987). *Adolescent relations with mothers, fathers, and friends.* Chicago: University of Chicago Press.

ఇ 10 ೧

From Research Project to Nationwide Programme: The Mother–Child Education Programme of Turkey

SEVDA BEKMAN

The focus of this paper is on the development, expansion, and dissemination processes of the Mother–Child Education Programme of Turkey. The review of literature aims to provide an overview of some of the successful intervention programmes and to illustrate similar examples around the world rather than being a comprehensive coverage. An attempt is also made to describe the context such as educational level and the early childhood education system in the country within which the Programme was developed and implemented. An account of the different developmental phases of the Programme and its components is followed by a detailed discussion of the research evaluation of the Programme after it became nationwide. The paper concludes with a discussion of the results of the research, factors contributing to success of the Programme, and challenges encountered.

A Rationale for Early Intervention

It is society's responsibility to provide care and protection for young children, especially for those who are vulnerable due to their environmental conditions. It is more beneficial for children, families and society to prevent the distressing effects of such conditions through early intervention rather than seeking a remedy later through treatment (Shankoff & Meisels, 1990).

The underlying rationale of intervention programmes is that cognitive and social development should be enhanced by encouraging intellectual stimulation and by strengthening the developmentally appropriate characteristics of the child's environment (Campbell & Ramey, 1994). It is believed that children from empowered environments enter school more prepared and with a higher likelihood of success in comparison with their less advantaged peers. Early school success leads to later academic success and success in life (Schweinhart, Barnes, & Weikart, 1993). It has also been argued that children who have participated in intervention programmes and can meet the demands of the school system are also perceived as successful by their teachers, thus reinforcing their success and increasing the likelihood of their academic progress and performance. All these factors affect readiness for success in adult life (Berrueta-Clement et al., 1986; Myers, 1992; Woodhead, 1986). Although this framework suggests certain cause–effect relations, it does not provide evidence for the specific connections, but simply identifies the causal conditions, which make the effect more likely to occur. These causes are considered as contributing factors (Schweinhart & Wiekart, 1980).

Existing programmes, which aim to empower the development of children from risk environments, adopt different strategies. One strategy is "delivering a service directly to children". The immediate goal of this approach is to enhance the child's overall development and the programme often takes place in "centres" outside the child's home. However, interest in how a child's environment affects growth and development has led to a shift from a child centred approach to an ecological approach in programmes to promote early childhood development. Thus, an approach that emphasizes the importance of the interrelationships between the child, the family, and social support systems (Bronfenbrenner, 1979; Weiss & Jacobs, 1984; Zigler & Berman, 1983) is adopted in many early intervention programmes. It is the transactional interpretation of development (Sameroff, 1975), and Bronfenbrenner's (1979) view of the family as a system embedded in a larger ecological framework of systems that constitute the underlying philosophy of programmes which target the familial context. Here, the aim is to give equal attention to the child and his or her environment.

There is ample evidence of the positive effects of both types of intervention programmes on the child's short-term development, and long-term healthy adjustment, educational and occupational achievement (Ramey, Yeates, & Short, 1984). Evidence of success of centre based intervention is provided by the Perry Preschool Project that yields empirical data not only for short-term but also for long-term positive effects (Schweinhart et al., 1993). The report of the Consortium for Longitudinal Studies (Lazar & Darlington, 1982) which reviewed 11 studies indicated successful long-term effects of centre based interventions on the cognitive development of children, such as less need for special education, less grade retention, better achievement test scores, and more achievement-oriented attitudes in research studies with the involvement of parents at different levels (Beller, 1974; Deutsch, Deutsch, Jordan, & Grallo, 1983; Gray, Ramsey, & Klaus, 1982; Karnes, Teska, & Hodgins, 1970). These programmes also have a specific impact on the mother's child rearing style and employment opportunities (Berrueta-Clement et al., 1986; Royce, Darlington, & Murray, 1983; Upshur, 1990).

The effects of parent focused intervention programmes also reveal promising results. Increase in IQ (Andrews et al., 1982; Slaughter, 1983) and children's improved school performance (Cochran & Handerson, 1985; Levenstein, O'Hara, & Madden, 1983; Slater, 1986) are some of the short-term effects of parent education programmes. It has been found that children are less likely to be enrolled in special education classes for as long as 7 years after the termination of the programme (Jester & Guinagh, 1983) and show better health and development indicators (Palti, Mansbach, & Kurtzman, 1987). There is also evidence of the positive effects of these programmes on maternal behaviour, such as positive and facilitative language with the child, and better child rearing attitudes (Andrews et al., 1982; Dickie & Gerber, 1980; Lambie, Bond, & Weikart, 1974). Parents involved in intervention programmes adopt better parenting skills and have better parent–child interactions, and experience less social isolation (Morgan, Jeanette, & Allin, 1990; Pehrson & Robinson, 1990; Telleen, Herzog, & Kilbane, 1989). The Yale Child Welfare Project provided long term evidence of the positive effects of self-support, continuing education, and small family size (Seitz, Rosenbaum, & Apfel, 1985). Further, the positive effects of caregiver focused interventions on children and mothers were observed by Olds, Henderson, Tatelbaum, and Chamberlain (1988), and Larson (1980). Gomby, Culross, and Behrman (1999) reviewed the evaluation of six family focused programmes implemented by home visits. The evaluation results revealed that for all the six programmes, programme benefits did not impact all the families participating in the programmes. If benefits were found they were fairly modest. Furthermore, programmes faced difficulties in enrolling, engaging and retaining families.

On the basis of their extensive review of intervention research, Seitz and Provence (1990) concluded that although it is not possible to decide whether child focused or caregiver focused intervention is better, due to the limited information available for disadvantaged environments, caregiver focused interventions probably lead to more comprehensive changes for families and, in turn, result in a broader range of beneficial outcomes for children than a child focused approach. Furthermore, it has been suggested that interventions should focus on the environments of children whose development is threatened by environmental conditions. Although such approaches may be more time consuming, difficult to implement and expensive, they have a higher chance of success than introducing preschool programmes (Farran, 1990).

SETTING FOR THE MOTHER–CHILD EDUCATION PROGRAMME

A characterization of Turkey in terms of the educational facilities provided to the population yields an insight into the setting in which the Mother–Child Education Programme (MOCEP) was implemented and the various roles it has played in that setting.

According to 1995–96 figures, literacy rate in Turkey was 83 per cent. The literacy rate varied for males (91 per cent) and females (76 per cent). When male and female populations were considered separately for the 1990–99 period, 74 per cent of the eligible male population attended primary school as compared to 71 per cent females. According to the 1995–99 figures, among the enrolled population, 99 per cent reached the last year of elementary school.

The enrolment rate for secondary school was 70 per cent for males and 50 per cent for females (UNICEF, 2001). At the time when these statistics were compiled, compulsory education in Turkey was 5 years of elementary school. In 1997, a law was passed extending compulsory education to 8 years. Of a population of 65,546,000, 6,659,000 persons are under the age of 5. According to the 1996 figures, 1,415,000 infants are born each year. The mortality rate for infants and for those under 5 decreased during the 1960–96 period. The mortality rate for the population under 5 was 219 for every 1,000 children in 1960, this decreased to 133 in 1980, and further to 68 in 1999. While the decline in the mortality rate was 2.5 per cent during 1960–80, it increased to 6.5 per cent during 1980–96 (UNICEF, 2001).

Turkey does not have a standardized widespread system of early childhood education. Nearly all the services are centre based and located in the large cities. Only 16 per cent of 5-6-year-olds attend some type of institution. When the whole target population is considered (0-6) the percentage decreases further.

An investigation of the quality and effectiveness of the system reveals a picture that is no more positive than that reflected by the quantitative data. The government not only aims to go to scale with only a centre based education model but also adopts a very narrow definition of the target group of the early childhood education system. Attempts by the government to improve early childhood education and development policies have nearly always been confined to the 5-6 years age group. The consequence of this narrow definition and adoption of a single model of early childhood education and development is that the level of the population reached will always be unsatisfactory. The absence of adequate state supported early childhood care and education facilities has negative consequences especially for children from unstimulating home environments, since most of the facilities available (preschool centres, daycare centres, nursery classes) are privately owned and charge a tuition fee. Thus, the existing system does not target children from high risk environments. State resources have been allocated mainly to compulsory education which leaves public services in early childhood education and development at a rudimentary level.

The present services are distinctly divided into two categories with respect to their aims: custodial and educational. Unfortunately, the number of custodial centres far outweighs the number of educational ones (Bekman, 1993; Kagitcibasi, Sunar, & Bekman, 1988). The existing early childhood development and education services are far below minimum standards. It is these concerns and the existing status of early childhood education in Turkey which gave rise to the development of the Mother–Child Education Programme. The Programme targets the group with low education and socioeconomic characteristics. The majority of mothers and fathers participating in the Programme have completed compulsory elementary school education (5 years) and are engaged in unskilled or semi-skilled jobs. They constitute recent migrants from rural areas to the towns and cities. Following migration from rural to urban areas, families assume the characteristics of nuclear families since they either leave the extended family members behind or upon migrating to urban areas remain in close proximity to their extended family but live in separate houses.

In line with the review of successful programmes discussed earlier, the Programme follows the lessons learnt from many intervention programmes in that it aims to stimulate the child intellectually and strengthen the child's environment to foster his development. Thus, it promotes contributing factors for success in life. In doing so, equal attention is focused on the child and his environment. As mentioned earlier, the Programme targets children whose environmental conditions threaten their development.

The Mother–Child Education Programme

The origins of the Mother–Child Education Programme (MOCEP) date back to 1982 and are rooted in the research project—the "Turkish Early Enrichment Project" (Bekman, 1990; 1995; 1998a; 1998b; Kagitcibasi, 1991; 1992; 1996; 1997; Kagitcibasi, Bekman, & Göksel, 1995; Kagitcibasi, Sunar, & Bekman, 1988). This 4-year longitudinal study aimed to assess the impact of both centre based education and home intervention on the overall development of the child. The project did not introduce centre based education, but the existing centres were studied in terms of their orientation: custodial vs educational.

At that time the home intervention programme comprised two main elements: a programme to foster the overall development of the child, and a programme to foster his cognitive development. The first element, developed by the research team and entitled the "Mother Enrichment Program" (Kagitcibasi, Bekman, & Sunar, 1991), took the form of group discussions on topics designed to increase the mother's sensitivity to the child's social and emotional needs and to help her foster the child's social and personality development. The programme to foster cognitive development was a Turkish translation and adaptation of the Home Instruction Program for Preschool Youngsters (HIPPY) developed by the Research Institute of Innovation in Education at Hebrew University, Jerusalem (Lombard, 1994) and comprised the cognitively-oriented element of the mother training programme. The Programme was spread over two periods of 30 weeks for 4- and 5-year-olds. It was implemented through group meetings and home visits. The original project lasted 4 years (1982–86) and in the fourth year assessments were made of the short-term effects of the Programme. A follow-up study was conducted 6 years later in 1991–92 to assess the long-term effects. Both short- and long-term effects were positive and impressive (Bekman, 1990; 1995; 1998a; 1998b; Kagitcibasi, 1991; 1992; 1996; 1997; Kagitcibasi, Bekman, & Göksel, 1995; Kagitcibasi, Sunar, & Bekman, 1988).

Short-term results yielded extensive data on the context of development (educational, custodial, and home care) and mother training (compared with no training). Educational daycare centres were found to be superior to custodial daycare centres and home care for all indicators of cognitive, social, and emotional development as well as school achievement. The same trend was also observed for children who had been exposed to the intervention. On all measures of cognitive, social and emotional development, children of the trained group exceeded the control group.

The effects of mother training on mothers were also impressive. The main difference was observed in the area of mother–child interaction. Trained mothers were observed to be more responsive, used higher levels of verbalization, and had higher aspirations and expectations for their children. Direct effects on the mothers indicated higher intrafamily status within the family and greater optimism for the future.

The findings of the follow-up research revealed improved cognitive functioning, higher school grades, better attitudes toward school, and a larger number of children still in school for the group whose mothers were trained. This group also enjoyed better family relations. The long-term results in the case of mothers revealed that the mother training programme had long-term benefits for mother–child interaction as well as for the mothers themselves. Mothers developed closer relations with their children and were more likely to provide a stimulating environment. These mothers also had the final say in decision making at home.

Applications of the home intervention programme began even before the completion of the project. An 11-episode television series was produced for the first component, which aimed to sensitize mothers to the overall development of the child. Limited applications followed with funding from various groups, including parent–teacher associations, women's groups, and the private sector. Partial and full applications of the mother training programme were implemented as a public service mainly in Istanbul. The main developments began with the collaboration of UNICEF and the Ministry of National Education. The mother enrichment element of the programme was included in the adult education programmes of the Ministry of National Education to train child-minders.

Since the implementation of the project in 1983, the mother training programme that focuses on the different needs of target groups in a variety of contexts has been revised thoroughly for application in the community. The most important modification was made in the duration of the programme, it was reduced from 60 to 25 weeks. Furthermore, the programme no longer targets both 4- and 5-year-olds, but only 5-year-olds since it aims to reach children before they begin formal schooling. Akin to these changes, a new cognitive training programme was developed by the original project team to replace HIPPY. Although the number of topics in the mother enrichment element remained unchanged, the content was revised and enlarged to include a new component—reproductive health and family planning—in the programme. The programme is now implemented through weekly group meetings instead of a combination of home visits and group meetings as was done previously. The programme with all its components was named the Mother–Child Education Programme (MOCEP). Following these modifications, the programme became a public programme targeting national coverage instead of limited applications. In 1993, the Mother–Child Education Foundation (MOCEF) obtained the copyright of the programme and the programme began to be implemented with the collaboration of the MOCEF and the Ministry of National Education.

The Mother–Child Education Programme comprises three main elements: a programme to foster cognitive development of the child, a programme to sensitize mothers to the overall development of the child, and a programme to sensitize mothers to reproductive health and family planning. Spread over 25 weeks, the programme targets children who are "at risk" due to their environmental conditions.

THE PROGRAMME TO FOSTER COGNITIVE DEVELOPMENT OF THE CHILD

The Cognitive Development Programme was developed in 1991 (Kagitcibasi, Bekman, Özkök, & Kusçul, 1991) and revised in 1995 (Kagitcibasi, Bekman, Kuscul, Özkök, & Sucuka, 1995). The primary aim of this component is to prepare the child for school, by fostering his preliteracy and numeracy skills.

Weekly group meetings are held at an adult education centre and mothers are given 20–25 pages of worksheets. Each week's materials contain various daily exercises to be used by the mother with the child, which take about 15 to 20 minutes to complete. Each day of the week has specific worksheets which are marked to help the mother keep track of the activities for different days. The level of difficulty of the worksheets progressively increases over time. The exercises cover the areas of eye–hand coordination, sensory discrimination, preliteracy (recognition of letters, and recognition of letter sounds) and prenumeracy skills (recognition of numbers, addition and subtraction), language development, classification, seriation, concept formation (direction, size, and place), learning of colours and shapes, problem solving skills, and general ability.

In addition to these worksheets, 8 picture storybooks (Alpöge, 1995) are used for training in listening comprehension, verbal description, vocabulary, question–answer activities, and reasoning. Interactive shared book reading activities are given particular emphasis since the origins of emergent literacy are believed to lie in early mother–child interaction in activities involving picture books and reading materials. These interactions carry the character-istics of a scaffolding dialogue. Correlation between the frequency of shared book reading and the child's language development and later reading has been well observed (Crane-Thoreson & Dale, 1992; Rowe, 1991).

THE MOTHER ENRICHMENT PROGRAMME

The Mother Enrichment Programme was developed in 1982 and subsequently revised in 1995 (Kagitcibasi, Bekman, Özkök, & Kusçul, 1995). It aims to increase the mother's sensitivity to the cognitive, social, and emotional development of the child, and to assist her in creating a home environment more conducive to the child's development. In addition, it aims to support the mother in developing consistent and positive interaction with the child.

Included in this programme are children's health, nutrition, cognitive, social, and physical development, creative play activities, and importance of play. Issues such as discipline, methods for changing negative behaviours, and other facets of mother–child interaction and communication are also discussed. Group discussions focus on expressing and listening to the feelings of the child and their acceptance. Generalizations are made to other human relations, including spousal relations. Some meetings also focus on the mother's feelings about being a woman and a mother. Throughout the programme, mothers are encouraged to develop a positive self-concept, as the group discussions are oriented toward supporting mothers in developing feelings of competence, efficacy and self-confidence.

THE REPRODUCTIVE HEALTH
AND FAMILY PLANNING PROGRAMME

This programme was developed in cooperation with institutions active in the area of family planning. The programme covers 23 topics with the first part comprising 14 topics that focus on the importance of reproductive health and the factors that influence it. This part sensitizes mothers to their reproductive system and suggests ways to prevent basic illnesses of this system, it also defines healthy pregnancy, and safe motherhood. The second part concentrates on different methods of family planning, which are discussed in 9 weekly meetings.

How the Mother–Child Education Programme (MOCEP) Works

The Mother–Child Education Programme targets both the child and the child's immediate environment. To promote the child's overall development, the mother is targeted as she is the significant person in the child's home context, the aim being to foster cognitive and psychosocial development in the home environment. In this respect, the programme is influenced by the ecological approach which underlines the role of the child's environment.

The programme also aims to promote school readiness by providing cognitive enrichment to the child and by creating an environment that is conducive to optimal psychosocial health and nutritional development. This necessitates fostering the role of the parents in the cognitive, social, and emotional development of the child. Child management methods and communication with the child, emotional security and self-esteem of the mother, family planning, and reproductive health are also targeted in the programme. Thus, the programme combines both adult education as well as child development.

Timing has always been an issue for intervention programmes (Campbell & Ramey, 1994; Roberts & Wasik, 1994). There are contradictory views regarding programme duration and time of initiation. It is believed that there are periods in the parents' lives when they are more open to new information, for instance, immediately before and after the birth of a child may be a good time to introduce support. The Mother–Child Education Programme reaches children and parents just before the child begins formal schooling. The underlying reason is that mothers would be more receptive to new information during this period.

Different approaches are adopted for the implementation of the various components of the programme. For two of the three components, Mother Enrichment and Reproductive Health and Family Planning, a group dynamics approach was found to be more appropriate. Mothers attend group discussions and are expected to implement group decisions at home. In subsequent meetings, the group leaders follow the consequences of these decisions. The expectation is that mothers would be more responsible for the decisions taken and followed by the group since they know that they have the support of the group if faced with resistance for the decisions taken at home. This process is believed to facilitate attitude and behaviour change more than the other means of disseminating information which often view the participants as passive receivers (Kagitcibasi, 1997).

For the Cognitive Training Programme, a mediated learning approach is adopted. The aim is to promote school readiness through interaction with an adult who is instructing the child. Mothers, therefore, become the teachers of their children. They provide scaffolding in order to maximize intellectual competence and growth of the child. Mothers are expected to conduct exercises with their children especially in prenumeracy and literacy skills. During these exercises, by asking questions, making suggestions, instructing and answering questions, mothers help their children to develop and integrate their cognitive skills and create an opportunity to function in their zone of proximal development.

IMPLEMENTATION OF THE MOTHER–CHILD EDUCATION PROGRAMME

During the 25 weeks of the programme, mothers attend weekly group meetings held at adult education centres, which are found in each district of each province in Turkey. Each group comprises 20–25 mothers. Adult education teachers who are trained by the staff of the Mother–Child Education Foundation supervise the meetings. In the first part of a meeting that week's topic of the Mother Enrichment Programme is discussed for nearly 90 minutes. Mothers are encouraged to actively participate in the group discussions by asking questions, expressing opinions, and sharing ideas and experiences. The second part of the meeting focuses on the Reproductive Health and Family Planning Programme which is discussed for 15 minutes. Here, the main aim is to pass information in the context of a group. This makes it possible for mothers to share their own experiences and learn about others' experiences in the area of family planning and reproductive health.

In the last part of the meeting, groups of five or six mothers are formed and they learn the exercises of the Cognitive Development Programme through role playing. Each group has an aide (one of the mothers) who is responsible for the correct implementation of the programme in that group. All the mothers in the group take turns and role play the activities that they would later perform with their children. Each mother is given an opportunity to experience the role of the mother as well as that of the child. To ensure that the implementation is effective at home extra effort is made to teach the worksheet of that week correctly to mothers. The entire meeting lasts approximately 3 hours.

Empirical Study[1]

The short- and long-term evaluation of the Mother Training Programme implemented on a small scale was carried out and it revealed impressive results. Despite positive outcomes it was apparent that there was a need for further research to assess the effects of the revised programme (the Mother–Child Education Programme), which was implemented on a wide scale, and targeted both children and mothers.

The first phase of the research, which studied the short-term impact of the programme on both children and mothers, followed a pre–post, control group, quasi-experimental design. Thus, children and mothers were assessed on several variables both before the introduction of the programme and after it was terminated. The time interval between these two assessments was 8 months.

Follow-up research examined (*a*) whether an early enrichment programme providing the child with school readiness skills enabled the child to start ahead and enjoy initial success in primary

[1] Research is funded by the Bernard Van Leer Foundation.

school, and (*b*) whether positive changes in the home environment were long lasting. With these aims, the experimental and control groups were compared a year after the termination of the programme.

SAMPLE

The sample was drawn from four different provinces where the programme was being implemented. Children and mothers were selected from four different programme sites in each of the four provinces. Thus, data were collected from 16 programme sites. The control groups comprised comparable mother–child pairs who did not participate in the programme and were chosen from the same sites. For the selection of comparable control groups, criteria such as family housing conditions, education and occupation levels of mothers and fathers were matched. In total, there were 102 experimental and 115 control mother and child pairs in the study.

The follow-up phase of the research, which assessed initial school success, was able to contact the original sample of the first phase of the study. There was very little attrition of the original sample, all those who had started school were included in the follow-up research. However, 25 children had not begun school, 13 families could not be contacted, and 3 dropped out of the study. In total, there were 92 experimental and 85 control mother–child pairs in the follow-up study.

Children in the sample were between 61 and 72 months of age, and 98 of them were girls and 125 were boys. While 37.2 per cent of mothers were in the 27–30 years age group, 35.4 per cent were in the 31–34 years age group. The education level of the sample was generally low, as expected from a low socioeconomic status population. A majority of mothers and fathers were elementary school graduates (mothers 66 per cent, fathers 50 per cent). Most of the families had two children (52 per cent) and lived in apartment houses (60.4 per cent). Each household had 4 (48 per cent) or 5 (45 per cent) members. Nearly all the mothers (92 per cent) were housewives. More than half of the fathers was semi-skilled

(27 per cent) or skilled (28 per cent) workers. A large number of mothers (44 per cent) were city born, and the rest were born either in a rural village (34 per cent) or in a small town (17 per cent).

Data Collection Procedure

PRE-LITERACY SKILLS AND PRE-NUMERACY SKILLS INSTRUMENTS

To assess the immediate effects of the programme on children, preliteracy and prenumeracy skills were measured in the cognitive domain. The instruments measuring preliteracy and prenumeracy skills were designed by the research team, and assessed skills that are important for learning how to read and write and do mathematics in primary school. The Pre-literacy Skills Instrument comprised 26 items and the range of scores was between 0 and 167. The Pre-numeracy Skills Instrument comprised 15 items and the range of scores was between 0 and 149. Cronbach alpha for the Pre-literacy Skills Instrument was .87, and for the Pre-numeracy Skills Instrument it was .89.

LITERACY SKILLS AND NUMERACY SKILLS INSTRUMENTS

To assess the effect of the programme on children's primary school success in the follow-up study, two instruments—the Literacy Skills and the Numeracy Skills Instruments—were developed by the research team which measured literacy and numeracy skills respectively. Though these instruments tapped the same skills as the Pre-literacy Skills and Pre-numeracy Skills Instruments, the questions were more difficult since the aim was to assess the level at the end of the first year of primary school. The Literacy Skills Instrument contained 9 items and the range of scores was between 0 and 148. The Numeracy Skills Instrument also contained 9 items and the scores ranged from 3 to 134. Cronbach alpha for the Literacy Skills Instrument was .64, and .77 for the Numeracy Skills Instrument.

INTERVIEWS

Mothers were interviewed to assess the effect of the programme. The interview schedule included questions on demographic characteristics, child rearing attitudes, interest in the child's academic life, the mother's satisfaction with the child's school life, personal and family network of social relations in the family, and the mother's self-esteem. In addition to these assessments, teachers were interviewed to obtain their *evaluation of* the child with respect to his or her school life and school success. The interview schedule included questions related to the teacher's evaluation of the child in the social and cognitive domains, and to understand the nature of the teaching environment in the classroom.

Two scales were derived from the questions included in the interview schedule for teachers. The Teacher's Evaluation of Child's Cognitive Skills Scale measures such cognitive characteristics of the child as success in class, participation in class, curiosity, creativity, whether the child likes to explore things, interest in learning, attention level, and knowledge of responsibilities. Cronbach alpha for this scale was .96. The Teacher's Evaluation of Child's Personality Characteristics Scale included items that were related to the teacher's perception of how much the child is willing to share, whether the child is independent or not, whether his friends listen to him, whether he keeps his promises, and whether he is loving and caring to others. Cronbach alpha for this scale was .91. Both teacher and mother interviews were piloted before use.

DATE FOR READING AND AVERAGE GRADES

Date for reading and average grades were also collected separately. In Grade 1 in Turkey, class teachers keep a record of the date when the child is first able to read. Such information was collected for each child as well as passing grades for Grade 1.

THE ENVIRONMENTAL STIMULATION INDEX

An index was developed to identify the home environment of the child in terms of its stimulation level. The index included 10 variables such as the education level of parents, intensity of mother–child interaction, number and type of toys available at home, and the frequency of buying newspapers, magazines, and watching TV. Cronbach alpha for the index was .61. For each child, the home environment index was divided into two levels: high and low.

THE HOME STUDY ENVIRONMENT INDEX

In addition to the Environmental Stimulation Index, an attempt was made to evaluate the suitability of the home environment for studying. Variables such as place of study, the presence of TV and other people in the study area, the presence or absence of others when the child is doing homework, and the reactions of the child to these people were included in the Home Study Environment Index. There were 9 items in all and Cronbach alpha was .66. For each child, the study environment at home was divided into two levels: adequate and inadequate.

ANALYSIS

In the initial phase of the study, change scores were obtained for both the experimental and control groups for all the measures that assessed the effects of the programme on children. The main analyses included a comparison of these change scores using t-tests. Similarly, difference scores were obtained for mothers' interviews that assessed the effects of the programme on mother–child interactions as well as on the mothers themselves. For categorical items, comparisons between the two groups were done on the posttest results only. Of this categorical data, only those items that did not yield a significant difference between the groups in the pretest but showed a difference in the posttest have been reported.

In the follow-up phase of the research, t-test analyses were performed for all the measures that assessed the effects of the programme on children. This permitted an observation of the differences between the mother trained and non-trained children at the end of their first year in elementary school on different variables. Similarly, the effects of the programme on mothers were assessed either by using t-tests or chi square analyses. Variables were compared for trained and non-trained mothers. To examine the differences in the evaluation of teachers between trained and non-trained groups of children, teachers' self-reports on various factors were compared.

To examine the relations between predictor and outcome variables, multiple regression analyses and path analyses were performed. In path analyses, z-scores were computed for all the variables. Various stepwise multiple regression analyses were carried out with all the possible predictor and outcome variables. Predictor variables, which were significantly related to the outcome variables according to multiple regression analyses, were included in the model. Various possible models were examined by comparing the correlations computed in the model to the correlations obtained earlier for each pair of variables in the data. The model in which computed correlations reflected accurately the correlation coefficients computed for each pair was accepted (the difference between the correlations computed in the model and correlations in the main data were not higher than .11).

Results

PRELITERACY AND PRENUMERACY SKILLS

Analyses of the immediate effects of the programme on children revealed significant results. Comparisons of the change scores (pre–post difference) of the mother trained and non-trained groups revealed significant differences in both preliteracy and prenumeracy skills. The mean change scores of the trained group on preliteracy and prenumeracy skills were significantly higher than the mean change scores of the non-trained group (preliteracy: 33.40 vs 15.58, t (215) = 6.89, p = .01; prenumeracy: 47.24 vs 16.89, t (179) = 8.41, p = .01).

Figure 10.1
Preliteracy and Prenumeracy Scores

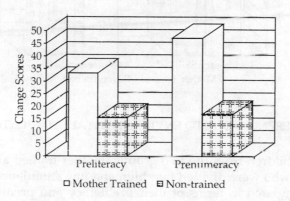

☐ Mother Trained   ☒ Non-trained

LITERACY AND NUMERACY SKILLS

Analyses of the literacy and numeracy scores obtained at the end of the first year of schooling revealed similar results. The mean scores of the trained group on literacy and numeracy skills were significantly higher than those of the non-trained group (literacy: 84.73 vs 73.69, t (169) = 2.99, p = .03; numeracy: 94.94 vs 82.78, t (173) = 3.15, p = .02). These results clearly revealed that the positive effects of the programme on children's cognitive development persisted for a year after the termination of the programme. These children were superior not only in preliteracy and prenumeracy skills, but also in literacy and numeracy skills at the elementary school level than those who had not participated in the programme.

Figure 10.2
Literacy and Numeracy Scores

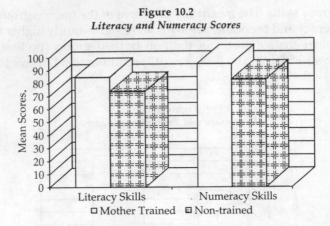

DIFFERENCES DUE TO ENVIRONMENTAL STIMULATION

Children from the two groups (mother trained and non-trained) who were divided into high and low stimulation levels were compared in terms of their preliteracy and prenumeracy mean change scores. The results revealed a distinct difference between the two groups. Children of the non-trained group of mothers from a stimulating environment had significantly higher preliteracy (24.00 vs 8.85, t (71) = 3.85, p = .01) and prenumeracy mean change scores (23.32 vs 10.85, t (70) = 2.65, p = .01) than children coming from a low stimulating environment of the same group. On the other hand, in the case of the mother trained group, no significant differences were obtained between children from stimulating and non-stimulating environments in terms of pre-literacy and prenumeracy mean change scores. Moreover, children of the mother trained group from different environments (stimulating and non-stimulating) had significantly higher mean change scores on both skills than children of the non-trained group of mothers from a stimulating environment.

When similar analyses were done for the literacy and numeracy scores of both groups, significant differences were obtained between the two groups. Children of the non-trained group from a stimulating environment had significantly higher mean literacy (85.33 vs 67.41, t (51) = 2.72, p = .01) and numeracy scores (94.33 vs 71.10, t (50) = 3.12, p = .01) than children from a low stimulating

Figure 10.3
Differences According to Environmental Stimulation Index:
Preliteracy and Prenumeracy Scores

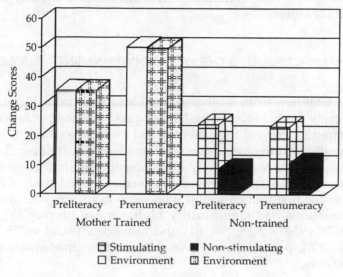

Figure 10.4
Differences According to Environmental Stimulation Index:
Literacy and Numeracy Scores

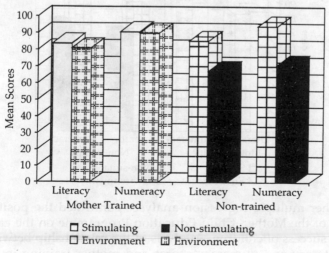

environment of the same group. In the case of the trained group, there were no significant differences between children from stimulating and non-stimulating environments on literacy and numeracy scores.

DIFFERENCES DUE TO THE STUDY ENVIRONMENT AT HOME

Children from mother trained and non-trained groups who came from adequate and inadequate environments were compared in terms of their literacy and numeracy scores. While no significant differences were obtained between children from adequate and inadequate study environments in the trained group, significant differences were found in the non-trained group. Children in the non-trained group who came from adequate study environments had significantly higher mean literacy (87.74 vs 68.70, t (58) = 3.28, p = .01) and numeracy (94.44 vs 75.34, t (59) = 2.84, p = .01) scores than children from inadequate environments.

Figure 10.5
Differences According to Study Environment at Home:
Literacy and Numeracy Scores

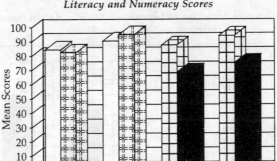

Further multiple regression analyses confirmed the positive effects of the Mother–Child Education Programme on the early school success of children. Analysis of the relationship between total literacy and numeracy scores and mother training in the inadequate study environment revealed that training was a predictor variable. Thus, literacy and numeracy scores were affected by training in the inadequate study environment (see Table 10.1). It is interesting that similar literacy and numeracy scores were obtained by children from adequate and inadequate study environments in the trained group and it may be argued that this was due to the effects of training on children from inadequate environments.

Average Grades

Report cards of Grade 1 children revealed significant differences between the average grades of trained and non-trained groups. The average grades of the trained group were significantly higher than those of the non-trained group (4.64 vs 4.08, $t(167) = 2.99$, $p = .02$). Multiple regression analyses of the average grades revealed that the variables of mother training and teacher's perception of the cognitive characteristics were predictor variables for average grades (see Table 10.1). Children in the trained group who were perceived by the teacher as being cognitively superior also had better average grades.

"Starts Reading" Date

As an indication of school success, the date at which each child began to read was obtained and compared. Data showed that children of the trained group began to read significantly earlier than the non-trained group of children ($\chi^2 (8, N = 168) = 20.85$, $p = .01$).
Better average grades and early reading in the case of the trained group revealed that children who had acquired skills which prepared them for formal schooling had an advantage at the time of entering school and enjoyed academic success in the first year of school.

Teacher's Perception of the Children

An attempt was made to determine whether there were differences in the teacher's perception of children of the trained and non-trained groups. Differences were obtained in the following variables.

Table 10.1

Multiple Regression for Total Literacy and Numeracy Score, Passing Grades and Teacher's Perception of Cognitive Characteristics of the Child

Variable	Total Literacy and Numeracy Score (Inadequate Study Environment at Home)		Passing Grades		Teacher's Perception of Cognitive Characteristics	
	B	SE	B	SE	B	SE
Mother training	.35**	.11	.18**	.07	-.03	-.04
Study environment at home	.16	.17	.14	.17	.03	.04
Teacher's perception of cognitive characteristics of the child			.29***	.04		
Teacher's perception of personality characteristics of the child			.08	.05		
Self-esteem of mothers			-.01	-.02		
Cognitive environment in the classrooms			.09	.11	-.04*	.02
Problems of the child in the school			-.05	-.06		
Mother's satisfaction with the child			.12	.13		
Mother's interest in schooling					.26**	.09
Cognitive readiness of the child					.29***	.06
Sex of the child					-.09	-.11
R^2	.12		.34		.32	
Adjusted R^2	.11		.32		.31	

Notes: *p < .05; **p < .01; ***p < .001.

According to the teachers, children of the trained group engaged in more appropriate behaviours at school than the non-trained group. The difference was significant (mean: 4.23 vs 3.91, t (174) = 2.38, p = .02). Further, teachers' evaluations revealed other significant differences between the trained and non-trained groups. Teachers evaluated children of the trained group as more attentive (4.11 vs 3.78, t (175) = 2.18, p = .03), more creative (3.85 vs 3.46, t (172) = 2.55, p = .01), and more curious (4.29 vs 4.00, t (175) = 2.10, p = .04) than children of the non-trained group.

Figure 10.6
Teachers' Evaluation of Children

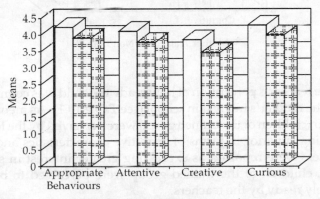

Means

□ Mother Trained ⊟ Non-trained

Teachers were also asked to evaluate children with respect to their school readiness and they reported that children of the trained group were more prepared cognitively (3.97 vs 3.48, t (163) = 2.76, p = .01) and socially (3.92 vs 3.60, t (162) = 1.93, p = .05) for school than the non-trained group.

Differences in the evaluation of teachers were not confined only to the behaviours of children from the two groups, but also covered the behaviours of their mothers. Teachers reported that the trained group of mothers attended school meetings more often (4.53 vs 4.19, t (175) = 2.14, p = .03) and they were more interested in their child's school behaviour (4.36 vs 4.00, t (175) = 2.62, p = .01) than the non-trained group of mothers.

Multiple regression analyses revealed that the teacher's perception of the cognitive characteristics of the child was predicted

Figure 10.7
Teachers' Evaluation of School Readiness

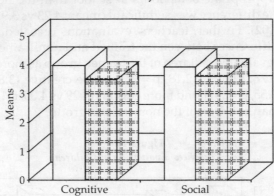

□ Mother Trained   ■ Non-trained

by the teacher's perception of how ready the child was cognitively and the mother's interest in school (see Table 10.1). As mentioned earlier, children of the trained group were perceived by the teacher as being superior in terms of cognitive characteristics and their mothers were reported as expressing greater interest in school. Thus, children of the trained group were perceived to be cognitively ready by the teachers.

MOTHERS' ATTITUDES TOWARD SCHOOL

The self-reports obtained from mothers revealed that the trained group of mothers was significantly more interested in the child's school activities than the non-trained group. The mean for the trained group was 4.47 and it was 3.93 (t (169) = 3.19, p = .02) for the non-trained group.

More trained mothers reported making an extra effort to encourage their child's success at school as compared to the non-trained group. The difference was significant: 80 per cent of trained mothers and 58 per cent of non-trained mothers stated making an extra effort for school success (χ^2 (1, N = 176) = 20.58, p = .01).

Figure 10.8
Mothers' Interest in Schooling

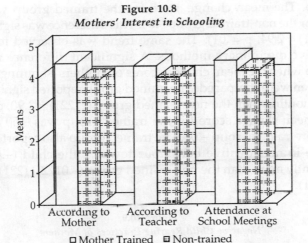

□ Mother Trained   ⊟ Non-trained

There was a significant difference between trained and non-trained mothers' views on their children's school readiness (χ^2 $(1, N = 177) = 20.58, p = .01$). All the mothers in the trained group (100 per cent) were of the view that their children were ready to begin school as compared to only 20 per cent of the non-trained mothers.

CHILD REARING ATTITUDES

The change in mother–child interaction was assessed by comparing the self-reports of mothers on their child rearing practices before and after the programme. The self-reports of the trained group were collected after they committed themselves to attend the programme but before the programme commenced. All the mothers in a group were included in the sample. These self-reports, collected through interviews, covered both the disciplinary methods used by the mother and their possible behaviours in certain situations.

An examination of the use of positive and negative disciplinary methods by mothers revealed a trend of significant decrease in the use of negative methods by the trained group as compared to the non-trained group. The trained group of mothers reported that they beat their children significantly less than the non-trained group. The mean change score for the trained group was −.38 and for the non-trained group −.04. This difference was significant: (t (221) = 2.94, p = .01). The same trend was observed for other negative disciplinary methods. A significant difference was obtained when the mean change scores of mothers' shouting at their children were compared. The trained group reported significantly less shouting than the non-trained group (t (221) = 2.90, p = .01). The mean change score for the trained group was −.50 and for the non-trained group −.06. The trained group also reported a decrease in nonattentive behaviour towards the child (−.42) significantly more than the non-trained group (−.0172, t (221) = 3.35, p = .01).

Figure 10.9
Negative Child Rearing Practices of Mothers

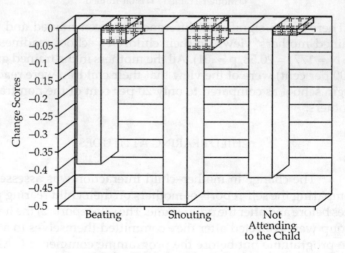

□ Mother Trained ⊟ Non-trained

It was found that trained mothers were not only less likely to use negative disciplinary methods, but also that they adopted more positive methods. Separate analyses revealed that the mean change score for explaining reasons of wrong behaviour (.08) was significantly higher for the trained group than the non-trained group (−.10), t (221) = 2.09, p = .04). The same trend was seen in relation to setting up rules of behaviour; this behaviour increased in the trained group (a change score of .20), whereas a negative change was observed in the non-trained group (–.05), t (221) = 4.15, p = .01). In the case of the positive disciplinary method of diverting the child's attention, the mean change score for the trained group was .26, but no change was observed in the non-trained group (.00), t (221) = 2.97, p = .01).

Figure 10.10
Positive Child Rearing Practices of Mothers I

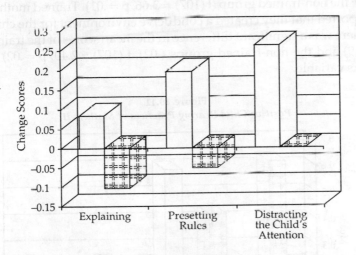

In order to determine whether the changes in mothers' child rearing attitudes obtained in the initial phase of the study were sustained over time, self-reports of the mothers were collected through interviews at the end of the first year of school.

An examination of mothers' use of positive and negative disciplinary methods confirmed that the trends obtained in the initial phase of the study persisted over time. The trained group made significantly less use of negative disciplinary methods than the non-trained group. Mothers in the trained group reported that they beat their children significantly less (mean .27) than those in the non-trained group (mean .62). The difference was significant: (t (170) = 3.64, p = .01). The same trend was observed in the case of the nonattentive behaviour of the mother when the child sought attention. The trained group manifested significantly less nonattentive behaviour (.26) than the non-trained group (.42), t (176) = 2.40, p = .02).

Separate analyses of each positive behaviour revealed that the mean score for explaining reasons of wrong behaviour was significantly higher for the trained group (.59) than the non-trained group (.24), t (151) = 3.39, p = .01). The same trend was also observed in relation to diverting the child's attention to something else; the mean score for the trained group was .24, and .02 for the non-trained group (t (107) = 3.66, p = .01). Trained mothers reported that they created a conducive environment for the child. There was a significant difference in the mean scores of the trained (.19) and the non-trained groups (.02), t (107) = 2.40, p = .02) on this variable.

Figure 10.11
Positive Child Rearing Practices of Mothers II

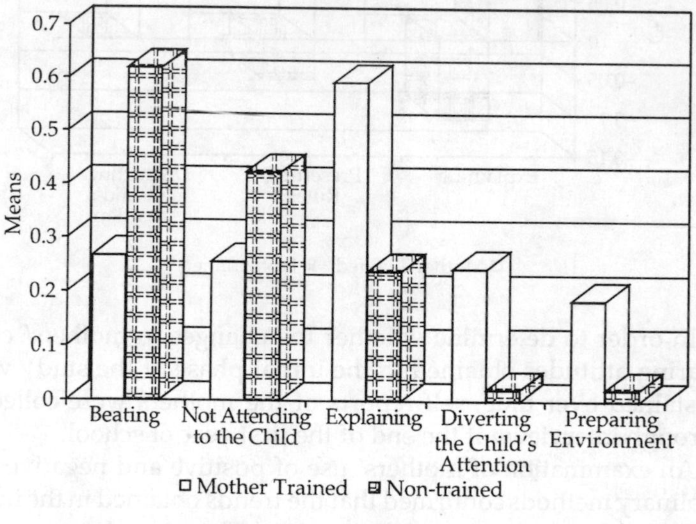

Chain of Effects

As indicated earlier, the aim of the follow-up research was to ascertain whether the chain of interrelated effects deriving from the programme developed into a positive cycle. The resulting path model is depicted in Figure 10.12. Statistically significant direct effects are represented by straight arrows, and arrows are omitted when path coefficients were not statistically significant. It can be seen from the model that the birth month of the child as well as environmental stimulation had significant effects on the level of preliteracy and prenumeracy skills at the time of introduction of the training. Environmental stimulation had a lesser effect on preliteracy and prenumeracy skills at the termination of the training. The reduced effect of environmental stimulation at the end of the programme implied that training interacted with the effect of environment.

Figure 10.12
Path Analysis

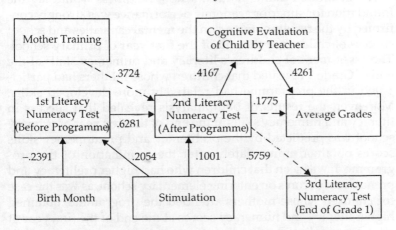

Although there is no direct path from training to Grade 1 performances, posttest of the preliteracy and prenumeracy scores of the child just before the school was affected by the training, which in turn had an impact on the literacy and numeracy skills and passing grades at the end of the first year. Also, posttest of both skills affected the teacher's cognitive evaluation of the child which in turn had a significant effect on passing grades at the end of Grade 1.

Discussion

The results of the research clearly reveal the positive impact of early home intervention, specifically the Mother–Child Education Programme, not only on children but also on one of the significant adults in the child's immediate environment—the mother—and on the relationship between the mother and the child. The results obtained immediately after the termination of the Mother–Child Education Programme revealed the effects of the programme on the cognitive development of children as reflected by the superior performance on the Pre-literacy Skills and Pre-numeracy Skills Instruments of children whose mothers attended the programme.

The likelihood that enhanced school readiness would lay the foundation for superior academic performance was strongly confirmed by the results obtained on the mental capacities and school success of children at the end of the first year of primary school. The assessment of children's literacy and numeracy skills at the end of Grade 1 revealed that children whose mothers had participated in the programme had relatively more developed skills. Moreover, the results of path analysis revealed that success in literacy and numeracy skills at the end of the first year of primary school was predicted by the preliteracy and prenumeracy skills scores obtained immediately after the termination of the programme. It was seen that children who had higher preliteracy and prenumeracy scores on entering elementary school, as was the case for children whose mothers attended the programme, obtained higher literacy and numeracy scores at the end of the first year of schooling, indicating that the effects of the programme on children's literacy and numeracy learning were carried over to formal schooling.

It seemed that the Mother–Child Education Programme mitigated the negative effects often associated with cognitively non-stimulating homes and inadequate study environments. Children who were exposed to the intervention programme that fostered their cognitive development performed far better than if they and their families had not been exposed to the intervention. The difference between groups, whose mothers were trained and non-trained in the stimulating and non-stimulating environments, revealed that when children were given a chance to participate in activities which facilitated the realization of their optimal potential, they performed better than their counterparts in spite of the existence of poor home conditions.

The significant difference between the average grades of children of trained and non-trained mothers and the earlier date for beginning to read were taken as basic indicators of initial school success. Thus, children from empowered environments were prepared when they entered school and this increased their chances of early success. School success was not only reflected in the performance of the child, but also in how others perceived the child's academic position and performance. Teachers perceived children from the trained group as socially and cognitively prepared for school. These children were found to be more attentive, creative, curious, and engaged in more socially well adjusted behaviours.

In this research, in addition to the child's cognitive readiness for school, school related behaviour and attitudes of mothers were also found to be influential factors. Teachers of the trained group of children, apart from perceiving them as more cognitively and socially prepared, also reported that their mothers were more interested in the child's school life and had a higher level of attendance at school meetings. The effect of the mother's interest in school on the teacher's perception of the child highlighted the importance of a supportive home context for the participation of the child in different settings, in this case the school.

Interestingly, the self-reports of trained mothers revealed that they perceived themselves as being more interested in their children's school and that they made extra effort to ensure the success of their children in school. All the trained mothers perceived their children as ready to begin school. These findings pointed to a home environment that was not only conducive to school performance and success, but also one that encouraged positive attitudes toward school and school performance. Thus, the programme was successful in preparing the child in terms of school readiness and in creating a supportive home environment.

The findings not only highlighted the importance of the experiences that the home environment provided to the child, but also demonstrated how the child and his environment were not independent of each other. Thus, mothers who provided cognitive and social stimulation to their children perceived them as ready for school and invested more in their school success. Likewise, children whose mothers perceived them to be ready for school and evinced an interest in their school life were successful. It is believed that the developmental changes observed in children as a result of the programme were the product of the interaction of children with the experiences provided by their families.

The programme was not only effective in creating an intellectually stimulating home environment, but also in fostering pleasant, understanding mother–child interaction, less punitive parenting which in turn led to a more pleasant home environment. The changes observed in mothers' disciplinary behaviours, where the trained group of mothers reported using less negative disciplinary methods were indicative of changes in the home environment. Similar findings obtained a year later revealed that the changes induced by the programme were maintained. Although the assessments in different domains indicated the continuation of the positive effects of the intervention at the end of the first year of primary school, there is a need for a follow-up study beyond Grade 1 to examine the further effects.

In sum, programmes like the Turkish Mother–Child Education Programme play an important role in the advancement of human development by overcoming some of the negative effects of unfavourable conditions in the home environment. A programme that empowers both the child and the mother, like the Mother–Child Education Programme, not only throws light on a successful early childhood education programme, but is also important for community development.

The results confirm the success of the Mother–Child Education Programme. At this point a discussion of the factors contributing to this success and the benefits obtained may be useful for policy makers, programme planners, and practitioners. It is believed that the outstanding results were mainly due to the principles that were accepted for implementation, the consistent adoption of those principles, and the follow-up of implementation by the programme staff. Special attention was given to both thorough training of the trainers, and close follow-up of implementation of two components—group meetings and home activities. Furthermore, the effectiveness of dissemination and implementation was continuously evaluated. Programme consultants were available when trainers were in need of assistance and periodic meetings were held during implementation to support the trainers. Trainers made an effort to ensure that each mother attended the weekly group meetings. When mothers failed to attend these meetings, trainers made additional home visits to inform them about the topics covered in the meeting. This not only ensured that mothers were able to follow subjects discussed in the mother empowerment component of the programme, but also provided a chance to observe mothers' use of the worksheets prepared for the children's cognitive development component. Mothers' own child rearing practices and attitudes were accorded due respect. All decisions were taken together as a group and trainers were sensitive to the need to build on mothers' strengths rather than underline their weaknesses.

As expected, there were various problems to be solved and challenges to be faced. One of the initial challenges was meeting the targeted enrolment rate and trainers made tremendous efforts to enrol mothers in the Programme in instances where it was first implemented in a community. Since the Programme was a new concept for the community, there were some misgivings. Following the participation of community members and the positive consequences of the Programme, these misgivings have largely been overcome. Similarly, some of the family members like mothers-in-law and husbands were not supportive of mothers attending such a programme. To solve this problem home visits were made. These are common problems faced in any new programme. Another challenge during the expansion phase of the Programme was working in partnership with the State and the need to work within bureaucratic regulations and limitations. Over time, these challenges led to the development of such skills as to establish a successful partnership between an NGO and the State. A primary lesson was the understanding that for the success of a parent training programme, equal weight and attention have to be given to all phases and components of a programme, including programme development, implementation and dissemination. The implementation of the Mother–Child Education Programme demonstrated that if a programme is useful and meets the needs of communities, it can secure the commitment of stakeholders and achieve success.

References

Alpöge, G. (1995). *Eight storybooks*. Mother–Child Education Publications No 3. Istanbul: Mother Education Foundation.

Andrews, S., Blumen-Chal, J., Johnson, D., Kahn, A., Ferguson, C., Lasater, T., Malone, P., & Wallace, D. (1982). The skills of mothering: A study of parent-child development centers. *Monographs of the Society for Research in Child Development*, 47(6, Serial no. 198), 1–181.

Bekman, S. (1990). Alternative to the available: Home-based vs center-based programs. *Early Child Development and Care, 58*, 109–119.

Bekman, S. (1993). Preschool education system in Turkey revisited. *OMEP International Journal of Early Childhood, 25*(1), 13–19.

Bekman, S. (1995). Research on HIPPY in Turkey. *Proceedings of the second HIPPY international research seminar*, 43–45.

Bekman, S. (1998a). Long term effects of the Turkish Home-based Early Enrichment Program. In U. Gielen & A.L. Comunian (Eds), *Family and family therapy in international perspective* (pp. 401–407). Italy: Edizioni Llint Trieste.

Bekman, S. (1998b). *Fair chance: An evaluation of the Mother–Child Education Program*. Istanbul: Mother–Child Education Publication.

Beller, E.K. (1974). Impact of early education on disadvantaged children. In S. Ryan (Ed.), *A report on longitudinal evaluations of preschool programs* (vol. 1, pp. 15–48). (DHEW Publication No. [OHD] 74–24). Washington, DC: US Government Printing Office.

Berrueta-Clement, J.R., Scheweinhart, L.L., Barnett, W.S., Epstein, A., & Weikart, D. (1986). Changed lives: Perry Pre-school Program on youths through age 19. In M.F. Hechinger (Ed.), *Better start: New choices for early learning* (pp. 11–40). New York: Wallker Company.

Bronfenbrenner, U. (1979). *The ecology of human development*. Cambridge: Harvard University Press.

Campbell, F.A., & Ramey, C.T. (1994). Effects of early intervention on intellectual and academic achievement: A follow-up study of children from low-income families. *Child Development, 65*, 684–698.

Cochran, M., & Handerson, C. (1985). *Family matters: Evaluation of the parental empowerment program*. Final report submitted to the National Institute of Education. Ithaca, NY: Cornell University.

Crane-Thoreson, C., & Dale, P.S. (1992). Do early talkers become early readers? Linguistic precocity, preschool language, and emergent literacy. *Development Psychology, 28*, 421–429.

Deutsch, M., Deutsch, J.P., Jordan, T.J., & Grallo, R. (1983). The IDS program: An experiment in early and sustained enrichment. In Consortium for Longitudinal Studies (Ed.), *As the twig is bent* (pp. 377–410). Hillsdale, NJ: Lawrence Erlbaum.

Dickie, J.R., & Gerber, S.C. (1980). Training in social competence: The effect on mothers, fathers, and infants. *Child Development, 51*, 1248–1251.

Farran, D.C. (1990). Effects of intervention with disadvantaged and disabled children: A decade review. In S.J. Meisels & J.P. Shankoff (Eds), *Handbook of early childhood intervention* (pp. 501–539). Cambridge: Cambridge University Press.

Gomby, D.S., Culross, P.I., & Behrman, R.E. (1999). Home visiting: Recent program evaluations—Analysis and recommendations. *The Future of Children*, *9*, 4–26.

Gray, S., Ramsey, B., & Klaus, R. (1982). *From 3–20—The early training project.* Baltimore: University Park Press.

Jester, R.E., & Guinagh, B.J. (1983). The Gordon Parent Education Infant and Toddler Program. In Consortium for Longitudinal Studies (Ed.), *As the twig is bent* (pp. 103–132). Hillsdale, NJ: Lawrence Erlbaum.

Kagitcibasi, C. (1991). The early enrichment project in Turkey. *UNESCO-UNICEF-WFP. Notes/comments.* (No. 193). Paris: UNESCO.

Kagitcibasi, C. (1992). Research on parenting and child development in cross cultural perspective. In M. Rosenzweig (Ed.), *International psychological science* (pp. 137–160). Washington, DC: APA.

Kagitcibasi, C. (1996). *Family and human development across cultures: A view from the other side.* Hillsdale, NJ: Lawrence Erlbaum Associates.

Kagitcibasi, C. (1997). Parent education and child development. In M.E. Young (Ed.), *Early child development: Investing in our children's future* (pp. 243–272). New York: Elsevier.

Kagitcibasi, C., Bekman, S., & Göksel, A. (1995). Multipurpose model of nonformal education: The Mother Child Education Program. *Coordinators' Notebook*, *17*, 24–32.

Kagitcibasi, C., Bekman, S., Kusçul, Ö.H, Özkök, Ü.S., & Sucuka, N. (1995). *Cognitive Training Program worksheets for 25 weeks.* Istanbul: Child Education Foundation Publication.

Kagitcibasi, C., Bekman, S., Özkök, Ü.S., & Kusçul,Ö.H. (1991). *Cognitive Training Program worksheets for 25 weeks.* Istanbul: Child Education Foundation Publication.

Kagitcibasi, C., Bekman, S., Özkök, Ü.S., & Kusçul, Ö.H. (1995). *Handbook of Mother Support Program.* Mother Child Education Foundation Publication No. 1. Istanbul: Mother Education Foundation.

Kagitcibasi, C., Bekman, S., & Sunar, D. (1991). *Handbook of Mother Enrichment Program.* Ankara: UNICEF Publications.

Kagitcibasi, C., Sunar, D., & Bekman, S. (1988). *Comprehensive preschool education project: Final report.* Ottawa: International Development Research Center.

Karnes, M.S., Teska, J.A., & Hodgins, A.S. (1970). The effects of four programs of classroom intervention on the intellectual and language development of four-year-old disadvantaged children. *American Journal of Orthopsychiatry*, *40*, 58–76.

Lambie, D.Z., Bond, J.T., & Weikart, D.P. (1974). Home teaching with mothers and infants. *Monographs of the High Scope Educational Research Foundation* (No. 2). Ypsilanti, MI: High Scope Press.

Larson, C. (1980). Efficacy of prenatal and postpartum home visits on child health and development. *Pediatrics*, *66*, 191–197.

Lazar, I., & Darlington, R. (1982). Lasting effects of early education: A report from the Consortium for Longitudinal Studies. *Monographs of the Society for Research in Child Development*, *47* (2 3, Serial No. 195).

Levenstein, P., O'Hara, J., & Madden, J. (1983). The mother child home program of the Verbal Interaction Project. In Consortium of Longitudinal Studies (Ed.), *As the twig is bent* (pp. 237–264). Hillsdale, NJ: Lawrence Erlbaum.

Lombard, A. (1994). *Success begins at home* (2nd ed.). Guilford, CT: The Dushkin Publishing Group, Inc.

Morgan, J.R., Jeanette, N.S., & Allin, D.W. (1990). Prevention through parent training: Three preventive parent education programs. *Journal of Primary Prevention, 10*(4), 321–332.

Myers, R. (1992). *The twelve who survive.* London: Routledge.

Olds, D.L., Henderson, C.R., Jr, Tatelbaum, R., & Chamberlain, R. (1988). Improving the life-course development of socially disadvantaged mothers: A randomized trial of nurse home visitation. *American Journal of Public Health, 78,* 1436–1445.

Palti, H., Mansbach, I., & Kurtzman, H. (1987). *An educational program for mothers to promote child development in primary care: The PROD program.* Jerusalem: Haddassah Medical Organization and School of Public Health and Community Medicine, Department of Social Medicine, Maternal and Child Health Unit.

Pehrson, K.L., & Robinson, C.C. (1990). Parent education: Does it make a difference? *Child Study Journal, 20*(4), 221–236.

Ramey, C.T., Yeates, K.O., & Short, E.T. (1984). The plasticity of intellectual development: Insights from preventive intervention. *Child Development, 55,* 1913–1925.

Roberts, R.N., & Wasik, B.H. (1994). Home visiting options within head start: Current practice and future directions. *Early Childhood Research Quarterly, 9,* 311–325.

Rowe, K.J. (1991). The influence of reading activity at home on students' attitudes towards reading, classroom attentiveness and reading achievement: An application of structural equation modelling. *British Journal of Educational Psychology, 61,* 19–35.

Royce, J.M., Darlington, R.B., & Murray, H.B. (1983). Pooled analysis: Finding across studies. In Consortium for Longitudinal Studies, *As the twig is bent* (pp. 411–460). Hillsdale, NJ: Lawrence Erlbaum.

Sameroff, A. (1975). Early influences on development: Fact or fancy. *Merrill Palmer Quarterly, 21,* 267–294.

Schweinhart, L.J., Barnes, V.H., & Weikart, D. (1993). Significant benefits: The High Scope Perry Preschool study through age 27. *Monographs of the High Scope Educational Research Foundation* (No. 10). Ypsilanti, Michigan: High Scope.

Schweinhart, L., & Wiekart, D. (1980). Young children grow up: The effort of Perry Preschool Program on youths through age 15. *Monographs of the High Scope Educational Research Foundation* (No. 7). Ypsilanti, MI: High Scope.

Seitz, V., & Provence, S. (1990). Caregiver-focused models of early intervention. In S.J. Meisels & J.P. Shankoff (Eds), *Handbook of early childhood intervention* (pp. 400–427). Cambridge: Cambridge University Press.

Seitz, V., Rosenbaum, L.K., & Apfel, N.H. (1985). Effects of family support intervention: A ten-year follow-up. *Child Development, 56,* 376–391.

Shankoff, J.P., & Meisels, S. J. (1990). Early childhood intervention: The evolution of a concept. In S.J. Meisels & J.P. Shankoff (Eds), *Handbook of early childhood intervention* (pp. 3–31). Cambridge: Cambridge University Press.

Slater, M. (1986). Modification of mother-child interaction processes in families with children at risk for mental retardation. *American Journal of Mental Deficiency, 91,* 257–267.

Slaughter, D. (1983). Early intervention and its effects on maternal and child development. *Monographs of the Society for Research in Child Development, 48* (4, Serial No. 202).

Telleen, S , Herzog, A , & Kilbane, T I. (1989) Impact of a family support program on mothers' social support and parenting stress. *American Journal of Orthopsychiatry, 59*(3), 410–419.

UNICEF. (2001). *The state of the world's children.* Oxford and New York: Oxford University Press.

Upshur, C.C. (1990). Early intervention as preventive intervention. In S.J. Meisels & J.P. Shankoff (Eds), *Handbook of early childhood intervention* (pp. 633–650). Cambridge: Cambridge University Press.

Weiss, H.B., & Jacobs, F.H. (1984). Family support and education programs—Challenges and opportunities. In H.B. Weiss & F.H. Jacobs (Eds), *Evaluating family programs* (pp. xix–xxix). New York: Aldine de Gruyter.

Woodhead, M. (1986). *Cross-cultural variation in early intervention processes and outcomes: Some issues for policy and practice.* Paper presented at the 8th International Congress of Cross-Cultural Psychology, Istanbul.

Zigler, E., & Berman, W. (1983). Discerning the future of early childhood intervention. *American Psychologist, 38,* 443–454.

❧ 11 ❧

Counting on Everyday Mathematics

ANITA RAMPAL

Introduction

Mathematics is often referred to as the "killer" subject and in India, as also elsewhere, most children fail in school because they cannot cope with the demands of the discipline. As mentioned in the preface to the report *Learning without burden* (1993), a large part of the problem of school "drop-out" can be attributed to the "burden of non-comprehension". An irrelevant curriculum, distanced from the lives of the majority, is normally rendered "boring and uninteresting" by outdated teaching strategies. In fact, it is now being acknowledged that if teaching in elementary schools in India had been more sensitive and relevant during the post-independence period, we would not have been faced with such high levels of non-literacy.

Interestingly, it was during our work with adolescents and adult learners that we first came to understand the yawning gaps between their learning strategies and the teaching methods devised for them. Unlike the captive audience in a school classroom, these learners are more demonstrative in their response to what is imparted to them. Moreover, we immediately realized that adults were not only keen to master the numeracy portion of the curriculum, but were already adept at performing oral arithmetic as part of their daily activities. They were also engaged in a host of other mathematical transactions, such as sorting, measurement, and estimation, as part of their livelihood and production processes. However, teaching practices related to these areas were completely divorced from their knowledge and skills, and were often even dismissive of the "non-standard" methods they used.

In order to understand how these unschooled adults had gained access to their knowledge and skills, we undertook to observe the processes of what we saw as "learning while doing" mathematics. We also attempted to document the rich cultural repertoire of folk mathematics still alive among the predominantly oral societies of India, and the cultural mechanisms used to preserve and appropriate such knowledge. It is through this exploration that we worked on devising a curriculum for adult learners, and also shared our experience with educators and activists across the country. Interestingly, our studies (Rampal, Ramanujam, & Saraswathi, 1998; 2000) have been extensively used not only by adult educators, but also by those who have been dissatisfied by the stunted techniques of teaching children, and have alternatively sought to make schooling more effective.

Studies of "Everyday Cognition"

Research on "everyday cognition" has shown that individuals perform better in everyday situations than in laboratory settings, in formally similar tasks. Not only has this area of research extended the arena of "contexts" for the study of cognition, but has also moved psychology beyond the individual, to look at human thinking through cultural, anthropological, social, and historical perspectives. Thinking, communicating and acting are now conceived more in terms of symbolic systems of knowledge construction, which could be linguistic, mathematical, scientific, metaphysical, folkloric, etc. (for a review of studies on everyday cognition see Schliemann, Carraher, & Ceci, 1997). In fact, the "context" is no longer a static conception, but is more dynamically linked to the nature of the activity, with the boundaries between the individual and the setting becoming increasingly blurred (Lave, 1996).

The early investigations among the Kpelle in Africa (Cole, Gay, Glick, & Sharp, 1971) had seen a major shift from the standardized investigations and interviews towards new ways of understanding cognition across cultures, through everyday practical activities. Today "everyday cognition" is a substantive field of study, with a vast range of investigations conducted either within the same culture or across cultures (Rogoff & Lave, 1984). Subjects engaged in activities ranging from tailoring, carpet weaving, navigation, fishing, vegetable selling to grocery shopping and even lottery betting have been studied.

The most popular and frequently examined area of everyday cognition is mathematics, since mathematical activities form a significant part of people's everyday lives even among unschooled communities. Some studies of mathematical thinking in different cultures have been documented in Carraher (1991), Gerdes (1985), Lancy (1983), Lave (1988), Nunes, Schliemann, and Carraher (1993), Saxe and Posner (1983), and Zaslavsky (1973). These broadly look at the creation of knowledge in everyday activities, through cultural tools and symbolic systems, its relation to knowledge acquired through schooled instruction and also raise questions about knowledge transfer across settings. Indeed, these studies have provided a sharp contrast between processes of cognition at school and cognition at work (or on the street), just as researches had earlier highlighted the differences in cognition in the laboratory versus everyday settings (Scribner & Cole, 1973). A striking difference in the two settings—the school and the street—lies in the processes of teaching and learning. In the "schooled" setting, even within a traditional adult literacy class, it is the sharp mismatch between the strategies of teaching and learning that makes most learners disheartened, despite being adept at performing mathematics as part of their daily transactions.

In a review of studies contrasting learning in and out of school, Resnick (1987; 1990) pointed out that while school learning focused on individual cognition, abstract thought and general principles, out of school learning depended on shared cognition, contextualized reasoning and situation specific strategies and competencies. Subsequently, Nunes, Schliemann, and Carraher (1993) demonstrated that the quality and effectiveness of the mathematical strategies employed depended on the symbolic systems and representations used. Rigid rule-bound solutions, taught in formal schools or non-formal adult literacy classes, provide learners with procedures and algorithms that do not carry meaning or help them solve problems in practical contexts. In contrast, the strategies they develop while "doing mathematics" in everyday contexts are flexible and help them to stay close to the meaning of the situation, and to the quantities involved. Thus, according to them, mathematics in school becomes an end in itself, often a meaningless manipulation of numbers, whereas street mathematics serves as a tool to achieve other goals, to give meaning to computations linked to people's life and labour.

We will briefly describe the Literacy Campaign in India, that led us to this study of adults' learning strategies, followed by a discussion of the deeper problem of innumeracy even among edu-cated adults in industrialized countries. We go on to present the sociocultural perspective of "situated" learning (Lave, 1996; Rogoff, 1995), which helped provide a theoretical framework for our study of everyday mathematics. In attempting to look at people's daily practices, we also present the historical under-pinnings of traditional techniques of measurement, to highlight that making a practical shift towards "standard" measures is also often related to a measured cognitive transition.

A Background of the Literacy Campaigns in India

During the last decade Mass Literacy Campaigns have been launched in over 500 districts in India, focusing on non-literate adults in the age group of 15–45 years. The campaign, unlike the earlier National Adult Education Programme, was designed to be a participatory one, with local teams planning and implementing it under the aegis of the district administration. However, in many places, sooner or later, it became a bureaucratic exercise, owing to the inability of the government functionaries to involve people in a truly democratic fashion. More significantly, the campaign was voluntary in nature, with teaching being carried out by millions of volunteers without any remuneration. In fact, the government bore a reasonably low cost (often less than US$ 2 per learner) for the campaign, while the community's contribution was greater, through volunteer teachers (VTs), space for literacy classes, food and shelter for the travelling theatre groups engaged in cultural mobilization, etc.

The innovative efforts towards community mobilization ensured that large numbers of adults initially attended the classes. However, the major problems surfaced later, in trying to sustain the motivation of learners and teachers through a series of three primers, or in restarting classes after a break. As a landmark decision in the history of Indian education, where textual materials are normally prepared in a centralized manner, the literacy campaign had called for the preparation of local primers at the district level. This, however, was not the case in all places, owing to the constraints of time, and more significantly, the lack of confidence that the curricula could indeed be designed locally. Nevertheless, some districts did prepare their own primers, and this was a major learning experience for their academic teams, since it gave them an opportunity to begin to engage with crucial issues related to adult learning.

These primers contained the literacy content as well as the numeracy parts, though the latter were often appended to each chapter in an ad hoc manner. As far as reading and writing were concerned, there seemed to be some consensual understanding that teaching methods must attempt to codify speech and verbal thought, through generative words, and not start mechanically from alphabets. However, there was no such attempt to understand the "meaning of numbers" and to locate the teaching of mathematics in the domain of the adults' lived experience. Numeracy was, therefore, the weakest area and, as has been observed across different programmes in the world, continued to dishearten adult learners attending the literacy classes.

A Mismatch between Teaching and Learning Strategies

The mismatch between teaching and learning strategies for mathematics has been a feature of most adult education programmes all over the world. During the International Literacy Year in 1990, some of the concerns expressed in the UNESCO report, *Arithmetic in daily life and literacy* (Dalbera, 1990), were strikingly similar to the problems we faced a decade later in our own campaign.

The UNESCO report points out that

only too often we find literacy programmes which include a highly "revolutionary" section aimed at providing access to written speech, increasing social awareness, encouraging development, etc. but a highly "reactionary" section providing access to written arithmetic. Adults find themselves faced with old-fashioned methods directly traceable to traditional primary education, childish and superficially adapted to the environment (marbles may have been replaced by eggs to create a "rural" impression), leading to poor results or none at all (Dalbera, 1990, p. 4).

An arithmetic programme must be able to transform the principal needs felt by adults into specific educational methods and content, by going directly to the most essential and useful matters. And quickly, for adults have only a limited time for learning. With them it is not possible, as it is at the school level, to put off the acquisition of more satisfying skills to a later time.... As we know, non-literates are almost always the poorest people, the most exploited and the most oppressed. They cannot be expected to agree to learn to read and write out of blind loyalty to moral or civic considerations, or out of free devotion to some noble cause for their benefit. In order not to waste their time literacy must offer them a real opportunity to help change their situation (Dalbera, 1990, p. 3).

Many of us involved in literacy campaigns in India, as voluntary resource persons or activists, had observed that adult non-literates routinely engage in everyday mathematics and are often capable of sophisticated mental computations. In fact, oral numeracy is more natural among unschooled adults than literacy, which means that they are more familiar with numbers, operations, measurements, etc. than with letters. Further, the strategies they use in oral arithmetic are often very distinct from the routine methods of written arithmetic.

We also realized that just as we do not begin by teaching adults how to speak before teaching them to read and write, we do not have to teach them to count simple numbers or to add before teaching them written numeracy. Moreover, adults are aware of the limitations of relying on only their memory for remembering numbers, especially when they tend to lose track of subtotals while doing complex calculations. They would find it extremely beneficial to be able to write numbers, but they do not want to be taught only how to write 1 or 8 or 22. They *quickly* want to learn to write larger numbers, and our numeracy programme must reach this level of teaching "useful" skills at an early stage. We realized that we must reinforce their mental arithmetic skills (instead of trying to replace or ignore them), and help them with different types of record keeping that are of practical use in their daily lives. Unfortunately, our adult literacy primers did not take into account any of these facts. The literacy primers, on the other hand, laboured through numbers in a boring and often absurdly linear fashion, with numbers 1–10 in chapter 1, numbers 11–20 in chapter 2, and so on. Normally, the first primer contained numbers 1–50 and simple addition and subtraction. The second primer dealt with numbers 1–100, some idea of place value, further exercises in addition and subtraction and an introduction to clock time. The third primer included operations of multiplication and division, measurement and basic concepts of decimals, fractions, money transactions, etc.

Thus, as part of the given curriculum adults are treated as children and are taught slowly and in a painfully linear manner. Pictorial illustrations, too, are borrowed from children's books, where they are asked to count eight ducks or five apples. The curriculum committee at the national level had tended to "dilute" the expected competencies each time it was compelled to deliberate on such issues. When the poor mathematical performance of adult learners was brought to its notice, its knee-jerk reaction was to remove the more challenging concepts, such as decimals or fractions, in a misguided attempt at further "simplifying" the curriculum.

On the contrary, the process of learning for an adult is far from linear. Moreover, adults want to quickly move on to more sophisticated and challenging tasks in mathematics, that can help them deal with market transactions confidently. A number such as 97 may seem large to a child but not to an adult, and therefore does not justify being relegated to the second primer. Operations of addition, multiplication, etc. make more sense as contextual problems, which can be stated in words, and adults are capable of doing "word problems" much before they learn to read and write. In fact, stating arithmetical problems in words helps provide a clear context and a link with the real world for adults. However, our curriculum planners, influenced by the school mathematics myth of "word problems are more difficult", diligently avoid using these even in the case of adults. In addition, various everyday calculations involving money, particularly related to profit and loss, simple interest on loans, or even the probability of winning or losing a lottery, which are considered to be important by the learners themselves, do not find a place in the curriculum.

Fractions cause a lot of heartburn among adult educators. However, an interesting observation we made during the course of our studies was that in many states of south India intricate fractions are part of everyday vocabulary. We also conjectured that this is similar to the markedly more intricate sound and beat patterns used for the percussion instruments in the classical Carnatic music. In Tamil and Malayalam, people still refer to "half of one fourth" as *araikaal* or "three fourth of one eighths" as *mukaal arakaal*. This is not found in the languages or the music of the north Indian states. However, the literacy primers of most regions in the south never attempted to incorporate such terms and concepts prevalent in everyday language, and instead proceeded to introduce fractions in the most artificial and "child-like" manner.

We had also observed that adults who attended literacy classes not only used their own oral arithmetical strategies, but also engaged in a host of other mathematical transactions, such as sorting, measurement, and estimation, as part of their daily activities. In this respect, too, teaching practices were completely divorced from their knowledge and skills, and often dismissive of the "non-standard" methods they used. For instance, metric units of measurement were defined as constituting the "standard" and "canonical" system, without any attempt to link those to the systems people normally used. As we will discuss later, the shift to the metric system has been seen in various civilizations to be a non-trivial one, and requires tremendous conscious and cognitive effort.

It is well known that adults do not acquire and internalize new skills, ideas or knowledge in a vacuum, but need to mediate them through the praxis of reflection and action. New ideas or skills have to be reinterpreted through their own mediatory mechanisms, of assigning meaning to them, codifying them according to the categories they have evolved and, more importantly, testing them out in real life settings. However, teaching practices used in adult literacy classes neither encouraged such mediation nor engaged learners in reflection of any kind. Thus, there existed a wide mismatch between the teaching and learning strategies of adults. It was evident that those who designed primers and teaching methods for adults were blissfully unaware of the learning strategies they used, and instead adopted outdated school based methods for teaching children. Thus, most literacy classes imposed on adults such routines that made no sense to them and only led to boredom, frustration and failure, similar to the "school math syndrome" suffered by millions of children. As a result, adults who had been mobilized to attend these literacy classes through tremendous efforts soon became disheartened and dropped out, often dampening the spirit of the campaign leaders.

Innumeracy among the Educated

In the last decade there has been much soul-searching in both the UK and the USA about large numbers of educated but innumerate citizens, who suffer from deep "maths anxiety" and are incapable of solving simple arithmetical problems. Despite having achieved universal schooling these industrialized countries are not only concerned about the level of mathematical performance of their adults, but are also questioning the efficacy of teaching mathematics in schools. Newspaper reports abound in "horror" stories about the abysmal level of everyday maths competence of the adult population, while politicians try to impose stricter norms and standardized tests on harassed schools and teachers. In the USA, the report of the National Committee for Excellence in Education (NCEE, 1983) caused some alarm, while subsequent assessment of students' mathematical abilities justified the concern. *The mathematics report card* (National Center for Educational Statistics, 1988), which discussed the results of the extensive National Assessment for Educational Progress, caused a furore after sampling 80 per cent of 17-year-olds at school. The study revealed that only 40 per cent of the nation's students could solve moderately sophisticated problems such as finding "87 per cent of 10", while only 6 per cent could locate the square root of 17 between two given consecutive integers.

These results were similar to those reported by the Cockroft Commission (Cockroft, 1982) in England some years earlier, after large-scale tests and interviews with adults. The most striking feature of the British study was the extent of anxiety, helplessness, fear, and guilt experienced by common people in the face of simple problems. It documented widespread inability to handle percentages; even those used everyday to calculate tips and sales tax. Many adults believed that a decline in the rate of inflation reported in the newspapers would cause a fall in prices. The Cockroft study also reported that many workers, who needed specific job related mathematics, managed by using methods and tricks passed on by fellow workers that had little connection with the methods taught at school.

In his immensely popular book *Innumeracy: Mathematical illiteracy and its consequences*, Paulos (1990) critiqued the education system and revealed that widespread innumeracy caused educated adults and even professionals to misinterpret statistics, leading to incorrect decisions. For instance, quoting a study done by two doctors at the Washington University, he showed that most doctors' assessments of the risks involved in various operations, procedures and medications were way off the mark by orders of magnitude. This theme has been analysed, through studies on people's beliefs, their understanding of probabilistic events and the rational basis for decision-making, by psychologists Kahneman, Slovic, and Tversky (1982). However, serious debate has followed in this area of logic and rationality, and how these relate to the decisions people take in everyday life. It has been argued that people's choices, in relation to their survival within diverse social environments, are far more problematic than simple textbook definitions of abstract logic or rationality (Gardner, 1985, pp. 370–379).

In the last decade there have been a number of international comparisons about mathematical performance of school students and the different strategies for teaching mathematics. A joint US–Japanese Commission, for instance, undertook studies to examine how Japanese children performed remarkably better in mathematics through the "open" teaching methods used in Japanese schools (Becker & Shimada, 1997). They recommended that teaching mathematics by promoting more than one way to solve their problems helped students to make better sense of the subject. The aim of these as well as other studies was to critically review teaching strategies and to examine possible methods that would instil greater confidence in learners and relate instruction to their life contexts.

However, it should be noted here that such international comparisons of school performance in mathematics have even acquired undesirable political overtones, compelling academics to often resist politicians' simplistic moves calling for "school reform". In the last decade, competitiveness in the global economy led the industrialized countries to correlate the superior performance of Japanese, Korean or Singaporean students on school mathematics to the economic advantage of these "Asian Miracles". Though there are no proven causal links between teaching strategies, children's performance on standardized tests, and national economic performance (Levin & Kelly, 1977), such inferences have indeed led to often questionable policies and an undue stress on "national standards" (Alexander, 2000, p. 42).

Finding vulnerable scapegoats for low economic performance in teachers and students, and to justify greater political control over schools through "national standards" is a matter of concern in many countries, and its repercussions have been seen in India too. In India, the "Minimum Levels of Learning" (MLLs) were developed, which were poorly formulated within a behaviourist framework, but they continued to shape most syllabi and textbooks during the last decade (for a detailed discussion on the MLLs by Rampal see PROBE, 1999, pp. 79–80).

"Learning while Doing"—Viewed from a Sociocultural Perspective

We have discussed that methods for the teaching of mathematics are divorced from the strategies people use for learning. We also saw how children in schools as well as adults in adult literacy classes do not make much headway in mathematics. Instead, most of them develop a deep sense of anxiety and helplessness, and attribute these to their innate inability to do mathematics. All over the world there has been concern regarding the need to improve the school math curricula and to make teaching more contextually related to the learners' life activities. However, there has not been enough effort to understand how people actually learn while doing mathematics, and the kind of strategies they adopt in diverse social and cultural settings.

"Learning" need not necessarily imply a lone struggle by an individual working in isolation, but as we will see, is also a collective social process. In most unschooled situations, learning takes place more as a "situated activity", grounded in specific transactions, through shared practices of everyday life. Even though there is no formal instruction, active learning takes place as people scaffold each other through "zones of proximal development", that are collective rather than individual, and attain new knowledge, skills, and strategies through the learning interaction. Unlike traditional cognitive theories that isolate and distance the learning "mind" from its experience, theories of situated learning do not separate thought, action, and feelings of the learners. Traditionally, knowledge is viewed as something static that is imported across a boundary, from the external to the internal. Thus, theories of cognitive "acquisition" of knowledge, concepts, skills, etc. tend to separate the actor from both the "acquired knowledge" as well as the social context.

Sociocultural studies of learning move away from the narrow focus on teaching and learning seen as "transmission and internalisation" of existing knowledge, towards understanding what constitutes "new knowledge". "New knowledge" is seen as a collective invention, adopted by people when faced with contradictions that may impede an activity. According to Lave, the difference between the traditional and the sociocultural perspectives lies in viewing knowledge as a collection of "real entities located in people's heads", learnt through a process of "internalisation", as opposed to a view of learning as engagement in changing processes of human activity. "In the latter case 'knowledge' becomes complex and problematic, whereas in the traditional perspective it is 'learning' that is problematic". In the situated view, learning occurs as part of an activity, and though it is very complex it may seem effortless because it is invisible. Learning is thus conceived as "the construction of present versions of past experience for several persons acting together" (Lave, 1996).

Knowledge in use is in a dynamic flux, always being constructed and transformed. Knowledge and learning are to be viewed as "distributed" throughout the complex structure of persons acting in a setting. Knowledge or learning cannot be pinned down to the head of an individual, or to the tasks undertaken, or to the external tools or the environment, but lie instead in the *relations* between all of them. Static theories of learning view knowledge or skills as entering people's heads and waiting passively for situations to occur later in which they may prove useful. Situated theories suggest that "learning disability" can have more to do with children who find themselves faced not by increasingly difficult but more "arbitrary" tasks at school, for which they are unable to define meaning and purpose, for its delayed use at some probable point in life. However, the same children may perform complicated mathematical or other tasks, which are part of the context of their activity.

According to McDermott, a static theory of learning normally relies on a static view of context. Thus,

> in all commonsense uses of the term "context" refers to an empty slot, a container, into which other things are placed. It is the "con" that contains the "text", the bowl that contains the soup. The soup does not shape the bowl, and the bowl most certainly does not alter the substance of the soup. Text and context, soup and bowl can be analytically separated and studied on their own without doing violence to the complexity of the situation. A static sense of context delivers a stable world (McDermott, 1996, p. 282).

The questions sought by sociocultural theories are therefore different. Instead of focusing on the relationship between persons and the contexts in which they act, what is observed is the relationship between local practices that contextualize the ways people act together, both in and across contexts. Further, the use of "activity" as the unit of analysis allows a reformulation of the relation between the individual and the sociocultural environment, where each is inherently involved in the other's definition (Rogoff, 1995). An "activity" is shaped by active contributions from individuals, their social partners, historical traditions and also materials and their transformations. According to Rogoff, the interdependence between the individual, the task, and the environment needs to be understood carefully through conscious "foregrounding" of specific activities, without losing the holistic background. For instance, in describing the functioning of an organ within an organism we may focus on the organ, but take care to keep in mind their interdependence. Thus, in foregrounding the functioning of the heart or the skin, we may describe their individual structure, but also remember that by themselves these organs do not have such structure or functioning, and only form a part of the human body. Similarly, we may foreground either a single person learning or the functioning of the whole community, but must not assume that they are elements separate from the activity.

At the beginning of the last century some educationists had highlighted the importance of the sociocultural context of learning. Dewey, whose work reflected a sociocultural approach, professed the important idea of "participation" in the social environment, with learning seen as a process of mutual "appropriation". As early as 1916 Dewey had written, in his classic book *Democracy and education*: "If the living, experiencing being is an intimate participant in the activities of the world to which it belongs, then knowledge is a mode of participation, valuable in the degree in which it is effective" (p. 393).

> The social environment is truly educative in its effects in the degree in which an individual shares or participates in some conjoint activity. By doing his share in the associated activity, the individual appropriates the purpose which actuates it, becomes familiar with its methods and subject matters, acquires needed skill, and is saturated with its emotional spirit (Dewey, 1916, p. 26).

Rogoff (1995, p. 152) argued that scholars such as Vygotsky also used the term "internalization", but not necessarily in a static sense, and similar to the idea of "appropriation", stressed the inherent transformation of the learner and what is learned during the process. She build on their ideas using the notion of "participatory appropriation", and viewed cognitive development as a dynamic, active and mutual process. She noted an important difference between the "participatory appropriation" and "internalization" perspectives in their inherent assumptions about time. In the internalization perspective, time is rigidly segmented into past, present and future, and treated as separate. According to her, critical problems arise about understanding the process of "transmission of knowledge" across time—about how individuals store memories of the past, how those are retrieved and used in the present, with plans made for and executed in the future. It involves a "storage model" of mind, with static elements held in the brain, and mysteriously difficult executive processes needed to explain how elements stored in one epoch are implemented in another epoch.

"Participatory appropriation" (Rogoff, 1995, p. 150) is a perspective on learning as an ongoing activity. People participate in activities and learn to handle subsequent activities in ways based on their involvement in previous events. There is no need to segment time into past, present and future, or to conceive of learning as internalization of stored units, achieved after external exposure to knowledge or skills. As a person acts on the basis of previous experience, the past is present in the participation, and contributes to the event by having prepared the ground for it. The present event is, therefore, different from what it would have been if the previous events had not occurred, and does not depend only on stored memory of past events. To explain this perspective of cognitive change, Rogoff used analogies from models of organizational or physical change. For instance, the shape, size and strength of a child's leg depend on the continuous process of its growth and use, without a need to refer to units of growth or exercise accumulated over time. The past is not stored in the leg, which continues to develop to be as it is in the present. Similarly, the present status of a company is seen to be the function of its previous activities, not of accumulated "units" of some specified parameters.

The new perspective throws up different questions about the nature of cognitive development. Transformations that occur during participation are developmental changes in particular directions, but are locally defined, and do not need universally specified end points or "milestones". To understand how people constitute learning, it is important to closely examine the processes through which they participate with other people in a cultural activity, and how they transform that process. In a sociocultural study of people's use of mathematics in a supermarket, it was noted that grocery shopping activity was constituted in a dialectic relation with the setting of the activity. For instance, a shopper would pause for the first time in front of the generic products section of the market, and having processed the new information regarding the unfamiliar "brandless" products and their relative low prices, the shopper devised different money saving strategies on a subsequent visit. The "setting" for grocery shopping had thus been changed by the activity itself, which in turn was also subsequently transformed (Lave, 1988). To understand learning in practice, it is therefore crucial to examine the details of how people are involved in activities, within specific settings, and how their participation changes from being peripheral, as in observing and performing secondary roles, to being responsible for managing such activities. Moreover, it is also important to examine how people construe the purpose of their activity and seek meanings in those situations. It is broadly within this perspective that we need to study the cultural repertoire of Indian adults, most of them unschooled, and yet very efficient in *doing* mathematics as part of their daily activities. In the following section we will attempt to give some idea of the rich traditions of folk mathematics still alive among the predominantly oral societies in India and the cultural mechanisms used to preserve and appropriate such knowledge.

Traditions of Counting, Sorting, Estimation, and Measurement

Oral societies have invested tremendous effort and ingenuity in devising mnemonic techniques to memorize, preserve and transmit to future generations their rich body of knowledge. *Shlokas, mantras* and *sutras* rendered through elaborate rhythmic patterns were means to ensure that the rich knowledge of such societies was made memorable for posterity. Moreover, verse and rhyme, which help in memorizing long pieces of complicated information, have been woven creatively with the empirical observations and philosophical moorings of oral civilizations (Rampal, 1992). Voluminous bodies of early scientific texts exist in purely oral form, composed and recited through the use of complex techniques. However, such poems, narratives, riddles, games, and songs exist not in the repertoire of classical oral literature, meant for the limited consumption of the "learned" elite, but more in the folklore of ordinary people. We found that older generations living in villages savour and enjoy this rich repertoire of folklore received through their ancient oral traditions.

We noted that a large repertoire of poetic riddles, puzzles and stories about numbers exist in the folklore of different regions of India, which are often non-trivial to solve, even with written algo- rithms. However, people enjoy enumerating these and try to give answers more through familiarity, often using intuitive and empirical strategies for finding solutions.

For instance, in one oral riddle a sparrow from a flock flying overhead calls out to one sitting on a tree and says: "We are not yet a hundred strong. We, a similar flock like us, one half of that, a half of that again, and you together will make one hundred". In order to calculate how many were flying in the flock, we would require an equation of the kind: $n + n + n/2 + n/4 + 1 = 100$ which yields the answer: $n = 36$. However, it would be more interesting to observe how people solve this orally. Similarly, there is another popular riddle that is used as part of an oral story, but which is not as simple to solve:

> If counted in pairs, one will remain,
> If counted in threes, two will remain,
> If counted in fours, three will remain,
> If counted in fives, four will remain,
> If counted in sevens, nothing remains.
> (*One hundred and nineteen*)

A poetic riddle, based on a rhythmic play of words and sounds, meant to tease and challenge the minds of learners, is a potent tool used by traditional oral societies to develop their faculties of creative thinking and imagination. Even today numerous such gems, amazing in their philosophical, lyrical or mathematical content, are recited by the older members of rural societies. Unfor- tunately, children, especially those who are schooled, no longer know these riddles or poems, and are systematically losing their folk knowledge.

We also conducted studies to examine how people perform oral arithmetic while transacting different objects as part of their daily life activities. In various studies of street mathematics it has been observed that people who depend on oral arithmetic make very few errors and adopt efficient ways to prevent deviating far from the correct answer. Detailed studies, comparing the strategies used by the same children first while selling their wares in street markets and later using written mathematics, were conducted for almost a decade in Brazil under a research programme of the Universidade Federal de Pernambuco, Recife (Nunes et al., 1993). Some of our own investigations (Rampal et al., 1998; 2000) were greatly influenced by the approach of the Brazilian studies. We will, however, not elaborate on our work on street mathematics in this paper, but will focus more on techniques related to measurement and estimation. In addition to market transactions, counting and sorting is done by people participating in specific production processes, through which they also acquire the ability to make accurate estimations. Estimations form the basis of all measurements, and there is a consensus as to which type of unit is to be used for measuring what and when. Even though people use a variety of units for different situations, they may not know how to convert from one type to another. This may be true of us too, who may not easily estimate heights of persons in the metric system, even though for cloth or distances we may have been using standard metric units.

A beautiful old poem in Tamil reveals an amazingly wide range of length measures from the atomic to an astronomical scale, through the use of rich life word imagery. Though the English translation cannot exactly capture the sense of rhyme and sounds of the original, nevertheless, it is presented here.

8 atoms	= 1 speck in the sun's rays
8 specks in the sun's rays	= 1 speck of cotton dust
8 cotton specks	= 1 hair point tip
8 hair tips	= 1 small sand particle
8 sand particles	= 1 small mustard seed
8 small mustard seeds	= 1 sesame seed
8 sesame seeds	= 1 paddy seed
8 paddy seeds	= 1 finger width
12 finger widths	= 1 span
2 spans	= 1 cubit
12 cubits	= 1 stick (kol)
500 kols	= 1 "koopidu dooram" (calling distance)
4 "koopidu doorams"	= 1 "kaadam" (about 1.2 km)

The measure *koopidu dooram* or "calling distance" is known to have been used as a traditional measure in early metrological systems. This suggests that folk and empirical knowledge acknowledged that sound travels only a finite distance and that different frequencies attenuate at different distances. In fact, the Saharan nomads developed an elaborate system of distance measurement, where the carrying distance of the human voice was distinguished from that for various other animals, leading to different comparative units.

Traditional versus "Conventional" Measures

The traditional measures we find in use even today have evolved over centuries, and have a social content, unlike the so-called "standard" measures, which are agreed upon purely by convention. Indeed, as pointed out by the economic historian Kula, the earlier measures were truly "representational" or those that "signified" something, and therefore had a social "meaning", determined through people's concrete activities of life and labour. It is implied that such folk measures should not be termed "conventional", while it is the metric system that is wholly arbitrary and dependent on convention (Kula, 1986; Wade, 1949).

The conventional metric units (metre, litre, etc.) are defined in terms of technical "invariables" and generally lack social significance, so that most people do not really know what these denote. For instance, not many of us today would be able to give the definition of a metre. The metre was first defined by the French as the 1/40,000,000th part of the earth's meridian, which was then considered to be immutable and unchanging. However, when it was realized that such distances were not wholly immutable, it was decided to resort to convention. A metre was chosen to be the length of a "specific" bar, made from an alloy of platinum and iridium, and kept guarded under fixed conditions of temperature and pressure. Subsequently, in the light of the need for greater accuracy and reproducibility, dependence on a singular physical entity was abandoned in favour of a more abstract and almost metaphysical definition, which has very little "meaning". What then is a "metre" and how many of us are confident of being able to define it? Surely, not many! I for one cannot remember that the metre is the length equal to 1,650,763.37 wavelengths of the orange light emitted by the Krypton atom of mass 86 *in vacuo*!! So much for the lack of meaning!

Historically, the earliest stage in the development of metrological concepts is "anthropomorphic", in which most measures actually correspond to parts of the human body. Thus, throughout the world there have been measures such as the foot (say, to mark distances while sowing potatoes), the pace, or the elbow or "ell" (to measure cloth, etc.). Moreover, as has been pointed out in the context of old Slavonic measures, the peasant fisherman would refer to his net as being "30 fathoms long and 20 ells wide", thus choosing different convenient measures for the length and the width (Kula, 1986, p. 5).

Similarly, the Saharan nomads, for whom the distances between one water hole and the next was often a matter of life and death, have developed a rich system of measures for long distances. They reckon distances in terms of a stick's throw or a bowshot, or the carrying distance of voice (either human or animal). Distance is also measured in terms of what can be seen from the ground level, by a person standing or from a camel's back. There are various units for "walking distances", as that covered by humans walking from sunrise to sunset, which is further differentiated into a man's walking distance without a load to carry, or with a laden ass, etc. Importantly, we need to acknowledge and build upon such measures, which are still in use today in many societies.

Techniques of production and transportation have also determined many of the measures used. The width of the loom for textiles, the size of the milling equipment for glass "panes", or the size of the "pig" for raw iron have given rise to units shaped by the production process. Similarly, transportation defines the cartload, the basketful for particular crops, and the boatload for sand, soil, etc. Discussing this with adults not only enhances their understanding of various systems of measurement but also helps them acquire a facility to switch to the more standard ones.

Scholars have argued that traditional measures were not only more functional, but were also technically sound for comparative purposes. For instance, for land measurement the hectare normally does not provide a directly "addable" measure, owing to the unequal quality of soils. The owner of 2 hectares is not twice as rich as the owner of 1 hectare, since the value of land depends upon many other parameters. Mechanically adding hectares is not technically correct, since every hectare is not "equal" to another. The traditional measures, based on qualitative factors, such as the labour time needed to till the land, or the amount of seed required for sowing a given crop, provided a more realistic value of a given piece of land. Indeed, historians find this dominance of qualitative over purely quantitative considerations in the social thinking of preindustrial societies most striking, and cite such sound functionality as the main reason for their reluctance to switch to modern "conventional" systems (Kula, 1986, p. 35).

Interestingly, such forms of measurement are widely prevalent in India even today, and coexist with the new standard systems. Ironically, most educators refuse to appreciate the ingenuity and significance of such measures, and dismiss them as "crude", inaccurate or "primitive". In this way they also thwart the possibility of a discussion with adults about the systems they use and the advantages of adopting more standard systems. This refusal to acknowledge people's lived knowledge often violently disrupts the process of learning and appropriation.

Another significant feature of the earlier system of weights and measures was that to account for different qualities of a commodity, the quantities were changed not the price. In addition, differences between the place of purchase and the place of sale, between regions with or without a surplus of foodstuffs, and between lender or borrower were expressed in a wide variety of differentiated measures, to cover costs of transportation, interest rates, etc. The "bushel sold" was different in size from the "bushel bought", and often a heaped container was bought from the farmer while a flat one was sold to a customer at the same price, to take care of the costs of the transaction. However, in industrial societies, the price is meant to reduce to a common denominator all the factors effecting the transaction, so that measures remain constant while the price changes.

Understanding the Problems of a Metric Shift

In trying to understand the learning strategies of adults we first need to be aware of the sociohistorical bases of the knowledge they already possess. Moreover, in attempting to affect a cognitive shift towards "modern" knowledge systems, the relevance of traditional systems, as well as the historical experience of other societies undergoing similar transitions cannot be ignored. In a way, the metric system sought a shift from the synthetic qualitative manner of thinking to a more abstract quantitative process. Through the metric system, we tend to abstract one out of the many different qualities of diverse objects, say, the length, and view them all from this single perspective. This single measure for length makes it more abstract and also distances the object from its particular context, leading to some amount of cognitive resistance to the use of metric units. So the pace of a woman, the length of her sari, the height of a tree, the thickness of a sheet of paper, or even the length of the earth's meridian are all contracted to the same measure. Further, the divisibility and cumulativeness of the metric system enables us to compare magnitudes diversely different—from that of the atom to the cosmos.

However, the fascinating poem in Tamil cited earlier reveals that the qualitative predisposition of thought had not constrained people in the past from thinking in more abstract quantitative ways about immensely diverse magnitudes. For, when they spoke of "8 atoms = 1 speck in the sun's rays", etc. they were indeed creatively comparing abstract quantities with deep insights about their qualitative attributes.

It is often thought that the metric system is "preferred" by human nature, "since the uneducated man counts on his fingers", and this is presumed to contribute to its simplicity and ready applicability. However, this has not been true historically, and the vigesimal system of base 20 has been more prevalent in various preindustrial societies. Indeed, mastering the principles of the decimal system has proved extremely difficult for the masses across the world, whenever a formal switch to the metric system was sought. The major drawback of the decimal system lies in the fact that the number 10 divides only once by 2 (while its divisibility by 5 is not of much practical use).

"Dichotomous divisibility" or repeated divisibility by 2 has been of crucial significance in the different counting systems used by ancient societies. Thus, in the duodecimal system the basic number 12 is twice divided by 2, and in the sex-decimal system the basic number 16 is four times divisible by 2. In this way people managed to halve and quarter quantities without resorting to fractions. In fact, in the early nineteenth century very few Europeans could use the decimal system, as is borne out by the following quote. The Commissioner for Weights and Measures had written (an apparently sexist letter) to the Finance Minister, stating that "Every girl and unlettered tailor knows what half a quarter-ell stands for; but we would lay a hundred to one that many professional accountants would be unable to assure you that half a quarter ell is equal to one hundred and twenty-five thousandths" (quoted in Kula, 1986, p. 83).

It has been seen that systems of groupings and division are a more basic and durable feature of a given system of measurement, than are the absolute values of its measures. It is, therefore, considered more feasible to change the values of measures, than alter the ways of dividing and multiplying that have been used for generations in the mental arithmetic practised by common people. Moreover, we observe the coexistence of many diverse systems of groupings in areas where different civilizations meet, because the system of divisions and multiples is the fundamental property of every metrological system. Similar dichotomous divisions and double multiples have prevailed almost everywhere among measures of fluid capacity, linear measures, and surface measures of cultivated land. Indeed, Kula noted that the extreme ease with which the traditional systems lent themselves to mental arithmetic without any writing was one of the chief barriers to the adoption of the metric system.

Our own research has shown that even today complex divisions and groupings are used in rural societies. We have noted earlier that the languages of south India contain words for intricate fractions such as half of one-fourth as *araikaal*, or even three-fourths of one-eighth as *mukaal arakaal*. Indeed, this rich system of divisions also had its effect on the sophisticated system of *taal* or rhythm used in Carnatic music, where each beat is divided into numerous different fractions.

MEASURED SHIFTS IN SOCIAL COGNITION

The metric system originated in France, as part of the French Revolution. It is interesting to note the different kinds of social education programmes organized by the new government to help people understand and accept the standard system of measures. Public "meters" were provided in places of gathering in order to settle disputes and public tuitions were conducted in prominent public places like the courtyard of the Louvre Museum in Paris. Schools were instructed to allot extra time for the teaching of the metric system. In addition, special encouragement was given to writers of appropriate manuals to be used by various professionals. However, historians have noted that these educational measures faced tremendous resistance, since the subject matter was difficult, and the new nomenclature unfamiliar. The new system appealed to the protagonists of the Revolution and to reformers who imagined that it would "release, for the good of the state, a great many additional hands (for work) by simplifying the reckoning in millions of daily calculations" (Kula, 1986). In reality, this system of reckoning turned out to be a major obstacle in the introduction of metric measures. The new terms were utterly alien to the French language; prefixes such as hecto, centi or even kilo were hard to master and this resulted in frequent misunderstandings.

Moreover, people had been attuned to thinking in terms of various measures for a different quality of a material or crop, such as a "better/larger" measure for poorer grain. Therefore, thinking in categories of invariable measures and variable prices (to adjust for the quality, purity, dampness, etc. of grain) amounted to a complete mental revolution. It was not enough simply to master the measures, or even to master the decimal way of counting. Even the most highly educated and professional groups had misgivings about the new system. The Agency of Weight and Measures repeatedly admonished government agencies, treasury officials, qualified civil servants or editors of journals for several years, for not adopting the new system.

Among the great many difficulties faced by the regimes attempting to introduce the metric system, the forces of social cognition, contrary to what the reformers had expected, proved the most intractable. People's routine reactions, habits of thought, technical difficulties with the new system, and the perceived practical advantages of the traditional measures all contributed to the delayed changeover. There were decades of fights and disputes between the administration and the people. However, despite successive changes in the administration and upheavals in the political system, attempts to reform the system through public education continued.

Similar experiences have been documented of the tumultuous change to usher in the metric system in other countries. In some industrialized countries even today the changeover has not been completely effected. However, the case of China needs to be mentioned as it highlights the strong cultural underpinnings of cognition. Even though the reform began as early as 1912, there were many difficulties owing to the new terminology, which used sounds that did not exist in the Chinese language. In 1959, the government attempted a different route that ultimately worked. It decided to retain many of the former names of measures, but instead standardized their dimensions and integrated them with the metric system. Thus *cheng* was made equal to the litre, the *tsin* to half a kilogram, and the *chi* to one-third of a metre. Old measures and weights were confiscated in thousands, melted down and then used to make new ones, so that there was considerable saving of raw materials and people were safeguarded against potential swindles. Within 5 months the new measures were available all over China and were made obligatory.

Conclusion

We have seen that innumeracy is linked not only to a lack of scriptural literacy, but also to the teaching methods, which are often divorced from adult learners' strategies and dismissive of their mathematical knowledge and skills. Adults do not acquire and internalize new skills, ideas or knowledge in a vacuum, but need to mediate them through the praxis of reflection and action. New knowledge needs to be reinterpreted through their own mediatory mechanisms, of assigning meaning to them, codifying them according to the categories they have evolved and, more importantly, testing them out in real life settings. However, teaching practices used in adult literacy classes never attempt to encourage such mediation and fail to engage learners in reflection of any kind.

Even educated adults suffer from deep math anxiety, helplessness, fear and guilt in the face of simple problems, leading to the need for serious rethinking about the traditional paradigm of school mathematics. A majority of children, especially in developing countries, who drop out of school owing to their inability to cope with school mathematics, manage to learn more efficient techniques while doing mathematics in everyday contexts. Studies of everyday cognition in mathematics provide a framework for redesigning teaching learning strategies, incorporating the folk and street mathematics of the community. This makes learning more meaningful not only for adult learners attending literacy classes, but also children who are encouraged to continue in school. Ultimately, it is hoped that a deeper understanding of everyday mathematics would provide a new paradigm for mathematics teaching in schools and across a variety of structured learning contexts.

The sociocultural as well as historical context of learning mathematics reveals that oral societies have collectively appropriated rich traditions of counting, sorting, measurement and estimation, through practice rooted in everyday activity, and also devised complex techniques for preserving their knowledge for posterity. In order to design effective teaching strategies for adult non-literates as well as school children, we need to observe the mathematical practices of those communities to acknowledge and build upon their folk knowledge. Historically, it has been seen that making a transition from traditional systems of measurement to modern conventional measures often requires a measured cognitive shift. Such transitions across contexts can be easily facilitated when educators themselves learn to count on everyday mathematics.

References

Alexander, R. (2000). *Culture and pedagogy: International comparisons in primary education*. Oxford: Blackwell Publishers.

Becker, J.P., & Shimada, S. (Eds). (1997). *The open-ended approach—A new proposal for teaching mathematics*. Reston, VA: National Council of Teachers of Mathematics.

Carraher, D. (1991). Mathematics in and out of school: A selective review of studies from Brazil. In M. Harris (Ed.), *Schools, mathematics and work* (pp. 169–201). London: The Falmer Press.

Cockroft, W.H. (1982). *Mathematics counts.* London: Her Majesty's Stationery Office.

Cole, M., Gay, J., Glick, J.A., & Sharp, D.W. (1971). *The cultural context of learning and thinking.* New York: Basic Books.

Dalbera, C. (1990). *Arithmetic in daily life and literacy.* Paris: UNESCO, International Bureau of Education.

Dewey, J. (1916). *Democracy and education: An introduction to the philosophy of education.* Macmillan: New York.

Gardner, H. (1985). *The mind's new science.* New York: Basic Books.

Gerdes, P. (1985). Conditions and strategies for emancipatory mathematics education in underdeveloped countries. *For the Learning of Mathematics, 5*(1), 15–20.

Kahneman, D., Slovic, P., & Tversky, A. (Eds). (1982). *Judgement under uncertainty: Heuristics and biases.* New York: Cambridge University Press.

Kula, W. (1986). *Measures and men.* Princeton: Princeton University Press.

Lancy, D.F. (1983). *Cross cultural studies in cognition and mathematics.* New York: Academic Press.

Lave, J. (1988). *Cognition in practice.* Cambridge: Cambridge University Press.

Lave, J. (1996). The practice of learning. In S. Chaiklin & J. Lave (Eds), *Understanding practice: Perspectives on activity and context* (pp. 3–34). Cambridge: Cambridge University Press.

Learning without burden. (1993). Report of the Yashpal Committee. New Delhi: Ministry of Human Resource Development.

Levin, H.M., & Kelly, C. (1977). Can education do it alone? In A.H. Halsey, H. Lauder, P. Brown, & A.S. Wells (Eds), *Education, culture, economy, society* (pp. 240–252). Oxford: Oxford University Press.

McDermott, R.P. (1996). The acquisition of child by a learning disability. In S. Chaiklin & J. Lave, *Understanding practice: Perspectives on activity and context* (pp. 269–305). Cambridge: Cambridge University Press.

National Center for Educational Statistics. (1988). *NAEP 1988: The mathematics report card.* Washington, DC: National Center for Educational Statistics.

NCEE. (1983). *A nation at risk: The imperative for educational reform.* Report of the National Committee for Excellence in Education. Washington, DC: United States Department of Education.

Nunes, T., Schliemann, A.D., & Carraher, D.W. (1993). *Street mathematics and school mathematics.* Cambridge: Cambridge University Press.

Paulos, J.A. (1990). *Innumeracy: Mathematical illiteracy and its consequences.* New York: Vintage Books.

PROBE. (1999). *The public report on basic education.* New Delhi: Oxford University Press.

Rampal, A. (1992). A possible "orality" for science? *Interchange, 23*(3), 227–244.

Rampal, A., Ramanujam, R., & Saraswathi, L.S. (1998). *Numeracy counts!* Mussoorie: National Literacy Resource Centre, LBS National Academy of Administration.

Rampal, A., Ramanujam, R., & Saraswathi, L.S. (2000). *Zindagi ka hisaab*. Mussoorie: National Literacy Resource Centre, LBS National Academy of Administration.

Resnick, L. (1987). Learning in school and out. *Educational Researcher, 16*(9), 13–20.

Resnick, L. (1990). Literacy in school and out. *Daedalus, 119*(2), 169–185.

Rogoff, B. (1995). Sociocultural activity in three planes. In J.V. Wertsch, Pablo Del Rio, & A. Alvarez (Eds), *Sociocultural studies of mind* (pp. 139–164). Cambridge: Cambridge University Press.

Rogoff, B., & Lave, J. (1984). *Everyday cognition*. Cambridge, MA: Harvard University Press.

Saxe, G.B., & Posner, J.K. (1983). The development of numerical cognition: Cross cultural perspectives. In H.P. Ginsburg (Ed.), *The development of mathematical thinking* (pp. 291–317). New York: Academic Press.

Schlicmann, A.D., Carraher, D.W., & Ceci, S.J. (1997). Everyday cognition. In J.W. Berry, P.R. Dasen, & T.S. Saraswathi (Eds), *Handbook of cross-cultural psychology* (vol. 2, pp. 177–216). Boston: Allyn & Bacon.

Scribner, S., & Cole, M. (1973). Cognitive consequences of formal and informal education. *Science, 182*, 553–559.

Wade, H.T. (1949). Weights and measures. In *Encyclopaedia of social sciences, XV* (pp. 389–392). New York: Seligman.

Zaslavsky, C. (1973). *Africa counts*. Boston, Mass: Prindle and Schmidt.

❧ 12 ☙

Current Issues and Trends in Early Childhood Education

LILIAN G. KATZ

The intent of this paper is to discuss some of the main trends, issues, and principles of practice in early childhood education, and their implications for practice. I begin, however, with the *caveat* that the ideas, observations and interpretations of the current situation in the field presented here are based on my own experience and study, largely obtained in the US. Thus, they may not fit very well with the traditions, constraints, and contexts in which Indians work.

However, my experience of working with colleagues in 40 odd countries over a period of some 30 years suggests that colleagues who are engaged in the same kind of work across countries often understand each other better than do their colleagues within their own countries who work in different sectors of the field. I am not suggesting by this point that, across countries, we all agree with each other. My hypothesis is that the nature of our work is probably a more powerful determinant of our assumptions, beliefs, and ideologies than is the larger national political and cultural context in which our work is carried out.

I would like to add that colleagues who work with young children in places where resources are limited, understandably often dwell on what they would do, could do, and wish they could do, if only they had more funds, space, materials, staff, and other desirable resources. It is easy to fall into this mode of thinking, and certainly very understandable. However, I assure you that I have come across preschool programmes for young children in which ten, or perhaps even a hundred times more is spent on facilities, materials, and personnel than is typical here in India, but in which—unfortunately—children's minds are no more engaged or enriched than I have observed here under less than ideal conditions.

Furthermore, I have worked with teachers in several large US cities who are not able to explore the neighbourhood with their pupils because the school is the only safe building within it! Similarly, many teachers in a rich country like the US cannot engage their children in a close study of their natural environment, not only because of danger lurking on the streets, but also because the phenomena of nature can no longer be seen in the neighbourhood!

Thus, the challenge facing teachers in many countries, both rich and poor, is to work under less than ideal conditions and yet to engage young children in experiences worthy of their lively minds and developing sensibilities. Today, there is widespread consensus among specialists in the field that any provision for young children that is less than top quality represents a missed opportunity to make a substantial contribution to the rest of their whole lives (cf. Myers, 1991). However, agreement on what constitutes top quality, and which or whose criteria should be used to judge it, is not so easy. In most countries and communities there are competing views about early childhood education.

My own views on these matters are presented here in two parts within the framework of a developmental approach to early childhood education and its implications for practice. The first part outlines the principles of practice underlying a developmental approach to early education, and the second part outlines a major element of early childhood practice implied by them.

Part I: Principles of Practice for Education in the Early Years

Anyone who intends to develop a curriculum, i.e., a plan for learning, for any group of learners, at any age, in any subject, must address the following four basic questions:

1. What should be learned?
   Answers to this question include an examination of the aims, goals, and objectives to be achieved by the programme.
2. When should it be learned?
   This question is the developmental one in that it deals with matters of the sequence and order in which experiences should be provided to ensure optimal learning, and addresses issues concerning the relationship between early experience and mature functioning.
3. How is it best learned?
   Combining the answers to the first two questions, the educator here considers the best pedagogical methods, materials, activities, etc. most likely to achieve the intended growth, development, and learning.
4. How can we tell how well we have answered the first three questions?
   This question addresses issues of evaluation and assessment of progress, a large topic that cannot be dealt with here. However, it is best to keep in mind the truism that those who control assessment very likely also control the curriculum. I propose to take up the main issues by shifting the order of the questions as follows: first, what does it mean to take a developmental approach to curriculum and teaching in early childhood education? Second, what should be learned? Followed by the third question concerning how it is best learned.

WHAT DOES IT MEAN TO TAKE A DEVELOPMENTAL APPROACH TO EARLY CHILDHOOD PRACTICES?

The issue of developmentally appropriate practice has been at the top of the early childhood education agenda in the US for at least 15 years (Bredekamp, 1987; Bredekamp & Copple, 1997). It became an issue in the early 1980s due to a strong trend to push the primary school curriculum further and further down the age levels to programmes for younger children so that they were judged by many to be prematurely subjected to formal instruction in academic skills.

The National Association for the Education of Young Children, the largest organization of early childhood professionals in North

America, decided to take a position against such premature formal instruction, and produced the position statement popularly known as DAP (Developmentally Appropriate Practice) (Bredekamp, 1987; Bredekamp & Copple, 1997). Over half a million copies of DAP had been sold by the mid-1990s, and it has been translated into at least 16 languages.

While it has enjoyed this widespread support, it has also been the subject of bitter criticism. It has been faulted for being too white, WASP, and middle class-oriented. Many such critics claim that minority group children—especially those from poor families—benefit most when the learning environment is formal, didactic and tightly structured, and one that clearly prepares them to cope with later schooling. Some critics assert that many minority children cannot relate to the kinds of subtlety embedded in middle class ways of speaking to, guiding and teaching children (Delpit, 1988). Other critics contend that such children have little "time to waste" on play, discovery learning, or investigation projects (Helm & Katz, 2000).

Others faulted DAP for underemphasizing the role of the teacher, and for neglecting the curriculum and teaching of children with special needs. I was privileged to serve on a committee to revise DAP, and found it one of the most difficult and challenging intellectual assignments. After three years of contentious meetings, the second edition was issued in 1997 (Bredekamp & Copple, 1997) and it continues to be criticized for a variety of reasons.

CRITERIA OF CURRICULUM AND PEDAGOGICAL APPROPRIATENESS

There are many possible criteria by which to judge the appropriateness of a curriculum and of pedagogical practices for a group of young children. Among them, are concepts and principles based on the body of knowledge of the psychology of development and learning. The latter may include considerations of such theories as social learning theory, behaviourist theory (though not really a developmental theory), constructivism, and psychoanalytic theories. Another criterion may be what we generally refer to as culture—particularly the norms and values of the culture into which children are born, and the culture—or we may say cultures—in which they are expected to participate when they are grown—to the extent they can be known. Other possible criteria may be the political, religious, and spiritual tenets of those being served, as well as of the official agencies that provide the programme. A more specific criterion, probably a subcategory of the psychological criterion and one often cited by teachers, is the extent to which children are "happy" in the programme.

A developmental approach to curriculum and teaching practices, however, is one that takes into account knowledge of development and principles derived therefrom—no doubt embedded also in the culture that produced them—as they apply to decisions about curriculum content, teaching methods, and the developmental progression of the learners. In other words, for those of us responsible for programmes for young children, whether for half day or the full day time of child care provisions, a major criterion for assessing the appropriateness of practices is what we know and assume about the nature of development, and the relationships between early experience and mature functioning.

It should be noted, however, that what may be judged appropriate by one of the criteria listed here may not be so judged by another. An example of conflicting criteria was reported to me by an Illinois kindergarten teacher working with children on a project on the post office in the course of which she suggested that it may be a good idea to write a letter to someone. When she asked the children to nominate someone to send a letter to, one child suggested George Washington, whose birthday had recently been observed. When she explained that this was not possible because he was no longer alive, the child responded indignantly, "You mean we had a birthday party for him and he's dead?" Thus, while it may be *culturally* appropriate to introduce young American children to legends about the founding-father George Washington, the topic may be *developmentally* inappropriate. Most teachers have similar experiences of young children's literal constructions of the legends of their cultural heritage, and the confusions—albeit temporary—that they can produce.

Culture, Heritage, and Bias

Another way of looking at the conflicting criteria of appropriateness is to assume that it *may* be culturally appropriate to expose young children to their heritage so that they appreciate and experience feelings of pride when significant adults make allusions to ancestors, historical events, and heroes. However, when developmental criteria are applied, these phenomena, though not harmful, may be too remote and abstract for meaningful understanding in young children.

I suggest that it may be helpful to distinguish between children's *heritage* and children's *culture*. The latter deals with their own first-hand experience; the former addresses the events, ideas, and persons of their family's ancestors. A developmentally appropriate curriculum, during the early years, helps children to extend and deepen their understanding of their culture, their first-hand experience, of the culture in which they are actually growing up. As children increase in age and the experience that accompanies that increase, the curriculum also helps them acquire knowledge and appreciation of, and identification with the events, ideas, and persons of their *heritage*, i.e., their culture's past. The focus of the early childhood educator is mainly on helping children deepen their knowledge and appreciation of the actual *culture* in which they are growing up and acquire some knowledge of their *heritage*.

Curriculum and pedagogical specialists in countries like the US, the UK, Canada, and Australia with increasingly diverse populations are now taken up by a growing literature on *multiculturalism* and the complex issues it involves. There is general agreement that teachers should be committed to deepening their understanding and knowledge of diverse cultures, beyond the "foods, fashions, and festivals" level. As Hyun (1996, p. 15) put it,

Within our field, ethnic diversity should be studied as pedagogical knowledge. Those at work with young children need help to develop multiethnic perspective-taking abilities. They can also be helped to recognize that cultural influences on learning and development become valuable pedagogical knowledge for them as they learn to adapt curriculum and instruction to the unique needs of students from diverse cultural, ethnic, gender, and social class groups. Early childhood teachers...will be more effective if they have and incorporate accurate information about their students' unique family culture and ethnic backgrounds within the learning environment.

This is not a simple goal. Cultures other than one's own are hard to know, understand, and appreciate, even with abundant good-will. It seems to me that the real underlying issue—at least in the US—is not just general ignorance of other cultures; rather, I suggest that the main issue is bigotry, discrimination, prejudice, racism and sexism, and other forms of bias. As is widely known, serious efforts are being made to develop so-called anti-bias curricula. These efforts must be strengthened and continued. Speaking from a developmental point of view, however, I often wonder if bias in young children, i.e., the view that their own family/group and its ways, its language, values, culture, etc. is *the* right or *the* best one, is developmentally inevitable; the problem is to help the young to outgrow such narrow ethnocentrism, racism, sexism, etc. as they mature. Many specialists in early childhood development and education have assumed that children are born "naturally" free of bias and learn it only from ill willed adults. But I am not so sure that we have not turned the developmental sequence upside down in this case! Bias in favour of one's own kind may be easy to learn in the early years, and—though difficult—important to outgrow and become in fact a mark of maturity.

PRINCIPLES UNDERLYING EARLY CHILDHOOD PRACTICE

In the following the focus is on how understandings of the nature of child development can be used to generate basic principles of practice for early childhood education in such a way as to co-satisfy criteria of developmental appropriateness.

Principle 1. A developmental approach to curriculum and teaching practices is one that addresses those aspects of learning that change with the age and experience of the learner.

A developmentally appropriate curriculum is one that is designed on the assumption that what children should learn, and the means by which they are most likely to learn it, change with their age and the accompanying physical developments, and the experience that accrues with age. In other words, in a developmental approach to curriculum design and teaching methods, answers to questions about what should be learned and how it would best be learned depend on what we know of the learner's developmental status and our understanding of the relationships between early experience and subsequent development and functioning.

As already suggested, developmental criteria must be considered in the context of a variety of other criteria by which the appropriateness of a curriculum and pedagogy can be assessed. Further, the nature of development is only one possible criterion for judging the appropriateness of a curriculum or of teaching methods. For example, when we apply psychological rather than developmental criteria, we can see that some curricula and teaching practices are always appropriate, regardless of the age and experience of the learner (to be respectful of the child, of his/her family, background, etc.). Similarly, some practices are never appropriate, no matter what the age of the learner (the use of timeout procedures for punishment, disrespect for the child's family, etc.). Since these criteria do not change with age they are psychological and ethical, or perhaps moral and philosophical, rather than developmental in nature.

Principle 2. A developmental approach takes into account two equally important dimensions of development.

The two dimensions of development, the normative and the dynamic, can be briefly defined as follows:

The *normative* dimension of development addresses the characteristics and capabilities of children that are typical or normal for their age group (such as the average age of first walking, the typical size of vocabulary of 4-year-olds, and of understanding numerical concepts).

Age norms provide useful starting points for curriculum planning. Knowledge of age-typical interests, activities and abilities can provide a basis for preliminary planning of a programme of activities, and the selection of equipment and materials. For example, the norms of development provide a basis for assuming that most—but not all—2-year-olds need daytime naps, most

4-year-olds understand calendar concepts poorly, or that typically, most 5-year-olds can begin to write their own names.

Age norms are also useful for alerting teachers to individual children whose patterns of development depart noticeably from those of their age group and who therefore warrant close observation to ascertain whether they require special curriculum and teaching strategies.

The *dynamic* dimension of development deals with an individual child's progress from immaturity to maturity. This dimension addresses changes over time within an individual and the long-term effects of early experience, rather than the normality or typicality of the behaviour and abilities of a particular age group. This dimension has three aspects: sequence, delayed effects, and cumulative effects.

Sequence refers to the order or stages of development through which an individual passes, for example, from babbling to talking in the course of achieving mastery of one's first language. Under this heading, the curriculum and pedagogical practices consider which learning and developmental tasks have to be completed before the next learning is most likely to occur. For example, it is reasonable to assume that starting to learn a second language is most likely to be beneficial following mastery of one's first language.

Delayed effects refer to the potential positive, negative or mixed effects of early experience that are not manifested at the time of occurrence, but may influence later functioning (for instance, early infant–caregiver attachment may influence later parenting competence, a hypothesis that has been fiercely discussed among developmental psychologists for many years).

This aspect of the dynamic dimension of development focuses on issues concerning practices that are effective in the short term but may have delayed or "sleeper" effects that are deleterious in the long term (such as rewards and punishments, and insecure early attachment of infants to caregivers). Similarly, some practices that may not seem important to development during the early years may have positive delayed effects later. Whether positive or negative, delayed effects are those effects that are not manifested until later in the course of development.

Cumulative effects refer to experiences that may have no observable effects (either positive or negative) if they occur occasionally or rarely, but may have powerful effects if they occur frequently (such as the cumulative positive effects of frequent block play or cumulative negative effects of frequent even if mild criticism). This view of development argues that just because children *can* do something, it does not mean that they should do it. Expressed as a principle of practice it is as follows:

Principle 3. A developmental approach is based on the assumption that what children should learn, and should do must be determined on the basis of what best serves their development in the long term— the dynamic dimension.

What Should Young Children be Learning?

The question of what young children should be learning is a surprisingly difficult one. Of course, when we talk in general terms there is agreement that children should learn to be productive, contributing, and competent members of their communities and society, they should be honest, responsible, cooperative, etc., and in other ways, realize their potential as much as possible.

However, when it comes to planning specific experiences for a given group of 4- or 5-year-olds, the question becomes problematic. I often ask groups of teachers to describe activities or topics they have taken up with their pupils. Their answers vary very little, even across a large country like the US. On the basis of extensive experience with programmes across the country, it appears to me that the question what should children be learning is typically answered by the alphabet, the calendar, colours and shapes, holidays, dinosaurs, and traditional stories. While these topics and their related activities are unlikely to be harmful, they are not likely to be mind engaging either.

Four Learning Goals

I suggest that curriculum planning is aided by taking into account four categories of learning goals: (*a*) knowledge, (*b*) skills, (*c*) dispositions, and (*d*) feelings. *Knowledge* includes facts, information, understandings, concepts/constructs, stories, songs, legends, etc. *Skills* are defined here as relatively small units of action that can be easily observed and inferred from behaviour, including physical, social and verbal skills, etc., of various levels of specificity. *Dispositions* refer to habits of mind—not mindless habits—with motivational and affective components that propel the manifestation of relevant behaviour, such as curiosity, cooperativeness, and quarrelsomeness (see Katz, 1995, for a fuller discussion of the problems of defining dispositions). *Feelings* are internal emotional states associated with most contexts and interactions (Katz, 1995).

I have listed knowledge and skills as the first and second of the four learning goals because educational programmes and institutions are uniquely charged by their communities with helping children acquire worthwhile knowledge and skills. Of course, both knowledge and skills are learned in many contexts other than educational or early childhood settings. Nevertheless, preschools and schools have the responsibility of helping the young to acquire knowledge and skills they judge worthwhile and essential for effective participation in the community.

The precise nature of knowledge has occupied professional epistemologists for hundreds of years and remains difficult to define. I note with some apprehension that the current literature on constructivism claims that "children construct their own knowledge" (Kamii & Ewing, 1996) when the real challenge to adults is helping children with their misconstructions! In some sense it seems reasonable to assume that all of us assimilate and accommodate "knowledge" in our own minds, that is, make up our own minds, as it were. Nevertheless, when children master such arbitrary "knowledge" as the alphabet or the calendar, it is somewhat misleading, if not confusing, to claim that they have "constructed" it by themselves. It would seem to me to be more appropriate to claim that children construct their own understandings and misunderstandings, say, of their experience (which also includes experience of being instructed!), and then to develop curricula and teaching strategies on that assumption, as discussed in the following.

No matter what curriculum, activities and pedagogical strategies are employed to accomplish the two learning goals: knowledge and skills, learners' dispositions and feelings are likely to be influenced by them, whether intentionally or by default. It seems appropriate, however, during the early years, to be especially intentional and deliberate about strengthening worthwhile dispositions (the disposition to learn, to hypothesize, conjecture, etc., and social dispositions such as to form friendships, and to be open to others who are different) and to engendering positive feelings (feelings of belonging, of competence, self-confidence, etc.).

Emphasis on explicit attention to strengthening worthwhile dispositions in the early years is recommended partly because undesirable dispositions may become more resistant to change with increasing age, and desirable ones, typically present at birth (such as the dispositions to learn, to be curious, and to become attached to caretakers), may be seriously damaged, weakened and even lost if not purposefully strengthened. Furthermore, once damaged or lost, these dispositions may be very difficult to re-instate or implant with increasing age. However, neither dispositions nor feelings are likely to be learned from instruction, exhortation or indoctrination.

Principle 4. Many important dispositions can be assumed to be inborn.

It is reasonable to assume, for example, that the dispositions to learn, to make sense of experience, to form attachments, relate to others, etc., are inborn in all human beings, more strongly in some than in others. Indeed, except for children growing up in completely chaotic and unpredictable environments, it is useful to assume that they all enter school with strong dispositions to make sense of their experience and to predict the effects they can cause. This assumption leads to a fifth principle of practice.

Principle 5. It is reasonable to assume that all children come to school with the dispositions to learn and to make the best sense they can of their experience, even though they might never have been read to, heard a story, looked at a book or held a pencil, or otherwise become "ready" for school.

This principle needs to be emphasized since it is easy to overlook the likelihood that because young children have not been exposed to the so-called school readiness activities should not be taken to mean that they do not have lively minds. The intellectual powers of all children tend to be underestimated; this is especially true of children without exposure to preacademic experiences and who often are from socioeconomically disadvantaged backgrounds.

Many dispositions—both the desirable and undesirable—are likely to be learned from being around people in whom they can be fairly easily seen. In addition, if dispositions are to be strengthened, they must be manifested or expressed with some frequency; in other words, dispositions cannot be strengthened unless they are expressed. Furthermore, the manifestation of dispositions must also be experienced as both effective and satisfying.

Thus, developmentally appropriate curriculum and teaching methods are those that provide contexts and pretexts for children to manifest desirable dispositions such as to cooperate, to resolve conflicts, to investigate, to hypothesize, to predict, and to persist.

Similarly, feelings are not likely to be learned from instruction or from exhortation. The capacities for some feelings like fear, anger, anxiety, and most probably joy are inborn. But many feelings are learned from experience: feelings of belonging and of not belonging, feelings of competence and incompetence, feelings of confidence: high or low, and numerous other feelings of concern to families and educators are learned in the course of experiences provided in the educational setting.

Many educators of young children are eager to help children develop self-esteem. Again, such feelings are unlikely to be learned from instruction, exhortation, indoctrination, certificates, prizes, and flattery. I suggest, first of all that it is a good idea to focus on the development of children's self-confidence and sense of competence, and on helping them to handle the inevitable low as well as high points in life. When it comes to self-esteem, the next principle of practice is important.

Principle 6. Children's self-esteem is most likely to be developed when adults esteem them.

To esteem children requires us to speak to them as people with minds, to give them ample and real opportunity to make decisions—right as well as wrong—to provide them with contexts and occasions for making choices, and to consult them on matters on which they might have ideas, etc.

In sum, a developmental approach to curriculum and teaching takes into account all four categories of learning goals: knowledge, skills, dispositions, and feelings, as well as the dimensions of development. Furthermore, all these four categories should be explicitly assessed. From a developmental perspective it is reasonable to assume that during the early years, strengthening desirable dispositions and engendering positive feelings should have a high priority when selecting from among alternative courses of pedagogical action.

> *Principle 7. The younger the children, the more important it is that the curriculum and teaching methods strengthen the children's disposition to look more closely at events and phenomena in their own environments and experiences worth learning more about.*

This developmental principle implies that curriculum and teaching methods are aimed at helping children make better, deeper, and fuller sense of their experiences and environment. However, as they grow older, i.e., develop, it is the responsibility of schools to help them make better, deeper and fuller sense of other people's experiences: people far away in both time and space. This principle of practice suggests that answers to the question "What should children be learning?" will include ways to involve children in close and detailed investigation of phenomena around them (see Katz & Chard, 2000).

> *Principle 8. The younger the children the more important it is that what they are learning about (knowledge) and learning to do (skills) have* horizontal *rather than* vertical *relevance.*

Horizontal relevance means that what children are learning about and learning to do are experienced as meaningful and purposeful at the time, on the same day, on the way home, and on the following weekend. Vertical relevance, on the other hand, refers to learning that is designed to prepare children for the next class, next grade, or next school, independent of whether it is meaningful at the time of learning.

To some extent pressure for vertically relevant learning can be attributed to a type of "pedagogical paranoia". Here, I have in mind cases where teachers judge their pupils as unready for given learning tasks, but nevertheless insist that their pupils master them in order to avoid being judged by the teacher of the next year or next class as incompetent teachers.

Principle 9. The younger the pupils, the more the curriculum and methods should emphasize mastery rather than coverage.

At every level of education all teachers face the coverage versus mastery dilemma: the more that is covered in the curriculum, the less that is mastered; conversely, the more mastery to be achieved, the less can be covered (Westbury, 1973). In other words, there is no way to do justice to both coverage and mastery, at any educational level.

It seems developmentally appropriate to tip the balance in favour of mastery rather than coverage in the early years. It seems to me that if we opt for mastery, children can be engaged in activities in the course of which we can support and strengthen important dispositions, especially the dispositions to pursue knowledge, understanding, insight, and skilfulness, i.e., dispositions of potential benefit throughout life. In as much as the sheer amount of rapidly accumulating knowledge cannot be covered adequately in most educational settings, strengthening the disposition to continue learning in this way would seem to warrant a high priority. If we opt for the coverage "horn" of the dilemma, the disposition to seek understanding cannot be strengthened and the disposition to "get through" the lessons and please the teacher may take precedence over the lifelong disposition to learn, ponder, inquire, etc.

Principle 10. When young children are introduced to formal instruction too early, too intensely and too abstractly, they may learn the knowledge and skills offered, but they may do so at the expense of the dispositions to use them.

For example, premature formal instruction in reading or arithmetic (especially through rote learning and memorization) may succeed in equipping children with the intended skills and knowledge at a rudimentary level; however, the processes of learning through such instruction may damage their dispositions to become readers and real users of the numeracy skills and concepts so painfully acquired.

The potential risk of premature formal instruction may be referred to as the *damaged disposition hypothesis* that may account for the common observation that children's natural dispositions to learn, explore and investigate subside (and often disappear) after a few years of schooling (see Donaldson, 1982). This phenomenon is also referred to as the second grade "wash-out" phenomenon. The potential damage may not be apparent early in the children's school lives. Most children during the early years are eager to please teachers and engage willingly in the activities provided for them. The damage is likely to be manifested as a cumulative effect of several years of excessive drill and practice of decontextualized skills that rely heavily on the practice of small bits of information and skills, and on rote memory. Thus, consideration is merited in curriculum planning of the potential long-term cumulative effects of early experiences on the dispositions to apply what is learned.

Principle 11. Learning, especially in the early years, generally proceeds from behavioural knowledge to representational (or symbolic) knowledge.

The distinction between behavioural and representational knowledge, for example, can be seen in language development. That is to say, preschoolers have the behavioural knowledge that enables them to use their mother tongue long before they can represent it in the form of abstract grammatical categories such as nouns and verbs. Similarly, young children can navigate their homes and immediate neighbourhoods correctly long before they can represent them in the form of maps or directional concepts such as "right" and "left" or "east" and "west."

A developmentally appropriate curriculum is one that broadens and deepens children's behavioural knowledge by providing a variety of first-hand experiences, and also helps them represent their experiences through a wide range of media, including verbal, literary and graphic languages, model construction, and dramatic play. In the processes of representing their understandings, adults can help children so that their understandings become deeper, fuller, more accurate, more finely differentiated, and in other ways, more fully developed. In this way young children can deepen and improve their understandings of what they already know (i.e., their own experience).

Another way of expressing this principle is that children's understandings are constructed and re-constructed by them in the processes of representing them, rather than "instructed into them" as it were, didactically.

Principle 12. Unless children have some experience of what it feels like to understand some topics in depth, their dispositions to seek in-depth understandings cannot be developed and strengthened.

Many curriculum and pedagogical practices in early childhood and elementary education emphasize superficial acquaintance with information and "smatterings" of knowledge of many things, series of "one-shot" activities, rather than the acquisition and construction of in-depth understandings of phenomena worthy of children's time and energy. Indeed, one of the issues that warrants discussion in many countries is the overcrowding of the early childhood and primary school curriculum, leading to fragmentation and strong emphasis on coverage versus mastery of disparate knowledge and skills. However, the disposition to seek in-depth understanding of complex phenomena worthy of children's and adults' attention is essential for competent participation in democratic processes—an important ultimate goal of education in countries like the US.

At this point it may be prudent to digress a bit and examine the distinction between academic and intellectual goals, both of which have to be considered. Academic goals and activities, as the term is currently used, are those focused on small specific bits of information, knowledge and skills that are either correct or incorrect, right or wrong. They are typically taught out of context in the form of disembedded exercises and worksheets, and are often to be memorized and regurgitated in correct form on tests. Such academic goals have a place as children grow older and as they must conform to the norms and requirements of the academy and master knowledge and skills that have no internal logic of their own.

Intellectual goals, on the other hand, focus on such dispositions as to analyse, synthesize, theorize, attribute cause and effect relationships, make predictions, speculate, and invent. However, from a developmental perspective, the younger the child, the more important it seems to me that we emphasize strengthening intellectual dispositions rather than academic skills. Not only are such dispositions apparent in most children—more so in some than in others—but, as I have already suggested, if they are lost through neglect or overemphasis on academic exercises, they may be difficult to re-institute later on, leading to another principle of practice.

Principle 13. When young children are frequently coerced into behaving as though they understand something adequately, when they really do not, their confidence in their own intellectual powers, observations and questions may be undermined, and in some cases may be abandoned.

The cumulative effect on young children of repeated experience in situations in which they must act without real or confident understanding may be a weakening or distrust of their natural dispositions to construct their own understandings of their experiences. For example, premature instruction in mathematical concepts, calendar concepts, the solar system, in which children are coerced into giving correct responses to teacher-generated questions without confident understanding, may cause children to dismiss their own questions and give up seeking assistance in achieving fuller understanding. This, in turn, may undermine their motivation to learn and to seek understanding and knowledge.

Principle 14. For young children, investigation and observation are just as natural ways of learning as is play.

Early childhood specialists and practitioners have for long asserted that play is the natural way that young children learn. Indeed, all young mammals play spontaneously, and in their play rehearse behaviour they would use in their maturity. Experience of living and working with young children confirms and strengthens our appreciation of the basis of this traditional emphasis on the educational value of play—one that may have developed at a time when children's play was not valued and when few play opportunities or materials were available for young children.

Nevertheless, this tradition should not diminish acknowledgment of the fact that it is just as natural for children to learn through direct observation and investigation as it is through play. It is common knowledge that the very young observe phenomena around them with great interest. Similarly, from infancy onwards, children invest tremendous amount of time and energy in investigating their physical and social environments—often exposing themselves to danger in the process. Young children are natural-born anthropologists, linguists, and scientists, granted that some are more effective in these endeavours than others, and some children receive more support and encouragement than others to enact these dispositions.

Most children spontaneously generate explanations and hypotheses to account for what they observe, whether the phenomenon in question is rain, worms, or cashiers in the supermarket. Their conjectures can be followed up with close observations, interviewing, and other fact-finding activities by which their predictions and hypotheses can be tested. In other words, a child-sensitive and developmentally appropriate curriculum is one that capitalizes on children's natural impulse to find out such things as what the objects around them are made of, how they work, where they come from, what they are used for, what they are called, what the people around them do, when and why they do what they do.

In short, a curriculum for young children that takes into account the nature of their development is one that addresses their natural dispositions to observe and investigate their surroundings. Furthermore, inasmuch as we share the goal of preparing our children to participate in and contribute to a democratic society, I suggest that what children should be learning from their observations and investigations should include an in-depth knowledge and understanding of the variety of ways others contribute to their lives, and not only of what these contributors do, but also of what they know.

How is It Best Learned?

Once it has been determined what young children should learn and when it is best learned, the next question is by what methods, activities, and strategies they are most likely to learn it.

Principle 15. The younger the learners, the more likely it is that they learn through interactive and active rather than reactive, receptive and passive experiences, through direct and first-hand experiences rather than indirect and second-hand experiences.

As children grow older, their capacities to benefit from passive learning, from indirect and second-hand learning increase. While young children do learn from passive experiences (for instance, stories, movies, and television), the major intellectual dispositions such as to inquire, hypothesize, explore, experiment, investigate, analyse and synthesize are strengthened in the early years through interactive experiences.

Principle 16. The younger the learners, the more important it is that they have opportunities to apply in meaningful contexts the knowledge and skills learned in the more formal parts of the curriculum.

Good project work in which children investigate events and phenomena in their environments worth learning more about, and represent the results of their investigation, provides meaningful contexts for children to apply the skills taught in the more formal parts of the curriculum (Katz & Chard, 2000). Indeed, involvement in project investigations often motivates children to seek help from teachers and others in strengthening their formal literacy and numeracy skills so that they can make use of them for representing their observations and findings.

Principle 17. The younger the learners, the wider the variety of pedagogical methods that must be used.

When a single method of teaching is used with a group of children that is diverse in background, development, experience, interests, abilities, aptitudes, etc., a significant proportion of them is likely to fail. When using a single method for teaching a whole class (say, teaching a group of more than a dozen young children, the same thing, the same way, on the same day, at the same time), chances are that about one-third of the children already know what is being taught, another one-third will learn it, and the remaining one-third is unlikely to grasp it; in this way, whole group instruction means that two-thirds of the children are likely to be wasting their time! As to the thoughts and feelings of these two-thirds at such times, we can only speculate that it is unlikely that interest or satisfaction are among them!

The use of a single method of teaching for a whole group of children can be described as the application of a homogeneous treatment to a heterogeneous group, which inevitably leads to heterogeneous outcomes. While we do not wish all children to become alike or homogeneous in every aspect (i.e., we value some heterogeneous outcomes), there are some desirable homogeneous outcomes. For example, we want all children to acquire minimal skills in literacy and numeracy, and achieve optimal self-confidence; we want all of them to experience feelings of belonging. If children differ from each other in significant ways (such as in terms of experience, background, language, ethnicity, aptitude, ability, and interests) and if we want a homogeneous outcome (i.e., all children to have the disposition to learn, competence in basic skills, etc.) then we must use heterogeneous treatments.

Principle 18. Children's dispositions to be interested, engaged, absorbed, and involved in intellectual effort are strengthened when they have ample opportunity to work on worthwhile topics over extended periods of time.

The term *interest* refers to the capacity to "lose oneself" in something outside of oneself. A curriculum characterized by a succession of brief one-shot activities completed in a few minutes and not resumed for further development, may weaken children's dispositions to become deeply absorbed in worthwhile pursuits.

Principle 19. The younger the learners, the larger the role of adults in helping them to develop social competence.

Research in the US has pointed out that children who fail to achieve at least minimal social competence by about the age of 6 are at significant risk for school failure, later mental health difficulties, dropping out of school, and similar other problems. Neither the extent to which these findings apply to the development of children in other cultures and contexts nor the incidence of early social difficulties in other countries is known. However, since all of us are concerned about supporting the development of social competence during the early years, I have included it here for your consideration.

As children grow older the problems of overcoming social difficulties increase. Children's social competence can be strengthened in the context of being engaged in activities which call for social understanding and social interactive skills in the presence of adults prepared to assist them. Project work is one part of a curriculum that can provide the context for the acquisition, manifestation, and strengthening of such skills.

In short, when these principles are taken together they highlight the need for young children to have frequent and continual opportunity to be engaged in small group efforts to investigate significant phenomena and events around them and to do so in depth. Good projects provide the context for learning in all four major categories: knowledge, skills, dispositions, and feelings, and include ample opportunity for the meaningful application and strengthening of the basic and essential literacy, numeracy, and social skills.

Part II: Curriculum Implications

Taken together, these principles imply that the curriculum and teaching methods for the early years should include a set of practices herein referred to as the project approach (Katz & Chard, 2000), the elements of which are outlined here.

The inclusion of investigation projects in the preschool and primary curriculum is not new. It was developed in the US around turn of the century by the followers of John Dewey, and was a major feature in infant schools in the UK during the so-called Plowden years from the 1960s to the mid-1970s. Today, project work is one of the most interesting features of preprimary education in the small northern Italian city of Reggio (cf. Edwards, Gandini, & Forman, 1998; Katz & Cesarone, 1995).

The re-introduction of project work in early education is timely because of what has been learned about young children's intellectual and social development since the 1960s. Furthermore, experience reveals that it can be undertaken by young children in most environments, even where educational resources and teacher–child ratios are less than ideal, as in the majority of early childhood and primary school settings in India.

WHAT IS A PROJECT?

A project is an extended in-depth study of a topic, ideally a topic worthy of children's time, energy, and attention. The defining characteristic of a project is that it is a piece of research involving children in finding out about something real, following up their questions in sufficient depth to achieve a sense of mastery of the topic.

A project is usually undertaken by the whole class, sometimes by a small group within the class, and occasionally by an individual child. Generally, the whole class is involved in the investigation of a topic by subdividing it so that small groups assume the responsibility for specific subtopics. Each subgroup also assumes the responsibility for ensuring that children in small groups other than their own will benefit from their findings. In the process of conducting the investigation, a wide variety of intellectual, and social dispositions as well as academic skills are called into play in ways that are clearly purposeful to the children, and are thereby strengthened.

Depending on the ages of the participating children, a wide variety of skills can be applied in the course of project work. These include verbal, cognitive, and social skills at all ages, and increasingly sophisticated literacy and numeracy skills as the children enter the primary school years. An important feature of good project work is that it is conducted and sustained over an extended period of time—ideally several weeks—though no matter how interesting it may be initially, it is likely that any topic will lose its appeal after a long period of intense focus.

Project Work and Other Parts of the Curriculum

As suggested earlier, project work is appropriate as a *part* of the curriculum for young children. In addition to project work, preschoolers also need to be provided regular opportunities for spontaneous play, music related experiences, physical activity, literature, arts and crafts, and—with increasing age—introduction to basic literacy and numeracy skills. During the preschool years, project work may be seen as a more formal or teacher structured part of the curriculum. Conversely, during the primary school years, projects would constitute the more informal, less teacher structured part of the curriculum. At both the preschool and primary levels, projects can be seen as complementary to the other aspects of the curriculum.

First, systematic instruction—the didactic and teacher directed aspects of the programme—assists children in the acquisition of basic skills, while project work provides them with an opportunity for the application of such skills in meaningful contexts. Second, in systematic instruction the teacher specifies the tasks to be undertaken on the basis of her or his expertise in how the skills are best learned, whereas in project work children are encouraged to make their own choices and decisions about what tasks to undertake and select the level of difficulty most comfortable for them. Third, during systematic instruction learners are in a passive and receptive posture; in project work learners take the initiative and are actively engaged in investigation and applying knowledge and skills in a wide variety of ways.

In project work the teacher's role is more consultative than instructional. The teacher is available for consultation at all times, and facilitates the work by maintaining a productive working environment through supervision and monitoring the children's progress. The teacher's observation of the children while they are at work provides cues concerning what kinds of instructional activities children may need and are ready for.

In sum, I suggest as a general principle of practice that young children's development and learning are well served when they have daily opportunity to engage in projects on worthwhile topics *and* when systematic instruction in basic skills is also available for those who cannot achieve mastery without adult assistance. Teachers are encouraged to balance the two important provisions for learning in the early years, and to eschew the tendency to offer one at the expense of the other.

CRITERIA FOR SELECTING PROJECT TOPICS

Experience suggests that the variety of kinds of potential learning accruing from project work is linked to the selection of worthwhile project topics. The suitability of a topic depends on many factors like the particular group of children, their previous experiences, their ages, and ongoing events of interest in the community.

An overarching principle of practice related to the selection of topics is that a major responsibility of teachers is to educate children's attention (Prawat, 1993) to aspects of their experience and environment worthy of their deeper understanding. Further, as part of our commitment to fostering the development of children for participation in a democracy, topics that deepen children's understanding and knowledge of how others contribute to their well-being should be a guiding principle in the selection of topics.

Some guidelines for identifying topics for projects during the preprimary and primary years are listed in the following (see also Katz & Chard, 1998; 2000). A topic is a good one if:

It helps children build on what they already know and will help them make better, fuller, deeper, and more accurate sense of their own experiences and environment.

It is related to the everyday experience/environment of many children.

It is more suitable for in-school than for out-of-school study, such as of local insects, plants, trees, and industries.

It is rich enough to explore over an extended period of time—at least a week.

It helps children understand and appreciate each other more fully.

It includes observational drawing, painting, model building, construction, direct handling of relevant objects, and the collection of relevant artifacts.

It has good potential for dramatic play—especially if the children are very young; children can readily discern roles to play, elements of the role, implements used by the role takers, etc. such as hospital, ambulance service, grocery store, and restaurant.

Parents can contribute materials, artifacts, and stories of their own experiences.

There are good community resources, such as a local museum, a local factory or industry that can be studied closely.

Phases of Project Work

It is useful to divide project work into three phases: phase I is the period of getting started; phase II is the time allocated to conducting the investigations; and phase III is the period of consolidating the findings and organizing culminating activities.

PHASE I: GETTING STARTED   During this phase, children and the teacher agree on the topic to be investigated. During an initial discussion they usually develop a web or conceptual map of the topic from which ideas for subtopics are developed.

The teacher then encourages children to discuss and to illustrate through drawings and stories (depending on their ages) the experiences they have had related to the topic. On the basis of the discussions the teacher determines what the children know and think, and what kinds of clarifications and new knowledge they need. The teacher encourages the children to share their own personal recollections related to the topic, and review their knowledge of it, using representational and expressive competencies such as dramatic play, drawing, and writing. The teacher can learn of the special interests of individual children and their parents from the sharing of current knowledge. The initial discussions help establish a baseline of understanding for the whole group involved in the project. During this period the teacher also encourages the children to raise questions, answers to which they would find through their investigation.

PHASE II: A PROJECT IN PROGRESS   In the process of reviewing their current understanding of the topic during phase I of the project, questions are raised related to various aspects of the topic. Often the questions reveal gaps in knowledge, or even misunderstandings which may form the basis for planning phase II of the project. As a consultant, the teacher is not too quick to correct misconceptions that emerge during phase I; these may be excellent resources for learning as the children investigate and test their theories against reality.

The main thrust of phase II, however, is acquiring new information, especially by means of first-hand, real world experience. The sources of information may be primary or secondary. Primary sources include field trips to real settings and events, such as a construction site, direct observations of the working of a machine, or the delivery section of a supermarket, handling objects related to the topic. Interviewing and talking to people who have direct experience of the topic also yield first-hand information.

The preparatory work includes identifying questions to be answered, people to talk to about their work, equipment, objects, and the materials used that they can observe closely. Children can carry simple clipboards and sketch or note down points (depending on their ages) of special interest to be used on return to the classroom. During the visit children can also be encouraged to count, note the shapes and colours of things, learn any special words for things, figure out how things work, use all their senses to deepen their knowledge of the phenomenon under investigation.

During phase II a field trip can be jointly planned by the teacher and the children. Field trips do not have to be elaborate or to distant places. These may be trips to places close to the school, stores, parks, construction sites, or neighbourhood walks, a street vendor of vegetables, a bicycle repair person in a nearby street, etc. In the case of the very young, they can be encouraged to tell the accompanying adults what they want to be noted down that would help them remember something of the trip when they return to the class.

After returning to the classroom, children can recall many details of their observations and impressions, and represent them in increasingly elaborate ways as they learn more about the topic. At this point they apply skills they have already learned: talking, drawing, dramatic play, writing, mathematical notation, measurement, diagrams, etc. Children's work can be filed in individual project folders, displayed on the walls, or noted in group record books so as to share it with others.

As the work progresses in phase II, children often develop a strong concern for realism and logic about the topic. Drawing real objects becomes an increasingly absorbing activity. In their observational drawing they can observe plants and animals closely, or see how the parts of a bicycle interconnect within the whole, note how the pattern inside a carrot dissected in different ways indicates the way water and other nutrients contribute to its growth, and so on.

Parents may also be able to contribute to the project in a variety of ways such as arranging places to visit, lending items for display, allowing children to interview them, and providing access to information, organizing trips for their own or for small groups of children to specific sites for close investigation during school hours as well as after school hours.

PHASE III: CONCLUDING A PROJECT   The main thrust of the last phase of a project is completion of the individual and group work, and summarizing what has been learned. For 3- and 4-year-olds, the last phase largely concentrates on dramatic play in their project constructions. Thus, if they have built a store or a hospital they will enact roles associated with the setting.

This phase of the project may include inviting people to view the work at an "open house" or the class next door to come and see some specimens of the children's work. It is satisfying for the children to share their ideas with the principal and other interested teachers. Preparations for the visitors offer a good debriefing experience for the class following the investment of considerable effort; such occasions provide a real purpose for a review of the work achieved. At this point children may be encouraged to evaluate their own work, to compare what the investigations have revealed with the questions they had generated during phase I.

Conclusion

I suggest that part of the curriculum for young children should engage them in extended investigations of events and phenomena around them worthy of their understanding and attention. Ideally, project work should be part of each day's work. At times, it takes up a greater part of the day, at other times, it is only a small part, depending on the phase and progress of the project. The work undertaken is complementary to other parts of the curriculum in that it provides the context for cooperation, application of growing competencies in basic skills, and strengthens desirable intellectual dispositions.

References

Bredekamp, S. (Ed.). (1987). *Developmentally appropriate practice in early childhood programs*. Washington, DC: National Association for the Education of Young Children.

Bredekamp, S., & Copple, C. (Eds). (1997). *Developmentally appropriate practice in early childhood programs* (rev. ed.). Washington, DC: National Association for the Education of Young Children.

Delpit, L.D. (1988). The silenced dialogue: Power and pedagogy in educating other people's children. *Harvard Educational Review, 58*(3), 280–287.

Donaldson, M. (1982). *Children's minds*. Glasgow: Fontana.

Edwards, C.P., Gandini, L., & Forman, G. (Eds). (1998). *The hundred languages of children. The Reggio Emilia approach* (2nd ed.). Greenwich, DT: Ablex.

Helm, J.H., & Katz, L.G. (2000). *Young investigators. The project approach in the early years*. NY: Teachers College Press.

Hyun, E. (1996). New directions in early childhood teacher preparation: Developmentally and culturally appropriate practice (DCAP). *Journal of Early Childhood Teacher Education, 17*(3), 7–19.

Kamii, C., & Ewing, J.K. (1996). Basing teaching on Piaget's constructivism. *Childhood Education, 72*(5), 260–264.

Katz, L.G. (1995). *Talks with teachers of young children*. Norwood, NJ: Ablex.

Katz, L.G., & Cesarone, B. (Eds). (1995). *Reflections on the Reggio Emilia approach*. Urbana-Champaign, IL: ERIC Clearing House on Elementary and Early Childhood Education.

Katz, L.G., & Chard, S.C. (1998). *Issues in selecting topics for projects*. Urbana-Champaign, IL: ERIC Clearing House on Elementary and Early Childhood Education.

Katz, L.G., & Chard, S.C. (2000). *Engaging children's minds. The project approach* (2nd ed.). Norwood, NJ: Ablex.

Myers, R.G. (1991). *Toward a fair start for children. Programming for early childhood care and development in the developing world*. Paris: UNESCO.

Prawat, R.S. (1993, Aug–Sep). The value of ideas: Problems versus possibilities in learning. *Educational Researcher*, 5–16.

Westbury, I. (1973). Conventional classrooms, "open" classrooms, and the technology of teaching. *Journal of Curriculum Studies, 5*(2), 99–121.

About the Editor and Contributors

Sevda Bekman is Professor at the Faculty of Education, Bogazici University, Istanbul, Turkey. Professor Bekman completed her doctorate from the University of London. She is interested in early childhood intervention and her contributions to the area include the development of intervention programmes for developmentally vulnerable children and their parents. She has also directed and contributed to two research studies investigating the effectiveness of intervention programmes. She had designed an educational TV programme for young children and their parents. Professor Bekman has published numerous articles in national and international journals and is the author of *A fair chance*.

John W. Berry is Professor Emeritus of Psychology at Queen's University, Kingston, where he worked from 1969 to 1999. He received his BA from Sir George Williams University, Montreal and his doctorate from the University of Edinburgh. He has been a lecturer at the University of Sydney, a Fellow of the Netherlands Institute for Advanced Study, and a Visiting Professor at the Universities of Nice, Geneva, Bergen, Oxford, Helsinki, Tartu, Baroda, and Kwansei Gakuin. Professor Berry has served as Secretary-General and President of the International Association for Cross-Cultural Psychology, where he is an Honorary Fellow. The Universities of Geneva and Athens conferred honorary doctorates on him. He is the senior editor of the *Handbook of cross-cultural psychology* and has authored, co-authored or edited 30 books in the areas of cross-cultural, social and cognitive psychology. Professor Berry is particularly interested in the application of cross-cultural psychology to public policy and programmes in the areas of acculturation, multiculturalism, immigration, health, and education.

Pierre R. Dasen is Professor of Anthropology of Education and Cross-Cultural Psychology at the Faculty of Psychology and Education, University of Geneva. He studied developmental psychology in Geneva, where he was an assistant to J. Piaget. Professor Dasen holds a doctorate from the Australian National University. He has done work on the cognitive development of aboriginal children in Australia, Inuit in Canada, Baoulé in Côte d'Ivoire, and Kikuyu in Kenya; and on cognitive anthropology among the Yupno of Papua-New-Guinea, and Bali. He has studied such topics as visual perception, the development of sensorimotor intelligence, the causes and effects of malnutrition, the development of concrete operations as a function of ecocultural variables and daily activities, definitions of intelligence, number systems, and spatial orientation. His current interests include everyday cognition, informal education, and parental ethnotheories. At present, he is involved in collaborative research in India and Nepal on language development and spatial concept development. Professor Dasen has co-authored or co-edited several volumes and textbooks on cross-cultural psychology and intercultural education.

Jodi Dworkin is a research assistant at the University of Illinois at Urbana-Champaign where she is working on her doctoral degree. Her research interests include adolescent experimentation and parenting adolescents.

Lutz H. Eckensberger obtained his Diploma degree in Psychology in 1964, and completed his doctorate in 1970. After Habilitation in 1973, he became a Professor at University of the Saarland (Saarbruecken), where he has been since 1976 (Development and Culture). In 1996, he moved to Frankfurt as Director of the German Institute of International Educational Research and Head of the Psychology Section, and has a Chair of Psychology at the Johann Wolfgang Goethe University. He was Fellow of the Center for Advanced Studies in Berlin (1985–86). Apart from his focus on methods and methodology, he is interested in moral development, the relation between affects and cognitions, which he has examined in diverse environmental and health contexts. He has published two monographs, has contributed over 90 articles to journals and books, and has edited 15 books.

Cigdem Kagitcibasi is Professor of Psychology at Koc University, Istanbul, Turkey. She holds a doctoral degree from the University of California, Berkeley. She has served as Vice-President of the International Union of Psychological Science, President and Honorary Fellow of the International Association for Cross-Cultural Psychology, and a member of the Turkish Academy of Sciences. She is the recipient of the American Psychological Association and the International Association of Applied Psychology Awards for Distinguished Contributions to the International Advancement of (Applied) Psychology. She has published extensively and has authored *Family and human development across cultures* and co-edited *Handbook of cross-cultural psychology* (vol. 3). She has taught or was a Visiting Scholar at the Universities of California (Berkeley), Harvard, Columbia, Duke, and Baroda. Her research interests include human development, parenting and family in a cultural context, as well as policy related work to enhance human capacity and well-being.

Lilian G. Katz is Professor Emerita of Early Childhood Education at the University of Illinois (Urbana-Champaign) where she is also Co-Director of the ERIC Clearing House on Elementary and Early Childhood Education. She has been Past President of the National Association for the Education of Young Children, and is Editor of the first on-line peer reviewed early childhood journal, *Early Childhood Research and Practice*. Professor Katz was founder-editor of the *Early Childhood Research Quarterly*, and served as Editor-in-Chief for the first six years. She currently holds the Chair of the Editorial Board of the *International Journal of the Early Years*. Her publications include *Young investigators: The project approach in the early years* (with J.H. Helm), *Talks with teachers of young children*, and *Engaging children's minds: The project approach* (with S.C. Chard).

Heidi Keller is Professor of Psychology at the University of Osnabrück, Germany. Her research interests include the analysis of ontogenetic development as integrating biological predispositions with cultural contextual information. Her theoretical approach has been published in various handbooks and encyclopaedias. Professor Keller's empirical programme focuses on cross-cultural studies of early socialization environments and their developmental consequences. She has taught in different cultural contexts including the USA, Latin America, and India.

Reed Larson is Professor in the Departments of Human and Community Development, Psychology, and Educational Psychology at the University of Illinois at Urbana-Champaign. Professor Larson has done work on the daily experience of adolescents and their parents. He has published *Divergent realities: The emotional lives of mothers, fathers, and adolescents* (with Maryse Richards), *Being adolescent: Conflict and growth in the teenage years* (with Mihaly Csikszentmihalyi), *The world's youth: Adolescence in eight regions of the globe* (with B. Brown and T.S. Saraswathi). His current area of interest is adolescents' experience in extra-curricular, community activities, and other structured voluntary activities during after-school hours. He holds a doctorate in Human Development from the University of Chicago.

A. Bame Nsamenang is a researcher at Cameroon's Institute of Human Sciences, Bamenda. He obtained his doctoral degree in Child Psychology from Ibadan (Nigeria) in 1984. Between October 1987 and May 1990 he was a Fogarty (postdoctoral) Fellow at NICHD, Bethesda, MD, where he worked with Dr Michael E. Lamb. Nsamenang's research interests are in the areas of ecology of infancy, socialization, parental knowledge, and collaborative cross-cultural work.

Anita Rampal is Director, National Literacy Resource Centre, LBS National Academy of Administration, Mussoorie. Dr Rampal has taught at the Faculty of Education, Jamia Millia Islamia, and has developed new courses on Science and Society and the Philosophy and Sociology of Science for the BEd and MSc Ed programmes. A recipient of the Nehru Fellowship (1987), she was affiliated to the Nehru Memorial Museum and Library, New Delhi, as a Research Scientist working in the area of cognition and communication of science. She has been actively associated with the All India Peoples' Science Movement in various developmental activities including mass literacy campaigns and has been a member of various national committees and task forces on elementary education and literacy. She has published extensively on education and is the co-author of the *Public Report on Basic Education (PROBE)*. Dr Rampal completed her doctoral and postdoctoral research in Theoretical Physics from the University of Delhi.

T.S. Saraswathi retired as Professor of Human Development and Family Studies at the Maharaja Sayajirao University of Baroda. She obtained her doctoral degree in Psychology from Iowa State University, Ames and was a Visiting Fulbright Scholar at Cornell University, Ithaca (1983–84). Her areas of interest are moral development, socialization in varied cultural contexts, child care and parental ethnotheories. She has published extensively and is the co-author of *The world's youth: Adolescence in eight regions of the world* (with B. Brown and R. Larson).

Alice Schlegel is Professor of Anthropology at the University of Arizona, Tucson. She has done work on the Hopi Indians of Arizona, and her first publication on adolescence was based on her research on the Hopi culture. Professor Schlegel has used the Standard Cross-Cultural Sample for both fieldwork and comparative studies. Her intensive research on adolescence began with a cross-cultural study entitled *Adolescence: An anthropological inquiry* (co-authored). Findings from that study led to further work in Germany, where she studied adolescent industrial apprentices; and in Italy, where she examined the participation of adolescents in the civil life of Siena. Her current interest is adolescent participation in adult centred economic and civil institutions.

The late **Durganand Sinha** was Professor and Head of the Department of Psychology, University of Allahabad, and Director of the ANS Institute of Social Studies, Patna. A UGC National Fellow (1973–76) and an ICSSR National Fellow (1987–89), he was also a past President and a Fellow of the International Association for Cross-Cultural Psychology (IACCP). Professor Sinha's wide ranging interests included cross-cultural psychology, the psychological dimensions of poverty and deprivation, and psychology in Third World countries. He contributed articles to reputed journals and edited volumes, and published *Psychology in a Third World country: The Indian experience, Social values and development: Asian perspective* (co-edited), *Effective organizations and social values* (co-edited), *Asian contributions to cross-cultural psychology* (co-edited), and *Ecology, acculturation and psychological adaptation* (co-authored).

Rama Charan Tripathi is Director, G.B. Pant Social Sciences Institute, Allahabad. He was Professor and Head of the Department of Psychology and Centre for Advanced Study in Psychology at the University of Allahabad. He received his doctoral degree from the University of Michigan where he has been a Fulbright Scholar. He was a Visiting Professor at the Wake Forest and Tilburg Universities. His publications include *Environment and structure of organizations, Deprivation: Its social roots and consequences* (with D. Sinha and G. Mishra), and *Norm violation and intergroup relations* (with R. De Ridder). He is the Editor of *Psychology and Developing Societies: A Journal*. His research interests include social change, intergroup relations, and organizational socialization.

Suman Verma is Head, Child Development Department, Government Home Science College, Chandigarh. She has published extensively in the areas of time use and daily life experiences of adolescents in the family, school stress, time sensitization and life skills education for the youth, and street and working children. She has co-authored an annotated bibliography, *Adolescent development in India: Contemporary perspectives*. She was a Visiting Scholar at the Center for Advanced Study in the Behavioral Sciences, Stanford, working on a volume on "How adolescents spend their free time across countries".

Subject Index

abilities, 57, 64, 181, 205, 343
absolutism, 52
academic goals, 370
academic/school performance, 43, 139, 179, 185, 288
academic success, 288, 309
acculturation, 38, 54, 61, 66, 134, 146–47, 154
action(s), 31, 36, 58, 76, 77–79, 80–81, 96–97, 134, 150, 363; instrumental, 81–83, 87, 93; primary, 84–86, 89; reflection and, 333, 350; secondary, 86–89, 94; tertiary, 89–93
adaptability, adaptiveness, 75, 171
adaptation, 38, 51, 52, 55, 58, 60, 106, 107, 109, 134; cultural, 53–54, 146, 147–48; ecological, 53–54
adolescence, adolescents, 33, 41–42, 141, 174, 175; emotional state, 273–74; exclusion from adult life, 245–48; universality of, 239–40
adult centered settings, 236, 246–47, 248, 255; see also peer
adult learning, literacy, 43, 327, 328–29, 350–51
adults, adulthood, 147, 152, 156, 228, 239–40, 242, 244, 246, 262, 326–27, 330–34, 336
affluence, 60, 171
affordances, 106, 134
African: educational thought and practice, 214, 222–24; social intelligence, 177; worldview, 29, 33,

150, 153, 214, 216;—and conception of personhood, 215–18
Afrocentric perspective, 214, 218, 221
age segregated, 246, 247
agency, 38, 40, 76, 81, 83–84, 93, 96, 168, 172, 173, 176
aggregation, 30, 63
antisocial behaviour, see behaviour, anti-social
apprenticeship, 41, 247, 249, 251–52
authoritarian, authoritarianism, 42, 198, 259, 262, 277
authoritative parenting, see parenting, authoritative
autonomous relational self, see self, autonomous relational
autonomy, 40–41, 91, 94, 167, 168–69, 170–76, 183, 184, 216, 229, 230, 259, 260, 262

barriers and obstacles, 86–89, 91
behaviour, 24, 25, 29, 33–35, 38, 40, 52, 54–56, 64–66, 76, 81, 102–03, 112, 141–42, 151, 184, 219, 222, 229, 238, 248, 279, 364, 371; anti-social, 244–45; cognitive, 59; contextual nature, 199–201; and culture, 24–26, 31, 65–66
behavioural knowledge, 369
biological adaptation, 147–48; conditions, 77–78; predispositions, 106; skills, 134; systems, 103

Author Index